Macroeconomic Theory and its Failings

DATE DUE

D1296925

Macroeconomic Theory and its Failings

Alternative Perspectives on the Global Financial Crisis

Edited by

Steven Kates

School of Economics, Finance and Marketing, RMIT University, Melbourne, Australia

Edward Elgar

Cheltenham, UK • Northampton, MA, USA

Published by
Edward Elgar Publishing Limited
The Lypiatts
15 Lansdown Road
Cheltenham
Glos GL50 2JA
UK

Edward Elgar Publishing, Inc.
William Pratt House
9 Dewey Court
Northampton
Massachusetts 01060
USA

A catalogue record for this book
is available from the British Library

Library of Congress Control Number: 2009937890

Mixed Sources
Product group from well-managed
forests and other controlled sources
www.fsc.org Cert no. SA-COC-1565
© 1996 Forest Stewardship Council

ISBN 978 1 84844 819 3 (cased)

Printed and bound by MPG Books Group, UK

Contents

Figures and tables

FIGURES

TABLES

Contributors

Peter J. Boettke is the BB&T Professor for the Study of Capitalism at the Mercatus Center, and University Professor of Economics at George Mason University, Fairfax, VA. He has been the editor of the *Review of Austrian Economics* since 1998.

Tim Congdon is an economist and businessman, who has for over 30 years been a strong advocate of sound money and free markets in the UK's public policy debates. He was a member of the Treasury Panel of Independent Forecasters (the so-called 'wise men') between 1992 and 1997. Often regarded as the original 'Thatcherite monetarist', he founded the economic research consultancy, Lombard Street Research, in 1989. A collection of his papers, with the title *Keynes, the Keynesians and Monetarism*, was published in September 2007 by Edward Elgar. His latest work, on *Central Banking in a Free Society*, was published by the Institute of Economic Affairs in March 2009. He writes columns on economics for *Standpoint* and the IEA's journal, *Economic Affairs*. He was awarded the CBE for services to economic debate in 1997.

Robert Costanza is the Gordon and Lulie Gund Professor of Ecological Economics and founding director of the Gund Institute for Ecological Economics at the University of Vermont at Burlington. His transdisciplinary approach integrates the study of human beings and the rest of nature to address research, policy and management issues at multiple scales, from small watersheds to the global system. He is co-founder and past president of the International Society for Ecological Economics, and was founding chief editor of the society's journal, *Ecological Economics*. His awards include a Kellogg National Fellowship, the Society for Conservation Biology Distinguished Achievement Award, and a Pew Scholarship in Conservation and the Environment.

Ben Fine is Professor of Economics at the School of Oriental and African Studies, University of London. The fifth edition of *Marx's Capital*, co-authored with Alfredo Saad-Filho, is in press (Pluto Press). Recent books include *From Political Economy to Economics: Method, the Social and the Historical in the Evolution of Economic Theory*, awarded the Gunnar Myrdal Prize for 2009, *From Economics Imperialism to Freakonomics: The*

Shifting Boundaries Between Economics and Other Social Sciences, awarded the Isaac and Tamara Deutscher Prize for 2009 (both with Dimitris Milonakis, Routledge, 2009), and *Theories of Social Capital: Researchers Behaving Badly* (Pluto Press). He is an appointed member of the Social Science Research Committee of the UK's Food Standards Agency.

J. Patrick Gunning studied economics and public choice under Gordon Tullock and James Buchanan at Virginia Polytechnic Institute and State University at Blacksburg in the early 1970s. He was a victim of the 'revival' of Austrian economics in the 1970s. Since that time, he has published articles and books in both Austrian economics and public choice. He is currently a visiting lecturer at Bryant University in Rhode Island, USA, after a long stint in a number of universities in several countries outside the USA. Much of his work is devoted to showing the affiliation between the earlier generations of Austrians, including especially Ludwig von Mises, and the early neoclassical economists. He has argued that later neoclassical economics took a Keynesian, mathematical and statistical turn away from the action-based neoclassical economics that preceded it. His chapter in this volume aspires to be in the tradition of both Ludwig von Mises and the early neoclassicals.

Steven Horwitz is Charles A. Dana Professor of Economics at St Lawrence University in Canton, NY. He has published in the areas of monetary and macroeconomic theory, monetary history, the history of economic thought, political economy and the economics of the family. He considers his professional work to be in the tradition of Ludwig von Mises, Friedrich Hayek and the Austrian school.

Steven Kates has just completed an appointment as Commissioner on the Australian Productivity Commission and has commenced an academic career in the School of Economics, Finance and Marketing at RMIT University in Melbourne, Australia. For most of his career he worked for the private sector, having been for a quarter of a century the chief economist for the Australian Chamber of Commerce and Industry. His professional interests have therefore been closely related to the formation of economic theory in line with the needs of policy. His *Say's Law and the Keynesian Revolution* (Edward Elgar, 1998) discussed the loss to economic theory of the disappearance of the classical theory of the cycle. He describes himself as a classical economist.

Steve Keen is Associate Professor of Economics and Finance at the University of Western Sydney, Australia, and author of *Debunking Economics* (Pluto Press, 2001). He has over 40 academic publications on topics as diverse as financial instability, the money creation process, mathematical flaws in the conventional model of supply and demand, flaws in Marxian economics, the application of physics to economics, Islamic finance, and the role of chaos and complexity theory in economics. Since 2006 he has been publishing a monthly report explaining the economic dangers of excessive private debt. He is a specialist in Minsky's financial instability hypothesis, and produced the first mathematical model of a debt-induced economic crisis in 1995.

J.E. King teaches economics at La Trobe University in Melbourne, Australia. A strong believer in pluralism in the teaching of economics, he has sympathies with several heterodox approaches, including institutional and ecological economics. His principal attachments, however, are with post-Keynesian and Marxian political economy, with Michał Kalecki serving as a bridge between them.

Mervyn Lewis is Professor of Banking and Finance in the School of Commerce at the University of South Australia. Previously he was Midland Bank Professor of Money and Banking at the University of Nottingham and Course Director of the MBA in Financial Studies. He was also a consultant to the Australian Financial System Inquiry, visiting scholar at the Bank of England and inaugural Securities Commission–University of Malaya Visiting Scholar. In 1986 he was elected a Fellow of the Academy of the Social Sciences in Australia. Professor Lewis has authored or co-authored 21 books, 65 articles and 76 chapters. Recent volumes are *Handbook of Islamic Banking* (Edward Elgar, 2007), *Islamic Finance* (Edward Elgar, 2007) and *Untangling the U.S. Deficit: Evaluating Causes, Cures and Global Imbalances* (Edward Elgar, 2007). His latest volume is *An Islamic Perspective on Governance* (Edward Elgar, 2009).

William J. Luther is a research fellow at the Mercatus Center and a PhD student in economics at George Mason University.

Robert E. Prasch is Professor of Economics at Middlebury College, in Middlebury, Vermont, USA. He teaches courses on monetary theory and policy, American economic history, macroeconomics and the history of economic thought. His teaching and research take seriously the proposition that 'history matters', including the history of ideas. While his research has been informed and inspired by a number of scholars, his monetary economics is closely aligned with the post-Keynesian and institutionalist schools of economics. His most recent book is *How Markets Work: Supply, Demand and the 'Real World'* (Edward Elgar, 2008).

Martin Ricketts is Professor of Economic Organization at the University of Buckingham, UK. His work has been particularly influenced by writers such as Ronald Coase, Armen Alchian, Harold Demsetz and Oliver Williamson, who developed 'the new institutional economics'.

Jan Toporowski is Reader in Economics and Head of the Economics Department at the School of Oriental and African Studies, University of London; and Research Associate in the Research Centre for the History and Methodology of Economics, University of Amsterdam, The Netherlands. He has worked in fund management and commercial and central banking. He has published books and articles on monetary and financial economics and on the history of economic thought inspired by his reflections on Kalecki, Keynes, Schumpeter, Minsky and Steindl. He is currently working on an intellectual biography of Michał Kalecki.

Charles J. Whalen is Executive Director and Professor of Business and Economics at Utica College, NY and Visiting Fellow in the School of Industrial and Labor Relations at Cornell University, NY. His research interests include macroeconomics, labour and employment relations, and the history of economic thought. He describes himself as a post-Keynesian institutionalist, influenced by institutional labour economists in the tradition of John R. Commons and by post-Keynesian macroeconomists such as Hyman P. Minsky.

L. Randall Wray is Professor of Economics at the University of Missouri–Kansas City, Research Director of the Center for Full Employment and Price Stability, and Senior Scholar at the Levy Economics Institute of Bard College, Annandale-on-Hudson, NY. A student of Hyman Minsky, Jan Kregel and Marc Tool, Wray works within the post-Keynesian and institutionalist traditions.

Acknowledgements

In any book, never mind one with 14 other authors, there are many to whom a great deal is owed.

Firstly, I have to thank all of the contributors for their exceptionally interesting and insightful discussions of what is an unusually difficult period of economic instability and policy experiment. But I think such excellence is to be expected from the particular authors who have agreed to participate in this collection.

For myself as editor, what I am especially grateful for has been the willingness of all 14 authors to meet what was quite a tight schedule in getting this into print. Their meeting every one of the deadlines along the way towards final publication has allowed the book to go to press with no delays during the whole of the production process. Anyone familiar with academic publishing will know how difficult that can be.

I must also thank Laura Elgar, the commissioning editor at Edward Elgar Publishing, for her immediate recognition that such a book might be of interest and then for her willing assistance at every stage in allowing this book to reach its final completion. In this, I would also like to thank all of those at Elgar's who have worked to turn a series of individual articles into the high-quality publication that this has now become.

Finally, I must thank my family for their interest and support. My sons, Benjamin and Joshua, have put up with my many hours of discussion dealing with macroeconomic theory and its failings. Their patient tolerance of my obsessions has made this journey to final publication easier and more pleasant than it would otherwise have been.

The book is, however, dedicated to my wife, Zuzanna, the best natural economist I know, but whose greatest contribution has been her encouragement in allowing me the time to see this through to the end. My debts to her, of course, extend far beyond her help in seeing this book finally into print.

The publishers also wish to thank the following who have kindly given permission for the use of copyright material.

The Social Affairs Unit for the article by Tim Congdon (2009), 'The unnecessary recession', *Standpoint*, Issue 13, June, 40–45, published here in revised form as Chapter 2.

The Center for Economic Research and Social Change for Ben Fine (2009), 'Looking at the crisis through Marx', *International Socialist Review*, **64**, March–April, 40–47, published here in revised form as Chapter 4.

Quadrant Magazine Co. Inc. for Steven Kates (2009), 'The dangerous return of Keynesian economics', *Quadrant*, March, No. 454 (Vol. LIII, 3), 5–10, published here in an expanded and revised form as Chapter 7.

Every effort has been made to trace all the copyright holders but if any have been inadvertently overlooked the publishers will be pleased to make the necessary arrangements at the first opportunity.

Introduction

Steven Kates

> The financial crisis that is spreading out from countries with the most 'advanced' financial systems to the rest of the world has not been well served by economic theory.
>
> Jan Toporowski (this volume, Chapter 13)

This is a book about the global financial crisis and the economic theories that have been used first to understand its causes and thereafter to contain the damage it has brought. But it is more than that. It is a book about the inadequacies of the economic theories that are being used to deal with the present global economic meltdown. The one and only unifying feature of the articles collected together within these covers is that each and every one of the authors disagrees with the standard mainstream neoclassical macroeconomic models that have been applied in attempting to comprehend what has gone on and then, more importantly, have been used to devise policies to bring this recession to an end.

This book is thus about the usefulness or otherwise of existing textbook economics to deal with the present crisis. But while all disagree with the standard mainstream model, it should also be understood that the various authors in this collection do not necessarily agree with each other. There is, in fact, a very wide disparity of views. The perspectives provided range across the entire breadth of economic theory from free market to highly interventionist. The intention in putting this collection together has been to provide a single platform for the different sets of views that are often drowned out by the standard-bearers of the mainstream.

Moreover, all the contributors to this volume have had longstanding beliefs, even before our present problems began, that today's standard economic models are inadequate, if not actually wrong. It is the ideas and theories of these economists, all of whom are serious scholars, that are being employed to provide alternative explanations of the economic events of the past two years and to discuss alternative remedies that might now be applied.

Theory in economics is indispensable. Little about the operation of economies is understandable without being viewed through the lens of an economic theory to make sense of what is actually taking place. Until theory brings them together, most things that happen within an economy are no more than a set of unrelated economic events. What the contributors to this collection have done is to apply their own theoretical understanding to the facts of the world to comprehend what has gone on and to think through what policies now need to be adopted.

Not only is there an economic crisis, there is also a major crisis potentially brewing in economic theory itself. The adequacies of existing theories are being tested as seldom before. Whether textbook theory as it is now taught will remain unaffected by the events of the world which that theory is intended to depict and explain is far from certain. Concerns aplenty will build should there not be a reasonably rapid return to strong rates of non-inflationary growth accompanied by low rates of unemployment.

First, there are the concerns that surround the management of our economies in the lead-up to the financial crisis. Even with the wisdom of hindsight, it is far from clear what went wrong. There is no consensus on what caused these problems or why they spread so rapidly.

There is certainly no consensus on what ought to have been done instead to prevent these problems from building. At its most basic, there is not even a consensus on whether the problems were due to inherent flaws in the economic system or were instead due to the policies adopted by governments.

But these are questions about the past – only a prelude to thinking about what to do next. The more important questions are about the future. The questions that are mounting deal with the actions that ought now to be taken to fix our present problems, whatever may have been their origins. Beyond that, there may now be further questions that relate to repairing any additional damage caused by the first sets of policies used to deal with the downturn. Lastly, there are the questions for the longer term, surrounding what should be done to forestall a repetition of the present downturn, assuming anything can be done at all.

There are two central issues that in many ways overlap. There are, first, questions that relate to whether governments should take actions to hasten growth by adding to the level of aggregate demand. A second set of questions relates to the extent to which greater regulation of markets, particularly financial markets, is needed. Both sets of questions come back to the basic question of economic theory: whether markets should be left to sort things out or whether more direct government involvement can push them in particular directions to achieve better results sooner and to ensure that the actions of participants in particular markets do not undermine the common good.

THE ECONOMIC STIMULUS

The first set of questions relates to the economic stimulus that governments across the world have been injecting into their economies to encourage a return to faster rates of growth and lower unemployment. There is certainly no agreement within the economics community over whether the increased levels of public spending and the massive increases in deficits have been the proper response to our problems; nor is there agreement on the longer-term implications. This is despite the fact that at the core of mainstream analysis is a model of the economy that at some level endorses every step that has so far been taken. It is a model that instructs governments to increase expenditure without guidance on what that expenditure ought to be on. Anything, so far as these models are concerned, will apparently do. These models support deficit financing and increased public debt without indicating what that spending should be on, or how high debt may go before it needs to be reined in.

It is a model that governments have therefore embraced during the current downturn without obvious concern for the implications about the long-term potential for harm. Whatever short-term benefits there may be, and even the existence of such short-term benefits remains debatable, the question is whether future costs, involving, for example, the repayment of debt or additional inflationary pressures, will be so high that they far exceed any short-period good that may have been done.

THE STANDARD MODEL

Some sense of the structure of the modern macroeconomic model and the kinds of guidance it gives are useful in understanding the actions that governments have taken. The focus here is on the introductory macroeconomic model taught to first-year economists. This model, although refined with additional features and nuance in later years of study, nevertheless provides the core conceptual reasoning that underpins the shared framework of both academic economists and the makers of economic policy. It is what every economist learns and is the basis for the macroeconomics of virtually every student who has taken only a single course in economics.

The relevant theory is often called Keynesian, after the English economist John Maynard Keynes. It was his *General Theory of Employment, Interest and Money*, published in 1936, that became the point of origin for the standard macroeconomic model now in general use. Although there are fundamental disagreements among economists over the message that Keynes was trying to impart, there is no disagreement that it is from

Keynes's scholarly work that modern macroeconomic theory began its voyage.

It should however be emphasized that a significant proportion of those who describe themselves as followers of Keynes would not accept many, and possibly most, elements of the standard macroeconomic model as their own.

The model that has descended to the modern textbook level is generally referred to as the neoclassical synthesis, the melding of Keynesian ideas with the ideas of Keynes's predecessors. As taught today, within this neo-classical model the single most important factor in understanding fluctuations in the level of output is fluctuations in the level of aggregate demand – the demand for everything produced.

Moreover, the underlying assumption in such models is that in an economy in recession, if it were left to itself, the level of aggregate demand would not recover, or if it did, the process would take far too long. Active government involvement to restore economic growth is seen as essential and overwhelmingly beneficial.

Even where supply-side factors may have in the first instance caused the economy to slow and unemployment to rise, for example through the higher cost of oil, it is nevertheless in a stimulus to aggregate demand that the solution is to be found.

The basic framework for discussing macroeconomic theory and policy today is generally a model based on aggregate supply and aggregate demand (AS–AD). To raise output and push employment higher requires an increase in either aggregate demand or aggregate supply; that is, either through an increase in total spending or through an increase in the under-lying productivity of the economy.

Positive changes in even short-run aggregate supply are, however, either relatively long term in nature – such as requiring an increase in physical capital, improvements in technology or increased workplace skills and abilities – or are related to factors largely beyond the reach of a national economy, such as a general fall in the price of oil. Indeed, improvements in productivity can even lead to a fall in the demand for labour.

It is for this reason that policies based on AS–AD are generally related to aggregate demand. These are seen to be more immediate and available for adjustment by those who manage the domestic economy. They are also seen as being more able to provide a direct stimulus to the level of economic activity since a response from business as an intermediary is not required but can be applied directly by the government on its own, using its vast powers to spend. Almost all policies that have been adopted during the early stages of the present economic downturn have therefore involved taking steps to encourage an increase in aggregate demand.

Aggregate demand is related to expenditure. Increasing the level of spending is seen as the key to increasing the level of economic activity. Going back to its origins in the early Keynesian models, the components of aggregate demand are identified as consumption, investment, government spending and net exports (exports minus imports). The standard formulation as an equation, with national output designated by the letter Y, is this:

$$Y = C + I + G + (X - M)$$

It is entirely arguable that this is not an equation at all but an identity. The level of GDP is *defined* by the sum of consumption, investment, government spending and net exports, but is not directly governed by them, which is why the same expression used in the national accounts is presented as an accounting identity:

$$Y \equiv C + I + G + (X - M)$$

But in treating this expression as an equation, economic policy has been designed to raise the level of production on the left-hand side by increasing the elements that appear on the right-hand side. Therefore, to raise the level of national output, policy has been centred on raising expenditures by consumers, investors, governments and international buyers of domestically produced goods and services. The more that is spent, the faster the economy is expected to grow, with the faster growth rates leading to a rise in the number of persons employed.

TEXTBOOK EXAMPLES

Some examples from modern texts by leading authors provide an indication of the instruction given to economics students. The first is from the fourth edition of Gregory Mankiw's *Principles of Economics* (Mankiw, 2007: 772):

> Any event or policy that raises consumption, investment, government purchases, or net exports at a given price level increases aggregate demand.

Similarly, in the text co-authored by Ben Bernanke, the Chairman of the Federal Reserve in the USA, we find the same sentiment (Frank and Bernanke, 2007: 826):

> For any given value of inflation, an exogenous increase in spending (that is, an increase in spending at given levels of output and the real interest rate) raises

short-run equilibrium output, shifting the aggregate demand (AD) curve to the right.

In a text co-authored by John Taylor, who devised the Taylor Rule used in interest rate determination around the world, we find this (Taylor and Moosa, 2002: 310):

> Imagine that government expenditure rises. We know from our analysis of spending balance in the previous chapter that an increase in government expenditure leads to an increase in real GDP in the short run.

Then in the eighteenth edition of Samuelson (first published in 1948 and now Samuelson and Nordhaus, 2005: 489) is found:

> Only with the development of modern macroeconomic theory has a further surprising fact been uncovered: Government fiscal powers also have a major *macroeconomic* impact upon the short-run movements of output, employment, and prices. The knowledge that fiscal policy has powerful effects upon economic activity led to the *Keynesian approach to macroeconomic policy*, which is the active use of government action to moderate business cycles.

There is no end of caveats to these bare statements found in each of these texts, as well as in the many others that tell the same story. Moreover, the further one studies economics, the more qualifications to these basic statements one finds. But in the end there is no practical point to discussing aggregate demand and public expenditure unless the conclusion being reached is that in recession one of the actions that governments can take is to raise the level of its own demand. Standard macroeconomic theory is unambiguous: higher public spending during recession is one of the actions governments should consider when unemployment rises and the level of economic activity falls.

The fact that governments around the world have done exactly this is directly related to the economic theory that economists are almost universally taught. Governments have not taken this course on their own initiative. In increasing the level of public spending, they have taken the advice of their professionally trained economic advisers. If these policies fail, there will be a major case to answer that it was the economic theories encouraging these actions that will have themselves been shown to have failed.

REGULATION

As important as the issue of the fiscal stimulus has been, so too is the role of regulation of markets, and particularly financial markets. Although various actions have already been taken to deal with perceived vulnerabilities, over the longer term there are certain to be ongoing debates on what governments can and should do to minimize economic instability while maintaining healthy rates of growth.

Within economic theory there is a strong predisposition towards a generally hands-off approach to economic management. For most economic activities, the economist's response is to assume that intrusive regulation of markets is unnecessary and, whatever might be the perceived benefits, will tend to do more harm than good.

For all markets, it is assumed that the participants know more than any outsider could possibly know. Moreover, about the unknowable future, the assumption deep within economic theory's DNA is that since no one can know what is going to happen next, and all actions based on the future must of their nature be a form of guesswork, markets are able to adjust to circumstances more smoothly, with more accuracy and with more assurance than any group of government officials could ever hope to do. If such judgements are left to people with their own money on the line, the incentive to get things right will lead to the optimal outcome, although surprises will frequently upset many an applecart along the way.

Regulators are too distant and lack the requisite knowledge to make appropriate real-time decisions. Regulation therefore inhibits markets and leads to a suboptimal outcome. The economy is worse for being subject to too many regulations and regulations of the wrong kind.

We should also consider the role of self-interest. Within economics, it is generally assumed that individuals acting on their own behalf and risking their own money will be prudent. Government intervention is by a nine-to-five bureaucracy whose involvement will in most instances do more harm than good. Indeed, not only would such attempts at detailed regulation of markets cause them to perform poorly, they are unnecessary because the market supplies its own discipline.

It is now a central question whether the current crisis in the USA began because of the actions of market participants in the finance industry and the housing market, or whether it was due to specific decisions by governments that allowed, if not actually caused, forces to be unleashed that would otherwise have been contained. Many policy questions will ride on the answer to this question alone.

While one may recognize the harm that has been done by the global downturn, the question remains whether the business cycle is the price that must be paid for the benefits that accrue when markets are allowed to find their own level. Cyclical activity may be impossible to avoid. If there is little that can be done to prevent periodic downturns, or to dampen their amplitude, then intrusive regulation will limit growth only in real incomes but do nothing to prevent the instability and personal insecurities that are embedded in the nature of things.

There is therefore the predisposition within the economics mainstream towards the self-regulation of markets where a culling process of the unprofitable and less competent is expected to ensure that those who should not be in business are removed and the capital they have been employing set free for other businesses to use in their stead. That is part of what the recessionary phase of the cycle is intended to achieve.

The basic framework of a free enterprise economy is tied to the ancient notion of the 'invisible hand'. Adam Smith's most famous passage even today remains an important part of an economist's understanding of the operation of markets:

> [A merchant] generally, indeed, neither intends to promote the public interest, nor knows how much he is promoting it . . . He intends only his own security; and by directing that industry in such a manner as its produce may be of the greatest value, he intends only his own gain, and he is in this, as in many other cases, led by an invisible hand to promote an end which was no part of his intention. Nor is it always the worse for the society that it was not part of it. By pursuing his own interest he frequently promotes that of the society more effectually than when he really intends to promote it. (Smith, 1976 [1776]: Book IV Chapter II)

An important modern manifestation of this principle is referred to as the 'efficient market hypothesis'. Financial markets are so well constructed, it is argued, that all the relevant information available is already part of the price of any financial product. No one can enter the market with more knowledge; increased regulation can only make markets less efficient since those who do the regulating will never know as much as those who are already engaged in the market and have their own money at stake.

It is this conclusion, which is embedded within standard neoclassical theory, that the global financial crisis has put on notice. Are there regulations that can be introduced that will make economies perform better, make them less susceptible to downturns, and make whatever downturn that does occur shallower and shorter?

Or is the attempt to add new regulations to those that already exist futile? Would such regulations cause only net harm by reducing the ability of markets to respond to changed circumstances and limit financial market innovation? Would such regulation in fact diminish economic stability and make jobs less secure?

These are questions of the greatest significance that will be discussed for years on end, just as similar questions were discussed following the Great Depression. They are the kinds of question that are a perennial part of the discourse among economists.

THE INVITATIONS TO PARTICIPATE

All contributions to the present volume were specially written for inclusion within this collection. Each contributor received some variant of the following letter, which was emailed to a number of economists identifiable from their previous writings for their rejection of the standard neoclassical model. The message line read: 'Seeking your Contribution to an Elgar Publication on the World Financial Crisis'. This was the relevant part of the letters that were sent:

> I am writing to ask if you would be willing to participate in a publishing venture that I believe could have enduring interest and value.
>
> I am editing a book to be published by Edward Elgar with the provisional title: *Alternative Perspectives on the World Financial Crisis*. The aim of this book is to gather together in one place the views of members of non-neoclassical schools of economic thought dealing with the financial and economic upheavals that are presently taking place across the world. The definition of the neoclassical model being used as the basis for this analysis is outlined below.
>
> What is being sought is an article of around 5000 words divided into three separate sections, not necessarily of equal length, which would cover each of the following issues:
>
> 1) How does your understanding of the operation of the economy differ from the standard neoclassical model?
> 2) From your understanding of how economies work, what have been the fundamental causes of the global financial crisis and the sharp downturn in economic activity and employment?
> 3) From your understanding of how economies work, what policies should governments now follow in returning the world economy to prosperity?
>
> These are amongst the major economic questions of our time. Governments will be taking action based on some variant of the standard neoclassical model which, for the purposes of this analysis, encompasses the following principles:
>
> - the most appropriate framework for macroeconomic intervention is some version of the aggregate supply–aggregate demand model
> - based on the AS–AD model, higher levels of government spending, involving large and increasing budget deficits, may be required to hasten recovery if not actually allow recovery to take place at all
> - although the market mechanism and individual decision making are the appropriate means to allocate resources in the vast majority of cases, greater levels of government regulation of the financial sector, as well as increased regulation of other sectors of the economy, may nevertheless be necessary to maintain economic stability in the future.
>
> This is obviously only a first approximation, but it is based on the models found in the majority of introductory texts on economics in use today. If you believe there are any other aspects of the standard model that are relevant, please include these in your own analysis.

The article being sought will hopefully not require much if anything in the way of research. It seeks a brief summary of the framework you bring to economic issues and the application of this framework to understanding our present economic problems.

The article would also ideally not include statistics or mathematical analysis. The intention is to make each article as accessible as possible to the widest range of readers, many of whom will not be economists but all of whom will be deeply interested in understanding the different perspectives on our current economic and financial troubles.

This book is intended to be of enduring interest long beyond the present. It is intended to be a reflection of the range of economic understanding at the start of 2009.

The enduring interest in a volume such as this is in having a series of essays contemporary with the events of the global financial crisis. A major part of its value is to provide conceptual guidance to those who are making policy decisions to bring this recession to an end and then to ensure that mistakes that were made are not repeated.

LONGER-TERM PERSPECTIVE

There is a longer-term perspective that is also an important part of the direct intention of putting these contributions together, but which is almost entirely unrelated to policy. The aim is to provide economists, historians and others in the future with a date-stamped on-the-ground perspective of these events as they were experienced by members of the economics community at the time.

None of us contributing to this volume know what will happen in the years to come. If we think in terms of the timeline of the Great Depression, the chapters have been written in the first half of 1930. It is early days in what may be a recession of relatively short duration or in what may end up being the start of a period of prolonged instability with many different bends in the road before we again reach satisfactory levels of output growth and employment.

Even the term we now use to describe our economic conditions, calling it as we do the 'global financial crisis', may not last the distance. A crisis is a momentary event of great intensity. A long-drawn-out recession would eventually lead to a new name being given to what many at this moment believe will be no more than a brief downturn, followed by a return to robust economic health. Only time will tell whether this is the same bravado that accompanied the soldiers of the First World War to the battlefields of Europe, who believed they would be home by Christmas. In 1930, the Great Depression was not called by that name either.

It is for those who live in times to come that this book is to an important extent intended. A major part of the reason that this collection has been brought together is to assist those who are interested in looking back at us from some vantage point in the future to do so.

PERSPECTIVES ON THE CURRENT CRISIS

In spite of its reputation for disagreement, economics is no more fractious than any other science, but with this one difference. It is within the public arena and among non-economists that a significant part of our economic debates takes place. Moreover, the answers that economists provide have a major impact on the lives of millions. The conclusions reached by economists matter.

There is a mainstream. There are textbook theories and practices that are learned and understood by all economists. But whatever is the mainstream at any moment in time, some economists reach the conclusion that the mainstream – the core beliefs of the profession – are in some important ways wrong. This has always been the case. It is how economic theory develops. Some members of the profession disagree with the mainstream position, and over time their points of view become the mainstream in its place.

It is the macroeconomic side of these economic theories that is now under the microscope in this volume by economists who take sharply different points of view from the majority of the profession. But the different perspectives provided here are not from a single direction but from across the entire range of positions found in different economic traditions. The different traditions from which the chapters in this volume have been written are listed below in alphabetical order:

- Austrian
- Classical
- Environmental
- Institutionalist
- Islamic
- Marxist
- Minskyite
- Monetarist
- Post-Keynesian.

No attempt is made to define any of these in this introduction. That is up to each individual author. The list of contributors provides a brief statement of the intellectual allegiances of each of the authors. Readers with a greater knowledge of economic theory and its subdivisions will have no difficulty in recognizing the different points of view.

And although one might describe some of the members of this list as belonging to 'schools' of economic thought, that would be too confining in most cases. As the chapters make clear, there are overlapping points of view and a number of key concepts shared across a number of the perspectives are presented. Each author has been allowed to describe his own approach to economics in his own way. The chapters are in alphabetical order according to the author's name. No precedence has been given to any point of view.

But what is important is that each of the authors as a representative of one of these perspectives has something of value to contribute to this debate. For each of these, there is an historical tradition that goes back to the earlier years of the study of economics. Each of the economists is the present incarnation of a perspective on economic issues that has been pursued by a succession of economists who have learned their economics within those traditions. None of these perspectives was the invention of the economist who has written the chapter for this publication. Each is a descendant from a longer, deeper tradition.

Even so, economists have a common language. Because they have been economically trained, there is a framework within which discourse can take place. But when all is said and done, within each tradition there is a separate way of understanding the various dynamic operations of an economy. There are important differences on what matters and how it matters. There are differences over what governments can and cannot do successfully. There are differences over the consequences of different policies and over how policies will matter in the short run in comparison with the long run. There are differences in the categories by which to classify and aggregate. There are, in fact, differences over whether discussing economic issues in terms of aggregates is even coherent.

Yet so far as this collection is concerned, it has been designed to be read widely by those with no economic training whatsoever. The purpose has been to make these essays accessible so that the different points of view can be understood by the interested non-economist. There would be no point to this volume if its only audience were other economists. The aim is to reach beyond the confines of the economics discipline to the wider community to present the diversity of views among economists on these major questions.

There is, it should be understood, not just one school of economic thought. There isn't only one answer given by economists to the complex and perplexing issues that surround us. There is a wide variety of possible policy responses that should be examined and considered.

Those who make policy decisions usually do not have prior training in economics. They should therefore be aware of these other perspectives, which are too often obscured by the mainstream. The narrowness of policy debates has often led to the adoption of a course of action that may have long-term consequences and potentially cause major damage to productive potential because other options were not considered.

The aim of this book is to bring into focus views of other traditions within economics that those who must make policy in the midst of events would seldom normally consider. But given the complexity of the task before us, and the distinct possibility that the policies that have so far been adopted will fail to bring about the desired result, these chapters have been brought together to ensure that alternative perspectives are examined as future decisions are made.

REFERENCES

Frank, Robert H. and Ben S. Bernanke (2007), *Principles of Economics*, 3rd edn, New York: McGraw-Hill.

Keynes, John Maynard (1936), *General Theory of Employment, Interest and Money*, London: Macmillan.

Mankiw, N. Gregory (2007), *Principles of Economics*, 4th edn, Mason, OH: Thomson South-Western.

Samuelson, Paul A. and William D. Nordhaus (2005), *Economics*, 18th edn, Boston, MA: McGraw-Hill Irwin.

Smith, Adam 1976 [1776], *An Inquiry into the Nature and Causes of the Wealth of Nations*, edited by Edwin Cannan, Chicago, IL: University of Chicago Press.

Taylor, John B. and Imad Moosa (2002), *Macroeconomics*, 2nd edn, Milton, Queensland: John Wiley & Sons.

1. The ordinary economics of an extraordinary crisis

Peter J. Boettke and William J. Luther

INTRODUCTION

It is amazing how the economics profession succumbs to mass hysteria in times of adjustment. Why do we even talk of 'depression economics'? Do the lessons of economic science drastically change in times of recession? Would it make sense to talk of 'depression physics' or 'depression biology'? If economics is indeed a hard science, its claims – like those in physics and biology – must be universal.

Admitting that institutions matter does not transform the principles of economics. Those principles transcend time and place; but the manifestation of those principles in action are context dependent. The basic teachings of economics do not go out the window when governments engage in fiscally irresponsible behavior, pursue expansionary monetary policy, and regulate (or even nationalize) industries. In fact, it is the teachings of economics in that context that allow us to predict the results of such a policy path. Extraordinary times call for ordinary economics.

A HISTORY OF IDEAS

That most modern economists cannot articulate ordinary economics should come as no surprise. Ordinary economics has been out of fashion for some time. While not lost entirely, it has taken a back seat in recent years to model jockeying and equilibrium theorizing. This was not always the case. And, with some luck, the economics discipline might turn once again to a more process-oriented approach. Until then, we must rely on the classics and a handful of scholars who have kept the tradition of ordinary economics alive.

The body of theory developed by Smith, Hume, Ricardo and Say traced out tendencies and directions of change. Except in the simplest of cases – and then only to illustrate the underlying process – classical economists

14

rarely bothered with point prediction of exchange ratios. The price system was depicted as a dynamic process, adjusting to accommodate tastes and technology. In sharp contrast to the omniscient actors assumed to exist in modern equilibrium models, the classical economists assumed merely that self-interested producers and consumers would weed out persistent error. They assumed market participants would draft plans and modify behaviors until all mutual gains were exhausted. Relying on entrepreneurial alertness and action, the classical theory of the market economy was one of economic activity, not a state of affairs.

In the late nineteenth century, the scientific demands on economic theory shifted from a theory of price formation to one of price determination. With the analytical focus centered on settled equilibrium states, the idea of economic activity was nearly lost. This is not to say that classical economics was not in need of repair – it certainly was. Prevailing theories of value and cost could not explain several paradoxes that demanded resolution for scientific refinement. It is an unfortunate fact of history that the economists who resolved these paradoxes tended to focus not on the adjustments to changing conditions, but rather on the settled state of affairs that results when all change has ceased. Consequently, the classical view of the market system as an active process was slowly and subtly replaced by equilibrium analysis while the key components of the market economy's self-regulating nature – property, prices and 'profit and loss' – were taken for granted.

With the underlying process removed from economic analysis, the focus shifted further to aggregate variables. The ideas of the past were deemed unsatisfactory in explaining what was perceived to be excessive unemployment. Rejecting Say's Law, Keynes postulated that a general glut – where aggregate supply exceeds aggregate demand – was responsible. This was all remediable, according to Keynes, with sufficient fiscal policy; government spending would overcome market imperfections. Ordinary economics – which emphasized individual actors engaged in the market process – slipped further into the shadows, as Keynesian macroeconomics took center stage.

Since the 1940s, economic policy worldwide has been dominated by Keynesian ideas. Even when claiming to break away from this tradition, research in economics was primarily Keynesian. Keynesian ideas led to Keynesian models. Keynesian data were generated to test these models and explore the efficacy of Keynesian policies. All that oscillated was whether one should be 'liberal' or 'conservative'; but everyone – certainly everyone in power – was fundamentally Keynesian.

The neo-Keynesian consensus entailed a commitment to macroeconomic fine-tuning through fiscal and monetary policy and microeconomic regulation (or nationalization in the UK). The results of this policy consensus were revealed to be disastrous. By the 1970s, economies in the Western democracies were failing. Soviet bloc nations were crumbling from within, as political corruption mixed with an economic system incapable of aligning incentives for state-owned firms to produce efficiently and meet consumer demands (let alone spur technological innovation!). And we must not forget the third world crises of the 1970s and 1980s – Mexican debt, Latin American instability, African dictatorship and Indian brain drain. All of these economic realities were a consequence of neo-Keynesian policies and socialist aspirations.

After the 1987 Crash, Reagan was asked whether this meant the rehabilitation of Keynesian economics. He responded by telling the audience that Mr Keynes didn't even have a degree in economics. Despite Reagan's rhetoric, his diagnosis of the crash was one of aggregate demand failure. His policy response was an attempt to stimulate consumption. Within two minutes of questioning the credibility of Keynes, Reagan endorsed the policy prescriptions of the *General Theory*, exhorting Americans to 'Buy, buy, buy!'

The 'Washington Consensus', an era of so-called *laissez-faire* following the Reagan revolution, was, in reality, much closer to the policy prescription of John Kenneth Galbraith than that of Milton Friedman. Sure, Friedman's rhetoric was employed; but Galbraith's policies were pursued. Galbraith argued for activism via a weird mix of Marx, Veblen and Keynes. The basic prescription involved government both as referee and active player in the economic game. This, of course, was only nominally different from the same old policies implemented since the 1940s.

Friedman used the logic of economic theory and empirical examination to point out the consequences of government activism. When it came to macroeconomics, however, Friedman was fundamentally a Keynesian. Rather than rejecting the bankrupt methodological and analytical framework of Keynes, Friedman articulated a sort of 'conservative' Keynesianism. As such, his intellectual victory did not translate into a fundamental change in the structure of public policy either in the USA or abroad.

Nonetheless, conceptual confusion and historical inaccuracy blame our current problems on an era of small government and *laissez-faire* policy that never really existed. We have deluded ourselves into believing that politicians who freely adopted the language of the great economists were actually persuaded by their arguments and ready to follow that advice. They were not ready. Instead, they constantly intervened in the economy, either by abandoning principles or in the name of principles. As a result, the language of economics has been corrupted – reduced from science to mere opinion.

Keynes isn't the intellectual solution to our current economic woes. His ideas are one of the primary reasons we are in this mess. He was wrong in 1936. He was wrong in 1956 and 1976. He is still wrong in 2008. Bad economic ideas result in bad economic policy, which, in turn, results in bad economic consequences. That simple linear relationship is true across time and place. While there may be macroeconomic problems, there are only microeconomic solutions. We do not need more of the same old bad economic ideas that have persisted for most of the last century. What we need, instead, is a return to ordinary economics.

EXPLAINING A CRISIS WITH ORDINARY ECONOMICS

Many claim that economics as a scientific discipline has been rocked by current events. They cite a failure to 'predict' the economic downturn and an inability to 'fix' it with a consensus on the right public policy as evidence. To be sure, these are dark days for economists – but certainly no darker than the 1930s and 1940s. Unemployment, reported at 9 percent in March of 2009, hit a record-breaking 24.9 percent in 1933. The so-called crisis of this century pales in comparison to the actual crisis of the last century. But what has been until now a severe recession might result in a crisis if we have not learned from the mistakes of our past.

There are basically three explanations for the Great Depression, two of which place blame on the government. First, we have the Austrian story. From 1922 to 1928, while technological innovation put downward pressure on prices, the general price level was kept more or less stable as a newly established and inexperienced Federal Revenue (the Fed) drastically expanded the money supply in fear of deflation. This generated a boom–bust cycle, which began to swing south by the end of the decade. Second, we have the Monetarist claim that the Fed acted incorrectly in the 1930s, contracting the money supply when expansionary policy would have remedied the situation. And, finally, we have the Keynesian explanation, which points to aggregate demand failure.

Austrian and monetarist explanations need not be at odds with one another. For one, the Austrians address the cause of the Depression while the monetarists deal with how it could have been prevented. They pertain to two different time periods. Both pinpoint government as the source of the problem. Most importantly, though, both are far enough removed from the claim of aggregate demand failure to avoid being implicated by the shortcomings of fiscal policy. The lesson to be learned from the 1930s is that the depth and length of the Great Depression cannot be attributed to monetary distortions (either credit expansion or monetary contraction). A host of policy missteps prevented markets from adjusting to changing circumstances.

After the stock market crashed in 1929, market corrections were immediately set in motion. Prices adjusted to the new realities and resources were reallocated accordingly. By June of 1930, the Dow Jones Index had largely recovered. Then the economy was hit with a massive policy shift on tariffs. The Smoot–Hawley Tariff Act effectively raised the prices of 20 000 imported goods by up to 50 percent. As a consequence, trade was destroyed. The natural process of market correction, which works through the vehicle of trade, came to a screeching halt. In other words, policy shocks transformed the pain of correction into the pain of a crisis.

In hindsight, the Great Depression should come as no shock. Credit expansion followed by monetary contraction created a business cycle and magnified its downturn. Then, just when things were looking up, poor fiscal policy and trade restrictions made reallocating resources exceedingly difficult. Government actions promoted malinvestment and resource mismanagement. Government actions prevented the market from engaging in the natural process of correction. Government actions resulted in the Great Depression. Unfortunately, it seems as though we have not learned from the mistakes of our past. As a result, history may very well repeat itself.

In many ways, the current economic situation is a perfect storm of policy mishaps. In addition to the breakdown of fiscal restraint, which started nearly a century ago, credit expansion under Greenspan (Chairman of the Fed) following the dot-com bubble bursting in 2000 and the stock market downturn of 2002 encouraged individuals to own homes they could not otherwise afford (see Schwartz, 2009: 19).[1] In the absence of cheap credit, these ventures would have been unprofitable and, thus, foregone. Expansionary policy gave lenders an incentive to lower standards, extending loans to those who would be less likely to repay. Below-market-level interest rates – initiated and perpetuated by the Fed – generated malinvestment in the housing market.

To make matters worse, the Fed's efforts to increase home ownership were magnified by government meddling. Under the Clinton Administration, government-sponsored entities, including the Federal National Mortgage Association (Fannie Mae) and the Federal Home Loan Mortgage Corporation (Freddie Mac), were directed to increase the number of mortgage loans extended to low-income families. In 1996, Fannie Mae and Freddie Mac were told that '42 percent of their mortgage financing had to go to borrowers with incomes below the median income in their area' and '12 percent of all mortgage purchases by Fannie and

Freddie had to be "special affordable" loans, typically to borrowers with incomes less than 60 percent of their area's median income' (Schwartz, 2009: 20). Under the Bush Administration, these programs were continued, even extended (see Bergsman, 2004: 55–6). The target for 'special affordable' loans increased to 20 percent in 2000; by 2005, it was 22 percent (Schwartz, 2009: 20). Although shares in Freddie Mac and Fannie Mae were owned privately since 1968, 'their congressional charters suggested that if they got into trouble, Congress would bail them out (as it did, in fact, in September 2008)' (Friedman, 2009: 6). As such, they followed the directives of politicians. And politicians on both sides of the aisle were in agreement: every American ought to own a home.

While their intentions may have been pure, government officials failed to realize why these individuals were unable to get low-rate mortgages in the first place. The mere act of extending loans did not change the fact that these individuals were poor candidates for receiving loans. Instead, good intentions bred poor policies and resulted in an even worse state of affairs. Had they been more familiar with the teachings of ordinary economics, they would have known that *ought* cannot presuppose *can* (see Horwitz, 2009: 34–6).[2]

Lenders, pressured to lower standards, attempted to hedge this additional risk by adopting new, untested means of securitization. Technological development is always a risky venture. However, the risk is usually spread among many firms employing multiple strategies and each firm is held accountable for the amount of risk it takes on. In this particular case, though, institutional structures developed to rate credit risk had been eroded by government regulation, effectively granting firms a free pass to act irresponsibly (see White, 2009). As such, financial institutions leveraged to the hilt at the below-market interest rate. And rather than waiting for a tried and true method to emerge, they invested heavily in mortgage-backed securities. The nature of these securities meant that firms would be able to repay their loans only if the housing market continued to trend upward.

While the portfolios of lenders were becoming less and less stable, borrowers continued to take out loans. And as the interest rate fell, the credentials of those borrowers offered loans sank as well. These new borrowers were often first-time homebuyers with few or no assets to put up as collateral and a limited understanding of adjustable rate mortgages (see Zandi, 2009: 54). Most importantly, these individuals had been shielded from the market's natural tendency to discipline participants. The 1990s was a high-growth decade fueled, at least in part, by expansionary monetary policy. Expecting the upward trend to continue, individuals got comfortable living beyond their means. Even at the exceptionally low interest rates, many of these new borrowers were barely able to service their loans. When rates began to ratchet back up to the market level, they were unable to repay.

The financial fiasco that has followed the bursting of the housing bubble is not a consequence of market instability, but of the inability of government to engage in apt intervention. Politicians presume they have the necessary knowledge to effectively tackle the problems that, ironically, they have brought about. In reality, they do not possess this knowledge. They cannot possess this knowledge. This knowledge is dispersed throughout society, with each market participant holding information of a particular time and place that is often unknown to others and, in some respects, impossible to articulate. Even if politicians were capable of collecting the necessary knowledge – and, to reiterate, they are not – that knowledge would be outdated before it could be used. We live in a dynamic world where things are constantly in flux. And, to the dismay of politicians, the instantaneous collection of knowledge by one entity – which would be required for apt intervention – is beyond the realm of possibility. Breaking down the institutional structures of an economy to engage in apt intervention when it is impossible to accomplish what is intended ends predictably in catastrophe.

What we are witnessing at present is the endogenous creation of a crisis. Policy failures are compounding the problem. Similar to how in the post-Hurricane Katrina debacle the folly of man worsened the fury of nature, the policy path taken in response to the bursting housing bubble and subsequent financial system shake-up has turned a market correction of government-induced distortions into a potential system-wide collapse. Make no mistake: market correction is a painful process. Businesses fail and unemployment rises. Some families must uproot and relocate in order to find new jobs. Others have to retrain, as the skills they possess are no longer deemed valuable by the market. Parents must explain to their children why fewer presents will be under the Christmas tree; why the annual vacation must be postponed; why they are unable to help with those college expenses this year. The process of market correction is not enjoyable, but it is necessary.

It is natural, in the midst of a recession, to think that times are much worse than they should be. But in fact times were much better in the preceding period than they should have been. The boom experienced was artificial, a period of wasteful malinvestment that led to insolvency. And the time for correcting this malinvestment has come. Credit-induced booms are unsustainable – they will come to an end. The only question is when this adjustment will take place. Implementing policy that softens the pain of correction merely prolongs the process of adjustment.

Unfortunately the Fed and the Treasury have acted as if the only lesson to be learned from the Great Depression is that lack of liquidity can cause a crisis. This is not the relevant lesson for today. Inflation is damaging, deflation is damaging. As Mises once put it, trying to cure the problems created by one by following up with the other is analogous to backing up over a man to undo the damage of driving your car over him in the first place. Expansionary monetary policy and government intervention that prevents market correction when malinvestment is revealed do not get you out of trouble. Instead, they merely mask the problem for another day. The truth is, we have been postponing the adjustment period for decades. Bailouts, stimulus packages and easy credit cannot be sustained indefinitely. Postponing the adjustment for yet another round will only make us less equipped to deal with the underlying problem in the future.

Distortions to market signals caused by government manipulation are real. The perverse incentives created by bailouts will be with us for years and the costs of rent-seeking are accumulating. $700 billion becomes $850 billion. Rather than investing in productive ventures, entrepreneurs form special interest groups to swarm DC for their share of the funds. Just as the policies pursued during the Great Depression extended the period of correction, the decisions politicians make today will certainly have an impact on the length and depth of the adjustment that lies ahead.

MOVING FORWARD

Ordinary economics emphasizes the reality of scarcity: there is no such thing as a free lunch. This applies to those acting in the name of government just as much as to anyone else. With this in mind, it is foolish to talk about government spending without also discussing how those expenditures are to be financed. Government can raise revenue in one of three ways: tax, borrow or inflate. To be clear, the second of these is only a temporary means of raising revenue. Eventually, borrowed funds must be repaid through taxation, inflation or a combination of the two.

The natural proclivity of democratic governments is to pursue those public policies that concentrate benefits on the well organized and well informed, and disperse costs on to the unorganized and ill informed. Additionally, there are strong reasons to believe that policy-making will be biased toward shortsightedness – pay out the benefits now, worry about the costs down the road. Thus the natural tendency for elected officials is to borrow (rather than tax) and then inflate (rather than tax). In other words, politicians prefer to spend in the short run to meet electoral promises. Then, when the bill comes due, they print more money in order to pay back in cheaper currency. Hence current deficits are financed by massive amounts of public debt; and this debt is repaid, at least to some extent, by monetization.

Milton Friedman taught us that inflation is everywhere and always a monetary phenomenon. Wage-pull or cost-push inflation stories do not make sense. The oil shocks of the 1970s, for example, explain a relative price change, but not a change in the general price level. The general price level is determined by the supply and demand for money. While Friedman's dictum is correct, Tom Sargent's work on hyperinflation suggests it could benefit from modification: hyperinflation is everywhere and always preceded by fiscal imbalance. Or, put simply, the natural proclivity of government has consequences.

In the 1970s, the Irish government attempted to boost aggregate demand by implementing expansionary fiscal policies. Public infrastructure projects were taken on; government agencies expanded to offset unemployment; and transfer payments increased. Predictably, fiscal expansion was financed with deficit spending. By 1977, public sector borrowing rose from 10 to 17 percent of GNP (Powell, 2003: 433). In the end, however, these Keynesian-style macroeconomic policies were not effective at stimulating the economy. Ireland's average annual growth rate was a meager 2.2 percent from 1973 to 1992 (Hall and Luther, 2009). To make matters worse, efforts to stimulate the economy left the Irish government with a fiscal crisis.

Fortunately, Ireland was a member of the European Monetary System (EMS), which effectively prevented the government from monetizing its debt via inflation. Since previous tax increases had failed to raise sufficient revenue, the only remaining option was to cut spending. By 1987, the current operating budget was cut by 3 percent (Powell, 2003: 435). With government spending under control, Irish policy-makers were able to create a more competitive tax system. Although these reforms were adopted to deal with a fiscal crisis, they helped pave the way for Ireland's economic take-off.

Unfortunately, the USA is not as restrained as Ireland was. What is more frightening is the near-universal belief in the USA that we can spend our way out of trouble. Government spending would likely be deficit financed and the monetization of this debt will cause even more inflation, distorting market signals further. Likewise, it makes no sense to encourage private spending with easy credit, as this very policy created the problem we are dealing with and would only exacerbate it further. The only solution is to allow the market to correct.

Successful politicians at present claim we must move past the dead ideologies of the past and the 'do-nothing' arguments that have failed time and time again. The reality, of course, is that those arguments have not been actively pursued since Grover Cleveland. Hoover, and then Roosevelt, was actively involved with the economy. Both attempted to manipulate the market. Both were guilty of the fatal conceit. Both failed miserably.

The economic problems of the present are not the result of dead ideologies, but instead a live political pragmatism. Wealth creation results from realizing the gains from trade and the gains from innovation, not government investment. Citizens and statesmen alike have forgotten the basic ideology that made possible the great growth of the wealth of nations. The foundation of Western civilization – a system of property, contract and consent – has allowed for freedom of trade and social cooperation under an international division of labor. Without this foundation, Western civilization would cease to exist. For this reason, government, rather than being unleashed, must be constrained. It must be constrained in such a binding way that it is not possible for elected officials to pursue their natural proclivities to provide privileges to political favorites by concentrating benefits and dispersing costs. It must be prevented from monetizing its debt. It must be minimized.

How do we get out of the present mess? Not by curtailing market adjustment, that's for sure. Instead, we must allow the market to weed out unproductive investments promoted by the credit-induced boom. If bankrupt businesses are not bailed out, they will fail. The stock market will go down and unemployment will rise. But resources will not go into a black hole. They will be reallocated to more productive uses. Malinvestment, generated and perpetuated by government meddling, will be cleared away.

The political and legal infrastructure that has made the US economy an attractive economic environment and a land of entrepreneurial opportunity throughout its history must be reinforced. When the gains from trade and the gains from innovation are continually realized, long-term economic growth wipes out the consequences of financial miscues relatively quickly. As Robert Lucas noted, 'Once one starts to think about [economic growth], it is hard to think about anything else' (Lucas, 1988: 5). This assumes, of course, that the policy regime in place does not completely distort the fundamental structure that makes economic growth possible. If we were to fundamentally change the political and legal structures that have, however imperfectly, secured property rights, ensured the consensual transference of property and upheld the contracts of individuals, the trend of long-term growth would be reversed.

To date, the absorptive power of the US economy in dealing with government stupidity has been amazing. Remember that the twentieth century encompassed the First World War, the Second World War, the Korean War, the Vietnam War, the Cold War and turmoil in the Middle East. It was the century of the panic of 1907, the Great Depression, stagflation in the 1970s, the 1987 Crash, and the 1997 Asian contagion. It was a century full of regulations, mismanaged money and irresponsible fiscal policy. It was a century of protectionist legislation and pork-barrel politics. Yet it was also a century of amazing technological innovations. The century started with horse and buggies and ended not only with automobiles, but also with the ability to fly around the world and rocket a man to the moon. During the twentieth century, the cost of domestic trade fell swiftly as train, truck and plane enabled coast-to-coast transactions. International trade reached from the USA to the remotest corners of the world. More so than at any other time in human history, Schumpeterian gains from innovation and Smithian gains from trade have swamped the stupidity of government action. This would not have been possible without a political and legal structure that accommodates property, prices and 'profit and loss'.

CONCLUSION

Hayek argued in the early 1930s that the fate of the economist was to be called upon to address questions of pressing political concern, only to have his advice discounted as soon as it was uttered. Why? Because economics, as a science, puts parameters on the utopias of man. It gives us primarily 'negative' knowledge. Economics tells us that we live in a world of scarcity, that there is no such thing as a free lunch. It reminds us that we cannot assume what it is that we hope to prove. It requires us to face reality: *ought* cannot presuppose *can* and *can* does not always imply *ought*. As Hayek wrote, 'The curious task of economics is to demonstrate to men how little they know about what they imagine they can design' (Hayek, 1988: 76). To this degree, it has failed as a discipline.

Most individuals have no idea what economic science is. In their minds, economics is concerned merely with practical business, or worse, a tool to espouse political ideology. They know nothing of the laws of economics, despite living by them every day. We economists have permitted this. We have allowed politicians and the public to demand of our discipline results that cannot be produced. To our shame, we have pretended to produce those results in order to obtain power and prestige.

Fortunately, all is not lost. There is still time to realize the power of markets to utilize self-interest, coordinate dispersed information and spur entrepreneurial discoveries. It is not too late to point out government inefficiency; crowding out of wealth-creating investment; systemic errors produced by knowledge problems; vested interests seeking privileges; and a precarious inclination toward deficits, debts and debasement. As a discipline, economics must learn to recognize once again the importance of a dynamic market process. Even in times of extraordinary crisis – indeed, especially in such times – we must rely on the lessons of ordinary economics.

NOTES

1. As Schwartz explains, 'An asset boom is propagated by an expansive monetary policy that lowers interest rates and induces borrowing beyond prudent bounds to acquire the asset.' See also Gjerstad and Smith (2009) and Taylor (2009).
2. As Horwitz notes, '"Oughts" without "cans" – ethical pronouncements without economics – are likely to lead to disastrous public policies.'

REFERENCES

Bergsman, Steve (2004), 'Closing the gap', *Mortgage Banking* (February): 55–6.
Friedman, Jeffrey (2009), 'A crisis of politics, not economics: complexity, ignorance, and policy failure', *Critical Review*, **21** (2–3): 127–83.
Gjerstad, Steven and Vernon L. Smith (2009), 'Monetary policy, credit expansion, and housing bubbles: 2008 and 1929', *Critical Review*, **21** (2–3): 269–300.
Hall, Joshua C. and William J. Luther (2009), 'Ireland', in Mehmet Odekon (ed.), *Booms and Busts: An Economics Encyclopedia*, Armonk, NY: M.E. Sharpe.
Hayek, F.A. (1988), *The Fatal Conceit*, Chicago: Chicago University Press.
Horwitz, Steven (2009), 'Ought implies can', *The Freeman*, **59** (4): 34–6.
Lucas, Robert (1988), 'On the mechanics of economic development', *Journal of Monetary Economics*, **22** (1): 3–42.
Powell, Benjamin (2003), 'The case of the Celtic Tiger', *Cato Journal*, **22** (3): 431–48.
Schwartz, Anna J. (2009), 'Origins of the financial market crisis of 2008', *Cato Journal*, **29** (1): 19–23.
Taylor, John B. (2009), *Getting Off Track: How Government Actions and Interventions Caused, Prolonged, and Worsened the Financial Crisis*, Stanford, CA: Hoover Institution.
White, Lawrence J. (2009), 'The credit rating agencies and the subprime debacle', *Critical Review*, **21** (2–3), 389–99.
Zandi, Mark (2009), *Financial Shock: A 360-Degree Look at the Subprime Mortgage Implosion, and How to Avoid the Next Financial Crisis*, Upper Saddle River, NJ: FT Press.

2. Did Bernanke's 'creditism' aggravate the financial crisis of 2008?

Tim Congdon

Keynes once described a rival's work as 'an extraordinary example of how, starting with a mistake, a remorseless logician can end up in Bedlam'.[1] Since September 2008 the world economy has been closer to Bedlam than at any time since the end of the Second World War. Turmoil in stock exchanges and commodity markets has been accompanied by almost constant public wrangling between politicians, financial regulators and bankers. Even worse, output and employment have been on a drastic downward slide, causing many comparisons to be drawn with the Great Depression of the early 1930s.

Is there an intellectual mistake which, by the remorseless logic of events, has ended up in the international financial Bedlam of late 2008 and early 2009? Of course the current crisis is complex and multifaceted, and has many causes. However, the argument here is that one particular line of thought has to carry a large share of the blame for what went wrong. Only now is a rather different set of ideas being heard, perhaps foreshadowing a radical move to better policies and a sharp improvement in the economic situation.

Our starting point is a recondite article in the May 1988 issue of the *American Economic Review*, on 'Credit, money and aggregate demand' by Ben Bernanke and Alan Blinder. Both authors later became prominent in the Federal Reserve (the Fed), with Bernanke receiving the ultimate accolade when he was appointed chairman of the board of governors in February 2006. The article's emphasis was on 'the special nature of bank loans' (Bernanke and Blinder, 2006: 435–9). Following the lead of the Harvard economist Professor Benjamin Friedman (not to be confused with the redoubtable Milton Friedman of Chicago), Bernanke and Blinder referred to 'new interest in the credit–GNP relationship'. By 'credit' they meant bank lending to the private sector.

The 1988 article received numerous citations in other economists' journal articles, the key metric of academic stardom. In 1995 Bernanke was encouraged by this success to write a further article, with Mark Gertler, on 'the credit channel of monetary policy transmission' (Bernanke and Gertler, 1995). The heart of their argument was that 'informational frictions in credit markets worsen during tight-money periods', with the difference in cost between internal and external funds to companies enhancing 'the effects of monetary policy on the real economy'. The remarks on 'informational frictions' were a dutiful allusion to Jo Stiglitz, awarded the Nobel prize for economics in 2001, who had written on 'asymmetric information' as a cause of imperfections in financial markets. Bernanke and Gertler further differentiated between so-called 'balance sheet' and 'bank lending' channels 'to explain the facts', although – curiously – they added a warning that comparisons of actual credit aggregates with other macroeconomic variables were not 'valid tests' of the theory. We shall return to this later.

Bernanke, Blinder, Gertler, Benjamin Friedman and Stiglitz are American, and all of them have had teaching spells in the great East Coast universities (Harvard, Columbia, Princeton, Yale). They are a motley crew, and are far from sharing the same politics or agreeing about everything. However, in economics as in other walks of life, branding makes a big difference to the marketability of what is produced. To non-economists – and indeed to most economists – the intellectual output of the East Coast universities more or less defines the latest and best in the subject. With all these distinguished names writing about credit and its importance, isn't it a fair deduction that credit – and, more specifically, bank lending to the private sector – must be vital to the health of an economy?

Such is the influence of the top East Coast universities that, when the financial crisis broke in autumn 2007, a universally held view among policy-makers was that everything possible must be done to sustain the flow of new bank lending to the private sector. The lending-determines-spending doctrine was accepted without question. Few clearer statements can be found than those from the UK's own prime minister and Treasury ministers. As the crisis escalated in September and October 2008, Gordon Brown emphasized that official action was needed to sustain extra bank lending and that his government's approach went 'to the heart of the problem'. In his view, banks had a 'responsibility' to maintain credit lines to small companies and family businesses.

But there is a problem with bank lending to the private sector. Because borrowers may not be able to repay, lending is risky. Banks must therefore have capital to absorb possible losses in their loan portfolios. So, the remorseless logician proceeds, not only is bank credit central to the nation's economic well-being, but public policy must concern itself with the quantity and quality of the banking system's capital. Because bank lending to the private sector matters so basically to the economy, the government is entitled to interfere with the banks, and to tell them how much capital they should have and what form it should take.

If the reports and accounts prepared by tens of thousands of internal and external auditors are to be believed, in the first half of 2008 the UK's banks were profitable and solvent. Indeed, not only was their capital in positive territory; it was also sufficiently positive to comply with regulations agreed with the Financial Services Authority (FSA). However, in late September and early October 2008 a number of officials at the Treasury, the Bank of England and the FSA got it into their heads that the economy was in deep trouble and that the banks were at risk of failure.[2]

It was certainly true that the closing of the international wholesale money markets in August 2007 had cut off the flow of funds for some banks. With these markets shut down, the banks were having difficulty rolling over their interbank borrowings and so were restricting new credit. However, the problem could have been tackled easily enough, either by loans (at a penalty rate) from the Bank of England or by state guarantees on interbank borrowing (with an appropriately high charge for the guarantee fee). A large body of precedent from earlier crises suggested that answers on these lines ought to be made available and would work.

The package put together by UK officialdom did include guarantees on interbank borrowing. But that was only one element. The lending-determines-spending doctrine was so strongly and widely held that the authorities added a major qualification. The guarantees would be available only if banks had sufficient capital to continue lending during the downturn. Whereas two banks (Royal Bank of Scotland and Barclays) issued press releases saying they were not seeking extra capital, officialdom insisted that large amounts of new capital had to be raised. Further, if private shareholders would not cough up the money, the government would subscribe the money instead. Against the banks' protests that macroeconomic conditions were not too bad and a recovery could be envisaged in a few quarters, the Bank of England put together a planning scenario with a deep, long-lasting recession. This scenario implied that large amounts of extra bank capital had to be made obligatory.

In days (and often nights) of ferocious bargaining during October 2008, some of the world's largest financial organizations – organizations that have been household names in the UK for decades, and had long been widely admired around the world for their efficiency and expertise – were bullied into raising capital that they themselves did not think was necessary. The UK government brushed aside such niceties of market capitalism as shareholders' rights and management independence. The East

Coast economists applauded Brown's effort. The Nobel prize winner, Paul Krugman of Princeton, said in his *New York Times* column that the UK was 'playing a leadership role', with Brown's bank recapitalization programme being superior to the US Treasury's plans to buy up toxic assets from the banks (Krugman, 2008).[3] Backed by Krugman's endorsement, Brown claimed that he was 'rescuing the world'. Intriguingly, press reports suggested that Bernanke at the Fed was instrumental in persuading US Treasury Secretary, Hank Paulson, that US policy should move in the UK direction.

Over a year later, at the World Economic Forum in Davos, Switzerland, UK Chancellor of the Exchequer Alistair Darling described the underlying rationale for official policy in two sentences. 'We have got to recapitalize first. You've got to get the expansion of lending.'[4] It was the imperative of 'more lending' – motivated by the theories of the East Coast economists – that justified the intimidation of the banks. As Marcus Agius, chairman of Barclays, told his shareholders, the banks had faced 'an existential threat'.[5]

Almost nine months later the questions have to be asked, 'Was the government right in its views on the economic outlook?' and 'Has the case for large-scale and rapid capital raising in the banking industry been validated?' On the face of it the shocking deterioration in economic conditions and the recent announcement of large losses in banks' loan portfolios vindicate the stance taken by the government and its regulatory agencies. But that conclusion is too hasty. Banks are unique and rather odd institutions that occupy such a central position in a modern market economy that their behaviour can interact with the business cycle in unexpected ways.

In a 1933 academic article in *Econometrica*, one of the USA's most influential economists, Irving Fisher, proposed 'the debt-deflation theory of great depressions'. Starting from a boom in which people had borrowed heavily, he suggested that an unforeseen deterioration in business conditions might cause large repayment of bank debt. The repayment of bank debt would reduce the amount of money in the economy (which he called 'deposit currency'), which in turn would cause a fall in prices, with a disproportionate effect on profits, the value of businesses and asset prices, leading to further repayments of debt, another round of reductions in bank deposits, a further fall in prices and so on. The disaster was rather like the capsizing of a ship. In Fisher's words, under 'normal conditions' a ship is always near 'a stable equilibrium', but 'after being tipped beyond a certain angle' it 'no longer has this tendency to return to equilibrium, but, instead, a tendency to depart further from it' (Fisher, 1933: 339).

The problem with October 2008's bank recapitalization exercise was that it capsized the UK economy. (The same comment is true of similar exercises in other economies, but there is no space here to go into details.) The warnings of a big recession were particularly foolish and counterproductive, since they caused an abrupt step downwards in business expectations. The shock to the banks was so sudden and severe that they reacted not by increasing the availability of credit, as officialdom had intended, but by restricting it further. (The Bank of England publishes a monthly series for 'sterling unused credit facilities'. It had started falling in mid-2007, but the pace of decline accelerated in the immediate aftermath of the bank recapitalization exercise.)

Just as Irving Fisher warned over 60 years ago, a restriction of bank credit stops the growth of households' and companies' deposits. The lack of money in the economy hits spending, profits and asset prices, and asset price falls lead to an unexpectedly high level of losses on banks' loan assets. The result is a self-feeding and unstable downward spiral of retrenchment. In the 1933 article Fisher emphasized the sometimes paradoxical nature of this downward spiral. People repay bank debt in order to improve their financial circumstances, but – if everyone does so at the same time – the resulting fall in bank deposits (i.e. in the quantity of money) causes a drop in prices and possibly an increase in the *real* value of the remaining debts. To quote from him again, 'the mass effort to get out of debt sinks us more deeply into debt' (Fisher, 1933: 344).[6]

The October 2008 bank recapitalization package did not protect the economy from a deep recession. On the contrary, it accelerated the onset of recessionary forces and intensified them. By February 2009 the UK's policy-makers were desperate.[7] In October 2008 they had put together a package that they regarded as clever in conception, and appropriate and proportionate in its implementation. Indeed, their efforts had been praised by trend-setters of international opinion, including the *Financial Times* which judged that the UK's measures created 'a global template'. Many leading economists – including the US economists who had theorized about credit and its role in business – recommended programmes similar to the UK's for their own countries. But demand, output and employment were deteriorating more rapidly after bank recapitalization than before. Although interest rates had been slashed almost to zero, banks were still cutting back on credit lines and stock markets continued to decline. The year 2009 would be the worst year for the UK economy since the early 1980s.

As usual in cyclical downturns, some economists urged fiscal reflation – higher government spending unmatched by extra taxes or outright tax cuts – in order 'to boost demand'. This is an ancient tribal custom of Keynesian economists who believe that the mere invocation of their hero's name can overwhelm experience and logic. Careful tests of the effectiveness of fiscal policy are needed, comparing changes in the cyclically adjusted budget deficit with concurrent or subsequent changes in total demand. The results of such tests are disappointing and show, quite simply, that fiscal policy does not work. (The International Monetary Fund website provides a database with values of both the structural, cyclically adjusted budget balance and the output gap for most of the world's economies since 1980. An appendix to this chapter shows the results of regressing the change in the output gap on the change in the structural budget balance for the G7 economies from 1981 to 2008. The change in the budget balance did not have a statistically significant impact on output in any of them.)

Japan exemplifies the wider argument. Since the early 1990s it has been the target of constant criticism from foreign economists, particularly Krugman, who assert that the answer to its chronic demand weakness is fiscal expansion. In fact, over the last 20 years Japan has had prolonged phases in which the budget deficit has increased and demand grown at a beneath-trend rate or fallen, and prolonged phases in which the budget deficit has decreased and demand has grown at an above-trend rate. Although Darling mentioned Keynes at the time of the 2008 Pre-Budget Report, the idea of a discretionary fiscal boost in the UK had been forgotten when the Budget itself was announced in March 2009.

At the bleakest moments of the crisis, in January and February 2009, a major policy rethink seems to have started at the Bank of England. (If public statements are to be taken at face value, nothing comparable occurred at the Treasury.) In his 1988 paper Bernanke had proposed the lending-determines-spending doctrine as an alternative to 'standard models of aggregate demand' (as he termed them), which paid more attention to money than to loans. In fact, Bernanke saw the 'money-only framework' as 'traditional' and regarded his own work as an innovation. He even coined the word 'creditist' to describe a central bank with a special alertness to credit developments. Implicitly he was contrasting 'creditism' with 'monetarism', where monetarism is understood as the claim that the quantity of money – nowadays dominated by bank deposits – is crucial in the determination of national income. Bernanke said in forthright terms that in some circumstances 'a credit-based policy' would be 'superior' to 'a money-based policy'.[8]

Throughout the financial crisis of late 2007 and 2008 the monetary alternative to the lending-determines-spending doctrine had always been there. For many years the Bank of England had been agnostic over major theoretical issues. It may have veered towards the creditist side in the creditist/monetarist debate, but it had not made a final commitment. With base rates down to a mere 0.5 per cent, further significant cuts in the *price* of money were out of the question. The Bank decided to refocus on the *quantity* of money. On 5 March 2009 it announced a programme of so-called 'quantitative easing', in which enormous purchases of gilt-edged securities, mostly from non-banks, would deliberately add to the level of bank deposits (i.e. the quantity of money).[9]

Credit and money are often confused, and confusions in a subject as arcane as banking theory are understandable enough. However, credit and money are distinct. Lending to the private sector is a totally different entry on a bank balance sheet from the figure for deposits. Increases in banks' loan portfolios add to assets and require extra capital to anticipate the risk of default; increases in bank deposits expand liabilities and may not need any more capital at all. The point is that banks can grow their deposit liabilities by acquiring assets with a negligible risk of default. These assets are of two main kinds – claims on the government (Treasury bills and gilt-edged securities) and claims on the central bank (their so-called 'cash reserves'). When the quantity of money increases as a result of banks' acquisition of such assets, no new bank capital is required.

Reports about quantitative easing in the media have been muddled. Many journalists remain imprisoned in the lending-determines-spending box and believe that the purpose of quantitative easing is to stimulate more lending. Again, the mistake is understandable, as the phrases 'the quantity of money' and 'the money supply' are used interchangeably, and the second of these gives the impression that banks are 'supplying money' (that is, 'making loans'). However, it must be emphasized that 'the money supply' consists of deposits, not loans. The money supply and bank lending are different things.

The intention of the Bank of England's programme of quantitative easing is to increase the quantity of money by direct transactions between it and non-banks. Strange though it may sound, monetary expansion could occur even if bank lending to the private sector were contracting. In its essence the mechanism at work is very simple: the Bank of England adds money to the bank accounts of holders of government securities to pay for these securities. (The details can be of mind-blowing complexity, but need not bother us now.) Roughly speaking, the quantity of money in the UK is about £2000 billion. Gilt purchases of £150 billion over a six-month period would therefore lead by themselves to monetary growth of about 7.5 per cent or, at an annual rate, of slightly more than 15 per cent. This is a very stimulatory rate of monetary expansion.

The objection is sometimes raised that the major holders of gilts are pension funds and insurance companies, and they will not 'spend' the extra money in the shops. But the big long-term savings institutions are reluctant to hold large amounts of money in their portfolios, because in the long run it is an asset with negligible returns. At the end of 2008, UK savings institutions had total bank deposits of about £130 billion. They will be reluctant to let the number double, but – if the £150 billion were allowed to pile up uselessly – that would be the result.

What is the likely sequence of events? First, pension funds, insurance companies, hedge funds and so on try to get rid of their excess money by purchasing more securities. Let us, for the sake of argument, say that they want to acquire more equities. To a large extent they are buying from other pension funds, insurance companies and so on, and the efforts of all market participants taken together to disembarrass themselves of the excess money seem self-cancelling and unavailing. To the extent that buyers and sellers are in a closed circuit, they cannot get rid of it by transactions between themselves. However, there is a way out. They all have an excess supply of money and an excess demand for equities, which will put upward pressure on equity prices. If equity prices rise sharply, the ratio of their money holdings to total assets will drop back to the desired level. Indeed, on the face of it a doubling of the stock market would mean (more or less) that the £150 billion of extra cash could be added to portfolios and yet leave UK financial institutions' money-to-total-assets ratio unchanged.

Second, once the stock market starts to rise because of the process just described, companies will find it easier to raise money by issuing new shares and bonds. At first only strong companies will have the credibility to embark on large-scale fundraising, but they can use their extra money to pay bills to weaker companies threatened with bankruptcy (and also perhaps to purchase land and subsidiaries from them).

In short, although the cash injected into the economy by the Bank of England's quantitative easing may in the first instance be held by pension funds, insurance companies and other financial institutions, it soon passes to profitable companies with strong balance sheets and then to marginal businesses with weak balance sheets, and so on. The cash strains throughout the economy are eliminated, asset prices recover, and demand, output and employment all revive. So the monetary (or monetarist) view of banking policy is in sharp contrast to the credit (or creditist, to recall Bernanke's term) view. Contrary to much newspaper coverage, the monetary view contains a clear account of how money affects spending and jobs. The revival in spending, as agents try to rid themselves of excess money, would occur *even if bank lending were static or falling*.[10]

The important variable for policy-makers is not the level of bank lending to the private sector, but the level of bank deposits. (Remember Irving Fisher's reference to 'deposit currency'.) Indeed, because companies are the principal employers and the representative type of productive unit in a modern economy, bank deposits in company hands need to be monitored very closely. If these deposits start to rise strongly as a by-product of the Bank of England's adoption of quantitative easing, the recession will be over.

Is quantitative easing working? Lags between economic policy and its effects are unpredictable, and celebration would be premature. Nevertheless, the early months of quantitative easing have seen startling improvements in several areas. Most obviously, the UK stock market has soared by 30 per cent and corporate fundraising has been on a massive scale. Anecdotally, companies are saying that cash pressures are less severe. Business surveys have also turned upwards, with a key survey of the services sector suggesting earlier this month that almost as many companies planned to raise output as to reduce it. If there are more output-raising than output-reducing companies, the recession will be over.

The debate about quantitative easing, and the larger debate between creditism and monetarism to which it is related, will rage for the rest of 2009 and probably for many years to come. Much will depend on events and personalities, as well as on ideas and journal articles. But there is at least an argument that Bernanke's creditism was the mistaken theory that, by a remorseless logic of citation, repetition and emulation, spread around the world's universities, think tanks, finance ministries and central banks, and led to the Bedlam of late 2008. The monetary approach – which Bernanke himself saw as standard and traditional – argued that measures such as quantitative easing, rather than bank recapitalization, were appropriate in September and October 2008. Why were large-scale expansionary open market operations – operations targeted directly to increase bank deposits – not adopted at that stage? And would not hundreds of thousands of jobs, and thousands of businesses, have been saved if the Treasury and the Bank of England had bought back vast quantities of gilts then instead of bullying the banks? (This is not to propose that the banks are perfect and angelic. They had been silly, naughty and greedy in the years leading up to the crisis of 2008. But they tend to be silly, naughty and greedy in the years leading up to most crises, and recessions as severe as the current one are not normally visited on innocent bystanders.)

The academic prestige attached to the lending-determines-spending doctrine and other credit-based macroeconomic theories is puzzling. As noted earlier, Bernanke and Gertler included in their 1995 article an observation that comparison of actual credit magnitudes with macroeconomic variables was not a valid test of their theory. One has to wonder why. They claimed that bank lending was determined within the economy and so was 'not a primitive driving force'. (In jargon, bank lending was endogenous and determined by the economy, not exogenous.) Bernanke and Gertler must have known that the relationships between credit flows and other macroeconomic variables were weak or non-existent, casting doubt on their whole approach.

In the event, their reservations about the predictive power of credit aggregates were neither here nor there. In late 2008, policy-makers were bossy and crude in their demands that the banks lend more and have enough capital to support the new loans. More bank lending was deemed to be good, without ifs or buts. To repeat Darling's words, 'We have got to recapitalize first. You've got to get the expansion of lending.' Bluntly, the statistics justified neither official policy nor Darling's hectoring and aggressive tone, while Brown's claims to be 'rescuing the world' and Krugman's praise of UK policy-making now look ridiculous. In no economy are there reliable relationships between bank lending to a particular sector and activity in that sector or the wider economy. In that sense the bank recapitalization exercises were sold on a false prospectus.

Another enigma here is that the alternative view – that over the long run national income is a function of the quantity of money – has clear and overwhelming substantiating evidence from all economies at all times. Both evidence and standard theory argue that the expansionary open market operations that are the hallmark of quantitative easing, not bank recapitalization, should have been policy-makers' first priority in autumn 2008. In the next crisis they must accept that money, not bank credit by itself, is the variable that matters most to macroeconomic outcomes.

NOTES

1. Keynes's remark was in a highly critical review, which originally appeared in 1931, of Hayek's *Prices and Production*. See Moggridge and Johnson (1973), p. 252.
2. See the October 2008 issue (no. 24) of the Bank of England's *Financial Stability Report* for a description and rationalization of official policy. Perhaps the key claim appeared on p. 42: 'Recent events have illustrated that banks can now incur losses much faster than they can recapitalise themselves in stressed conditions.' The report contained numerous references to 'liquidity' and 'credit', but at no point were the phrases 'the quantity of money' or 'the money supply' used.
3. According to Krugman, 'we do know . . . that Mr. Brown and Alistair Darling . . . have defined the character of the worldwide rescue effort, with other wealthy nations playing catch-up.'
4. 'UK weighs "bad banks"', *The Wall Street Journal*, 4 February 2009.
5. See report in the *Financial Times* on Barclays' annual general meeting on 23 April 2009.
6. 'Then we have the great paradox which, I submit, is the chief secret of most, if not all, great depressions. *The more the debtors pay, the more they owe* [Fisher's italics]. The more the economic boat tips, the more it tends to tip. It is not tending to right itself, but is capsizing' (Fisher, 1933: 344).
7. The 16 February 2009 issue of the *New Statesman* carried a 2500-word article on 'The New Depression' by Martin Jacques. A quote appeared on the front page, 'The political and business elite are [sic] flying blind. This crisis has barely started and remains

      completely out of control.' I understand that, at meetings held in the Treasury at this time, both officials and politicians were in utter despair and could see no end to the deterioration in macroeconomic prospects.

8.   See the last three pages of the Bernanke and Blinder article (Bernanke and Blinder, 1988), which include both the word 'creditist' and the phrase 'the credit channel', with this latter phrase appearing seven years before the 1995 Bernanke and Gertler article for which it was part of the title.

9.   The Bank of England website contained an interview between the Governor, Mervyn King, and the BBC journalist, Stephanie Flanders, in which King made clear that the intention of quantitative easing was to increase the quantity of money on a broad definition (i.e. the quantity of bank deposits, in effect).

10.   In their 1995 article Bernanke and Gertler claim that economists do not have a clear account of the transmission mechanism from the quantity of money to the economy, so that the relationship between money and the economy is inside a 'black box'. The claim has to be described as astonishing, since – from David Hume's 1752 essay 'Of money' onwards – numerous accounts of the transmission mechanism are given in the relevant literature. Irving Fisher's contributions (in his 1911 *Purchasing Power of Money* and 1912 *Elementary Principles of Economics*) and Patinkin's *Money, Interest and Prices* (2nd edn, 1965) are particularly important here. In my own work I have emphasized that a coherent account of the transmission mechanism is easiest to present with an all-inclusive or broadly defined money measure, and that money in this sense is relevant to the determination of the nominal values of *both* wealth and income. Indeed, sharp changes in the rate of money growth seem to have their earliest effects on asset prices, and these asset price changes then affect demand, output and employment. See Congdon (2005: 22–47).

REFERENCES

Bank of England (2008), *Financial Stability Report*, No. 24 (October).

Bernanke, Ben S. and Alan S. Blinder (1988), 'Credit, money and aggregate demand', *American Economic Review*, **78**: 435–39.

Bernanke, Ben S. and Mark L. Gertler (1995), 'Inside the black box: the credit channel of monetary policy transmission', *Journal of Economic Perspectives*, **9**: 27–48.

Congdon, Tim (2005), *Money and Asset Prices in Boom and Bust*, London: Institute of Economic Affairs.

Fisher, Irving (1933), 'The debt deflation theory of great depressions', *Econometrica*, **1**, 337–57.

Krugman, Paul (2008), 'Gordon does good', *New York Times*, 12 October.

Moggridge, Donald and Elizabeth Johnson (eds) (1973), *The Collected Writings of John Maynard Keynes, Vol. XII – Economic Articles and Correspondence: Investment and Editorial*, London and Basingstoke: Macmillan for the Royal Economic Society.

The Wall Street Journal (2009), 'UK weighs "bad banks"', 4 February.

APPENDIX: IS FISCAL POLICY EFFECTIVE?

The equations below are of change in output gap regressed on change in structural (i.e. cyclically adjusted) budget balance, annual data, both as a percentage of potential GDP. Note that the budget concept is 'the balance', i.e. it is negative when a deficit is recorded. (As explained in the text, the data source is the IMF's website and the data relate to the 1981–2008 period.

According to standard Keynesian theory, when the deficit increases, that is, when the cyclically adjusted budget balance becomes more negative, demand and output should grow more strongly than would previously have been the case. If fiscal influences on demand are dominant, the change in the output gap ought to respond positively to the increase in the deficit. So the Keynesian view on the effectiveness of fiscal policy would be validated if:

1. The regression coefficients in the equations were negative;
2. The regression coefficients were statistically significant, with a t-statistic of at least 2;
3. The regression coefficients took a value of over one, consistent with the idea that the multiplier was a valid concept, and
4. The equations had a good fit with the data (i.e. R^2 of, say, over 0.5, so that fiscal policy was 'explaining' at least half the variation in the change in output relative to trend).

1. The USA

Change in output gap = 0.04 + 0.20 Change in general government structural balance

- t-statistic on regression coefficient   0.9
- R^2 of equation   0.03

2. Japan

Change in output gap = −0.04 + 0.36 Change in general government structural balance

- t-statistic on regression coefficient   1.83
- R^2 of equation   0.114

Macroeconomic theory and its failings

3. Germany

Change in output gap $= -0.01 - 0.19$ Change in general government structural balance

- t-statistic on regression coefficient -0.79
- R^2 of equation   0.023

4. France

Change in output gap $= -0.02 - 0.28$ Change in general government structural balance

- t-statistic on regression coefficient -1.07
- R^2 of equation   0.042

5. The UK

Change in output gap $= 0.01 + 0.19$ Change in general government structural balance

- t-statistic on regression coefficient   1.23
- R^2 of equation   0.055

6. Italy

Change in output gap $= -0.06 - 0.22$ Change in general government structural balance

- t-statistic on regression coefficent -1.26
- R^2 of equation   0.057

7. Canada

Change in output gap $= -0.06 + 0.06$ Change in general government structural balance

- t-statistic on regression coefficient   0.22
- R^2 of equation   0.002

What is the Verdict?

1. The regression coefficients were positive in four of the seven equations.
2. None of the regression coefficients was statistically significant, according to the usual tests.
3. None of the regression coefficients took a value of above 0.4, casting doubt on the empirical relevance of the multiplier concept. (In any case, in the nation in which the value of the regression coefficient was almost 0.4, Japan, the coefficient had the wrong sign.)
4. The hypothesis did not fit the data at all, with an R^2 above 0.1 only in Japan, where – as already noted – the regression coefficient took the wrong sign.

Conclusion

Contrary to hundreds of textbooks, an increase in the budget deficit does not stimulate demand and output. Naïve Keynesianism – the supposed theory of fiscal stimulus – is not supported by the facts.

3. Toward a new sustainable economy
Robert Costanza

The 2008 financial meltdown was the result of underregulated markets built on an ideology of free market capitalism and unlimited economic growth. The fundamental problem is that the underlying assumptions of this ideology are not consistent with what we now know about the real state of the world. The financial world is, in essence, a set of markers for goods, services and risks in the real world, and when those markers are allowed to deviate too far from reality, 'adjustments' must ultimately follow and crisis and panic can ensue. This problem was identified as far back as the work of Frederick Soddy in the 1930s (Soddy, 1933). To solve this and future financial crises requires that we reconnect the markers with reality. What are our real assets and how valuable are they? To do this requires both a new vision of what the economy is and what it is for, proper and comprehensive accounting of real assets, and new institutions that use the market in its proper role of servant rather than as master.

The mainstream vision of the economy and model of development (also known as the 'Washington Consensus') is based on a number of assumptions about the way the world works, what the economy is, and what the economy is for (see Table 3.1). These assumptions were created during a period when the world was still relatively empty of human beings and their built infrastructure. In this 'empty world' context, built capital was the limiting factor, while natural capital and social capital were abundant. It made sense, in that context, not to worry too much about environmental and social 'externalities' since they could be assumed to be relatively small and ultimately solvable. It made sense to focus on the growth of the market economy, as measured by GDP, as a primary means to improve human welfare. It made sense, in that context, to think of the economy as only marketed goods and services, and to think of the goal as increasing the amount of these goods and services produced and consumed.

But the world has changed dramatically. We now live in a world relatively full of human beings and their built capital infrastructure. In this new context, we have to recognize what the economy is and what it is for. We have first to remember that the goal of the economy is to sustainably

Table 3.1　*Basic characteristics of the current development model and the emerging sustainable and desirable 'ecological economics' development model*

	Current development model: the 'Washington Consensus'	Sustainable and desirable development model: an emerging 'Green Consensus'
Primary policy goal	More: economic growth in the conventional sense, as measured by GDP. The assumption is that growth will ultimately allow the solution of all other problems. More is always better	Better: Focus must shift from merely growth to 'development' in the real sense of improvement in quality of life, recognizing that growth has negative by-products and more is not always better
Primary measure of progress	GDP	GPI (or similar)
Scale/carrying capacity	Not an issue since markets are assumed to be able to overcome any resource limits via new technology and substitutes for resources are always available	A primary concern as a determinant of ecological sustainability. Natural capital and ecosystem services are not infinitely substitutable and real limits exist
Distribution/ poverty	Lip service, but relegated to 'politics' and a 'trickle-down' policy: a rising tide lifts all boats	A primary concern since it directly affects quality of life and social capital and in some very real senses is often exacerbated by growth: a too rapidly rising tide lifts only yachts, while swamping small boats
Economic efficiency/ allocation	The primary concern, but generally including only marketed goods and services (GDP) and institutions	A primary concern, but including both market and non-market goods and services and effects. Emphasizes the need to incorporate the value of natural and social capital to achieve true allocative efficiency
Property rights	Emphasis on private property and conventional markets	Emphasis on a balance of property rights regimes appropriate to the nature

Table 3.1   (continued)

	Current development model: the 'Washington Consensus'	Sustainable and desirable development model: an emerging 'Green Consensus'
		and scale of the system, and a linking of rights with responsibilities. A larger role for common property institutions in addition to private and state property
Role of government	To be minimized and replaced with private and market institutions	A central role, including new functions as referee, facilitator and broker in a new suite of common asset institutions
Principles of governance	*Laissez-faire* market capitalism	Lisbon principles of sustainable governance

Source: Costanza (2008)

improve human well-being and quality of life. We have to remember that material consumption and GDP are merely means to that end, not ends in themselves. We have to recognize, as both ancient wisdom and new psychological research tell us, that material consumption beyond real need can actually reduce our well-being. We have to better understand what really contributes to sustainable human well-being, and recognize the substantial contributions of natural and social capital, which are now the limiting factors to sustainable human well-being in many countries. We have to be able to distinguish between real poverty in terms of low quality of life, and merely low monetary income. Ultimately we have to create a new vision of what the economy is and what it is for, and a new model of development that acknowledges this new full-world context and vision.

QUALITY OF LIFE, HAPPINESS AND THE REAL ECONOMY

There is a substantial body of new research on what actually contributes to human well-being and quality of life (Costanza et al., 2008). This new 'science of happiness' clearly demonstrates the limits of conventional economic income and consumption in contributing to well-being. Kasser (2003) points out, for instance, that people who focus on material consumption as a path to happiness are actually less happy and even suffer higher rates of both physical and mental illnesses than those who do not. Material consumption beyond real need is a form of psychological 'junk food' that satisfies only for the moment and ultimately leads to depression.

Easterlin (2003: 11182) has shown that well-being tends to correlate well with health, level of education and marital status, and not very well with income beyond a certain fairly low threshold. He concludes:

> People make decisions assuming that more income, comfort, and positional goods will make them happier, failing to recognize that hedonic adaptation and social comparison will come into play, raise their aspirations to about the same extent as their actual gains, and leave them feeling no happier than before. As a result, most individuals spend a disproportionate amount of their lives working to make money, and sacrifice family life and health, domains in which aspirations remain fairly constant as actual circumstances change, and where the attainment of one's goals has a more lasting impact on happiness. Hence, a reallocation of time in favor of family life and health would, on average, increase individual happiness.

Layard (2005: 147) synthesizes many of these ideas and concludes that current economic policies are not improving happiness and that 'happiness should become the goal of policy, and the progress of national happiness should be measured and analyzed as closely as the growth of GNP.'

Frank (2000) also concludes that some nations would be better off – overall national well-being would be higher, that is – if we actually consumed less and spent more time with family and friends, working for our communities, maintaining our physical and mental health and enjoying nature.

On this last point, there is substantial and growing evidence that natural systems contribute heavily to human well-being. Costanza et al. (1997) estimated the annual, non-market value of the earth's ecosystem services at $33 trillion per year, substantially larger than global GDP at the time, and almost certainly a conservative underestimate. The Millennium Ecosystem Assessment (2005) is a global compendium of the status and trends of ecosystem services and their contributions to human well-being.

So, if we want to assess the 'real' economy – all the things that contribute to real, sustainable, human well-being – as opposed to only the 'market' economy, we have to measure and include the non-marketed contributions to human well-being from nature, from family, friends and other social relationships at many scales, and from health and education. One convenient way to summarize these contributions is to group them into four basic types of capital that are necessary to support the real, human-well-being-producing economy: built capital, human capital, social capital and natural capital.

The market economy covers mainly built capital (factories, offices, and other built infrastructure and its products) and part of human capital (spending on labor, health and education), with some limited spillover into the other two. Human capital includes the health, knowledge and all the other attributes of individual human beings that allow them to function in a complex society. Social capital includes all the formal and informal networks among people: family, friends and neighbors, as well as social institutions at all levels, such as churches, social clubs, local, state and national governments, non-governmental organizations (NGOs) and international organizations. Natural capital includes the world's ecosystems and all the services they provide. Ecosystem services occur at many scales, from climate regulation at the global scale, to flood protection, soil formation, nutrient cycling, recreation and aesthetic services at the local and regional scales.

ARE WE REALLY MAKING PROGRESS?

Given this definition of the real economy, are we making progress? Is the mainstream development model really working, even in the 'developed' countries? One way to tell is through surveys of people's life satisfaction, which has been relatively flat in the USA and many other developed countries since about 1975. A second approach is an aggregate measure of the real economy that has been developed as an alternative to GDP called the Index of Sustainable Economic Welfare (ISEW – Daly and Cobb, 1989) and more recently renamed the Genuine Progress Indicator (GPI – Cobb et al., 1995).

Let's first take a quick look at the problems with GDP as a measure of true human well-being. GDP is not only limited, measuring only marketed economic activity or gross income, it also counts all of this activity as positive. It does not separate desirable, well-being-enhancing activity from undesirable well-being-reducing activity. For example, an oil spill increases GDP because someone has to clean it up, but it obviously detracts from society's well-being. From the perspective of GDP, more crime, more sickness, more war, more pollution, more fires, storms and pestilence are all potentially good things, because they can increase marketed activity in the economy.

GDP also leaves out many things that *do* enhance well-being but are outside the market. For example, the unpaid work of parents caring for their own children at home doesn't show up, but if these same parents decide to work outside the home to pay for child care, GDP suddenly increases. The non-marketed work of natural capital in providing clean air and water, food, natural resources and other ecosystem services doesn't adequately show up in GDP either, but if those services are damaged and we have to pay to fix or replace them, then GDP suddenly increases. Finally, GDP takes no account of the distribution of income among individuals. But it is well known that an additional $1 worth of income produces more well-being if one is poor rather than rich. It is also clear that a highly skewed income distribution has negative effects on a society's social capital.

The GPI addresses these problems by separating the positive from the negative components of marketed economic activity, adding in estimates of the value of non-marketed goods and services provided by natural, human and social capital, and adjusting for income-distribution effects. While it is by no means a perfect representation of the real well-being of nations, GPI is a much better approximation than GDP. As Amartya Sen and others have noted, it is much better to be approximately right in these measures than precisely wrong.

Comparing GDP and GPI for the USA shows that, while GDP has steadily increased since 1950, with the occasional dip or recession, GPI peaked in about 1975 and has been flat or gradually decreasing ever since. From the perspective of the real economy, as opposed to just the market economy, the USA has been in recession since 1975. As already mentioned, this picture is also consistent with survey-based research on people's stated life satisfaction. The USA and several other developed countries are now in a period of what Herman Daly has called 'un-economic growth', where further growth in marketed economic activity (GDP) is actually reducing well-being on balance rather than enhancing it. In terms of the four capitals, while built capital and human capital have grown, social and natural capital have declined and more than canceled out the gains in built capital.

A NEW SUSTAINABLE, ECOLOGICAL MODEL OF DEVELOPMENT

A new model of development consistent with our new full world context would be based clearly on the goal of sustainable human well-being. It would use measures of progress that clearly acknowledge this goal (i.e. GPI instead of GDP). It would acknowledge the importance of ecological sustainability, social fairness and real economic efficiency.

Ecological sustainability implies recognizing that natural and social capital are not infinitely substitutable for built and human capital, and that real biophysical limits exist to the expansion of the market economy. Climate change is perhaps the most obvious and compelling of these limits.

Social fairness implies recognizing that the distribution of wealth is an important determinant of social capital and quality of life. The conventional development model, while explicitly aimed at reducing poverty, has bought into the assumption that the best way to do this is through growth in GDP. This has not proved to be the case and explicit attention to distribution issues is sorely needed. As Frank (2007) has argued, economic growth beyond a certain point sets up a 'positional arms race' that changes the consumption context and forces everyone to consume too much of easily seen positional goods (like houses and cars) at the expense of non-marketed, non-positional goods and services from natural and social capital. Increasing inequality of income actually reduces overall societal well-being, not just for the poor, but across the income spectrum.

Real economic efficiency implies including all resources that affect sustainable human well-being in the allocation system, not just marketed goods and services. Our current market allocation system excludes most non-marketed natural and social capital assets and services that are huge contributors to human well-being. The current development model ignores this and therefore does not achieve real economic efficiency. A new, sustainable ecological development model would measure and include the contributions of natural and social capital and could better approximate real economic efficiency.

The new development model would also acknowledge that a complex range of property rights regimes is necessary to adequately manage the full range of resources that contribute to human well-being. For example, most natural and social capital assets are public goods. Making them private property does not work well. On the other hand, leaving them as open access resources (with no property rights) does not work well either. What is needed is a third way to 'propertize' these resources without privatizing them. Several new (and old) common property rights systems have been proposed to achieve this goal, including various forms of common property trusts.

The role of government also needs to be reinvented. In addition to government's role in regulating and policing the private market economy, it has a significant role to play in expanding the 'commons sector', which can propertize and manage non-marketed natural and social capital assets. It also has a major role to play as facilitator of societal development of a shared vision of what a sustainable and desirable future would look like. Strong democracy based on developing a shared vision is a prerequisite to building a sustainable and desirable future (Prugh et al., 2000). This new vision implies a core set of principles for sustainable governance.

PRINCIPLES OF SUSTAINABLE GOVERNANCE

The key to achieving sustainable governance in the new full world context is an integrated (across disciplines, stakeholder groups and generations) approach based on the paradigm of 'adaptive management', whereby policy-making is an iterative experiment acknowledging uncertainty, rather than a static 'answer'. Within this paradigm, six core principles (the Lisbon principles) that embody the essential criteria for sustainable governance have been proposed (Costanza et al., 1998). Some of them are already well accepted in the international community (e.g. Principle 3); others are variations on well-known themes (e.g. Principle 2 is an extension of the subsidiarity principle); while others are relatively new in international policy, although they have been well developed elsewhere (e.g. Principle 4). The six principles together form an indivisible collection of basic guidelines governing the use of common natural and social capital assets.

- *Principle 1: Responsibility.* Access to common asset resources carries attendant responsibilities to use them in an ecologically sustainable, economically efficient and socially fair manner. Individual and corporate responsibilities and incentives should be aligned with each other and with broad social and ecological goals.
- *Principle 2: Scale-matching.* Problems of managing natural and social capital assets are rarely confined to a single scale. Decision-making should (i) be assigned to institutional levels that maximize input, (ii) ensure the flow of information between institutional levels, (iii) take ownership and actors into account, and (iv) internalize costs and benefits. Appropriate scales of governance will be those that have the most relevant information, can respond quickly and efficiently, and are able to integrate across scale boundaries.
- *Principle 3: Precaution.* In the face of uncertainty about potentially irreversible impacts to natural and social capital assets, decisions concerning their use should err on the side of caution. The burden of proof should shift to those whose activities potentially damage natural and social capital.
- *Principle 4: Adaptive management.* Given that some level of uncertainty always exists in common asset management, decision-makers should continuously gather and integrate appropriate ecological, social and economic information with the goal of adaptive improvement.
- *Principle 5: Full cost allocation.* All of the internal and external costs and benefits, including social and ecological, of alternative decisions

concerning the use of natural and social capital should be identified
and allocated. When appropriate, markets should be adjusted to
reflect full costs.

- *Principle 6: Participation.* All stakeholders should be engaged in the
  formulation and implementation of decisions concerning natural
  and social capital assets. Full stakeholder awareness and participation contributes to credible, accepted rules that identify and assign
  the corresponding responsibilities appropriately.

SOME POLICIES TO ACHIEVE REAL, SUSTAINABLE DEVELOPMENT

The conventional development model is not working, for either the developed or the developing world. It is not sustainable and it is also not desirable. It is based on a now-obsolete empty world vision and it is leading us
to disaster.

We need to accept that we now live in a full world context where natural
and social capital are the limiting factors. We could achieve a much higher
quality of life, and one that would be ecologically sustainable, socially fair
and economically efficient if we shifted to a new sustainable development
paradigm that incorporates these principles.

The problem is that our entire modern global civilization is, as even
former President Bush acknowledged, 'addicted to oil'. It is also addicted
to consumption and conventional development model in general. An
addictive substance is something one has developed a dependence on,
which is either not necessary or harmful to one's longer-term well-being.
Fossil fuels (and excessive material consumption in general) fit the bill. We
can power our economies with renewable energy, and we can be happier
with lower levels of consumption, but we must first break our addiction
to fossil fuels, consumption and the conventional development model,
and as any addict can tell you; 'that ain't easy'. But in order to break an
addiction of any kind, one must first clearly see the benefits of breaking it,
and the costs of remaining addicted, facts that accumulating studies such
as the IPCC reports, the Stern Review (2007), the Millennium Ecosystem
Assessment (2005) and many others are making more apparent every
day.

What else can we do to help break this addiction? Here are just a few
suggestions.

- Create and share a vision of a future with zero fossil fuel use
  and a quality of life higher than that of today. That will involve

understanding that GDP is a means to an end, not an end itself, and that in some countries today more GDP actually results in less human well-being (while in others the reverse is still true). It will require a focus on sustainable scale and just distribution. It will require an entirely new and broader vision of what the economy is, what it's for, and how it functions.

• Convene a 'new Bretton Woods' conference to establish the new measures and institutions needed to replace GDP, the World Bank, the IMF and the WTO (World Trade Organization). These new institutions would promote:

  – Shifting primary national policy goals from increasing marketed economic activity (GDP) to maximizing national well-being (GPI or something similar). This would allow us to see the interconnections between built, human, social and natural capital, and build real well-being in a balanced and sustainable way.
  – Reforming tax systems to send the right incentives by taxing negatives (pollution, depletion of natural capital, overconsumption) rather than positives (labor, savings, investment).
  – Expanding the commons sector by developing new institutions that can 'propertize' the commons without privatizing them. Examples include various forms of common asset trusts, like the atmospheric (or sky) trust (Barnes et al., 2008) payments for depletion of natural and social capital, and rewards for protection of these assets.
  – Reforming international trade to promote well-being over mere GDP growth. This implies protecting natural capital, labor rights, and democratic self-determination first and *then* allowing trade, rather than the current trade rules that ride roughshod over all other societal values and ignore non-market contributions to well-being.

CONCLUSION

The long-term solution to the financial crisis is to move beyond the 'growth at all costs' economic model to a model that recognizes the real costs and benefits of growth. We can break our addiction to fossil fuels, overconsumption, and the current development model and create a more sustainable and desirable future. It will not be easy: it will require a new vision, new measures and new institutions. It will require a directed evolution of our entire society (Beddoe et al., 2009). But it is not a sacrifice of quality of life to break this addiction. Quite the contrary, it is a sacrifice not to.

REFERENCES

Barnes, P., R. Costanza, P. Hawken, D. Orr, E. Ostrom, A. Umana and O. Young (2008), 'Creating an earth atmospheric trust', *Science*, **319**: 724.
Beddoe, R., R. Costanza, J. Farley, E. Garza, J. Kent, I. Kubiszewski, L. Martinez, T. McCowen, K. Murphy, N. Myers, Z. Ogden, K. Stapleton and J. Woodward (2009), 'Overcoming systemic roadblocks to sustainability: the evolutionary redesign of worldviews, institutions and technologies', *Proceedings of the National Academy of Sciences*, **106**: 2483–89.
Cobb, C., T. Halstead and J. Rowe (1995), *The Genuine Progress Indicator: Summary of Data and Methodology*, San Francisco, CA: Redefining Progress.
Costanza, R. (2008), 'Stewardship for a "full" world', *Current History*, **107**: 30–35.
Costanza, R., R. d'Arge, R. de Groot, S. Farber, M. Grasso, B. Hannon, S. Naeem, K. Limburg, J. Paruelo, R.V. O'Neill, R. Raskin, P. Sutton and M. van den Belt (1997), 'The value of the world's ecosystem services and natural capital', *Nature*, **387**: 253–60.
Costanza, R., F. Andrade, P. Antunes, M. van den Belt, D. Boersma, D.F. Boesch, F. Catarino, S. Hanna, K. Limburg, B. Low, M. Molitor, G. Pereira, S. Rayner, R. Santos, J. Wilson and M. Young (1998), 'Principles for sustainable governance of the oceans', *Science*, **281**: 198–9.
Costanza, R., B. Fisher, S. Ali, C. Beer, L. Bond, R. Boumans, N.L. Danigelis, J. Dickinson, C. Elliott, J. Farley, D.E. Gayer, L. MacDonald Glenn, T. Hudspeth, D. Mahoney, L. McCahill, B. McIntosh, B. Reed, S.A.T. Rizvi, D.M. Rizzo, T. Simpatico, and R. Snapp (2008), 'An integrative approach to quality of life measurement, research, and policy', *Surveys and Perspectives Integrating Environment and Society*, **1**: 1–5.
Daly, H.E. and J. Cobb (1989), *For the Common Good*, Boston, MA: Beacon Press.
Easterlin, R.A. (2003), 'Explaining happiness', *Proceedings of the National Academy of Science*, **100**: 11176–83.
Frank, R. (2000), *Luxury Fever*, Princeton, NJ: Princeton University Press.
Frank, R. (2007), *Falling Behind: How Rising Inequality Harms the Middle Class*, Berkeley, CA: University of California Press.
Kasser, T. (2003), *The High Price of Materialism*, Cambridge, MA: MIT Press.
Layard, R. (2005), *Happiness: Lessons from a New Science*, Harmondsworth, UK: Penguin.
Millennium Ecosystem Assessment (2005), *Ecosystems and Human Well-being: Synthesis*, Washington, DC: Island Press.
Prugh, T., R. Costanza and H. Daly (2000), *The Local Politics of Global Sustainability*, Washington, DC: Island Press.
Soddy, F. (1933), *Wealth, Virtual Wealth, and Debt: The Solution of the Economic Paradox*, Boston, MA: E.P. Dutton.
Stern, N. (2007), *The Economics of Climate Change: The Stern Review*, Cambridge, UK: Cambridge University Press.

4.   Looking at the crisis through Marx – or is it the other way about?

Ben Fine

INTRODUCTION

Orthodox economics has in part seen financial markets as an efficient way of mobilizing and allocating resources, and thereby coordinating information through the market system and across its agents. As the variously infamous former US Treasury Secretary, Chief Economist at the World Bank, and Head of Harvard Larry Summers has described the efficient market hypothesis, cited in Davidson (2008a),

> The ultimate social functions are spreading risks, guiding investment of scarce capital, and processing and dissemination the information possessed by diverse traders . . . *prices always reflect fundamental values* . . . The logic of efficient markets is compelling [original italics].

The logic today is less compelling, not least to the bankers themselves, who had previously deployed it to rationalize what is now being revealed to be a reality of inefficient, dysfunctional and parasitical markets. At best, the mainstream sees this as some combination of corruption, imperfect coordination of markets, and their imperfect institutions and regulation. What is notably absent is any systemic understanding of finance in its relationship to capitalism in general and to its current character. Such approaches, from Keynes through to varieties of post-Keynesianism, with Minsky to the fore, have been marginalized by the mainstream in light of its obsessive preoccupation with the optimizing, if imperfectly coordinated, individual.

Even before the current crisis, the idea that finance more or less efficiently mobilizes and allocates resources on behalf of the real economy bordered on the ridiculous. In the UK, formerly the workshop of the world, does it take half a million workers to do this and 25 per cent of GDP? Perhaps this can be excused on the grounds of the weight of international financial services provided. That cannot be said of South Africa. Finance has been its fastest-growing sector since the overthrow of apartheid, now taking up

20 per cent of GDP. Yet, 40 per cent of the population do not benefit from any financial services at all. Such services have, in any case, been deployed to financialize and globalize the operations of previously internationally constrained, highly concentrated, domestic conglomerates – that is to export domestic capital and surplus generated within the economy. Effectively, far from contributing 20 per cent of GDP, finance has appropriated a quarter of it, claiming this to be a contribution to what has been produced.

At times of crisis, Marx is always dug up and paraded for popular consumption, much as neoliberals suddenly rediscover a love of the state to rescue themselves from themselves, something that Marx, incidentally, pointed out in his study of banking legislation as sacrosanct only between crises. Marx offers a particularly sophisticated understanding of the nature of the capitalist financial system, and how it relates to the functioning of capitalism as a whole. The purpose here is to give a brief account of his approach and of its relevance for current circumstances.

FROM ACCUMULATION TO FINANCE

Marx's political economy is based upon the notion of capitalism as a mode of *production* (of surplus value), and Volume 1 of *Capital* is primarily focused on how (industrial) capitalists do this and with what consequences. As accumulation proceeds, more machine-intensive and large-scale techniques of production tend to be deployed, requiring the centralization of capital in larger blocs. Such restructuring, however, extends far beyond the sphere of production, incorporating economic restructuring more generally (in markets, finance and distribution of income), spatial restructuring (both nationally and internationally, with Marx pointing to relations between town and country), and social reproduction and transformation (with Marx emphasizing impoverishment of certain sections of the workforce, for example). For Marx, a major lever for bringing about economic restructuring is the credit system, since it is capable of both gathering together lesser units of finance and redistributing them on a larger scale.

In contrast to Volume 1, Volume 2 of *Capital* is concerned with the circulation of (surplus) value through the exchange system on the basis of given value relations within production. What is involved is the simultaneous, but structured and sequenced, balancing (if not equilibrium) of values, exchange values and use values. The circulation of commodities and money is the single most important mechanism for coordinating developments in the accumulation process. What is demonstrated by Marx's schema of reproduction in Volume 2 is both that capital accumulation can proceed under its own dynamic despite the economic and social tensions that it creates, and that, equally, the balances of reproduction are consistent with depressed or even crisis levels of activity.

Volume 3 of *Capital* seeks to bring Volumes 1 and 2 together, but at a more concrete if still abstract level, exploring how the accumulation and circulation of capital give rise to more complex economic forms through which the tensions in the accumulation process are at most temporarily resolved and which result in crises from time to time. In this respect, most attention in the literature has understandably been focused upon the law of the tendency of the rate of profit to fall. This has been variously interpreted (and rejected), but the perspective offered here is that the law (and counteracting tendencies) are primarily a shorthand way of pointing to the tensions generated by the accumulation process and a questioning of whether and how the processes of exchange can accommodate these (Fine and Saad-Filho, 2010). In particular, can both the restructuring and accumulation of capital proceed without crisis and, if not, in what form do crises appear? Necessarily, Marx's theory of finance and of capital in exchange more generally is of paramount importance in addressing these issues.

FROM FINANCE TO FINANCIALIZATION

Marx's theory of finance takes the structural separation between spheres of production and spheres of exchange as the starting point. Apart from being used by (industrial) capitalists to produce surplus value, money capital can also be utilized within the sphere of exchange purely for the purpose of facilitating exchange and drawing a profit from doing so (but without creating any surplus value). This is most obvious in the case of merchant capital, for which specialized traders buy and sell at different prices, the difference covering costs and profitability. For Marx, merchants buy commodities below value and sell commodities at value since they themselves produce no value. There is no reason why the rate of profit for merchant capital should not be equalized to that of industrial capital. Otherwise, there would be flows of capital in or out of merchanting just as there are between sectors of industrial capital. Not surprisingly, though, the rate of profit is reduced by the presence of merchant capital, and would be higher if it were less. This does not mean that it is advantageous to eliminate it. The point of merchant capital is that there is a division of functions between capitalists, and this can reduce the costs of circulation relative to industrial capitalists managing it for themselves. None the less, there is the logical possibility of over-extension of merchant capital, of replicating costs as merchants seek both to appropriate and to create opportunities for sale. This is transparent in the numbers of estate agents (realtors) competing for the same business or in competitive advertising to the extent that it leaves overall sales and (imagined) use values unchanged.

With merchant capital as a logically distinct category for Marx, and with the emergence of finance, money capital can be used in exchange for other purposes, not least in being made available to investors in the form of what he calls interest-bearing capital. This is a generic term for the money capital that is loaned for the specific purpose of undertaking or extending an industrial circuit of capital. Marx's theory of interest-bearing capital has eight fundamental features. First, whilst they are mutually interdependent, with industry producing surplus value and interest-bearing capital financing it to do so, there is a conflict of interest between the two. This is reflected in the division of surplus value between profit of enterprise and interest, which is the second feature. One can gain only at the expense of the other. Third, as industrial capitalists compete by accumulating, by scale of operation and, hence, by access to interest-bearing capital, so competition *within* the sector of finance is different. For, whilst there can be formation of new financial institutions, this will be tempered by the unwillingness of those operating in the financial sector to offer the capital to create a rival. Fourth, competition within the financial sector depends upon gathering surplus money capital and loaning it to industrial capitalists (or others). Competitiveness of individual and blocs of finance, national financial systems for example, depends upon how restricted or not are the conditions under which loans can be made. Greater restrictions reduce both the vulnerability to crises and the capacity to undertake financial operations profitably.

This point is universally recognized across the financial literature and practice. But its significance within Marx's approach is distinctive. In the case of interest-bearing capital, a loan is made in order to initiate a circuit of industrial capital for which the production and realization of surplus value is prospective and by no means guaranteed. The division of that surplus value between interest and profit of enterprise depends upon the successful completion of the circuit, without which one, other or both of interest and profit must suffer, a reflection of the conflict of interest between the two fractions of capital.

Fifth, thus Marx argues that interest-bearing capital necessarily gives rise to what he terms fictitious capital. This is a paper claim to the ownership of capital that exists independent of the capital itself in material terms. Of course, there is the possibility that interest-bearing capital will be advanced on the basis of entirely corrupt and fictional schemes, with no possibility of generating the rewards anticipated. This is not generally the case. None the less, the financial system does proceed on the basis of paper claims to rewards that have yet to be realized. Such fictitious capital is itself traded in financial markets.

Sixth, this leads Marx to ask when an accumulation of fictitious capital corresponds to real accumulation. It is not possible to give an answer since outcomes differ from intentions. A genuine attempt to make profit out of an industrial loan may fail. And loans made for non-commercial purposes, to fund consumption for example, may allow an industrial enterprise to reap its own and other's financial returns from the realization of commodities produced. More generally, as emphasized by Marx himself, the financial system can be extraordinarily powerful in mobilizing and allocating finance for the purpose of real investment. But, by the same token, it can both trigger and amplify monumental crises.

Seventh, this needs to be situated in the context of Marx's theory of accumulation and reproduction. For this, commodities are always being reduced in value as accumulation generates productivity increase, and this means that capitals are being devalued even as they are expanded through accumulation. So devaluation is the consequence of the production of surplus value. But, to the extent that the latter fails, the accumulation of fictitious and real capital diverges, and the capital is what Marx terms 'depreciated', effectively destroyed or reduced by the failure to produce surplus value rather than because it has done so in a world of declining values. Generalized devaluation of capital is synonymous with a period of successful accumulation. Generalized depreciation is the result of financial or other crisis. It sharply raises the issue of whether real or fictitious capital, industry or finance, will bear the costs of adjustment.

Last, it should be emphasized that this is a highly abstract analysis, focusing exclusively on the pure relations between finance and industry for the purpose of initiating circuits of industrial capital. Marx is well aware that, in practice, this process is embedded in a range of other ways in which borrowing and lending take place, including a credit system, with the payment of interest without involvement of production. Marx uses the term 'loanable money capital' to represent the ensemble of credit relations to which interest-bearing capital is attached, into which it is embedded. This embeddedness of interest-bearing, and fictitious, capital in other forms of commerce is the embryonic form of what I think has increasingly been the defining characteristic of the capitalist system over the past 40 years – its financialization – and which accordingly sheds light on the nature of the current crisis.

FROM FINANCIALIZATION TO CONTEMPORARY CAPITALISM

Significantly, the explicit literature on financialization is both limited and marginalized from mainstream thought, although this may change in light of recent events. Stockhammer (2004: 720) offers an overview of financialization, acknowledging that it 'is a recent term, still ill-defined, which summarizes a broad range of phenomena including the globalisation of financial markets, the shareholder value revolution and the rise of incomes from financial investment'. His own focus is upon 'changes in the internal power structure of the firm'. Others have emphasized the extraordinary rewards that have accrued to those working in finance. From Keynes's euthanasia of the parasitic rentier, we are suddenly confronted with the heroic financial entrepreneur who creates nothing but fictitious value (Erturk et al., 2006). And, from a labour movement perspective, the restructuring of productive capital is sacrificed for realization of short-term gains or shareholder value. As Rossman and Greenfield (2006: 2) put it,

> What is new is the drive for profit through the elimination of productive capacity and employment . . . This reflects the way in which financialization has driven the management of non-financial companies to 'act more like financial market players'.

But similar developments are to be found across each and every aspect of our (or others') economic and social lives. Indeed, as the *Financial Times* journalist Martin Wolf has put it,[1]

> The US itself looks almost like a giant hedge fund. The profits of financial companies jumped from below 5 per cent of total corporate profits, after tax, in 1982 to 41 per cent in 2007.

On the other hand, a point taken to be crucial in arguing for the presence of financialization itself, non-financial corporations have been accruing increasing proportions of their profits from financial activity. Stockhammer (2004: 720), in particular, defines financialization as 'the increased activity of non-financial businesses on financial markets', and finds that, '(f)or France, financialisation explains the entire slowdown in accumulation, for the USA about one-third of the slowdown. Financialisation, therefore, can potentially explain an economically significant part of the slowdown in accumulation' (ibid.: 739).

There is no reason to treat these definitions as competitive or mutually exclusive. By financialization is meant here that finance has penetrated all commercial relations to an unprecedented *direct* extent. I emphasize 'direct' because the role of finance has long been extensive both in promoting capital accumulation and in intensifying its crises, most notably in the Great Crash of 1929 and the ensuing recession. But finance is different today because of the proliferation of both purely financial markets and instruments, and the corresponding ranges of fictitious capitals that bridge these to real activities. Most obviously, and a major element in the financialization literature, especially in the USA, is the drawing in of personal finance in general and of pension funds in particular. Yet the compass of financialization goes much further than institutionalized investment funds, as finance has inserted itself into an ever-expanding range of activities, not least in managing personal revenues, as emphasized by Lapavitsas (2009) and dos Santos (2009).

Before turning to the effects of financialization, three further elements need to be added. The first is the role of the state (and international organizations) as regulator of the monetary and financial systems, and as a major agent in the provision of financial instruments, not least through its own indebtedness – paper bonds as a form of fictitious capital. Second is the nature and role of world money: how it is that the relations, properties and functions of money in general are realized on a global scale in light of the presence of numbers of national currencies and assets. And third is historical specificity in relation to both of the previous two elements and their interaction, reflecting particular patterns of accumulation at a global level. In this respect, there are generally identifiable and agreed historical periods in which the roles of nation-states and of world money are distinct, most recently the rise and fall of the Bretton Woods system (see, e.g., Arrighi, 2003 for a deeper and longer account).

At the broader, macroeconomic level, what is apparent empirically, irrespective of how it is situated analytically, is that the current world financial system has become even more dependent on the US dollar as world money even as the US economy itself has experienced relative decline at a global level with peculiarities of its own. Financialization of the US economy has been attached to a domestic consumer-led boom based both on a housing asset bubble and on extraordinary levels of indebtedness to the rest of the world. Although China has been at the forefront, other developing countries have, ironically, been safeguarding themselves against currency volatility by accumulating dollar reserves at great expense to themselves, having been forced to relinquish exchange controls under US-led neoliberalism.

FROM FINANCIALIZATION TO NEOLIBERALISM

From Marx's analysis, especially within *Capital*, it is possible to tease out the analytical categories appropriate to address the current crisis – with financialization explaining both the slowdown of growth over the last 30 years or more, and why the crisis should be able to originate within housing and not be amenable to state control and intervention. As dos Santos (2009: 180–81) dramatically puts it for the subprime mortgage crisis,

> By many historical measures the current financial crisis is without precedent. It has arisen from neither an industrial crisis nor an equity market crash. It was precipitated by the simple fact that increasing numbers of largely black, Latino and working-class white families in the US have been defaulting on their mortgages.

Financialization as economic restructuring will now proceed with a vengeance, the exact course of which will be almost impossible to predict.

It will, however, be contingent upon the role of the state as it seeks to hold back both the collapse of the financialized pack of cards and the real accumulation of capital to which it is attached. Does this mean that neoliberalism is dead or, more broadly, that some form of ideological restructuring is on the agenda? When neoliberalism first emerged, it seemed possible to define it relatively easily and uncontroversially. In the economic arena, the contrast could be made with Keynesianism and emphasis placed on perfectly working markets. A correspondingly distinctive stance could be taken in respect of the role of the state as corrupt, rent-seeking and inefficient as opposed to benevolent and progressive. Ideologically, the individual pursuit of self-interest as the means to freedom was offered in contrast to collectivism. And, politically, Reaganism and Thatcherism came to the fore. It is also significant that neoliberalism should emerge soon after the postwar boom came to an end, together with the collapse of the Bretton Woods system of fixed exchange rates.

This was all 30 or more years ago and, whilst neoliberalism has entered the scholarly if not popular lexicon, it is debatable whether it is now or, indeed, ever was clearly defined. How does it fare alongside globalization, the new world order, and the new imperialism, for example, as descriptors of contemporary capitalism? Does each of these refer to a similar understanding but with different terms and emphasis? And how do we situate neoliberalism in relation to Third Wayism, the social market and so on, whose politicians, theorists and ideologues would pride themselves as departing from neoliberalism but who, in their politics and policies, seem at least in part to have been captured by it (and even vice versa in some instances)?

So, given its diversity and elusiveness, does neoliberalism exist or not? If it does exist, what is it? If it does not exist as such, does it remain a useful and progressive term for the purposes of political and ideological engagement? The salience of these questions is particularly powerfully brought to the fore as the USA takes into public ownership the bad debt of its financial institutions to the tune of what will ultimately be in excess of a trillion dollars, even more remarkable for emanating from those across Bush as president, through Treasury to the Federal Reserve, who might previously and still be considered to be ideal representatives and guardians of neoliberalism. Yet here we have state ownership and intervention to such an extent that we might refer to a creeping if not galloping socialism, albeit confined to the bankers. Marx himself might be chuckling in his grave. In Volume 1 of *Capital*, he polemically asserts that '(t)he only part of the so-called national wealth that actually enters into the collective possessions of modern peoples is – their national debt'(ch. 31). Now it seems we are to own the private debt as well! To put this figure in proportion, a mere $45 billion was required to calm the markets after 9/11 (Davidson, 2008b). And, remarkably, while in a crisis, there is no difficulty in finding billions to support finance, in more normal times, such funding for health, education, welfare and poverty relief would be viewed as the height of fiscal irresponsibility.

So, in the capitalist market, we are all equal, although some are more equal than others when it comes to finance and crisis. For finance must be saved in order to save the economy as a whole. But strip out all those financial services and would the rest of the economy need to go to the wall? There does not seem to be a compelling reason why production, distribution and exchange should not continue as before in the absence of so many financial instruments. Such instruments are, after all, of relatively recent vintage and without them even advanced capitalist economies could previously prosper. There are, of course, the inflated and distorted demands for goods that derive from the expenditure of those who have made their fortunes out of finance. A little redistribution of that demand to the poor and needy should surely be both manageable and warranted.

But I digress from my theme of the uncertainties that surround the notion of neoliberalism. To the extent that they can be, I seek to resolve the corresponding conundrums attached to neoliberalism through a two-pronged assault upon them. The first, in characterizing neoliberalism, is to distinguish between its rhetoric (advocacy or ideology), its scholarship and its policy in practice. Each of these is shifting in content and emphasis (across time and place) and, although they have connections with one another, these too are shifting and by no means mutually consistent. In addition, there is a complex and shifting relationship between neoliberalism across these three elements and the reality that they purport both to represent and to influence. And the shifts can be both dramatic and acrobatic. There are those, increasingly rare, who continue to blame the current crisis on too much state intervention. It might even be claimed in a perverse way that the state has got in the way of finance spontaneously creating its own regulatory safeguards and that, as now overtly revealed, as lender if not subsidizer or nationalizer of last resort, it has positively encouraged undue risk-taking and speculative activity. Such neo-Austrianism and its belief in the natural order that springs from individual freedom, not least through the marketplace, is understandably less than popular among the banking fraternity currently as it clamours for more not less state intervention.

Neoliberalism, then, both lavishes praise on the market at the expense of the state and calls upon the state to rescue the markets from themselves and not just provide an orderly environment in which to operate. So, unpicking neoliberalism's chameleon-like character, around its shifting diversity across rhetoric, scholarship, policy and realism, is a challenge, one that can best be met by acknowledging the significance of financialization. As already emphasized, financialization has extended finance beyond the traditional to the personal and broader elements of economic and social reproduction. For the latter, it is not simply that neoliberalism is associated with privatization, commercialization and commodification, but, where these do prevail, financialization will not be far behind – may be even in the lead.

But it is not merely a matter of the extent to which financialization has thereby rendered contemporary capitalism subject to crises of potentially greater depth *and* breadth, of both origin and incidence. Financialization is also complicit in the persistence of slowdown of accumulation since the end of the postwar boom. It has created a dynamic in which real accumulation is both tempered and, ultimately, choked off by fictitious accumulation (although this may be preceded by bubbles of excessive accumulation, fictitious or real); it has undermined the role of the state as an active agent of economic restructuring; and it has also undermined the role of the state as an agent in furnishing the more general economic and social conditions conducive to accumulation, in health, education and welfare, for example, that alongside industrial policies underpinned the postwar boom as opposed to Keynesianism as such.

In this light, it is possible to suggest in broad terms that neoliberalism has experienced two phases. The first, following upon the collapse of the postwar boom, was akin to a sort of shock therapy of greater applicability than to the transition economies of Eastern Europe at a later date. This phase is marked by the state intervening to promote private capital in general as far as possible and financial markets in particular. The second phase exhibits two aspects. One has been for the state to intervene to moderate the impact of this financialization, most notable now in the support given to rescuing financial institutions themselves. But, as is thereby evident, the second and more important aspect is for the state to be committed to sustain the process of supporting private capital in general and of financialization in particular.

Where does this leave 'neoliberalism'? Here, the distinctions around rhetoric, policy, scholarship and realism are imperative if subject to subtle application. Of course, opponents of neoliberalism but proponents of capitalism will claim that the second phase is a departure from neoliberalism. And, in a limited sense, they are correct, for the rhetoric and the scholarship are not neoliberal even if swayed in that direction by comparison with Keynesian/welfarism. Indeed, the new market and institutional microfoundations within orthodox economics, which emphasizes the need for targeted correction of imperfections to the market and its governance, and Third Wayism as its political expression, are ideal complements for the new phase of neoliberalism since they rationalize piecemeal, discretionary intervention in deference to moderating and promoting the market in general. And, making markets work in general increasingly means making financial markets work in particular. What is going on now in support of financial markets is both an acute and a striking illustration of these postures.

For the era of financialization entrenches new modes of corporate governance and assessment of performance, privatization and state support of it rather than public provision, lack of coherent and systematic industrial and agricultural policy, pressure for user charges for health, education and welfare, and priority to macroeconomic austerity to allow for liberalization of financial capital. In this context, market imperfection economics is not only weaker than Keynesian/welfarism, it is so in a context where it needs to be much stronger to be effective. As Stiglitz (2008: 2) puts it, 'The left now understands markets, and the role they can and should play in the economy . . . the new left is trying to make markets work.' But where we see 'markets', we should read 'capital in general', and where we see 'capital in general' we should read 'finance in particular'.

WHAT IS TO BE DONE?

The policy dilemmas posed by this situation were beautifully anticipated by Sir Josiah Stamp some 70 years ago, as revealed in the following quote:[2]

> Banking was conceived in iniquity and was born in sin. The bankers own the earth. Take it away from them, but leave them the power to create money, and with the flick of the pen they will create enough deposits to buy it back again. However, take it away from them, and all the great fortunes like mine will disappear and they ought to disappear, for this would be a happier and better

world to live in. But, if you wish to remain the slaves of bankers and pay the cost of your own slavery, let them continue to create money.

How do Stiglitz and his left know that by making markets work, they will do no more than hand 'the flick of a pen' back to finance? What we can recognize is that the current plans to rescue finance from its predicament in the second phase of neoliberalism do not even get as far as Stamp's first step of taking wealth away from bankers (although the markets themselves are doing this more than the state). Indeed, they seem to be a step in the opposite direction, as the state is throwing money at the financial institutions in order that they can continue to create money. In this light, the issue is not the more or less orderly and justifiable rationale upon which such funds are allocated. Instead, it is the question of whether levels of economic and social provision should be subject to the dictates of a financial system that is so dysfunctional. Yet, whilst financialization has shifted the modes of interaction and balance of power across vested interests, it does not rigidly determine outcomes. These remain contingent, especially in the wake of the continuing weight of state intervention, upon struggles to sustain alternatives, not least in seeking insulation against the logic of finance. If neoliberalism is not a temporary illusion, it is only because it is inextricably linked both to the state and to financialization.

It is surely time not only to reverse rather than to sustain the financialization of our lives, but also to throw off the chains of slavery that reside in the banker's flick of a pen. Indeed, we need to turn this neoliberal world upside down if not inside out. If socialism is good enough for the bankers without regard to the rest of us, surely it is good enough for us without regard to the bankers? Consider, for example, the role of housing finance and the irony of the rescue of HBOS (Halifax–Bank of Scotland) by Lloyds in the UK to create a mortgage provider that takes 30 per cent of the market, a higher share than was disallowed on monopoly grounds in a proposed merger just a year before. Both competition and state withdrawal are neoliberal sacrificial lambs in a crisis. As the politician, and perhaps a neoliberal, says, these are my principles and if you don't like them, I will change them – and perhaps the audience was made up of bankers. Historically and ironically, HBOS had been a building society or not-for-profit mortgage provider until it became a bank-for-profit in 1997. The same is true of Bradford and Bingley, now nationalized like Northern Rock, by UK government as its share prices collapsed towards nothingness. Significantly, the billions of state funding being thrown at the mortgage sector to stem the crisis could have been used directly to fund the provision of housing. Further, and more generally, as revealed by Hall

(2008, 2009), the level of support now on offer to the financial system is more or less equivalent to the total revenue realized from all the privatizations that have taken place. And the turn to public–private partnerships as a way of providing social and economic infrastructure is collapsing for want of private participation and demand for greater contributions from the state.

Similarly, in commodity markets, we have futures trading at its most bizarre with carbon offsets. Commodity fetishism has surely arrived at perfection when we can buy and sell in a market for not producing something in the future (especially when, in fact, carbon trading is about allowing that undesirable carbon to be produced for you by someone else as well as yourself on the grounds that they might produce less of it than you would if you were producing what they produce as well as what you yourself will carry on producing). Down on earth, futures trading and speculation more generally in 'commodities' is endemic. In 2006, the US Permanent Senate Committee came to the view that at least a third of the then $60 price of a barrel of oil was due to speculative futures trading. Presumably, we may well have to have added a further $40 since then (Davidson, 2008a). And futures trading in commodities more generally has increased by 20 times since 2003 alone to a level of $260 billion. But, as this is a trade in which you have to lay out only a small proportion of the cost of what you buy (you are, after all, never going to consume it), the actual trades are ten or more times larger. It is tragic that, alongside other triggering factors, the speculative ebb and flow of trading in commodities futures should so inflate the prices of food that hundreds of millions will be added to those at risk from starvation.

This suggests that the immediate goal is not so much to restore the financial system as to do so only by placing priority on what is to be delivered, whether it be industrial restructuring, poverty alleviation, employment generation, or health, education and welfare. It now seems that the put-down should be applied to capitalism not socialism – that it is all very well in theory but it just does not work in practice. On the other hand, whilst the earlier period of Keynesian/welfarism did place finance in more of a subordinate position, there must be grave doubts whether this can be restored without being subject to the flick of the banker's pen. For this to run dry is not merely a matter of the right policies. It also requires the subordination of fictitious to real accumulation through the active participation of those who produce and use in the processes of provision at the expense of those who enrich themselves at a distance.

NOTES

1. 'Why it is so hard to keep the financial sector caged', *Financial Times*, 6 February, 2008, cited in Michael Perelman, 'How to think about the crisis', http://www.monthlyreview. org/mrzine/perelman131008.html.
2. See http://en.wikipedia.org/wiki/Josiah_Stamp,_1st_Baron_Stamp.

REFERENCES

Arrighi, G. (2003), 'The social and political economy of global turbulence', *New Left Review*, **20**: 5–71.

Davidson, P. (2008a), 'Securitization, liquidity and market failure', *Challenge*, **51**(3): 43–56, viewed at http://econ.bus.utk.edu/faculty/davidson/securitization-price%20talk10.pdf.

Davidson, P. (2008b), 'Crude oil prices: 'market fundamentals' or speculation?', *Challenge*, **51**(4): 110–18, viewed at http://econ.bus.utk.edu/faculty/davidson/challenge%20oilspeculation9wordpdf.pdf.

dos Santos, P. (2009), 'On the content of banking in contemporary capitalism', *Historical Materialism*, **17**(2): 180–213.

Erturk, I. et al. (2006), 'Agency, the romance of management pay and an alternative explanation', Centre for Research on Socio-Cultural Change, CRESC Working Paper, No. 23, University of Manchester.

Fine, B. (2009), 'Looking at the crisis through Marx', *International Socialist Review*, **64**, March–April, 40–47.

Fine, B. and A. Saad-Filho (2010), *Marx's Capital*, 5th edn, London: Pluto Press.

Hall, D. (2008), 'Economic crisis and public services', Public Services International Research Unit, note 1, December, http://www.psiru.org/reports/2008-12-crisis-1. doc.

Hall, D. (2009), 'Economic crisis and public services: a crisis for public–private partnerships (PPPs)?', Public Services International Research Unit, note 2, January, http://www.psiru.org/reports/2009-01-crisis-2.doc.

Lapavitsas, C. (2009), 'Financialised capitalism: crisis and financial expropriation', *Historical Materialism*, **17**(2): 114–48.

Rossman, P. and G. Greenfield (2006), 'Financialization: new routes to profit, new challenges for trade unions', *Labour Education, Quarterly Review of the ILO Bureau for Workers' Activities*, no. 142, http://www.iufdocuments.org/www/ documents/Financialization-e.pdf.

Stiglitz, J. (2008), 'Turn left for sustainable growth', *Economists' Voice*, September, 1–3.

Stockhammer, E. (2004), 'Financialization and the slowdown of accumulation', *Cambridge Journal of Economics*, **28**(5): 719–41.

5. Incentive divergence and the global financial crisis

J. Patrick Gunning

Price bubbles and cycles due to reliance on financial intermediaries are ordinary characteristics of market interaction in a market economy. So long as people are free to interact, they will often err and be misled. It is possible that such errors and mistaken reliance on others can accumulate, leading to unusually large changes in demand and supply conditions.[1] The global financial crisis that began in 2007 was partly a manifestation of these ordinary phenomena. The phenomena were magnified and exaggerated in the USA, however, by a set of laws and government-created institutions. The most important were (1) regulation of financial intermediation by the Federal Reserve Bank (the Fed), the Federal Deposit Insurance Corporation (FDIC) and the Securities and Exchange Commission (SEC) and (2) the manipulation of money.

This chapter explains the crisis by focusing on 'incentive divergence'. Incentive divergence refers to a condition in which an actor's action in his own interest causes either benefits or harm to others whom he does not take into account.[2] I attribute the crisis to the incentive divergence (1) that exists under normal conditions in an otherwise pure market economy and (2) that is introduced by the regulation of financial intermediation, the manipulation of money, and other regulations related to the monetary system and monetary policy.

Unfortunately, space considerations prevent a full exposition of this explanation. In this chapter, I omit discussion of monetary factors. I recognize this as a significant gap. A consequence is that I will be unable to fully defend my recommendations. I hope that some other author adequately presents the Austrian economists' case for maintaining a constant quantity of money, the elimination of deposit insurance, and abolition of government-controlled fractional reserve banking.

I have a good reason for emphasizing the incentive divergence that occurs in the absence of regulation. It seems likely that government measures to deal with the crisis, which was caused mostly by regulation, will themselves consist of regulation, albeit of a different sort, rather than deregulation. The regulations will change but no doubt the new regulations will be a major factor helping to cause future crises. Since it is uncertain what these future regulations will be, a chapter that identifies defects in a previous regulatory regime is likely to be irrelevant for the future. However, the incentive divergence that occurs in the absence of regulation will continue to exist, so long as some segments of the economy remain unregulated. For this reason, an explanation of the recent crises that focuses on market incentive divergence is likely to have greater relevance for explaining future crises. Moreover, if one's goal is either to justify non-intervention or to construct the optimal regulatory regime, one must account for the incentive divergence that would exist without regulation. A hypothesis about how a financial crisis could occur in the absence of regulation, then, has direct policy relevance.

Sections 1–3 describe the incentive divergence that is present in ordinary market interaction. Section 4 tells how incentive divergence is increased by regulation of financial intermediation. Section 5 presents my recommendations. A brief glossary is provided at the end of the chapter, since I use several terms that may be unfamiliar to readers.

1.   INCENTIVE DIVERGENCE IN A MARKET ECONOMY

The starting point for modern economics is the theorem of consumer sovereignty (see Gunning, 2009).This theorem applies strictly only to a complete private property system. Ludwig von Mises defined such a system as a situation in which each actor receives all of the benefits that result from his action, including the benefits that are felt by others, and in which he is responsible for all of the harm to others that he causes (Mises, 1966: 655). In the market economies we know, such a situation is rare if it exists at all. Recognizing this, I regard the complete private property system assumption partly as a paradigm for comprehending and describing the extent to which consumer sovereignty prevails in real market interaction.

I aim to invoke this paradigm to explain why there can be a sudden disruption in the satisfaction of consumer wants of the type that occurs during a financial crisis. To achieve this goal, I identify situations of incentive divergence. Incentive divergence leads consumer sovereignty to be compromised because an actor may make decisions in his own interest that harm others and because he may fail to act when the benefits to others are much greater than the costs to him in terms of money.[3]

Incentive Divergence in Market Interaction

By definition, no incentive divergence could exist in a Crusoe situation – the one-person society. However, specialization causes it to be pervasive in a market economy. Whereas Crusoe has an incentive to produce and use knowledge that he believes will satisfy his wants, the specialist in a market economy ordinarily has very little incentive to produce knowledge about how to produce the goods that she consumes. This lack of knowledge exposes a person to harm due to others' errors, to misjudgments about others' future actions and to deceit or fraud.

In a market economy, communication by means of markets, prices and contracts helps individuals reduce much of the incentive divergence that would otherwise exist. For example, although the employer makes job offers in his own interest, his announcement sends a signal of a potential gain to prospective employees. This gives them an incentive to apply for the jobs. Thus a specialized employer who could benefit potential employees actually does so by means of his job offers and eventual employment. A large-scale milk manufacturer produces milk because she expects to sell her milk to consumers. Consumer responsiveness in the past and her belief that their choice conditions have not changed significantly give her confidence that she can earn a profit. The specialized milk producer's knowledge benefits milk consumers by enabling them to use money to buy milk in a market. An electrician acquires an incentive to install the electrical network for a new house by receiving a promise from a builder to pay for his work after he sells the house. The contract enables the building contractor and ultimately the house buyer to gain from the specialized knowledge and work of the electrician.

Observations of such signaling and responses to signals led F.A. Hayek to refer to the price system as a marvel (Hayek, 1945: 527) in that it economizes on the production and use of specialized knowledge. The market economy is also a marvel in that each person knows next to nothing about how to produce the vast majority of the economic goods she consumes. Indeed, it is the fact that individuals need not acquire such knowledge that best characterizes the gains from specialization in market interaction (ibid.).

Nevertheless, as pointed out above, when a person depends on others to produce goods for her, she renders herself vulnerable (1) to their errors, (2) to her own misjudgments about the actions that the others will take and (3) to their deceit and fraud. On the one hand, she may misjudge contractual or implicit promises. The employer may not pay after the work is done, the milk may be tainted, and the electrical wiring may cause a fire. On the other hand, the market conditions that led others to send signals upon which a person comes to rely may change. The employer may lay off workers who expected to keep their jobs because of a reduction in demand or a rise in costs; the milk producer may go out of business; and electrical contractors may drastically raise their prices after the builder has already made a substantial investment in house construction. In both cases, the theorem of consumer sovereignty is violated. The reason, as I define it, is incentive divergence.

In sections 2 and 3, respectively, I describe two classes of events that can result from incentive divergence in a pure market economy that lacks complete private property rights. The first is a housing bubble, which results from incentive divergence in market signaling and in selling house mortgages. The second is a reliance cycle in financial intermediation, which results from incentive divergence associated with the principal–agent relationship in the supply of financial services and corporate governance.

2. HOUSING BUBBLE THEORY

I distinguish a price bubble from a sustained price increase. A sustained price increase is common in markets for highly durable resources like houses and land. A continuing unexpected migration of people from one place to another causes a continuing rise in demand. Increases in supply lag behind the increases in demand. Land and/or house prices persistently rise. Eventually, the migration slows and increases in supply catch up with increases in demand. The price stops rising and may even fall if suppliers have made the error of anticipating further increases in demand.

Incentive Divergence Leading to the Housing Bubble in the USA

Bubbles in such markets are also common. My theory holds that bubbles are caused by two separate sources of incentive divergence: novice speculators and cunning salespeople. I define a novice speculator as someone who has no special information about the reason why a price will rise or fall. The novice speculator uses statistical extrapolation to make decisions to buy or sell. Statistical extrapolation refers to a decision-making rule that predicts the future consequences of a choice entirely on the basis of the past consequences of the same, or similar, choice. Its most pure form is the application of mathematical formulae and past numerical data.

Statistical extrapolation is extremely successful in the material world. The successes of physical scientists and engineers in conquering the forces of nature and in enabling the mass production of the numerous goods that have improved the human condition is largely due to the reliability of extrapolation. Statistical extrapolation is also highly successful in every-day life. Numerical statistics on past weather conditions at different times during the year help people decide when and where to live and travel, and how to best exploit the resources of the sun, wind and water. Statistics on the previous consequences of various medical treatments help people decide which treatment to use for a particular ailment.

In spite of its success in science and everyday life, statistical extrapolation should not be used by someone who aims to predict others' actions. He/she should use 'the understanding' (Mises, 1966: 117–8). That is, he/she should assume that the others are actors with ends and means. Beginning with this assumption, one makes judgments about the nature of the ends and perceived means. Then, one uses these judgments as a basis for building images of the others' choices. This, of course, is what economists also do. 'The understanding' is appropriate both for succeeding in market interaction and in trying to predict others' actions in social science.[4]

Speculative demand for houses rises

Novice speculators were especially active in the US housing market between 2003 and 2005, when the rate of price increase in new homes averaged more than 8 percent per annum. An increasing number of prospective buyers of houses based their decisions to buy on the expectation that the price increases of the past would continue. Their decisions to bid higher prices sent signals to house suppliers and also to other prospective novice speculators. Because supply was slow to respond, house prices on average increased at a gradually increasing rate (Shiller, 2005: 13).

I define a 'cunning salesperson' as a person whose goal is to profit by using deception and/or fraud to facilitate an exchange between one person and another, whom he persuades. The profit is usually in the form of a sales commission. In the case of a housing bubble, a cunning salesperson deceptively or fraudulently persuades a person that she can improve her well-being by buying a house because house prices have been rising. Perhaps the simplest deception is the representation of the facts of the past. The salesperson may draw a graph to show the history of house prices and present a chart to represent how much the novice speculator can gain if she later decides to sell or refinance. Then, if the novice speculator objects that she cannot afford the downpayment, he offers an adjustable rate mortgage, a negative amortization mortgage, a piggyback loan or some other inducement.[5] Such a salesperson does harm to the buyer while benefiting himself. His actions manifest the most extreme form of incentive divergence in a peaceful society with protection against theft and violence.

Some house buyers do not need the prodding of salespeople to make the decision to speculate on the assets they purchase. They are already prone to use statistical extrapolation. But many would not enter the market if it were not for the persuasive techniques of the salespeople.

Suppliers respond

Partly as the result of novice speculators and cunning salespeople, suppliers of houses during the 2003–05 period received signals that there was a sustained and continuing increase in the demand for houses. They then sent further signals to resource suppliers that there would be a more or less indefinite increase in demand for resources. Producers of electrical wiring, plumbing supplies, house fixtures, construction work etc. all received and sent signals up their respective supply chains. Throughout all of the supply chains related to producing a house, signals were received to produce more. Upon receiving such signals the entrepreneurs upgraded, invested in R&D and embarked on human capital production programs.

Since most houses are purchased with borrowed funds, signals were also sent up the supply chains related to mortgage financing. Mortgage finance entrepreneurs sent signals to intermediaries who, in turn, sent signals to savers to the effect that they could earn income by saving in the form of assets the value of which depended on the repayment of mortgage loans. As savers responded to these signals, they changed their patterns of demand for near and more distant future consumer goods. In the process, the financial intermediaries upgraded, invested in R&D, and produced new human capital and other resources related to their work.

During the latter stages of a housing bubble, the supply of houses rises faster than the non-speculative demand. More experienced speculators begin to signal their expectations of a decrease in the rate of price increase or even a price decrease. As these signals compete with those of the cunning salespeople, the salespeople find it increasingly difficult to persuade novices to speculate. As speculative demand tapers off, the bubble starts to burst. When this occurs, most speculators whose decisions caused house prices to be exaggerated in the first place find that they have done damage to themselves. The capital gains they expected were not forthcoming. In addition, they and the cunning salespeople by whom many of them had been persuaded damaged all of the unwary entrepreneurs who operated businesses along the relevant supply chains for houses and mortgages. Most of these suppliers suffered losses and abandoned their longer-term upgrading and investment projects.

Incentive Divergence

The thesis of this section is that incentive divergence due to novice speculation and cunning salespeople is sufficient to explain a housing bubble.

Moreover, it is reasonable to attribute these phenomena to ordinary activity in a market economy. The incentive divergence due to the novice speculator is manifest in the signals that are sent up the supply chains for resources. The loss borne by any particular novice speculator from using a poor method of economic prediction is only a part of the total loss due to her error. Numerous other actors are likely to be misled by the signals sent by house buyers who use statistical extrapolation. Perhaps the most important are future novice speculators since they also use increases in past house prices to predict future house prices and future increases in house prices. Cunning salespeople contribute to this incentive divergence by means of their persuasive actions.

A person could avoid all of the harm due to incentive divergence by not relying on others. Becoming a hermit would eliminate exposure to a housing bubble. Even a participant in market interaction could invest in acquiring the knowledge to more effectively apply 'the understanding'. One must assume that because people do participate, do not acquire knowledge, and do not effectively apply 'the understanding', in general they gain more than they lose from such interaction. The crucial issue is whether some kind of government intervention can improve matters or whether it is likely to make people worse off from the perspective of consumer sovereignty.

The Housing Bubble of the 2000s

It would be completely wrong, of course, to attribute the recent housing bubble in the USA entirely to sustained migration, novice speculation and cunning salespeople. The Fed engineered massive increases in the quantity of money in 2001 and again in 2003. There can be little doubt that the low interest rates accompanying these increases helped to sustain the housing bubble. Moreover, in 2005, when the Fed reduced money growth, the rise in interest rates had the effect of compelling many subprime, adjustable rate mortgage borrowers to default.[6] So one could argue that the bursting of the bubble was also engineered by the Fed. There was also some regulatory and legislative pressure on financial intermediaries to lend to subprime borrowers. My purpose in this section is not to provide a causal explanation of the bubble but to show how a bubble could occur even without the manipulation of money and regulation.

3. RELIANCE IN FINANCIAL INTERMEDIATION

The recent housing bubble was spurred partly by another type of incentive divergence that is typical of financial markets – the principal–agent

relationship (see glossary). The principal–agent relationship is the underlying cause of what I shall call a 'reliance cycle'. In financial markets
it is manifest in the following way. A financial intermediary builds a
reputation for being reliable, many savers (*qua* investors) become reliant
on him and reduce their monitoring of his activities; he or a surrogate
proceeds to violate savers' trust by acting recklessly or using deceit or
fraud. Guaranty and insurance promises may not be kept. After current
savers lose large sums of money, future savers become more cautious than
usual in turning over control of their funds to an agent. In the case of the
global financial crisis, the entire set of financial corporate chief executive
officers (CEOs) can be conceived as playing the role of agent. Numerous
financial intermediaries, many acting independently but some acting in
concert, misled and were partly misled themselves about the security of
the assets they acquired for themselves on behalf of savers, investors and
stockholders.

Fundamentals of Financial Intermediation

The vast majority of savers in a market economy who wish to earn a
return on their savings lack specialized knowledge about profit-making
opportunities and know it. As a result, they have incentives to turn
over control of their money to financial intermediaries. The most basic
financial intermediary service offered to savers is to find either borrowing producers who can earn a profit or households who are willing to
pay interest to borrow. Thus the incentives of savers to earn income on
their savings provide opportunities for financial intermediaries to gain by
offering various risk–rate of return options along with a second service of
giving advice, or otherwise enabling the saver to gain from the intermediary's specialized knowledge about which alternative is best. The savers'
incentives provide the environment; financial intermediaries operate in
that environment.

Guaranty is common in such transactions. Guaranty is a promise to
perform some action if certain events are observed to take place. In financial intermediation it is used to assure savers that their principals and
interest on loans will be paid. It typically consists of a promise to transfer
the ownership of property, which most often consists of money, if the
principal and interest are not paid as promised. A financial intermediary
may provide the guaranty herself. Or she may purchase it for a fee from
a specialized guarantor or insurer. The guaranty relationship is also a
principal–agent relationship, although it is more complex.

The CEO of a firm that manufactures and sells a product is an agent
for his stockholders. In supplying governance, he also supplies financial

intermediation services for them. The CEO of a financial intermediation firm is thus an agent for two different sets of savers: his stockholders and the savers and investors who entrust their funds to the firm he governs. Such a CEO is in a position to cause harm to both sets.

The history of financial intermediation is filled with cases in which, facing this environment, unscrupulous intermediaries have swindled savers out of their wealth. Nevertheless, if such swindles were too frequent or large, a saver would be reluctant to turn her money over to an intermediary in the first place. In general and in the long run, the expected gain from financial intermediation must be positive. Financial intermediation performs an economic function and the financial intermediary entrepreneurs, in performing that function, act according to the theorem of consumer sovereignty.

Reliance Cycle Theory

A reliance cycle in the supply of financial intermediation services can be divided into three periods. In the first, savers are extremely reluctant to entrust their savings to financial intermediaries. Their use of 'the understanding' leads many of them to recognize incentive divergence and to be wary. In the second, the intermediaries proceed to build trust in various ways but primarily by persistently paying higher returns than savers can earn without the assistance of intermediaries. During this period, savers gradually come to entrust more of their savings to the intermediaries. They become accustomed to earning high returns. In the third period, savers gradually reduce their alertness to potential intermediary actions that would lead them to regret entrusting their funds. They begin to think that the high returns will occur regardless of their trust and alertness. Also during this period, many intermediaries become more careless. They more often resort to statistical extrapolation to make lending decisions. As a result, they tend to make reckless loans. In order to increase sales, the intermediaries may also become deceptive and fraudulent, concealing information from savers or lying to them about the safety of their savings. At the end of the third period, the poor quality of loans is revealed. A wave of caution and unwillingness to trust develops among savers, the intermediation business shrinks, and borrowers find it unusually difficult to borrow. The interest rate rises sharply on loans of a given type. The conditions that were present during the first period are repeated.[7]

A reliance cycle may be local, regional, national or international. It may be large or small. The nature of any particular cycle depends very much on liability law and social norms.

Reliance Cycles in the US Economy

The reliance cycle is a normal occurrence in a specialized economy where the purchasing power of savers' savings must be transferred either to unrelated individuals who carry out entrepreneurial ventures or to unrelated dissavers. The US financial crisis was actually a combination of several reliance cycles in several financial markets. Moreover, they were triggered largely by the housing bubble, which itself was spurred partly by the manipulation of money by the Fed. In addition, government regulation and guarantees played an important role. To untangle the various causes is a daunting task. In this section, I shall consider how, during a housing bubble, incentive divergence in an otherwise pure market economy could cause a combination of cycles in different financial markets, leading to something like a crisis of the type that occurred. I delay discussing the influence of regulation until section 4.

Types of Reliance

In the following I identify three different kinds of reliance that were prevalent during the recent financial crisis and, it seems likely, could be present under the conditions of a market economy with incomplete private property rights. These are (1) reliance of savers on sellers of packaged securities and on the firms that rate such securities, (2) reliance of stockholders in large financial corporations on their CEOs and ratings firms, and (3) reliance of large financial firms on insurers and hedge fund managers.

Reliance of savers on sellers of mortgage-backed securities and on ratings firms

The story of how a reliance cycle could contribute to a global financial crisis begins with the mortgage securitization.

Securitization of mortgages   The nationwide and even worldwide scope of the crisis was due to mortgage securitization and associated developments. Securitization refers to the process through which the owner of a collection, or pool, of mortgage loans transforms them into bonds (mortgage-backed securities – MBSs) which earn income based on mortgage payments by borrowers. Typically, a securitizing investment bank bundles a set of mortgage loans into a pool and employs a private agency such as Standard and Poor's or Moody's to attach a rating to the MBSs that are issued from the pool. Legal rights to share in the income, minus fees and commissions, are then sold to investors. This process nationalizes and, in the rapidly growing international financial intermediation market, internationalizes a mortgage market that would otherwise be financed only by local savers who are in the best position to evaluate the original mortgage lender and borrower.[8]

An increasing number of managers of investment funds, mutual funds, ordinary banks, and even the investment banks themselves were attracted to US-based MBSs after 2003. An especially large group of buyers of MBSs were foreigners, typically through some intermediary. It was estimated that more than half of MBSs were held by foreigners as the housing bubble expanded.[9]

Mortgage securitization has a history that goes back to the pre-Depression era.[10] Until 2003, however, it was dominated by agencies or enterprises created by the US government: Fannie Mae (Federal National Mortgage Association), Freddie Mac (Federal Home Loan Mortgage Corporation), and Ginnie Mae (Government National Mortgage Association). Between 2003 and mid 2006, while the housing bubble was expanding at its fastest pace, the market value of privately securitized mortgages grew from about 20 percent of the total to nearly 60 percent. The increase corresponded almost exactly with the increase in mortgages to subprime borrowers and other non-traditional loans, which appears to have increased the probability of default (England, 2006; USGAO, 2007: 49; Mayer et al., 2009: 28).

Since profitable private mortgage securitization has a very short history, it is not certain that a market economy would contain a large amount of it. Indeed, it is quite possible that many intermediaries and savers were lured into this market by cunning salespeople. The salespeople could point out the historical trend of high security and high yield of MBSs. At the same time, they could neglect to mention or they could under-emphasize the pre-2000 conservative policies of the government enterprises and the implicit government insurance against default, while attaching undue importance to ratings firms and the 'insurance' that could be purchased from private insurers to protect against unusual mortgage loan defaults. Depending on how much additional sales resulted from the prior government's involvement in issuing MBSs, the magnitude of the global financial crisis based on the housing bubble might have been several levels below what it actually reached and the crisis may not have spread far beyond US markets.[11] With this reservation, I proceed on the basis of the assumption that savers in distant places could be persuaded to purchase MBSs that have been rated by ratings firms.[12]

Ratings firms   A critical factor in the choice to securitize was the rating. MBS ratings firms attached a range of high-to-low ratings to bundles of mortgages that were securitized into MBSs. The ratings had long been (and still are) regarded by buyers as a way of judging risk. Everyone, including foreigners, can tell the difference between an AAA-rated MBS and one that is rated BBB.

There are three major ratings firms: Standard and Poor's, Moody's Investor Service and Fitch Ratings. However, Standard and Poor's claimed 92 percent of the US market (Morgenson, 2008). Since these firms perform direct services for buyers of MBSs, consumer sovereignty would probably be best served if the firms sold their ratings directly to consumers. Instead, the agencies provided the information free and charged fees to the investment banks that issued the MBSs. To compete with the market leader, Moody's apparently reduced its standards, although it is difficult to prove this claim. Threatened with a loss of market share, Standard and Poor's responded by offering ratings that were at least as high as those of its competitors. When asked by an investment banker to rate a package of mortgages that had previously been rated by one of the smaller raters, its policy was to accept the rating of the smaller rater out of concern for the possibility of losing the sale of its services to the investment banker who made the request (ibid.: 2008). Since Standard and Poor's had the better initial reputation in the USA, this strategy worked.[13] However, such a response implicitly incorporated Moody's rating models into practically all of MBS ratings. Although these models are proprietary, it is practically certain that they were statistical extrapolation models based on the assumption that housing prices would not fall.[14] Thus it seems reasonable to conclude that statistical extrapolation, as opposed to 'the understanding', became a systemic characteristic of mortgage pool ratings. This would not change until the crisis came.[15]

A ratings firm in an unregulated environment that was focused on its reputation and long-run profit would recognize that the use of statistical extrapolation could jeopardize its future sales. Apparently, however, the executives in these firms were not concerned with the long run.

In such an environment, investment bankers who were building MBS pools typically shopped for a high rating and, if needed, had the rating sanctioned by the industry leader. Moreover, the ratings firms actively participated, for a fee, in helping an investment bank structure a pool of mortgages in order to assure that the pool would achieve the highest rating or set of ratings according to its objective tests (Rosner, 2007).[16] This arrangement gave ratings firms opportunities to increase short-term profit albeit at the expense of reducing their reputations as unbiased raters.

Those who relied on ratings firms also used statistical extrapolation. If they had used 'the understanding', they might have recognized the conflict of interest. On the one hand, they might have paid attention to the vulnerability of subprime borrowers, especially on adjustable rate mortgages, to a fall in house prices, to a recession, and to a rise in the indices used to determine adjustable rate mortgage payments. In addition, they might have recognized the prospect for increased deception and fraud by mortgage applicants and mortgage originators or they might have expected the level of these activities to increase due to the very large increase in funds available to lend, and subsequent increase in independent mortgage originators. On the other hand, they might have recognized that the ratings firms could not be trusted to employ 'the understanding' in a timely fashion.[17]

Reliance of stockholders in large financial corporations on corporate executives and ratings firms

Economists have long recognized the incentive divergence associated with the corporation, or joint stock company. This is a special case of the principal–agent relationship. The CEO is the agent and the stockholders are the principals. The CEOs of corporations that are owned jointly by many small stockholders cannot be given the same incentive to manage efficiently as an owner–manager of a sole proprietorship. As a result, a corporate CEO is likely to make substantially more errors from the point of view of the theorem of consumer sovereignty than those made by a sole proprietor of the same kind of business. He is also unlikely to be as diligent in his oversight. He may even use deceit and fraud to the detriment of stockholders and consumers. In the case of fraud, if stock ownership is dispersed, the incentive of any single stockholder to sue a CEO for damages is not strong because he would receive only a part of the total gains to stockholders if his suit were successful. The larger the corporation and the more dispersed its shareholders, the lower the incentive of a single stockholder to sue.

Corporate CEOs cannot become too inefficient without inviting takeover by corporate raiders. Thus there is a limit on the incentive divergence in a corporation. On the other hand, if incentive divergence creates a potential personal gain situation, as it did in the case of investment banks, ordinary banks and other investment funds during the global financial crisis (see below), a raider may be able to gain by taking over a corporation whose CEO has been very efficient and acted in the interests of stockholders. The raider immediately adopts risky policies to increase short-term profit, causing stock prices to rise. He then sells his newly bought shares for a handsome personal gain.

Incentive divergence in financial services corporations During the housing bubble period, the more important effect of incentive divergence due to corporate financial intermediation occurred in large financial services corporations such as investment banks and large insurance (or default swap

– see below) companies like American International Group (AIG). The CEOs and top employees of such companies are in a position that is different from their positions in major production firms in two respects. First, they are typically more highly specialized, since choosing from among the possible methods available to manage the risk of loss in making financial investments is a highly specialized task. Second, the diversity of potential financial investments, combined with the large amount of speculation, implies that CEOs face a tradeoff between investments that are expected to yield higher long-term profit and those that are expected to yield higher short-term profit. Given some initial allocation of funds to different investments, a competent CEO will recognize that he can earn higher expected short-term profit if he is willing to incur a sacrifice of lower expected long-term profit or even expected loss.

As a result of these facts, incentive divergence takes a special form for large financial corporations. The gains to a CEO and other top executives in deciding how to deal with the above-mentioned tradeoff depend upon how they are rewarded for their choices. If the more permanent stockholders are well informed, they will want a balanced tradeoff between short-term and long-term profit because such a balance maximizes the long-run price of their shares. The stockholders will set up a reward system that constrains the CEO to limit the pursuit of higher short-term profit. However, because the governance of a financial services corporation is a highly specialized task, stockholders are unlikely to be well informed. In this circumstance, the stockholders can be persuaded to give large cash bonuses and/or sales commissions to those who contribute to the short-term profit. Once such a reward system is in place, the CEOs and salespeople can earn large short-term incomes by pursuing a short-term profit strategy. Moreover, the highly specialized nature of their skills means that their role in causing the harmful effects to the more permanent stockholders may never be discovered. Finally, even if a CEO is ultimately replaced at stockholder initiative, his expertise assures that he can find a job that yields comparable income, minus the bonuses and/or commissions, elsewhere. Alternatively, he can expect to retire and live off of the large bonuses and/or commissions that he will have earned in the short run.

There is a fine line between the CEO's (1) shift from long-term to short-term profit maximization and (2) malfeasance. So the executive who is not careful may end up the object of a lawsuit by stockholders or even the target of a fraud investigation. However, so long as he avoids outright illegal activity, he can usually do well – provided he can persuade stockholders to reward him with bonuses and/or sales commissions for activities about which they lack knowledge and about which they are unlikely to learn.

Large CEO bonuses and high sales commissions were widespread in the financial services industry during the period before the housing bubble burst and before the weakness of financial institutions became evident. Apparently, CEOs had been able to persuade stockholders to allow these.

Reliance of large financial firms on 'insurers' and hedge fund managers
A critical part of the process of making investments is the management of risk. It is the saver's concern with this fact that makes her hesitate to turn over her money to an intermediary in the first place. It is the reason that providing guaranty is a function in a market economy. Consider a CEO of a financial services corporation who perceives a financial investment opportunity that will substantially raise short-term profit but that risks reducing long-term profit by too much to justify to stockholders. If he can purchase insurance on all or part of the risk, both he and the stockholders may come to see the investment as wise and prudent. Their interests will converge. Of course, the insurer must herself be trustworthy and she must possess sufficient wealth to pay off if the investment project fails. As mentioned above, a guarantor (or insurer) is also an agent. If the CEO and stockholders believe the insurer's promise but the insurer fails to keep sufficient reserves to cover all of her insurance obligations, their calculations will have been wrong. Because of this, the possibility of buying investment insurance may add to the incentive divergence.

As we have seen, the relationship between the CEO of a financial services corporation and the stockholders is one of incentive divergence. The CEO may have an incentive to purchase insurance for short-term investments even though doing so is against the interests of stockholders. Suppose that the CEO suspects that an insurer of a short-term project will default on the insurance payoff if the investment fails. Stockholders, however, are unaware of the high probability of the insurer's default. Then the CEO may buy the insurance anyway because doing so helps him persuade stockholders to allow him to borrow in order to finance the project. Alternatively, since the loss to him is less than the loss to the collective of stockholders, he may not ask about the capacity of the insurer to meet her obligations or he may employ statistical extrapolation to help make his judgment. As before, the incentive of the CEO depends on the reward system. A CEO who can persuade stockholders to pay a bonus for raising short-term profit has an incentive to buy such bogus insurance.

It is essential to realize that providing insurance against business risk is a very different activity than providing insurance against material risk or risk in nature. As I have pointed out, science relies on the assumption that the future will be like the past. Scientists can be confident in applying statistical extrapolation as a fundamental mode of reasoning in cases where events in the material world are uncertain. One can confidently construct a series of risk premiums on the basis of observed material facts. In the social and economic world, however, this mode is inappropriate because, by definition, events are caused by human choice. A human being can certainly agree to be responsible for the economic losses incurred by another. However, unless she uses 'the understanding' to evaluate the probability of the losses, she is likely to lose her money. And if she relies on past experience alone to predict whether an insurer will be able to pay off on a business insurance claim, she is likely to err. She is a prime candidate for becoming a victim in a reliance cycle or principal–agent relationship.

Market events cannot be insured against in the proper sense of the term. If someone hopes to earn profit from insuring against economic events, she must be capable of predicting the insured party's long-run profitability. She must act as an entrepreneur, which means that she is not, strictly speaking, an insurer. She is betting on what she regards as a superior ability to appraise resources. She is sharing in the insured party's profit and loss, albeit indirectly. Properly understood her income is profit from the project she insures. She is like a co-investor.

During the period prior to the breakdown of the international financial system, CEOs of the largest investment banks bought insurance directly or indirectly in the form of credit default swap (CDS) deals.[18] The largest seller of such insurance may have been AIG. It is impossible to know whether the CEOs were themselves persuaded that the guarantors who offered CDSs were reliable or whether, not being persuaded, they dealt with them anyway partly as a means of appeasing stockholders.[19] It turned out that the insurers were not reliable. When Lehman Brothers went bankrupt, those financial firms that had bought CDSs to insure their bond holdings in Lehman Brothers lost their insurance and, as a result, suffered substantial loss. Had AIG also gone bankrupt, the hit on financial firms would have been much greater.[20]

Unfortunately, there is no way, at least for an outsider like myself, to know whether the executives whose firms participated in these markets realized how fragile the system was. It is at least conceivable, however, that a number of insiders were quite aware and that they feasted on high bonuses and commissions in the short run, realizing that when the crisis came, they could escape the fallout relatively unscathed.

Hedge funds   A major set of players in the global financial crisis were the 'hedge funds'. In formal terms, a hedge fund is merely an investment fund in which financial investors turn over their money to a fund manager to invest in their interests. A hedge fund is subject to much looser regulation than other funds and may be completely unregulated, except for a limit on the number of investors who can participate.[21]

Hedge funds come and go. Some make huge profits; others go bankrupt. What is important for this chapter is their relationship to large banks. During the period of the housing bubble, hedge funds often provided a market for the lower-rated MBSs (Morris, 2008: 108–9). At the same time, they were important clients of investment banks, which brokered their stock and bond trades (ibid.: 111). Moreover, they often made credit default swaps possible by being willing to sell or buy a swap that no other market participant would sell or buy. Finally, they played a large role in the gambling market that developed on various economic events. Besides the real market on credit default swaps and other financial assets, there was a shadow market in which individuals and firms bet against each other on future economic events, such as a fall in the price of a particular kind of bond.[22] The connection between banks and hedge funds makes a bank vulnerable to losses in the event that a hedge fund fails. The bank may own a credit default swap guaranteed by a hedge fund, its brokerage branch may have extended a credit line to a hedge fund, it may rely on the hedge fund's brokerage demand, and so on. Any relationship with a hedge fund other than merely providing banking services is likely to increase the bank's risk. Links to hedge funds were apparently largely responsible for Lehman Brothers' downfall.[23] I have not sufficiently studied the matter to know how important the hedge funds were to the problems suffered by other large investment banks, commercial banks and other financial institutions.

As with insurance, a bank's relationship with a hedge fund increases the incentive divergence by increasing the complexity of the decision-making process faced by stockholders. Also, as in the case of insurers, it is not possible to know whether a particular CEO of a bank made an honest error or used the hedge fund relationship as a means of persuading stockholders to allow bonuses and high individual sales commissions.

4. INCENTIVE DIVERGENCE DUE TO GOVERNMENT REGULATION OF FINANCIAL INTERMEDIATION

Government intervention in markets contains a large set of incentive divergence classes. I believe that the most important interventions that were relevant to the global financial crisis are the manipulation of money and credit, regulated fractional reserve banking, and deposit insurance. Also important were the actions of the so-called government-sponsored enterprises – Fannie Mae and Freddie Mac – and the Community Reinvestment Act. However, discussion of these is beyond the scope of this chapter. I confine this section to the incentive divergence introduced by financial market regulation. Examples of regulatory agencies that were relevant to the crisis are the Fed, FDIC (Federal Deposit Insurance Corporation), and SEC.

The regulation of financial intermediation is intended to reduce the incentive divergence associated with deceit and fraud. Some of it, such as regulation of banks, aims to block potential victims from putting themselves into positions where they can be victimized. By far the majority of such regulation, however, aims to achieve its primary goal by restricting the behavior and actions of financial intermediaries. By and large, regulation that aims to accomplish either of these goals is futile. There are four reasons. First, in all but the most extreme cases, the knowledge needed to accurately judge whether deceit or fraud has occurred is either impossible for regulators to acquire or too costly to be worthwhile trying to acquire. Second, regulators' incentives and ability to achieve their assigned goals are constrained by law, which makes regulatory agencies into bureaucracies. Third, regulators are at a disadvantage in the regulation game and, as a result, their actions and behavior tend to be greatly influenced, in the long run, by the very individuals they initially aim to regulate. The regulators are 'captured'. Fourth, regulators may be impeded by political opportunism on the part of legislators and their assistants. In this section, I discuss each of these reasons. In addition, I suggest that the institution of regulation can be a source of error due to the adolescent mentality, which views regulators as performing a necessary function.

Deceit, Fraud and the Cost of Government Error in Judging whether Deceit or Fraud has Occurred

Consider regulation designed to deter or prevent the harm due to persuasion and fraud by enterprisers. The proposed role of the authorities is to deter deception and fraud, while encouraging principal–agent relationships that entail truthful information. The problem is that there is a fine line between an effort to deceive and defraud, and an effort to help someone as an agent by either providing information or performing some action that the actor can reasonably presume is in the principal's interest. This line is not fixed. The kind of information that people can gain from receiving, the means of deceiving and defrauding, and the technology used to deceive and defraud are continually changing. In light of these characteristics of situations in which deceit and fraud are most likely to occur, it is only possible in the extreme cases for the authorities to accurately judge whether an agent for a principal has done intentional harm or failed to exercise reasonable care. This is especially true in the case of financial intermediation. The reason is the complexity of the task, which I have already discussed. Only rarely is it reasonable to expect judges or appointed lawyers for the prosecution in fraud cases to possess the expertise of the CEOs, investment fund managers, hedge fund managers and so on. Yet without this expertise, they cannot adequately judge whether the agent has been cheating a principal or performing an entrepreneurial function.[24]

I now focus on less extreme cases. If the authorities try to make judgments in these cases, they are bound to make errors due to their limited knowledge. Suppose that the regulatory agency is charged with making judgments in such cases or with deciding whether an agent should be permitted to provide a service that would enable him to commit deceit or fraud. Then the prospect for errors by the regulator would most likely increase the incentive divergence associated with the principal–agent relationship. The agent's worry about being prosecuted by regulators for deceit or fraud would be enough to deter some prospective agents from offering their services and thereby reduce the benefits to members of society from the principal–agent relationship. Consumers would be less well served.

Bureaucracy

A second source of incentive divergence due to regulation is associated with bureaucracy. The reason for bureaucracy is well known. If a government employee is permitted to use discretion, as opposed to following bureaucratic rules, she may use her power to profit by making decisions that are demanded by pressure groups and other special interests, political incumbents and new candidates for political office. In the most extreme cases, her decisions may threaten the continuation of the government in its present form. She may use her discretion to start a revolution. To allow a government employee too much discretion introduces such huge incentive divergence that makers of democratic constitutions demand provisions designed to avoid it. The abuse-of-power threat is typically avoided in a democracy by subjecting government employees to bureaucratic rules (see Gunning 2003, ch.14). The behavior of each of the employees of a regulatory agency is constrained by such rules.

There is an obvious conflict between the desire to regulate any enterprise and bureaucratic rules. Because entrepreneurial profit and loss conditions are continually changing, and because entrepreneurs are expected to possess and exercise imagination, creativity and inventiveness, no lawmaker with insight would want regulation to be so rigid that it restricts entrepreneurship. Yet a lawmaker cannot anticipate the entrepreneurial actions that are likely to best satisfy consumer wants. Such a legislator must admit that consumer benefits are the consequence of the entrepreneurial production and use of specialized knowledge which is practically impossible for her to know and to anticipate. If she hopes to succeed, she realizes that she must rely on an expert regulator. Such a regulator would have to possess wide discretion in gathering and interpreting information and in making judgments about who should be punished and rewarded. Yet legislators cannot grant regulators wide discretion to command additional resources, if needed, without risking the abuse of power.

This is the conflict. It results in a general lack of ability on the part of regulators of financial intermediaries to make the kinds of decisions that are necessary to reduce the incentive divergence associated with deception and fraud. The regulator gets constrained by bureaucratic rules. If she passively follows the rules, she ends up being totally ineffective. The only result is a waste of regulatory resources. If she decides to be active, the existence of rules puts her at a disadvantage in the regulation game. The CEO she aims to regulate has an incentive to outwit her. Most likely the regulator will get duped. The necessary bureaucratization of regulation results in even greater incentive divergence than otherwise.

The Regulation Game and Capture

The third source of incentive divergence is the disadvantage faced by regulators with respect to the parties they aim to regulate. The mere existence of regulators as an instrument of government coercion creates opportunities for enterprises to manipulate the regulators into positions where they can achieve greater monopoly power and other objectives. To understand how, it is necessary to realize that making and enforcing regulations is like a game. The regulator tries to constrain the actions of the regulated individuals. Since such constraints reduce the options available to the regulatees, they try to evade the regulations and to influence the making of them. While the rewards to regulators from winning this game must be limited due to the abuse-of-power conflict, the rewards to regulatees can be large. For example, a government regulatory agency may be created to detect and deter instances in which savers or stockholders are likely to be deceived or defrauded by a CEO. Yet, when confronted with the deep pockets of a prospective deceiver and defrauder, it may institute new rules that make it easier to deceive and defraud. The regulator may simply decide that the game is not worth winning *to him*. Or he may try his best to win but lack the resources that he would need to win. Or perhaps he will succumb to bribery and corruption or persuasion. Failing this, he may be further constrained by the politicians who oversee the regulatory agency. The politicians may be enlisted by lobbyists or bribers to thwart the efforts of well-intentioned and dedicated regulators. In any of these cases, the actions of the regulator may come to be controlled by the very people his actions were designed to regulate. In other words, the regulators are prone to be *captured* by those they aim to regulate (Stigler, 1971).

For example, mortgage lenders, investment bankers and regular bankers were permitted by regulators at various times to use accounting procedures that obscured the true market value of their assets and liabilities from stockholders. Once they adopted these procedures, they were in a better position to employ ratings firms to help induce customers to buy their MBSs and other products. And they could more easily persuade the stockholders to allow them to receive large bonuses for their contribution to short-run profit through their sales, while staving off corporate raiders.[25]

Political Opportunism

Besides the bureaucracy problem, the laws and rules that guide regulatory agencies are subject to political opportunism. Pressure groups form in an effort to divert the rules or their enforcement so that they help achieve purposes that are different from those intended. In the game of political opportunism, citizens with the deepest pockets or loudest voice typically have an advantage. For example, the agencies assigned by the government to guarantee and securitize mortgage loans (Fannie Mae and Freddie Mac) were required, or persuaded, by politicians and regulators to help implement laws aimed at assisting otherwise unqualified borrowers to obtain loans. Many banks that specialized in mortgage loans were also given incentives to incur higher risk by favoring subprime borrowers.[26]

Adolescent Mentality

Regulation has the potential to deceive savers and thereby add to incentive divergence. Why then do legislators try to regulate? My answer is the 'adolescent mentality'. Practically every growing child who does not encounter day-to-day violence on the part of the government goes through a stage during which she conceives of the agents of government as functionaries in a grand system of benevolent authoritarian control. The mailman performs the function of delivering the mail, the public school teacher gives valuable education, the fireman puts out fires, the policeman helps people and maintains order, the president leads the country and so on. To the extent that savers have adopted the adolescent mentality, they think that the function of agencies like the Fed, the FDIC and the SEC is to protect their savings. They gladly hand over their funds to financial intermediaries, believing that even if the intermediaries would otherwise lie and deceive them, government regulations will keep the intermediaries in check. Regulation, combined with this mentality, adds to incentive divergence.

The adolescent mentality is particularly strong among some foreigners who see the USA as the most successful market economy and democracy. During the build-up to the crisis, it seems quite likely that the combination of regulation, high ratings by ratings firms, and insurance in the form of CDSs misled many Asians and Europeans into thinking that the MBSs and similar assets were sound investments. Their trust in ratings firms and insurance (the CDS) was undoubtedly partly due to their trust in the SEC to regulate such agencies and insurers. Unfortunately the trust in regulation was unwarranted.

5. RECOMMENDATIONS

Consumer sovereignty is the starting point for modern policy economics. It is the theorem upon which economists rely when they trumpet their support for capitalism over socialism. It applies strictly only to a pure market economy in which there are complete private property rights. Yet it is not possible to establish a society in which individuals reap the full benefits of their action or are fully responsible for the harm they cause. As a result, I conceive of the private property rights paradigm as a procedure for identifying cases in which consumer sovereignty does not fully prevail, due to incentive divergence.

There are many sources of incentive divergence in an unregulated market economy. This chapter has emphasized five of these in explaining how events comparable to the global financial crisis could occur in the absence of government intervention, including monetary policy: (1) specialization, which makes a person vulnerable to the errors made by others; (2) errors in decision-making, especially those caused by the use of statistical extrapolation; (3) a cunning salesperson's prospect for gain from persuading predictors of future prices to use statistical extrapolation; (4) the principal–agent relationship in financial intermediation; and (5) the principal–agent relationship in the corporation. The chapter has presented the theory of how the presence of these sources can lead to a substantial crisis.

According to the theory, a price bubble in a large segment of the market, such as housing, could occur as a consequence of changing migration patterns, the use of statistical extrapolation by house buyers and the presence of cunning salespeople. An increase in demand for mortgage funding that accompanies a housing bubble would, in turn, enable financial intermediaries to pay higher than normal returns. This would facilitate their attaining a position where savers would rely on them. In that position, the intermediaries would be able to take advantage of the propensity for their principals – savers – to use statistical extrapolation due to the complexity of making financial investment decisions. To simulate the recent financial crisis, I assumed that their means of doing so is to employ a new financial instrument – the rated MBS. The CEOs of financial intermediary firms (independent investment banks and investment banks that are part of larger commercial banks) could partner with ratings firms to deceive savers and other intermediaries who represent savers into believing that the savings are more secure than they really are. To earn income for themselves and their co-workers, they could persuade stockholders to permit high bonuses and sales commissions as rewards for higher short-term profit. And to allay stockholders' uncertainty, they could purchase insurance from large insurance firms and hedge funds in spite of their knowledge that such firms may not pay claims.

Such actions by the CEOs could harm stockholders and savers for whom the CEOs acted as agents. In some cases, it would threaten the survival of the firm. If enough financial firms were engaged in this practice, the banking system itself would be at risk.

The bursting of a housing bubble could cause the worst fears of stockholders and savers to be realized. At that point, the errors that are indigenous to the statistical extrapolation strategy would become evident to everyone. Subprime mortgage borrowers would default, MBSs would lose value, the false ratings of the ratings firms would be revealed, holders of MBSs would suffer a decrease in wealth, investment banks would become insolvent, hedge funds and insurers would go bankrupt, and banks would fail. The CEOs and salespeople would resign or be fired.

It might be thought that the key to preventing such a crisis is regulation. However, in a democracy, regulation is likely to make matters worse. The potential abuse of power leads citizens to limit the discretion that a regulator must have to compete in the regulation game effectively. In addition, regulated firms have a strong incentive to 'capture' the regulatory agency. As a result the regulator is apt to end up promoting the interests of those she is employed to regulate. In addition, regulation is influenced by wasteful rent-seeking and political opportunism.

Once it is accepted that regulation increases incentive divergence, one must admit (perhaps with an air of humility) that if the people of a nation want to enjoy the benefits of specialization and the division of labor, they must accept the incentive divergence that is endemic in a typical market economy. They must endure the inconvenience of occasional financial crises. The important questions are whether these are likely to be small or large in the absence of intervention, and whether there is any means available to reduce the effects on consumers.

To what extent is it possible to reduce the harm to consumers due to the periodic disruption caused by bubbles and reliance cycles? Regulation is not the answer. What, then? I cannot give a more complete answer to this question until I consider the effects of government manipulation of money, which is beyond the scope of this chapter. However, I will submit that a full understanding of the effects of such manipulation leads to the conclusion that the only function of government with respect to money – and it is a very important one – is to produce non-counterfeitable paper money and to keep the quantity in circulation as close to constant as possible. Such a policy would eliminate the prospect of a government's massive intervention in order to save a regulated fractional reserve banking system. It would allow the ordinary self-correcting mechanism to play itself out in the shortest possible time by increasing the responsibility of errant, deceitful and fraudulent financial firms and individuals for the damage they caused to their principals.

NOTES

1. The fact that such crises are ordinary is reflected by Reinhart and Rogoff's 2008 report on a number of similar crises under widely varying policy regimes.
2. The concept of incentive divergence has a long history in economics. Its most recent manifestation may be in the work of theorists involved in so-called 'mechanism design' (Maskin, 2008; Myerson, 2008).
3. Although use of the incentive divergence concept is a clear implication of Mises's praxeology-based economics, he did not often use it, to my knowledge. Nor did his students. The pioneers of practical work in applying the paradigm were the so-called property rights theorists of the 1960s and 1970s, following the lead of Ronald Coase and the new institutionalists (Furubotn and Pejovich, 1974; Klein, 2000). To my knowledge, no one has used the concept to explain the global financial crisis and to formulate or evaluate policy recommendations.
4. Mises's way of formulating this issue seems to me far superior to that of the modern literature. A recent paper in the *American Economic Review* presents a study of 'environments with players who are naive, in the sense that they fail to account for the informational content of other players' actions' (Esponda, 2008: 1269). In this 'mainstream' formulation, the author implicitly defines 'naive' as the character of a person who uses statistical extrapolation to make decisions. But in referring to 'informational content', he implies that knowledge of the *meaning* of others' actions is available to anyone who uses the correct interpretative formula. Such an implication suggests a superior view of what a person's actions actually reveal about what he/she will do in the future. It directs one's attention away from the intersubjective uncertainty that is characteristic of all market interaction and, therefore, away from what many Austrian economists

have called the 'market process'. Properly understood, the market process refers to how one can expect individuals to act in an environment in which they can earn profit by producing goods and services for others at a sufficiently low cost to attract them to buy. Such an environment provides incentives for individuals to bet that their appraisals of resources are superior to those of others. In turn, it gives the individuals an incentive to develop and employ methods to help understand the meaning of others' actions. Although modeling the processes that exist in environments described by Esponda (i.e. environments in which some individuals are 'naïve') is the only way to explain a crisis of the sort discussed in this chapter, the deeper question of why such environments exist necessarily lies beyond the scope of his analysis. For this chapter, it is the most important question. It is thus important to ask why so many additional novice speculators entered the housing market as housing prices rose as they did.

5. Many salespeople between 2003 and 2005 went far beyond this by defrauding both buyers of houses and mortgage lenders. Such salespeople defrauded borrowers by promoting themselves as agents for the buyers and then mis-stating the terms of the contract, which unwitting buyers chose to sign. They defrauded lenders by misrepresenting the character of borrowers. Consider the testimony of a loan officer of Novastar, a California company that specialized in originating loans. The loan officer

> who worked in California from 2002 to '03, told plaintiffs' lawyers that employees would apply an "X-Acto knife and some tape" to borrowers' W-2 forms and paychecks to qualify them for loans. The same employee said that on other occasions, the company would temporarily deposit $5,000 in the bank account of a potential borrower to inflate his or her assets. (Lubove and Taub: 2007)

6. Those who had borrowed on strictly adjustable rate mortgages began to default immediately. Most adjustable rate mortgages, however, carried rates that were fixed for two years. Defaults on these were delayed until the fixed rate period expired.

7. For many economists, the question would immediately arise as to why arbitrage would not prevent a reliance cycle from occurring. There is a ready answer. The effectiveness of arbitrage in eliminating overpriced and underpriced assets depends on the presence of individuals acting in the role of the entrepreneur who possess knowledge about the difference between the current and future price and who possess the wealth or access to it that is necessary to make the bet required for the underpriced asset to be purchased. Effectiveness also depends on the existence of a predictable political and regulatory environment. The persistence of overpriced assets during the build-up to a crisis is due to the lack of such knowledge. A more complete answer is provided in the appendix.

8. In addition to simple securitization of a mortgage pool, securitizers found that by attaching different legal rights to the pool of income received from mortgage payments, they could increase MBS marketability. Thus ratings firms (see below) were willing to give the top AAA rating to MBSs that claimed the right to, say, the first 70 percent of the income from a given mortgage pool, while assigning a much lower rating to MBSs that claimed only the right to, say, the last 5 percent of the pool income (Morris, 2008: 39–40). This process is called 'collateralization', and an MBS of this type was called a collateralized mortgage obligation. Other debts, such as credit card debt, have also been collateralized, so that a collateralized mortgage obligation is part of a larger class of collateralized debt obligations. The AAA-rated MBSs were attractive to pension funds and ordinary insurance companies because they paid a higher rate but were touted to be as secure as government bonds; the BBB-rated MBSs were attractive to hedge funds (see below) because of their high return and the possibility of balancing this risk against some other risk (ibid.: 108).

9. The buyers were often agencies of foreign governments, called 'sovereign wealth funds'.

10. The first effort at private securitization in the USA failed, along with a large number of other financial schemes, during the Great Depression (Jones, 1962; Weiss, 1989; Bartlett, 1989). Its revival was achieved through government intervention, which

provided the guaranty for mortgage loans. Significant private securitization re-emerged in the late 1990s.

11. The presence of government-sponsored securitization might help explain the difference between the magnitude of the effects of the collapse of subprime mortgage loan securitization and that of automobile loan securitization in the late 1990s (Hojnacki and Shick, 2008).

12. Coval et al. (2009: 23) are more skeptical.

13. Ratings firms are regulated in the USA by the government's Securities and Exchange Commission. Apparently, this agency failed in its mandate. In light of our discussion of regulatory agencies in section 4, this is not surprising.

14. When referring to how it rated financial instruments, Moody's executives referred to ratings by its 'models' (Jones and Tett, 2008).

15. A couple of articles in the *Financial Times* (Jones and Tett, 2008; Jones et al., 2008) report that Moody's knew about 'an error' in a computer program and that ratings should have been adjusted downward almost a year before they actually were.

16. This article also describes court cases in which stockholders of corporations have tried to recoup losses by suing a ratings firm for providing misleading ratings.

17. In this chapter, I have stressed the distinction between statistical extrapolation and 'the understanding'. To my knowledge, this would be regarded as a novel approach to modern economists. Yet listen to how similar ideas were recently expressed in a *Journal of Economic Perspectives* article by professors from Harvard and Princeton:

> As we have explained, these claims [that the market for structured credit will work itself out] are highly sensitive to the assumptions of 1) default probability and recovery value, 2) correlation of defaults, and 3) the relation between payoffs and the economic states that investors care about most. Beginning in late 2007 and continuing well into 2008, it became increasingly clear to investors in highly-rated structured products that each of these three key assumptions were systematically biased against them. These investors are now reluctant to invest in securities that they do not fully understand. (Coval et al. 2009: 23)

Presumably the last sentence has something to do with using 'the understanding'. However, the authors attribute the errors made by investors to 'biases'. Although a close reading indicates that such 'biases' were removed when investors came to realize they were tricked by the salespeople, the authors express their conclusions in the language of statistical extrapolation, as indicated by the terms they use to express the three reasons for their skepticism about the future of structured credit.

18. Matthew Phillips, writing for *Newsweek*, tells the story of a meeting of bankers in 1994 at which the idea of credit default swaps was hatched (Phillips, 2008). Swaps have a much longer history. They have been used with success for three decades in foreign exchange and commodities markets as means of hedging against unexpected changes.

19. A more important factor may have been regulators. Regulated financial firms must, by law, provide accounts that persuade regulators that they possess sufficient guaranty to protect investors. Failure to please regulators may not only affect their status as a licensed institution, but also their ability to raise funds and to maintain share values. Since I am trying to describe an environment in the absence of regulation, my assumption here is that CEOs of financial firms may have sufficient incentive to purchase insurance solely in order to reduce the uncertainty perceived by investors. For more on how CEOs used CDSs to avoid closer scrutiny by regulators, see Carney (2009).

20. See Gethard (2009) for a brief discussion of the AIG case.

21. Unfortunately, the term 'hedge' implies that the fund's business is to offset the risk associated with one asset by purchasing another investment of a different nature. This is regrettable because hedging performs an important and very different economic function in agricultural, mining and currency markets. In any case, our concern here is with the hedge fund, as it has been named in the business magazines. For a description of some major hedge funds in history see McWhinney (2005).

22. Richard Zabel (2008) writes that 'by the end of 2007, the CDS market had a notional value of $45 trillion, but the corporate bond, municipal bond, and structured investment vehicles market totaled less than $25 trillion. Therefore, a minimum of $20 trillion were speculative "bets" on the possibility of a credit event of a specific credit asset not owned by either party to the CDS contract.'
23. I base this partly on an article by Maurna Desmond (2008).
24. This conclusion differs from the suggestion by Milgrom (2008: 130) that making agents liable for disclosure of pertinent information would mitigate the incentive divergence problem.
25. Much of this deceit is related to so-called regulatory capital – the value of various categories of assets, as defined by regulator, that an investment bank (regulated by the SEC) or regular bank (regulated by the Fed and FDIC) must own. Businessdictionary. com defines regulatory capital as 'net worth of a firm defined according to the rules of a regulatory agency (such as securities and exchange commission)'. The regulator has substantial discretion in deciding what will count as regulatory capital. By allowing the regulated firm to use CDSs to increase the value of regulatory capital, the regulators in effect permitted CEOs to increase their risk of long-term loss. See Carney (2009). So-called regulatory capital arbitragers, like AIG, established special departments to create assets that they could sell to financial institution CEOs often for the sole purpose of increasing their regulatory capital. With more regulatory capital, the CEO could make additional short-term investments.
26. It is doubtful that the law and regulations that encouraged these changes added significantly to the housing bubble or the global financial crisis. However, they surely made the allocation of savers' funds less efficient in satisfying consumer wants than it otherwise would have been.

REFERENCES

Bartlett, William W. (1989), *Mortgage-Backed Securities: Products, Analysis, Trading*, New York: New York Finance Institute.
Carney, John (2009), 'How the banks used AIG's swaps to dodge banking rules', *The Business Insider: Clusterstock*, http://www.businessinsider.com/how-the-banks-used-aigs-swaps-to-dodge-banking-rules-2009-3.
Coval, Joshua, Jakub Jurek and Erik Stafford (2009), 'The economics of structured finance', *Journal of Economic Perspectives*, **23** (1): 3–25.
Desmond, Maurna (2008), 'Lehman bails out hedge funds', *Forbes.com* (10 April), http://www.forbes.com/2008/04/10/lehman-liquidation-losses-markets-equity-cx_md_0410markets25.html.
England, R.S. (2006), 'The rise of private label', *Mortgage Banking* (October), http://www.robertstoweengland.com/documents/MBM.10-06EnglandPrivateLabel.pdf.
Esponda, Ignacio (2008), 'Behavioral equilibrium in economies with adverse selection', *American Economic Review*, **98** (4): 1269–91.
Furubotn, E. and S. Pejovich (ed.) (1974), *The Economics of Property Rights*, Cambridge, MA: Ballinger.
Gethard, Gregory (2009), 'Falling giant: a case study of AIG', *Investopedia*, http://www.investopedia.com/articles/economics/09/american-investment-group-aig-bailout.asp.
Gunning, J. Patrick (2003), *Understanding Democracy: An Introduction to Public Choice*, Taipei, Taiwan: Nomad Press.

Gunning, J. Patrick (2009), 'Consumer sovereignty: the key to Mises's economics', Bryant University Working Paper, http://www.nomadpress.com/gunning/subjecti/workpape/cskeymis.pdf.
Hayek, F.A. (1945), 'The use of knowledge in society', *American Economic Review*, **35** (4): 519–30. Reprinted in *Individualism and Economic Order*, Chicago, IL: University of Chicago Press, 1948.
Hojnacki, Jared E. and Richard A. Shick (2008), 'The subprime mortgage lending collapse – should we have seen it coming?', *Journal of Business & Economics Research*, **6** (12): 25–36.
Jones, Oliver (1962), 'The development of an effective secondary mortgage market', *The Journal of Finance*, **17** (2): 358–70.
Jones, Sam and Gillian Tett (2008), 'Moody's to investigate staff over rating bug', *Financial Times*, 1 July, available at http://www.ft.com.
Jones, Sam, Gillian Tett and Paul J. Davies (2008), 'Moody's error gave top ratings to debt products', *Financial Times*, 20 May, available at http://www.ft.com.
Klein, Peter G. (2000) 'New institutional economics', in Boudewijn Bouckaert and Gerrit De Geest (eds), *Encyclopedia of Law and Economics. Volume I. The History and Methodology of Law and Economics*, Cheltenham, UK and Northampton, MA: Edward Elgar.
Lubove, Seth and Daniel Taub (2007), 'The subprime sinkhole', *Bloomberg* (July), http://www.bloomberg.com/news/marketsmag/subprime.html.
McWhinney, James E. (2005), 'Massive hedge fund failures', *Investopedia*, http://www.investopedia.com/articles/mutualfund/05/HedgeFundFailure.asp.
Maskin, Eric S. (2008), 'Mechanism design: how to implement social goals', *American Economic Review*, **98** (3): 567–76.
Mayer, Christopher, Karen Pence and Shane M. Sherlund (2009), 'The rise in mortgage defaults', *Journal of Economic Perspectives*, **23** (1): 27–50.
Milgrom, Paul (2008), 'What the seller won't tell you: persuasion and disclosure in markets', *Journal of Economic Perspectives*, **22** (2): 115–31.
Mises, Ludwig von (1966), *Human Action: A Treatise on Economics*, Chicago, IL: Henry Regnery Company.
Morgenson, Gretchen (2008), 'Credit rating agency heads grilled by lawmakers', *The New York Times* (22 October), http://www.nytimes.com/2008/10/23/business/economy/23rating.html.
Morris, Charles (2008), *The Trillion Dollar Meltdown: Easy Money, High Rollers, and the Great Credit Crash*, New York: Public Affairs/Perseus.
Myerson, Roger B. (2008), 'Perspectives on mechanism design in economic theory', *American Economic Review*, **98** (3): 586–603.
Phillips, Matthew (2008), 'The monster that ate Wall Street', *Newsweek*, (27 September), http://www.newsweek.com/id/161199.
Reinhart, Carmen M. and Kenneth S. Rogoff (2008), 'Is the 2007 US sub-prime financial crisis so different? An international historical comparison', *American Economic Review*, **98** (2): 339–44.
Rosner, Joshua (2007), 'Stopping the subprime crisis', *The New York Times* (25 July), http://www.nytimes.com/2007/07/25/opinion/25rosner.html.
Shiller, Robert J. (2005), *Irrational Exuberance*, 2nd edn, Princeton, NJ: Princeton University Press.
Stigler, George (1971), 'The theory of economic regulation', *Bell Journal of Economics*, **2** (1): 3–21.
USGAO (US Government Accountability Office) (2007), 'Home mortgage

defaults and foreclosures: recent trends and associated economic and market developments' (Briefing to the Committee on Financial Services, House of Representatives), October, http://www.gao.gov/new.items/d0878r.pdf.

Weiss, Marc A. (1989), 'Marketing and financing home ownership: mortgage lending and public policy in the United States, 1918–1989', *Business and Economic History*, **18**: 109–18.

Zabel, Richard R. (2008), 'Credit default swaps: from protection to speculation', *Pratt's Journal of Bankruptcy Law*, September, http://www.rkmc.com/Credit-Default-Swaps-From-Protection-To-Speculation.htm.

APPENDIX: WHY ARBITRAGE DID NOT MITIGATE THE RECENT RELIANCE CYCLE

To answer this question, I begin by trying to identify the precise arbitrage action that would have been necessary for the crisis to be mitigated. The way for an independent speculator to profit from arbitrage would have been to buy a CDS that rewards the buyer if an event occurs that causes the price of MBSs to fall. The seller of such a CDS might have been Lehman Brothers, Bear Stearns, AIG, or some other large investment bank. Investment banks themselves could have facilitated the arbitrage process by acting as intermediaries in locating speculators or hedgers who are willing to take the opposite position. In a relatively efficient market, a sufficient demand for such swaps would have made it very costly for an investor to purchase insurance against an event that would cause the price of MBSs to fall. As a result, the selling price of MBSs would have risen and the quantity demanded would have fallen on this account.

Why did these events not occur? My explanation is that an insufficient number of entrepreneurs who were in positions to bet on the prices of MBSs (i.e. who had the knowledge of how to bet, the willingness to bet, and the funds to back their bet) were aware (a) that there was extensive fraud in the mortgage origination business, (b) that adjustable rate mortgage borrowers could not afford to make payments on houses if the Fed tightened its policy, (c) that the response by such borrowers would seriously damage the wealth positions of speculative house buyers, and (d) that bond ratings firms had not taken these factors into account. Beyond this, it was not easy for a prospective arbitrager to predict that monetary policy would be tightened in 2005 and, if it were, and there was a large default on mortgages, to predict what the government, including the Fed, FDIC and other government agencies might do to mitigate the impending crisis. Moreover, a more sensible strategy, given that a speculative entrepreneur (arbitrager) predicted a crisis, might have been to make a large bet on rising MBS prices while paying close attention to the factors that would help predict exactly when the crisis would impact the MBS market. One who successfully predicted the downturn point could sell his MBSs just prior to that time and, simultaneously, buy the appropriate CDS. In short, few people had the knowledge or the willingness and ability to acquire the kind of knowledge that would have had to exist for the arbitrage market to work efficiently. This need not always be true and there is no doubt that both regulation by itself and uncertainty about what regulatory actions would be taken in the future increased the typical prospective arbitrager's lack of knowledge.

GLOSSARY

Credit default swap: a credit derivative contract between two counter-parties. The buyer makes periodic payments to the seller, and in return receives a payoff if an underlying financial instrument defaults. CDS contracts have been compared with insurance, because the buyer pays a premium and, in return, receives a sum of money if one of the specified events occurs (Wikipedia).

Cunning salesperson: a person whose goal is to profit by persuading one person to exchange with a second.

Incentive divergence: situations in which there are differences between the benefits and harm felt by an actor and the benefits and harm due to her actions that are felt by others.

Mortgage-backed security: a bond or share of stock whose income is a share of the receipts from mortgage borrowers, as filtered through agents who service the loan payments from mortgage borrowers, as they make payments on the mortgage.

Novice speculator: someone who has no special information about why a price or price index will rise or fall.

Principal–agent relationship: a relationship in which one person or entity (called the agent) acts on behalf of another (called the principal).

Regulatory arbitrage: any transaction that has little or no economic impact on a financial institution while either increasing its capital or reducing its required capital (riskglossary.com).

Reliance cycle: a four-period social cycle during which (1) principals are reluctant to trust, (2) an agent builds trust, (3) principals become increasingly willing to trust, and (4) the agent violates trust and principals become reluctant to trust again.

Securitization: the process through which a set of mortgage loans is transformed into a bond or share of stock.

Subprime mortgage borrower: a borrower 'with blemished credit and features higher interest rates and fees than the prime market' (USGAO, 2007: 8).

Theorem of consumer sovereignty: in a pure market economy, the entrepreneur function, by definition, acts in the interests of the consumer–saver role by bearing all uncertainty, producing all goods, and using methods of production that enable individuals in the consumer role to take the greatest advantage of the division of labor, except for errors in making predictions.

6. The microeconomic foundations of macroeconomic disorder: an Austrian perspective on the Great Recession of 2008

Steven Horwitz

Modern neoclassical macroeconomics has taken on the air of what John Kenneth Galbraith decades ago termed 'the conventional wisdom'. In particular, since Keynes, the economics profession has taken for granted a broad vision of macroeconomics that looks for the explanations of both booms and busts in the movements of various aggregate variables. The whole sub-discipline of 'macroeconomics' is premised on the belief that the standard microeconomic tools are not of much use in understanding the dynamics of growth and business cycles. Even with the rational expectations revolution purporting to set macroeconomics back on microfoundations, the language of aggregate supply and demand, oversimplified versions of the quantity theory of money, and the aggregative analytics of the Keynesian cross and simple models of functional finance still fill the textbooks and inform most policy debates. As we find ourselves in a significant recession that none of these models foresaw, nor seem to be of much help in extracting us, other approaches to macroeconomics have an opportunity to fill the explanatory vacuum. The Austrian school is uniquely positioned to fill that gap, as Austrians have long rejected the fundamental assumptions of modern macroeconomics and have developed an alternative approach to business cycles and economic growth that sheds a great deal of light on the current recession as well as suggesting ways to prevent future boom–bust cycles.

AUSTRIANS AND MODERN MACROECONOMICS

For Austrians, the start of economic analysis is the human actor trying to figure out what his ends are and how best to deploy his means to achieve them, but doing so in a world where his knowledge is fragmentary and often inarticulate and where the future is clouded by genuine, structural uncertainty. From the start, these preclude the use of standard neoclassical assumptions about rationality and self-interest. Austrians are not interested in describing the equilibrium outcomes of fully informed individuals and firms maximizing their utility and profits respectively. Such pictures of the world are useful, at best, as contrasts to the ways in which real-world human beings attempt to peer through the fog of uncertainty to better deploy their means for their desired ends, whether that is a single person engaging in economizing behavior or a firm searching for profits. All human action is, for the Austrians, speculative and entrepreneurial in that there is no assurance of success and genuine error and regret are possible (unlike neoclassical models, where the best decision possible given the data at hand is assumed to be made).

This depiction of human action translates into a conception of the market process. As individuals attempt, in Mises's (1966) words, to 'remove their felt uneasiness' by better deploying their means toward their desired ends, they have several options. First, they can engage in exchange and give up lesser-valued means for higher-valued ones. Exchange is mutually beneficial *ex ante* as both parties imagine they are being made better off by the trade, even if *ex post* they turn out to have erred. Such simple exchanges improve the subjective well-being of individuals or households, and as the inconveniences of barter take their toll, eventually traders discover the use of a medium of exchange. Monetary exchange brings with it the evolution of distinct money prices for each good, which in turn enables traders to more clearly calculate the gains and losses of various activities.

Money prices are also crucial to the second way in which people can improve their position: they can engage in roundabout processes of production. Rather than trade consumption good for consumption good, actors can gather together a variety of inputs and create a new output with them. This can be as simple as constructing a tool or as complex as producing automobiles. Carl Menger (1981 [1871]), the founder of the Austrian school, recognized the importance of intertemporal production by distinguishing between goods of the 'first order', or direct consumption goods, and goods of the 'higher orders', or capital goods that contribute to the production of first-order goods. In the Austrian vision, individuals see opportunities to improve their future consumption possibilities by consuming less now and using some of those resources to 'finance' multiple-stage production processes that will provide more output in the future. It is our current savings (i.e. the reduction in current consumption) that makes it possible for us to wait for the larger future output. Savings, for the Austrians, is the vehicle for long-run growth as it makes possible more roundabout processes of production.

Producers make their decisions about what to produce and how to produce it based on the signals provided to them by current prices and their judgments about what will be wanted in the future. This is the essence of entrepreneurship. Producers purchase raw materials, machinery, or other higher-order goods, as well as labor, and combine them to produce output that they believe can be sold at a price that exceeds the cost of the inputs plus the implicit interest rate required to wait for the output in the future. Because human beings, all other things equal, prefer the present to the future, the fact that production takes time means that the value of the final good must exceed not just the monetary costs of the inputs but also the value of the time the production takes. For Austrians, therefore, the interest rate plays a key role as the central price guiding intertemporal production. At lower interest rates, which reflect more patience on the part of consumers, production processes with more stages of production (i.e. those with more steps between raw materials and the final output) will be relatively more worthwhile, while higher interest rates and consumer impatience will make shorter processes relatively more desirable. The crux of the matter is the degree of 'intertemporal coordination', or the degree to which the roundaboutness of production plans are synchronized with the preferences of consumers for more or less consumption in the present or the future.

This conception of production and consumption has an important implication for how capital is understood. In neoclassical analyses capital is normally treated as a homogeneous aggregate; it is 'K' in various models. This is a crucial error from an Austrian perspective. Because capital is, for the Austrians, always embodied in specific goods, it cannot be treated as an undifferentiated mass. Entrepreneurs purchase inputs or build machines that are designed for specific purposes. They cannot be costlessly redeployed to an infinite number of other uses the way the homogeneous conception of capital might suggest. Austrians see capital as heterogeneous and having a limited number of specific uses (Lachmann, 1978 [1956]; Kirzner, 1966). The same is true of labor. The skills and knowledge workers have are not appropriate for all potential production processes, thus their human capital can be conceived of as heterogeneous and specific to a limited number of uses.

Capital is not only heterogeneous in this sense, it also might embody error. Given an uncertain future, producers are always making their best guess as to what to produce and how, so the range of capital goods in existence at any moment is likely to embody a variety of entrepreneurial errors. For example, if two producers buy up the inputs to produce a particular kind of running shoe, but the demand is sufficient only for one to be profitable, then the capital of the other has been misallocated. Of course, we cannot know that until the market process unfolds and the one firm's losses indicate that the value of their final product was not sufficient to cover costs including interest. This point is important because it implies that we cannot just add up the value of existing capital to get some aggregate measure of 'total capital'. That procedure would be valid only in equilibrium, where we knew that each higher-order good was deployed correctly. We cannot add up existing stocks of capital to get some aggregate. In thinking about capital we must pay attention to both where the capital (and labor) sit in the structure of production and factors that might distort price signals in ways that make it more difficult for firms to synchronize their production with the public's preferences about consumption.

The Austrian approach to macroeconomics can already be seen as being fundamentally microeconomic. What matters for growth is the degree to which microeconomic intertemporal coordination is achieved by producers using price signals, especially the interest rate, to coordinate their production plans with the preferences of consumers.[1] However, this coordination process can be undermined through economy-wide events that might well be called 'macroeconomic'. In particular, the very universality of money that makes possible the coordination that characterizes the market process can also be the source of severe discoordination. If there is something wrong with money, the fact that it touches everything in the economy will ensure that systemic 'macroeconomic' problems will result. When money is in excess or deficient supply, interest rates lose their connection to people's underlying time preferences, and individual prices become less accurate reflectors of the underlying variables of tastes, technology and resources. Monetary disequilibria undermine the communicative functions of prices and interest rates and hamper the learning processes that comprise the market.

More specifically, Austrians have offered a theory of the business cycle that brings together the themes outlined above.[2] According to the Austrian theory, the boom phase of the business cycle is initiated when the central bank attempts to supply more money than the public wishes to hold at the current price level. As these excess supplies of money make their way into the banking system, lenders find themselves able to provide more loans even though they have seen no increase in saving from the public. Central bank open market operations add to their reserves in a way indistinguishable from private deposits. This increase in the supply of loanable funds (note that 'loanable funds' need not equal 'private saving') drives down interest rates as banks move to attract new borrowers. These lower market rates of interest appear to signal to firms that the public is now more patient and more willing to wait for consumption goods. Had the expansion of loanable funds been financed by genuine savings, the lower interest rate would be sending an accurate signal about the public's wishes. However, when the expansion is caused by an excess supply of money rather than a shift in the public's time preferences, the tight relationship between market rates of interest and underlying time preferences is broken.

The lower interest rate signals to producers that the public is more willing to wait, they therefore engage in longer-term processes of production, i.e. ones that have more stages between raw materials and final consumer good. Longer processes are more productive, which is why they are desirable to producers, and the lower interest rate makes it economically rational to stretch out production in this way. Capital goods are created or purchased and refit to engage in these longer processes. Labor is bid away from markets closer to final goods and toward earlier stages of production. Prices and wages are bid up, and as Garrison (2001) argues, the economy can, at least temporarily, exceed its production possibilities frontier because, as we shall see, the projects being financed by the monetary expansion are ultimately not sustainable even as they create all the observed measures of a boom in the meantime. The boom cannot last because the underlying preferences of consumers have not changed and they are not willing to wait longer for output. So even as producers are shifting resources from producing goods for current consumption to earlier-stage goods, consumers continue to demand current goods with the same relative intensity as they did before the monetary expansion. The inflation-driven lower market rate of interest is sending out a false signal about the public's preferences.

The intertemporal discoordination becomes evident as a tug-of-war erupts between the attempts by some producers to purchase inputs for longer production processes, while others continue to bid up input prices for goods closer to consumers. Both groups cannot be successful given the realities of the resources available. Eventually those producers engaged in the longer processes find the cost of inputs to be too high, particularly as it becomes clear that the public's willingness to wait is not what the interest rate suggested would be forthcoming. These longer-term processes are then abandoned, resulting in falling asset prices (both capital goods and financial assets such as the stock prices of the relevant companies) and unemployed labor in those sectors associated with the capital goods industries. So begins the bust phase of the cycle, as stock prices fall, asset prices 'deflate', overall economic activity slows and unemployment rises. Key to the bust is the specificity of capital and labor noted earlier. The abandoned capital goods associated with the longer production processes cannot be instantaneously and costlessly converted in to new uses in the consumption goods sectors. The same is true of labor: unemployed workers must find their way into the particular sectors closer to final consumption where labor is needed; they will likely take a loss in income in the process, and may even require a different set of human capital to be successful. The bust is the economy going through this refitting and reshuffling of capital and labor as it eliminates the mistakes made during the boom. For Austrians, the boom is when the mistakes are made and it is during the bust that those mistakes are corrected.

Standard aggregative macroeconomics is not very helpful in understanding the process Austrian cycle theory describes. Most fundamentally, if GDP is conceived in terms of $C + I + G$, the idea that consumption and investment might trade off is difficult to comprehend. When investment is treated as an undifferentiated quantity, rather than the Austrian 'stages of production' approach, the whole notion of intertemporal discoordination and the problems raised by heterogeneous capital are also impossible to see. The ways in which artificially low interest rates distort the composition of 'I' rather than affecting the total quantity are obscured in the mainstream approach, yet are central to the Austrian understanding of the errors of the boom and the corrective process of the bust. Keynesian, and later, models that do not understand investment decisions, and the capital goods they lead to, in terms of the specific best guesses of a whole series of microeconomic entrepreneurs, will find it difficult to understand the distortive effects of artificially low interest rates. Hayek recognized this as early as his review of Keynes's *Treatise on Money*, when he wrote: 'Mr. Keynes' aggregates conceal the most fundamental mechanisms of change' (Hayek, 1995 [1931]: 128). Over 75 years later, that sentence remains a very pithy summary of the Austrian critique not just of Keynes, but of the whole class of models from a variety of schools of thought that comprise modern postwar macroeconomics. For Austrians, there are indeed macroeconomic questions, but there are only microeconomic answers.

AUSTRIAN MACROECONOMICS AND THE 'GREAT RECESSION' OF 2008

Austrian macroeconomics can offer a fairly comprehensive explanation of where we find ourselves in the current recession. One core concept in the Austrian approach is that although theoretical propositions are universally valid, they provide only the framework of a full historical explanation. In applying theory to specific historical episodes, Austrians recognize that the particular details of each episode may vary in important ways, even as the outlines of the episode conform to the pattern identified by the theory.[3]

In applying the Austrian cycle theory to specific historical episodes, therefore, the economist must pay close attention to the other kinds of factors in play that might have led to this particular episode's unique features.

The Austrian cycle theory emerged out of empirical data on the patterns of resource use and disuse that characterized nineteenth- and early twentieth-century business cycles. That the capital goods industries expanded during booms and contracted during busts was an empirical observation that demanded explanation in any theory of the cycle, and the Austrians believe they had provided it. Common explications of the Austrian theory normally make the claim that the excess loanable funds created by the central bank will find their way into producers' hands. Producers will then use them to invest in longer-term processes of production, as argued earlier. However, that claim is not a necessary feature of the cycle, rather a common one, especially in years past. Depending on the set of policies, institutions and incentives in place, the excess of loanable funds could end up in a number of specific places, although all of them where the lower interest rate makes longer-term economic activity less costly.

In the current recession, a series of such factors diverted the excess supply of loanable funds into the housing market, creating an asset bubble there that served as the basis for a set of ill-conceived financial instruments, all of which are now collapsing in the wake of the bursting of the housing bubble. The 'Great Recession' is not a product of the greed of *laissez-faire* capitalism, rather it is the unintended consequence of a pair of very significant interventions into the operation of the market process: the Fed's expansionary monetary policy and a set of policies that artificially reduced the costs and risks of homeownership, enabling the creation of highly risky loans that themselves then led to even riskier innovations in the financial industry. From an Austrian perspective, the eventual collapse of this house of cards built on inflation represents not a failure of capitalism, but a largely predictable failure of central banking and other forms of government intervention. To the details of this process we now turn.

The empirical evidence on various measures of the money supply and related interest rates makes quite clear the ways in which the US Federal Reserve System drove up the money supply and drove down interest rates since 9/11, if not earlier. This was very intentional policy on the part of the Greenspan Fed as it attempted to pull the US economy out of the small post-9/11 recession. The federal funds rate fell to the 1 percent range for a period, and stayed well below recent historic norms for much of the period prior to 2007. It is also worth noting the role played by the so-called 'Greenspan Put'. The Fed chair had made it clear that he believed that the central bank could do nothing to prevent the development of asset bubbles, but that it could cushion the effects when such bubbles burst.

What is notable is that Greenspan seemed ignorant of the role the Fed might play in causing such bubbles as well as the incentives this policy created for investors, who now knew that they would be, at least partially, saved from any losses they might suffer due to a collapsing bubble. The latter surely had a role in making financial markets feel as though there was no downside risk to the housing-related instruments developed during the boom.

For these inflationary funds to fuel a housing bubble and financial sector-driven boom more generally, government policy had to play an additional role. A state-sponsored push for more affordable housing has been a staple of several recent US administrations. At least since the Clinton Administration, the federal government has adopted a variety of policies intended to make housing more affordable for lower- and middle-income groups and various minorities. Among the government actions, those dealing with mortgage market government-sponsored enterprises were central. The Federal National Mortgage Association (Fannie Mae) and the Federal Home Loan Mortgage Corporation (Freddie Mac) are the key players here. Although they did not originate many risky mortgages themselves, they did develop a number of the low down-payment instruments that came into vogue during the boom. More important, they were primarily responsible for the secondary mortgage market as they purchased mortgages from others and promoted the mortgage-backed securities that became the investment vehicles *du jour* during the boom.

Fannie and Freddie are not 'free market' firms. They were chartered by the federal government, and although nominally privately owned until the onset of the bust in 2008, they have been granted a number of government privileges, in addition to carrying an implicit promise of government support should they ever get into trouble. With such a promise in place, the market for mortgage-backed securities was able to tolerate a level of risk that truly free markets would not. As we now know, that turned out to be a big problem. It is true that the problematic loans that were at the bottom of the current recession were generated by banks and mortgage companies and not Fannie and Freddie. However, their presence as 'big players' in the mortgage market dramatically distorted the incentives facing those truly private actors.[4] Their willingness and ability to buy up mortgages originated by others made private actors far more willing to make risky loans, knowing they could quickly package them up and sell them off to Fannie, Freddie and others. Fannie and Freddie had both various government privileges and the implicit promise of tax dollars if need be. This combination enabled them to act without the normal private sector concerns about risk and reward, and profit and loss. Their relative immunity from genuine market profit and loss sent distorting ripple effects through the rest of the mortgage industry, allowing the excess loanable funds coming from the Fed to be turned into a large number of mortgages that probably never should have been written.

Other regulatory elements played into this story. Fannie and Freddie were under significant political pressure to keep housing increasingly affordable (while at the same time promoting instruments that depended on the constantly rising price of housing) and extending opportunities to historically 'underserved' minority groups. Many of the new no/low down-payment mortgages (especially those associated with Countrywide Mortgage) were designed as responses to this pressure. Throw in the marginal effects of the Community Investment Act, which required lenders to serve those underserved groups, and zoning and land-use laws that pushed housing into limited space in the suburbs and exurbs, driving up prices in the process, and you have the ingredients of a credit-fueled and regulatory-directed housing boom and bust.[5] This variety of government policies and regulations was responsible for steering this particular boom in the direction of the housing market. Unlike past booms, where the excess of loanable funds ended up as credit to producers, this set of unique events that accompanied this boom was responsible for channeling those funds into housing.

The boom in the housing market drove prices to unprecedented levels. Those inflation-fueled rising housing prices enabled other parts of the financial industry to develop new instruments that took the mortgage payments of borrowers as a flow of income that could be parceled out among investors. The various fancy instruments that comprised the secondary mortgage market were all premised on the belief that housing prices would continue to rise, thereby enabling subprime borrowers to continue to see rising equity, which in turn would enable them to afford their payments. If housing prices were to fall, and subprime borrowers find themselves with mortgages greater than the value of their homes, this would in turn dry up the whole flow of income and bring these other instruments down like the houses of cards they were. Of course, this is exactly what happened when the boom finally came to an end: the housing industry found itself increasingly unable to find the resources it needed to build houses at prices that would be profitable and the flow of credit began to dry up. Once housing prices began to fall in 2006, the entire chain of investments built upon those rising prices was under threat. The stock market's large drop in the fall and winter of 2008–09 reflected the growing realization that the bust was under way and that the future earnings prospects of most firms had dimmed.[6]

The shrinkage of the housing and construction industries led those sectors to shed jobs and dramatically reduce investment in capital. The financial firms that began to bleed resources as their housing-dependent assets started to collapse in value also began to shed jobs and capital. These losses in employment and income have led to dropping demand throughout the rest of the economy. In addition, the losses of equity value in homes, along with the declines in the value of retirement accounts and other investments, caused further shrinkage in demand as households began to try to recoup through savings some of their lost wealth and/or saw absolute losses in investment income. All of these events together have led to the declines in the various macroeconomic indicators that we associate with recession.

From the Austrian perspective, the current recession has many features of the typical boom–bust process associated with the school's theory of the business cycle. The central bank fueled an unsustainable expansion of the economy that eventually would reveal itself leading to a bust that would begin to try to correct those mistakes of the boom. This recession, however, had some unique characteristics about it due to a whole host of government interventions and policies in the housing and financial sectors. The Austrian theory predicts that excess credit will flow to long-term production processes. In this case, that was housing, as the lower interest rates from the Fed's expansion artificially reduced the price of housing and led to the sequence of events we have outlined. As noted in the previous section, the Austrian theory does not attempt to predict the specific path inflation will take, only that it will generally conform to the pattern whereby it ends up in long-term investments as a result of lower interest rates. That in this case the excess credit went into housing is a particular feature of this cycle, completely consistent with the more typical features the theory identifies. Inflation by the government central bank, along with other government interventions and policies, account for both the typical and unique features of this cycle and are the direct causes of the current recession.

CAN POLICY CURE RECESSIONS?

Given the Austrian diagnosis of the problem, what does the theory recommend as the cure? Because the theory argues that government was responsible for the boom that produced the bust, it will not be surprising to find a great deal of skepticism about the ability of government to extract the economy from the mess it created. In fact, Austrian economics takes it as a very strong rule of thumb that governments should refrain from intervening in the corrective process of the recession. Even if there were some number of things government might do to help the situation, we cannot ignore the question of whether political actors have the incentive to do those things *and only those things* once we concede their role in the recovery. More fundamentally, however, Austrians do not believe that even well-motivated political actors can know exactly what policy steps would be needed to produce a true recovery. This argument emerges out of the claim that intertemporal discoordination that manifests as a 'macroeconomic' failure is ultimately a whole series of failures at the microeconomic level. Therefore attempting to correct those failures would involve both identifying where they occurred and knowing what the superior allocation of resources would look like. Given the Austrian emphasis on markets as processes for discovering just this kind of knowledge, their general policy recommendation is to allow markets to figure out where the errors are and where resources would be better used.

The first point can be dispatched with fairly quickly. The history of various stimulus and recovery programs does not suggest that governments can limit themselves to only those sorts of expenditures and policies that mainstream theory, assuming for the moment it is correct, suggests will be helpful. Once we open the door to political intervention as key to the cure, politicians will gladly make that an excuse to propose and pass a whole variety of items, regardless of whether they fit the economist's model of a pump-priming stimulus. The debate over the Obama Administration's stimulus package in the USA revealed just this sort of concern, as did the ensuing debate over the proposed budget. In both cases, the claim was made that these expenditures were necessary for economic recovery, yet a substantial portion of those expenditures, particularly the emphasis on health care, education and the environment in the budget, have no known relationship to economic models of recovery. This is a precedent set by the Roosevelt Administration during the Great Depression, when even Keynes was moved to note that many of its proposals seemed more like 'reform than recovery'. Even if theory suggested that government should have a significant role in recovery, the institutional incentives of the political process are such that it would be very difficult to limit government to just that role. When governments overreach, not only do they create additional costs (e.g. debt) that might offset any imagined gains, they can also retard private recovery by adopting policies that pose long-term threats to private property rights or that are constantly changing course. Both of these will create what Robert Higgs (2006) has termed 'regime uncertainty' and has blamed for the length of the Great Depression.[7]

This argument, however, is a mere sideshow for the Austrians. The more fundamental point is that even theory suggests that government can contribute little or nothing to the recovery process. The crux of the matter is that mainstream approaches to recovery are overly focused on macroeconomic aggregates such as consumption, investment and unemployment, which obscure the adjustment processes at the heart of the Austrian conception – those having to do with the reallocation of resources among sectors at the microeconomic level. Developing policies that will 'create jobs' or substitute aggregate net government spending for perceived insufficiencies of aggregate consumption or investment from the private sector neglects to ask the sorts of questions the Austrian theory suggests should be asked.

Recall that the core of the Austrian story is that the inflationary boom attracts both capital and labor toward the early stages of production as the artificially low interest rate makes longer-term projects look more profitable. As consumers continue to spend in their old patterns, in contradiction to what the interest rate seems to be saying they should do, industries closer to final consumption see demand staying constant and have to now out-bid producers in the early stages for various resources. For a period of time, as we noted earlier, this can drive the economy beyond its sustainable production possibilities frontier, as unemployment goes below the natural rate and capital owners use inputs with excessive intensity. The bigger point is that both capital and labor are misallocated among the various sectors, with capital in particular being 'malinvested' in the earlier stages of production. The Austrian theory is often wrongly termed an 'overinvestment' theory. It is true that there is 'overinvestment' for a short period of time, but the real problem is that resources are 'malinvested'. Traditional aggregates may not show any change in the total level of investment even as resources are misallocated between the earlier and later stages of production.

The downturn in economic activity we associate with the recession is, on the Austrian view, the economy attempting to shed capital and labor from where it is no longer profitable. Because markets are discovery processes that take place through real, historical time, and because human actors have fragmentary knowledge, moving those resources to where they will be more productive cannot happen instantaneously. Entrepreneurs at the earlier stages of production will idle capital and labor as their profitability shrinks. Entrepreneurs at the later stages will now have to consider whether to purchase new capital or hire new labor. They may well have to wait until prices and wages fall sufficiently to make the purchases worthwhile. They may also have to wait until workers can learn where the new opportunities are, and possibly get retrained, much as some capital might have to be refit to be valuable at the later stages.

This adjustment process takes time, but also requires the skillful judgment of entrepreneurs across the economy about whether idled labor or capital can be profitably redeployed. Here too, it is not a matter of too much or too little capital or labor, but of capital or labor that is not suitable for a particular stage of production in a particular production process. The Austrian emphasis on the heterogeneity of capital (and labor) is central here, as capital cannot be costlessly and instantly reallocated from the early stages to the later stages, as one might conceive it could be on the mainstream view of capital as an undifferentiated aggregate. The same can be said of government spending and investment, of course, as simply substituting G for I in the sum that comprises national income overlooks the shifts in capital and labor that would require, as well as the comparative efficiency of the two different lines of expenditure. The problem to be solved is not a matter of boosting aggregate measures of consumption and investment through any sort of government expenditure. The problem is ensuring that existing resources get reallocated away from sectors that were artificially stimulated by the boom to those sectors where consumers now wish to spend. Seeing the importance of the movement among the stages of production requires a different conception of capital and the production process – one that moves away from a focus on statistical aggregates toward one that takes time and human plans seriously.

The policy conclusion is that only those located in the context of the market have the knowledge and the feedback processes to ensure that this reallocation process takes place as quickly and effectively as possible. Government expenditures, even if we take out the inevitable politicization of the process, will never match the ability of the market to discover where the excesses were and where the current demand is. That sort of microeconomic discovery process is precisely why Austrians have long argued against more expansive visions of government intervention and planning, and those arguments hold with equal force in times of macroeconomic disorder. It is not accidental that the modern Austrian emphasis on the epistemological advantages of the market grew out of Hayek's participation in the two great debates of the 1930s: the socialist calculation debate and the debate with Keynes. The lessons of the former are also clearly evident in the latter.

Government actors must refrain from the huge temptation to step in and attempt to speed up the recovery process. Both theory and history suggest that doing so will be counterproductive and only slow the market's attempts to recover from the excesses of the boom. For the Austrians, the boom was when the mistakes were made and the bust is the market's way of correcting them. Interfering with that subtle and complex correction process is beyond the ability of government. Only the decentralized decision-making and learning processes of the market can accomplish the millions of corrections that have to take place in myriad individual microeconomic markets.

Is the Austrian perspective then left with a 'do-nothing' approach to recessions? At the level of 'stimulus' packages and similar sorts of specific policy interventions, the answer would be 'yes'. But in two other ways the answer is 'no'. First, saying that *government* should do nothing is hardly the same as saying 'we' should do nothing. In fact, recovery from recession depends upon active and creative entrepreneurship on the part of millions of economic actors. The Austrian perspective argues that it is *they* who should be 'doing something'. However, that perspective also recognizes that government policy-makers cannot know what it is that all of those actors should do, so for the entrepreneur-driven recovery process to happen quickly and effectively, policy-makers must refrain from interfering with that process and also take steps to ensure that policy creates a stable and predictable environment in which those entrepreneurs can operate. The primary objective for policy-makers should be to minimize Higgsian regime uncertainty and thereby facilitate the countless individual adjustments necessary for recovery to take place.

The second Austrian solution is a longer-term institutional one. At the root of the Austrian analysis is the ability of central banks to inflate without economic penalty and thereby set in motion the events of the cycle. For this reason, a number of Austrians have long argued for changes in the institutions of banking that would eliminate central banks and allow privately owned banks to issue currency competitively and enable banks to develop interbank institutions such as clearing houses to perform a variety of important functions that such institutions performed before they were abrogated by central banks.[8] Such a move to a 'free banking' system would put an end to the inflation that generates the boom and bust cycle and causes recessions and depressions. It would also break the link between government spending and monetary policy that often uses inflation as a way to monetize debt. As the stimulus plans endorsed by much of the profession continue to drive up the burden of government debt across the world, the temptation toward monetization will continue to grow. Unfortunately, should governments succumb to that temptation, it will only set in motion yet another chain of events that will create another, and possibly worse, boom and bust cycle. Separating money production from the state is the key institutional change that Austrians see as necessary not so much to recover from the current recession but to prevent future, possibly worse, ones.

CONCLUSION

Austrians themselves refer to their conception of the microeconomic market process as the factor that distinguishes them as a school of thought from the neoclassical orthodoxy (Kirzner, 1997). Elements such as uncertainty, fragmented knowledge, heterogeneous capital and the epistemological role of prices all matter for understanding macroeconomic phenomena as well, as Austrians see such phenomena as ultimately microeconomic in their causes and effects. It is the distortion of interest rates (which are prices) through expansionary monetary policy that initiates economy-wide disorder, and other government interventions in the market process will steer that disorder in particular directions. Finally, the Austrian conception of the market process provides reasons to be deeply skeptical of government stimulus programs as the appropriate solution to the very disorder that prior intervention has created. All of these microeconomic elements are on display in the Austrian understanding of the current recession and the appropriate ways to respond to it. Macroeconomic aggregates still, as Hayek wrote almost 80 years ago, conceal the most fundamental processes of change, and that observation provides the Austrians with their alternative, microeconomic, conception of the boom and bust cycle.

NOTES

1. Hayek (1984 [1928]) is the canonical article on the centrality of intertemporal coordination to the Austrian conception of the market.
2. Key contributions to Austrian business cycle and macroeconomic theory include Hayek (1966 [1933], 1967 [1935], 1975 [1937]), Mises (1966, ch. 20), Horwitz (2000) and Garrison (2001).
3. O'Driscoll and Rizzo (1996) distinguish between the 'typical' and 'unique' features of any historical event. Callahan and Horwitz (2010, forthcoming) apply this type of approach to Austrian cycle theory specifically.
4. On 'big players' see Koppl (2001).
5. On the role of land-use regulation, see Mills (2009).
6. This pattern, whereby the stock market is a slightly lagging indicator of a recession that has already started, is one we see historically (e.g. the Great Depression really started in the summer of 1929, months before the stock market crash). It is also consistent with Austrian theory in that the turning point of the boom into the bust is when the longer production processes become unprofitable. That knowledge will take some time to percolate through to investors, who will eventually see that unprofitability occurring economy wide, leading to broad-based reductions in stock prices. The stock market drop may also have reflected skepticism about the policy measures being taken to attack the recession. I turn to those questions in the next section.
7. Such regime uncertainty might also explain the ongoing lack of recovery, at least at the time of this writing, in the world economy. The lack of clear direction from the Obama Administration plus its apparent willingness to inject the federal government into firms such as General Motors might well lead private actors to be hesitant to engage in any long-term investment.
8. See White (1996) and Selgin (1988) on the argument for 'free banking'. Another group of Austrians has also argued for the abolition of central banking, but prefer instead a version of a 100 percent gold standard. See Rothbard (2008). My own view is that the White–Selgin perspective is superior. However, what matters for the point at hand is that both groups have a positive policy agenda for 'doing something' to prevent future recessions.

REFERENCES

Callahan, Gene and Steven Horwitz (2010), 'The role of ideal types in Austrian business cycle theory', *Advances in Austrian Economics*, forthcoming.

Garrison, Roger (2001), *Time and Money: The Macroeconomics of Capital Structure*, New York: Routledge.

Hayek, F.A. (1966 [1933]), *Monetary Theory and the Trade Cycle*, New York: Augustus M. Kelley.

Hayek, F.A. (1967 [1935]), *Prices and Production*, 2nd rev. edn, New York: Augustus M. Kelley.

Hayek, F.A. (1975 [1939]), *Profits, Interest, and Investment*, Clifton, NJ: Augustus M. Kelley.

Hayek, F.A. (1984 [1928]), 'Intertemporal price equilibrium and movements in the value of money', in Roy McCloughry (ed.), *Money, Capital and Fluctuations: Early Essays*, Chicago, IL: University of Chicago Press, pp. 71–117.

Hayek, F.A. (1995 [1931]), 'Reflections on the pure theory of money of Mr. J. M. Keynes', in Bruce Caldwell (ed.), *The Collected Works of F. A. Hayek, vol. 9: Contra Keynes and Cambridge*, Chicago, IL: University of Chicago Press, pp. 121–46.

Higgs, Robert (2006), 'Regime uncertainty: why the Great Depression lasted so long and why prosperity resumed after the war', in *Depression, War, and Cold War: Studies in Political Economy*, Oakland, CA: The Independent Institute, pp. 3–29.

Horwitz, Steven (2000), *Microfoundations and Macroeconomics: An Austrian Perspective*, New York: Routledge.

Kirzner, Israel (1966), *An Essay on Capital*, New York: Augustus M. Kelley.

Kirzner, Israel (1997), 'Entrepreneurial discovery and the competitive market process: an Austrian approach', *Journal of Economic Literature*, 35: 60–85.

Koppl, Roger (2001), *Big Players and the Economic Theory of Expectations*, New York: Palgrave Macmillan.

Lachmann, Ludwig (1978 [1956]), *Capital and Its Structure*, Kansas City, KA: Sheed Andrews & McMeel.

Menger, Carl (1981 [1871]), *Principles of Economics*, New York: New York University Press.

Mills, Edwin S. (2009), 'Urban land-use controls and the subprime mortgage crisis', *The Independent Review*, 13: 559–65.

Mises, Ludwig von (1966), *Human Action: A Treatise on Economics*, Chicago, IL: Henry Regnery.

O'Driscoll, Gerald P. and Mario J. Rizzo (1996), *The Economics of Time and Ignorance*, 2nd edn, New York: Routledge.

Rothbard, Murray (2008), *What Has Government Done to our Money?* 5th edn, Auburn, AL: The Ludwig von Mises Institute.

Selgin, George (1988), *The Theory of Free Banking: Money Supply Under Competitive Note Issue*, Totowa, NJ: Rowman & Littlefield.

White, Lawrence H. (1996), *Free Banking in Britain*, 2nd edn, New York: Routledge.

7. The crisis in economic theory: the dead end of Keynesian economics

Steven Kates

The Great Depression began, in most places, with the share market crash in 1929 and by the end of 1933 was already receding into history. In 1936, well after the Great Depression had reached its lowest point and recovery had begun, a book was published that remains to this day the most influential economics treatise written during the whole of the twentieth century.

The book was *The General Theory of Employment, Interest and Money*. The author was John Maynard Keynes. And his book overturned a tradition in economic thought that had already by then stretched back for more than one hundred years.

The dates are significant. The economics that Keynes's writings had overturned is today called 'classical theory',[1] yet it was the application of this self-same classical theory that had brought the Great Depression to its end everywhere but in the USA, where something else was tried instead. And at the centre of classical thought was a proposition that Keynes made it his ambition to see disappear absolutely from within economics. It was an ambition in which he was wildly successful.

Following a lead set by Keynes, this proposition is now almost invariably referred to as Say's Law.[2] It is a proposition that since 1936 every economist has been explicitly taught to reject as the most certain obstacle to clear thinking and sound policy. Economists have thus been taught to ignore the one principle most necessary for understanding the causes of recessions and their cures. Worse still, they have been taught to apply the very measures to remedy downturns that are most likely, from the classical perspective, to slow down the recovery process and potentially push their economies into a steeper downward spiral.[3]

Keynes wrote, and economists have since then almost universally accepted, that Say's Law meant full employment was guaranteed by the operation of the market. To accept this principle therefore meant that the models then used by economists could not be used to analyse recessions and unemployment because within these models was buried the tacit assumption of full employment.

After 150 years of capitalist development, with the business cycle having been the most unmistakably visible aspect of the operation of economies everywhere, Keynes in 1936 could still write that economists in accepting Say's Law had accepted 'the proposition that there was no obstacle to full employment' (Keynes, 1936: 26).

Keynes wrote that Say's Law meant that 'supply creates its own demand'.[4] In his interpretation of this supposedly classical proposition, everything produced would automatically find a buyer. Aggregate demand would always equal aggregate supply. Recessions would therefore never occur and full employment was always a certainty. That economists have accepted as fact that the entire mainstream of the profession prior to 1936 had believed recessions could never occur when in fact they regularly did shows the power of authority in allowing people to believe three impossible things before breakfast.

But what was important were the policy implications of Keynes's message. These may be reduced to two. First, the problem of recessions is due to a deficiency of aggregate demand. The symptoms of recession were its actual cause. And then, second, an economy in recession cannot be expected to recover on its own, and certainly not within a reasonable time, without the assistance of high levels of public spending and the liberal use of deficit finance.

The missing ingredient in classical economic theory, Keynes wrote, had been the absence of any discussion of aggregate demand. It was this missing ingredient that Keynes made it his mission to provide.

AGGREGATE DEMAND

And how successful he was. Aggregate demand has since 1936 played the central role in the theory of recession. Recessions are attributed to an absence of demand, and even where they are not, overcoming recessions is seen as dependent on the restoration of demand, which is the active responsibility of governments.

Until 1936, no mainstream theory of recession had so much as glanced at the notion of demand deficiency as a cause of recession. It was specifically to deny the relevance of demand deficiency as a cause of recession that Say's Law had been formulated in the first place. Accepting the possibility of demand deficiency as a cause of recession was then seen as the realm of cranks. How the world does change.

This, it cannot be emphasized enough, did not mean that the possibility of recessions was denied. There was, and is, no end of potential causes of recession that have nothing to do with demand failure.

Indeed, no one explains the causes of the present economic downturn, the global meltdown we are in the midst of, in terms of deficient aggregate demand. It would be absurd to suggest that the problems now being experienced have been caused by consumers no longer wishing to buy more than they have or savings going to waste because investors have run out of new forms of capital into which to invest their funds.

THE CLASSICAL THEORY OF RECESSION

Classical theory had taught that whatever might cause a recession to occur, it would never be a deficiency of aggregate demand. Production could never exceed the willingness to buy, and therefore treating the symptoms of a recession by trying to raise demand through increased public spending was utterly mistaken.

Governments could create value but their income was derived from taxation. Taking monies from those who were productively employed and directing production towards a government's own purposes remained acceptable so long as the level of such spending was limited and, most importantly, the government's budget remained in surplus.

These were the self-imposed restraints that Keynesian theory overturned. Public spending in combination with budget deficits, he argued, would propel an economy out of recession. It is this belief that is now accepted by a very large proportion of the economics community.

Yet for all that, no recession has been brought to an end through increased levels of public spending, but many recessions have been ended by a return to sound finance and fiscal discipline.

THE GREAT DEPRESSION

The history of public policy during recessionary periods has a number of lessons to teach, assuming we are capable of learning from them. In the UK, economic policy during the Great Depression saw the application of a full-scale classical approach. A policy of balancing the budget and the containment of expenditure was adopted. By 1933, the budget had been balanced and it was from 1933 onwards that the UK emerged from the downturn of the previous four years.

It is worth noting that it was balancing the budget that was seen to have made the all-important difference. In rejecting deficit financing during his budget speech of 1933, the British Chancellor of the Exchequer, Neville Chamberlain, made this explicit statement:

At any rate we are free from that fear which besets so many less fortunately placed, the fear that things are going to get worse. We owe our freedom from that fear largely to the fact that we have balanced our budget. (Quoted in Clarke, 1988: 203)

The same story could be told about Australia, where the decision was made by the Scullin Labor Government in adopting the 'Premiers' Plan', which sought a cut in public spending, a return to budget surplus and cuts to wages. In the light of later Keynesian theory, nothing would have been seen as less likely to have achieved a return to prosperity, but a return to prosperity was most assuredly the result. All this is perfectly captured in the following brief summary of events:

A strategy adopted in June 1931 by Australia's Scullin government to reduce interest rates and cut expenditure by 20 per cent, partly through slashing public-sector wages. The objective was to reduce Australia's huge budget deficit problems. Australia had to get its books in order if the country was to continue to get overseas finance. Devaluation had already been forced and increased tariffs tried. The rationale behind the Premiers' Plan was to revive business confidence. The plan was welcomed as an example of creative economic planning; Douglas Copland claimed it was 'a judicious mixture of inflation and deflation'. Later it was criticised as overly deflationary. (Carew, 1996)

Certainly it was 'later' criticized as overly deflationary after the Depression had passed and Keynesian economics had become the vogue, but at the time, that is while the Great Depression was an actual raging fact of life, rather than attracting criticism, it was the consensus view of the economics profession of Australia. And it worked. Australia was among the first countries to recover from the Great Depression. The trough was reached in 1932 and from then on there was continuous improvement year by year.

Contrast the UK and Australian experience with that of the USA. Roosevelt's New Deal applied a 'Keynesian' prescription before Keynes had so much as published a word. From 1933 onwards, public works, increased public spending and deficit financing were the essence of economic policy. And with what results?

With these results: Henry Morgenthau, Roosevelt's good friend and Secretary of the Treasury, after years of New Deal policies came to this conclusion:

'We have tried spending money. We are spending more money than we have ever spent before, and it does not work . . . I want to see the country prosperous. I want to see people get a job. I want to see people get enough to eat. We have never made good on our promises. I say, after eight years of this administration,

Macroeconomic theory and its failings

Table 7.1   *Unemployment rates (%): the USA, the UK and Australia,*
              1929–38

Year	United States	UK	Australia
1929	3.2	10.4	8.0
1930	8.7	16.1	12.7
1931	15.9	21.3	20.1
1932	23.6	22.1	23.0
1933	24.9	19.9	21.0
1934	21.7	16.7	17.9
1935	20.1	15.5	15.5
1936	16.9	13.1	12.6
1937	14.3	10.8	10.9
1938	19.0	12.9	8.9

Sources:
US data: US Bureau of Labor Statistics;
UK data: Garside (1990);
Australian data: Glen Withers, personal communication.

> we have just as much unemployment as when we started . . . and an enormous
> debt to boot.' (Folsom, 2008: 2)

Table 7.1 shows the unemployment rates in the USA, the UK and
Australia between 1929, the last pre-Depression year, through to 1938, the
last year before the UK and Australia went into the war.

None of these figures should be taken as anything more than indica-
tive since there were no official unemployment statistics at the time. All
are reconstructions based on incomplete data. But what these figures do
provide is an accurate reflection of the reality experienced on the ground at
the time. Although major pockets of unemployment remained, Australia
and the UK had by the mid-1930s left the Depression behind while the
USA did not do so until the war finally brought recessionary conditions
to an end.

THE POSTWAR RECOVERY

Only four years later the war itself had come to an end, by which time
much of the economics profession had been converted to Keynesian
theory. Although there was no evidence that the theory would actually
work in a peacetime economy,[5] a high proportion of economists advocated a continuation of the deficits and high levels of public spending that
had prevailed during the war.

The major debate took place in the USA. Only four years before, it was pointed out, the US economy had been in deep recession. Millions of its men and women, who had served overseas or in war-related industries, were returning to the civilian economy in which the resumption of recession seemed a genuine possibility.

Yet Harry Truman resisted the pressure to provide a fiscal stimulus to the US economy. In his State of the Union address, delivered in January 1946, the US President made his policy direction clear:

> It is good to move toward a balanced budget and a start on the retirement of the debt at a time when demand for goods is strong and the business outlook is good. These conditions prevail today.

Truman, in refusing to apply a Keynesian stimulus, touched off the most sustained period of economic growth in American and world history.

STAGFLATION

It has been argued that the slow development of the welfare state in the postwar period was the actual meaning of Keynesian policy. The 'fine-tuning' of the economy, as it was called, had in the eyes of some demonstrated the value of Keynesian policies. Whatever such fine-tuning did or did not involve, at no stage in the first quarter of a century following the war did Keynesian theory actually have to confront an economy in deep recession.

The first serious attempt to use Keynesian theory to deal with a major downturn did not occur until the late 1960s and early 1970s. Some have argued that President Kennedy had applied a Keynesian approach to end the mild recession of the early 1960s, but he had used tax cuts to stimulate growth. As with the Reagan tax cuts two decades later, this too was not a Keynesian approach. Keynesian economics is about increased levels of public spending.

Tax cuts are entirely classical in nature. They leave funds in the hands of those who have earned the income in the first place. Public spending diverts expenditure into directions of the government's own choosing. The first is market oriented, the second is not. The first would be expected to succeed under classical principles, the second would not.

The 1970s are in many ways a special case. It was a period that combined rapid growth in wages with huge increases in the cost of oil. But it also included an attempt to manufacture growth through a deficit-financed stimulus package on top of the expenditure related to the Vietnam War.

The result has gone down in history as the 'stagflation' of the 1970s. It was a period that pulled economies into a downward spiral, combining high inflation with low growth, the very outcome any classical economist would have foretold. It took well over a decade to return the world's economies to high and sustained rates of non-inflationary growth.

THE JAPANESE RECOVERY PROGRAMME

The most recent large-scale example of an attempt to use a Keynesian deficit-financed spending programme to restore growth to a depressed economy occurred in Japan during the 1990s. The end of the 1980s had seen brief recessions across the world from which most economies rapidly recovered.

Only Japan attempted to hasten recovery with a series of very large spending packages. Far from achieving recovery, this expenditure drove the Japanese economy into such deep recession that even today its economy, at one time the envy of the world, remains subdued. Yet, oddly, because economic theory continues to insist that the spending could only have been a positive, the example of the Japanese disaster is a lesson few have been prepared to absorb.

Consider, however, the following advice offered to the Japanese during the 1990s. It is the same advice offered to governments today, with the difference being that we at least now know the outcome in Japan.

Stanley Fischer, who in 1998 was the First Deputy Managing Director of the IMF, was very clear on the need for the massive increases in spending.[6] He wrote:

> Japan's economic performance is of course a matter of grave domestic concern. But given the prominent role of Japan in the world economy, and especially in Asia, it is also a legitimate matter for concern by Japan's neighbors and by the international community. There is little disagreement about what needs to be done. There is an immediate need for a substantial fiscal expansion . . .
> On fiscal policy, the recent suggestion of a package of 16 trillion yen, about 3 percent of GDP, would be a good starting point. But, unlike on previous occasions, the program that is implemented should be close to the starting point. The well-known reservations about increases in wasteful public spending are correct: that is why much of the package, at least half, should take the form of tax cuts. Anyone who doubts the effectiveness of tax measures need only consider the effectiveness of last year's tax increases in curbing demand.
> The IMF is not famous for supporting fiscal expansions. And it is true that Japan faces a long-term demographic problem that has major fiscal implications. But after so many years of near-stagnation, fiscal policy must help get the economy moving again. There will be time to deal with the longer-term fiscal problem later.

Another example of the same kind of advice is found in a 1998 editorial in *The Economist* (28 February: 21–2) under the heading 'Japan's feeble economy needs a boost':

> The [Japanese] government says it cannot afford a big stimulus because its finances are perilous. It is true that Japan's gross public debt has risen to 87% of GDP, but net debt amounts to only 18% of GDP, the smallest among the G7 economies. The general-government budget deficit, 2½% of GDP, is smaller than its European counterparts'. Rightly, the Japanese are worried about the future pension liabilities implied by their rapidly ageing population. But now is not the time to sort the problem out. Far better to cut the budget later, when the economy has recovered its strength.

Both took the view that Japan should immediately increase its spending and only afterwards clean up whatever problems were created. In Fischer's view, 'there will be time to deal with the longer-term fiscal problem later'. *The Economist* wrote that 'now is not the time to sort the problem out. Far better to cut the budget later, when the economy has recovered its strength.' These are conclusions that come directly from a Keynesian model that concerns itself with deficient demand as the cause of recession and looks to increased spending as its cure.

The Economist even added that 'just now, in fact, Japan is a textbook case of a country in need of fiscal stimulus'. Whatever may have been the case then, it ought to be the textbook case now for why all such forms of economic stimulus should be avoided. Say what you will about the causes of the Japanese downturn and the failure to recover, all major economies experienced the same deep recession at the start of the 1990s, but it is the Japanese economy alone that has never fully recovered its previous strength.

THE LEVEL OF DEMAND VERSUS THE STRUCTURE OF DEMAND

Recessions occur because goods and services are produced that cannot be sold for prices that cover their costs. There are countless possible reasons why and how such mistaken production decisions occur. But when all is said and done, the causes of recessions are structural. They are the consequence of structural imbalances that result from errors in production decisions, not the fall in output and demand that necessarily follows.

This cannot be emphasized enough. Modern macroeconomics is built around the notion of the *level* of demand, while before Keynes recessions were understood in terms of the *structure* of demand. The difference could not be more profound. To policy-makers today, the basic issue in analysing recessions is whether there is enough demand in total. To economists before Keynes, the central issue was to explain why markets had become unbalanced.

In modern economic theory, rising and falling levels of spending are for all practical purposes what matters. That is why increasing public spending and adding to deficits are seen as an intrinsic part of the solution, not as the additional problem such spending actually is.

Missing in modern economic debates is an understanding of the importance of structure: the parts of the economy must fit together. What's missing is an understanding that if the entire economic apparatus goes out of sync, recession is the result and recession will persist until all the parts once again begin to mesh.

Think of what caused this downturn in the first place. None of it is related to demand having suddenly evaporated for no good reason. All of the most visible causes can be brought back to distortions in decision-making that led to the production of goods and services whose full costs of production cannot now be met. Look at the list:

- The meltdown in the housing sector in the USA after financial institutions were encouraged to lend to borrowers who would not in normal circumstances even remotely be considered financially sound.
- The bundling of mortgages into financial derivatives whose value crashed with the crash in the value of housing and which has left the banking industry in a shambles.
- The massive US budget deficits that were allowed to continue for years on end largely because the Chinese chose to recycle the dollars received in the US money market without either allowing the value of the yuan to rise, as it most assuredly ought to have done, or using the funds received to purchase US goods and services.
- The phenomenal rise and subsequent fall in the price of oil, which radically changed production costs in one industry after another.
- The instability still being created across the world's economies over the actions that might or might not be taken to limit carbon emissions and reduce the level of greenhouse gases.
- The arbitrary and erratic use of monetary policy to target inflation, the results of which have been to raise interest rate settings at one moment and lower them at another, depending on assessments made by central banks.
- The plunge in share market prices across the world, with savage effects on the value of personal savings.

There have been few periods in which so many forms of financial and economic uncertainty have confronted the average business at one and the same moment. That business confidence has evaporated and an economic downturn has gained momentum is a matter of no surprise to anyone. The fact of recession is a certainty; only the depths to which it will descend and the length of time before recovery takes hold remain in question.

But just as the causes of this downturn cannot be charted through a Keynesian demand-deficiency model, neither can the solution. The world's economies are not suffering from a lack of demand and the right policy response is not a demand stimulus. Increased public sector spending will only add to the market confusions that already exist.

To try to spend our way to recovery will only compound these problems. The recession is likely to be deeper and more prolonged than if a fiscal stimulus had not been applied in the first place.

KEYNES'S FINAL THOUGHTS

In an article on the balance of payments published posthumously in 1946, Keynes wrote on one last occasion about the classical economics he had done so much to undermine. The Keynesian Revolution had ripped through the economics world and had by then displaced almost all previous thought on the nature and origins of the business cycle. In looking out on the monster he had created, Keynes wrote in some dismay about the importance and value of classical economics and its modes of thought. The specific issue he was addressing was international trade. The actual underlying issue was the need for free markets and decentralized decision-making. Here is what Keynes wrote:

> I find myself moved, not for the first time, to remind contemporary economists that the classical teaching embodied some permanent truths of great significance, which we are liable to-day to overlook because we associate them with other doctrines which we cannot now accept without much qualification. There are in these matters deep undercurrents at work, natural forces, one can call them, or even the invisible hand, which are operating towards equilibrium. If it were not so, we could not have got on even so well as we have for many decades past. (Keynes, 1946: 185)

In looking at the anti-market policies then finding their way into public discussion, he noted just how damaging they would be in practice. He had been advocating free market solutions, the 'classical medicine' of his description, but which others were reluctant to apply. Keynes wrote:

> We have here sincere and thoroughgoing proposals, advanced on behalf of the United States, expressly directed towards creating a system which allows the classical medicine to do its work. It shows how much modernist stuff, gone wrong and turned sour and silly, is circulating in our system, also incongruously mixed, it seems, with age-old poisons . . .
>
> I must not be misunderstood. I do not suppose that the classical medicine will work by itself or that we can depend on it. We need quicker and less painful aids . . . But in the long run these expedients will work better and we shall need them less, if the classical medicine is also at work. And if we reject the medicine from our systems altogether, we may just drift on from expedient to expedient and never get really fit again. (Ibid.: 186)

It is this 'modernist stuff, gone wrong and turned sour and silly', these 'age-old poisons' that are the economics of the present day. We have been adopting economic policies that may drag our economies into deep and ongoing recession and that will diminish our economic prospects possibly for years to come. We may, just as Keynes said, drift on from expedient to expedient and never get really fit again.

These are issues of immense importance. To get them wrong may well leave our market economies in the wilderness. The question before us really is whether markets should be allowed to find their way with only minimal government direction, or whether the economic system should be directed from above by elected governments and the public service.

This is not a mere matter of regulation but of actual direction and expenditure. No one disputes the importance of regulating the operation of markets. There is also a minor role that increased public sector spending might play in allowing some additional infrastructure projects to go forward while economic conditions are slack.

But to believe it is possible for governments to spend our way to prosperity would be disastrous. There is no previous occasion in which such spending has been shown to work, while there are plenty of instances in which it has not. On each and every occasion that such spending has been used, the result has been a worsening of economic conditions and not an improvement.

The concern is that the ruling paradigm in economics is a direct descendant from the *General Theory*. Modern mainstream macroeconomics, for all its developments since the 1930s, is still Keynesian and based on restoring aggregate demand.

The only lasting solution also consistent with restoring prosperity, growth and full employment is to rely on markets. The repeated attack on the market economy, and the role of the private sector, is a mindset begging for trouble.

Certainly there are actions that governments can take to relieve some of the problems of recession, but they are limited. Sure, this is a better time than most to build infrastructure. Absolutely, measures need to be taken to assist the unemployed. Yes, central banks should be lowering official interest rates and ensuring the viability of the banking sector. All such steps are mandatory and largely non-controversial.

But what must be explicitly understood is that recovery means recovery of the private sector. It is business and business investment that must once again take up the burden of moving our economy forward. It is the banking system that must be allowed to allocate funds. To expect and depend on anything else will take our economies down deflationary pathways that could require years to reverse.

The Keynesian model makes the engine of growth appear to be expenditure, irrespective of what that spending is on. And the most important element in the recovery process, according to these same models, is an increase in the government's own level of expenditure, and again it appears to matter not much at all on what that money is actually spent. Here is a passage from the *General Theory* that gives some idea of what's in store.

> If the Treasury were to fill old bottles with banknotes, bury them at suitable depths in disused coalmines which are then filled up to the surface with town rubbish, and leave it to private enterprise on well-tried principles of *laissez-faire* to dig the notes up again (the right to do so being obtained, of course, by tendering for leases of the note-bearing territory), there need be no more unemployment and, with the help of the repercussions, the real income of the community, and its capital wealth also, would probably become a good deal greater than it actually is. It would, indeed, be more sensible to build houses and the like; but if there are political and practical difficulties in the way of this, the above would be better than nothing. (Keynes, 1936: 129)

This is the earlier Keynes, the Keynes of the *General Theory*, the one who created and established the mindset in which policy is now devised. Productive government spending is rare and difficult to achieve. Wasteful profligate spending is easy and common as clay. There is now no end of projects coming forward, with hardly a one having been tested with any kind of rigour to ensure that funds are not being drained away into unproductive fiscal swamps.

The standard macroeconomic model, the model that the proposed fiscal expansion will be based upon, is a model that will endanger future economic prospects for years on end. If the Argentine economy is your idea of utopia, this is the way to bring it about faster and with more certainty than anything else that might conceivably be tried.

AN ECONOMIC DEAD END

Given the extent to which policy has followed almost completely the received theory, the future trajectory of the global economy should be viewed as the result of a radical experiment the likes of which the world has seldom seen.

The policies governments are using across the world to restore their economies to health are the precise instruments that modern economic theory tells them they should use. Governments have followed almost to the letter the instructions found in the standard macroeconomics texts, and if it turns out that what they have done is seriously misguided the responsibility must be brought home to where it belongs. And where it belongs is with the theories that governments have used to direct our economies into the dead ends into which they have gone.

For such governments, there has been no apparent pain in following the big-spending, high-deficit options they have chosen. It is no doubt pleasant to find that the actions they are compelled to take by the prevailing theory happen to coincide with the very things they would anyway like to do as political leaders.

Who, if in charge of managing an economy, would not like being told that what they must now do is spend money wildly, quickly and on anything at all? That was, in effect, what they were told, and that is what one government after another has now done.

These policies are the very essence of modern macroeconomics. It treats aggregate demand as if it is a completely separate entity from aggregate supply, when once it was understood that at the aggregate level they are both one and the same thing.

And what is even worse – worse because it is so obviously wrong and ought to be seen as indefensible at least among economists – modern macroeconomics treats public spending on anything at all as for all practical purposes equivalent to the demand that occurs naturally as part of the exchange processes of the market.

To unravel the problems embedded within existing macroeconomic theory, one should return to the theories that modern macroeconomics replaced. That is where the hunt for a replacement should begin. The question really is, however, whether the majority of macroeconomists are even capable of thinking about the nature of the business cycle without immediately reverting to thoughts about aggregate demand.

A MARKER IN THE SAND

A marker in the sand must be established now. There has been an absolutely undeniable use of Keynesian economic theory to bring this downturn to an end. If it does not work, it will not be because we have not seen Keynesian theory in action.

We have seen the real thing and then some. If it fails to deliver the strong robust upturn as promised, if recovery is slow and minimal, if real wages stagnate and debt remains an enduring problem, then Keynesian economics should go the way of all crank theories.

If the policies that have been used to hasten recovery are eventually recognized as having prolonged the downturn and delayed the return to better times, no one should be allowed to walk away from ownership of what may well be an unparalleled economic disaster.

And these are not the political consequences. They will take care of themselves. What is being referred to are the consequences for the teaching of macroeconomic theory and the future use of the Keynesian macroeconomic model in the formation of policy. If our economies end up in something like a lost decade, the entire theoretical apparatus that has led us down this path should be discarded for being the misleading and useless nonsense that it will have proven itself to be.

NOTES

1. 'Classical' was the name given to the economics of his predecessors by Keynes himself. The origins of the term as applied to economics and economists dates back to Karl Marx, who used it as a brush with which to tar his predecessors. Keynes, a polemicist of some genius himself, took up the term for exactly the same purpose, but extended its range to include his own contemporaries as well.
2. The term 'Say's Law' was not, it should be noted, an invention of Keynes's, nor was it classical in origin but had been introduced into economics at the start of the twentieth century by the American economist, Fred Manville Taylor. However, once the words appeared in the *General Theory*, they immediately entered the lexicon of the entire economics profession, where they have remained embedded ever since.
3. It might be hard for non-economists to appreciate just how absolute the rejection of Say's Law has been since 1936. Such attitudes are, however, not universal. Schumpeter, in full knowledge of what Keynes had written, was himself still able to write 'Say's Law is obviously true . . . It is neither trivial nor unimportant' (1986 [1954]: 617). But such statements are rare.
4. This phrase is practically the only statement from the whole of the economics literature that an economist is uniquely bound to know even if very few ever understand what it actually means or have the slightest clue as to its original source. The only other sets of words known to all economists are 'the invisible hand' of Adam Smith and, again from Keynes, 'in the long run we are all dead', both of which are also well known among non-economists.
5. Some point to the economic conditions during the war as evidence that Keynesian policy

actually works. But the war did no more than demonstrate that unemployment can be made to disappear if a large proportion of the workforce is removed from the workplace and a government-directed war economy is introduced. But the actual performance of the economy – as an institutional apparatus that will deliver goods and services to the community at reasonable prices – was dismal. Rationing and shortages of consumer goods existed throughout the war as one would expect.

6.   Remarks prepared for delivery to an Asahi Shimbun symposium, 'The Asian Economic Crisis and the Role of Japan', held in Tokyo on 8 April 1998. This advice, it might be noted, came after the Japanese had already been attempting for a number of years to stimulate growth through high levels of public spending and increased deficits. Not only had this policy had no success, but the economy continued to deteriorate further throughout this period.

REFERENCES

Carew, Edna (1996), *The Language of Money 3*, Website edition, Allen & Unwin, http://www.anz.com/edna/dictionary.asp?action=content&content=premiers_plan.

Clarke, Peter (1988), *The Keynesian Revolution in the Making 1924–1936*, Oxford: Clarendon Press.

Folsom, Burton W., Jr (2008), *New Deal or Raw Deal: How FDR's Economic Legacy has Damaged America*, New York: Threshold Editions.

Garside, W.R. (1990), *British Unemployment 1919–1939: A Study in Public Policy*, Cambridge: Cambridge University Press.

Keynes, John Maynard (1936), *The General Theory of Employment, Interest and Money*, London: Macmillan.

Keynes, John Maynard (1946), 'The balance of payments of the United States', *The Economic Journal*, **56**: 172–87.

Schumpeter, Joseph A. (1986 [1954]), *History of Economic Analysis*, London: Allen & Unwin.

8. The coming depression and the end of economic delusion

Steve Keen

1. NEOCLASSICAL FALLACIES AND THE FAILURE TO FORESEE THE CRISIS

My differences with the standard neoclassical model of the economy are legion and have literally filled a book. *Debunking Economics* (Keen, 2001) focused on the flaws in the micro side of neoclassical economics, because that is the wellspring from which all neoclassical economic fallacies emanate. As a derivative product of a flawed microeconomics, neoclassical macroeconomics is born deformed. But it adds key weaknesses of its own.

The most important of these are its obsession with equilibrium modelling, its ignorance of the role of credit and debt in a market economy, its refusal to acknowledge class divisions in economic function, income distribution and power, and lastly, in the associated realm of finance, the unjustified quarantining of finance from economics, and the reduction of uncertainty to risk.

It follows that my own perception of how the economy operates is that it is a demand-driven dynamic system that normally operates far from equilibrium, in which credit and debt dynamics play the primary role in determining demand, where class differences in both economic roles and income distribution play out in cyclical and sometimes secular trends, and where finance and economic performance are inextricably linked, because uncertainty about the future means that economic actors extrapolate current trends using simple 'rules of thumb' that have unexpected consequences over time.

My models of this system generate complex endogenous cycles, in which economic breakdown can occur when a rising level of debt overwhelms the economy's capacity to service that debt (Keen, 1995, 2000). I am also now developing strictly monetary models that can simulate a 'credit crunch', with changes in key financial flow rates – an increased rate of debt repayment, and a decreased rate of new money creation – being sufficient to generate depression-level unemployment (Keen, 2009). In terms of economic theory, my foundations are, in reverse chronological order, Minsky, Richard Goodwin, Schumpeter, Sraffa, Keynes and Marx. I regard Minsky's financial instability hypothesis as the crystallization of an alternative non-neoclassical thread that runs through all these authors, though each has to be individually consulted to shape a complete vision of how the economy operates.

This vision, and the history of economic thought behind it, couldn't be further removed from conventional neoclassical thought, whether that is 'old school' IS–LM/AS–AD thinking, or 'new wave' rational expectations, representative agent macroeconomics.

Both are inherently equilibrium frameworks – IS–LM and AS–AD are inherently static, while the pretensions to dynamics of SDGE models ('stochastic dynamic general equilibrium') would be laughed at in a proper dynamic discipline such as engineering.

They are also showcases of how little practising neoclassical economists actually know about neoclassical economics. Joan Robinson once described the IS–LM and AS–AD models as 'bastard Keynesian'; these modern neoclassical models are effectively bastard neoclassical, but carry falsified documents of paternity. Although they are touted as having 'rigorous microeconomic foundations', those foundations involve denying fundamental conclusions from 'rigorous microeconomic theory'.

These conclusions range from the impossibility of deriving 'well-behaved' market demand curves even if individual consumers' preferences are 'well behaved' (the so-called Sonnenschein–Mantel–Debreu or SMD conditions), through Sraffa's proof that the marginal productivity theory of income distribution does not hold in a multi-product world, to the erroneous calculus behind the 'model' of perfect competition (these and other issues are detailed in *Debunking Economics*).

Unaware of these underlying realities of rigorous microeconomics, today's neoclassical economists have built models that purport to analyse the macroeconomy using concepts that have all been debunked by microeconomic research. To take but one aspect here, the construct of the 'representative agent' is central to these models, yet one of the discoverers of the SMD conditions wrote that 'Only in special cases can an economy be expected to act as an "idealized consumer"' (Shafer and Sonnenschein, 1982: 672).

That such models have achieved an apparently close fit to past empirical data says more about the capacity of modern econometric techniques to manipulate parameter-dense models than the relevance of the models themselves to the real world. Their empirical fits would now be falling apart.

The old-fashioned IS–LM framework, based on the work of John Hicks, has already been thoroughly debunked – by John Hicks. As Hicks pointed out in his retrospective apology, 'IS–LM – an Explanation' (Hicks, 1990), the IS–LM model was inspired, not by Keynes's *General Theory*, but by a preceding and rightly neglected paper of Hicks's in which he tried to build a dynamic model of a 'bread economy' (Hicks, 1935). The intention of that paper, and some of the arguments in it, were laudable. Hicks observed that theories 'built upon the hypothesis of a stationary state [are] quite satisfactory under that hypothesis, but incapable of extension to meet other hypotheses, and consequently incapable of application'. He also noted that the then extant theories of capital were based on equalities that would apply in a steady state, since 'once we leave stationary conditions, these convenient equalities disappear, and theories based upon them cease to be applicable' (ibid.: 456–7).

Unfortunately, the final execution suffered. Being unaware of mathematical techniques to handle flows in continuous time, Hicks proceeded to introduce time by slicing the future into 'short sections, each of which can be treated as constant' (ibid.: 457), which he equated to a week. Every Monday – and only on Monday – the market opened, and set wages and the rate of interest. Production then ensued over the week, taking those prices as given. In effect, expectations of changes in prices over that week were set to zero: there would be no change in expectations for the production period.

Then, despite his correct opening argument that existing, static theories presumed equalities that applied only in a static state in equilibrium, he used equalities to decide how to handle key relations in his dynamic model (which was only stated verbally rather than in difference equation form). A key step here was the use of Walras's Law to argue that capital markets could be left out of his model because 'if the market for labour is in equilibrium, and if the market for bread is in equilibrium, the market for loans must be in equilibrium too' (Hicks, 1935: 465). He later used the same thinking to exempt the labour market from consideration when developing the IS–LM model.

Minsky, on the other hand, realized that a growing economy would be characterized by *dis*equilibrium, with aggregate demand *exceeding* aggregate supply, and therefore by debt rising over time.

> If income is to grow, the financial markets, where the various plans to save and invest are reconciled, must generate an aggregate demand that, aside from brief intervals, is ever rising. For real aggregate demand to be increasing, given that commodity and factor prices do not fall readily in the absence of substantial excess supply, *it is necessary that current spending plans, summed over all sectors, be greater than current received income* and that some market technique exist

by which aggregate spending in excess of aggregate anticipated income can be financed. It follows that over a period during which economic growth takes place, at least some sectors finance a part of their spending by emitting debt or selling assets. (Minsky, [1963] 1982: 7; emphasis added)

Imposing equilibrium conditions on a model of a growing economy is therefore oxymoronic, something that Hicks himself later came to appreciate (Hicks, [1980] 1982). Reflecting adversely on his creation, Hicks explained that while it may have been valid to hold expectations constant, and even to presume equilibrium in his model with its time period of a week, neither assumption was valid when considering a growing economy over the time period relevant to macroeconomics of at least a year. In particular, Hicks reasoned, the LM curve itself could not be derived if equilibrium – and hence constant expectations of the future – were assumed, because 'there is no sense in liquidity, unless expectations are uncertain' (ibid.: 152). Hicks concluded scathingly that:

I accordingly conclude that the only way in which IS–LM analysis usefully survives – as anything more than a classroom gadget, to be superseded, later on, by something better – is in application to a particular kind of causal analysis, where the use of equilibrium methods, even a drastic use of equilibrium methods, is not inappropriate . . .
   When one turns to questions of policy, looking towards the future instead of the past, the use of equilibrium methods is still more suspect. For one cannot prescribe policy without considering at least the possibility that policy may be changed. There can be no change of policy if everything is to go on as expected – if the economy is to remain in what (however approximately) may be regarded as its existing equilibrium. (Ibid.: 152–3)

The problems with Hicks's logic went further than Hicks himself was able to appreciate. The belief that a third market could be left out of consideration if the other two were in equilibrium did not apply out of equilibrium: thus even if the IS–LM model accurately characterized the economy, and even if the Walras's Law equalities applied in a growing economy, only at the point of intersection of the two curves could two curves only be used. Away from that point, the third market would not be in equilibrium and the dynamics become not two-dimensional, but three-dimensional.

Just as neoclassical developers of DGSE models are unaware of their bastard paternity, practitioners of old-style IS–LM neoclassical modelling are unaware of theirs. The IS–LM model continues to adorn neoclassical macroeconomic textbooks, with no mention of these problems, and those who are raised on these texts continue to invoke the names of Keynes and Hicks, without being aware that Keynes was not even midwife to this creation, while the father has disinherited his child.[1]

In addition to sharing dubious paternity, both old and new neoclassical models suffer from the key problem of model-building, 'omitted variable bias'. Neither class of models includes private debt as a variable, yet it should now be clear to everyone – even neoclassical economists – that excessive levels of private debt are *the* cause of the current crisis. Even without their other deficiencies, omission from consideration of this crucial argument means that their models would have failed to foresee this crisis.

My models do include debt, are explicitly disequilibrium in nature, and did predict this crisis as a feasible – though not inevitable – outcome of a debt-financed system, as long ago as 1995. A decade later, and much closer to the eventual crisis, neoclassical macroeconomists congratulated themselves on the apparent reduction in economic volatility in what they later dubbed 'The Great Moderation' (Bernanke, 2004a). Bernanke's comments on this, when he was a Federal Reserve governor, deserve to be recorded as the systemic equivalent of Fisher's unfortunate utterance about the stock market during the Great Crash:

> As it turned out, the low-inflation era of the past two decades has seen not only significant improvements in economic growth and productivity but also a marked reduction in economic volatility, both in the United States and abroad, a phenomenon that has been dubbed 'the Great Moderation'. Recessions have become less frequent and milder, and quarter-to-quarter volatility in output and employment has declined significantly as well. The sources of the Great Moderation remain somewhat controversial, but as I have argued elsewhere, there is evidence for the view that improved control of inflation has contributed in important measure to *this welcome change in the economy*. (Bernanke, 2004b; emphasis added)

By way of contrast, I concluded my 1995 paper with the statement that:

> this vision of a capitalist economy with finance requires us to go beyond that habit of mind which Keynes described so well, the excessive reliance on the (stable) recent past as a guide to the future. The chaotic dynamics explored in this paper should warn us against accepting a period of relative tranquility in a capitalist economy as anything other than a lull before the storm. (Keen, 1995: 634)

Technically, I use systems of ordinary differential equations to model the economy, rather than the mixture of comparative statics – and, in some cases, difference equations – that characterize most neoclassical modelling (and quite a bit of post-Keynesian economics as well). Although this modeling is initially more complicated than the simplistic mathematics used in standard neoclassical models, there is a substantial infrastructure of sophisticated dynamic modelling engines that make it relatively straight-forward as additional complexity is added.

Programs such as *Mathcad, Mathematica* and *Maple* make working directly in differential equations a breeze, while a multitude of 'systems engineering' programs (*Simulink, Vissim, Vensim*, to name but three) enable flowchart depictions and modelling of dynamic processes. Their widespread non-use in economics is a sign of how primitive this discipline is compared to the sciences and engineering when it comes to modelling dynamic processes.

These programs, and the mathematical techniques that underlie them, are also implicitly non-equilibrium in nature – designed to model the system when it is not in equilibrium. This removes the need for all the contortions neoclassicals get into when they try to model dynamic processes as if they are in equilibrium throughout, which are the main source of the apparent sophistication of these models. The maths is actually much easier when you don't have to force every last expression into an equilibrium straitjacket.

2.   LEVERAGE, BURSTING BUBBLES AND THE RECURRENCE OF 'IT'

The fundamental cause of the crisis was the bursting of a debt-financed speculative bubble, which is the fourth such bubble in the post-Second World War period (previous ones bursting in 1966, 1987–89 and 2000; see Figure 8.1). The first bubble manifested itself only in the stock market; the second and third bubbles occurred in both asset markets, while the third resulted in the highest levels of asset market overvaluations ever recorded (see Figure 8.1).

Each of these asset bubbles has been debt-financed: without leverage, asset prices could not have exploded so far above consumer prices and dividend flows. After each bubble burst, most of the debt still existed, and of course still had to be serviced. In a pre-Federal Reserve system, possibly the first and almost certainly the second would have induced a debt-deleveraging-driven depression, which, though painful, would have resulted in a secular reduction of debt levels. By 1990, debt had reached levels equivalent to those that had triggered the Great Depression – 175 per cent of GDP in the USA (see Figure 8.2). Although there is no necessary reason why this level of debt must trigger a depression, as Mark Twain put it, 'history doesn't repeat, but it sure does rhyme', and debt levels this high were on song for a secular crisis.

Instead, in what became known as 'The Greenspan Put' (http://

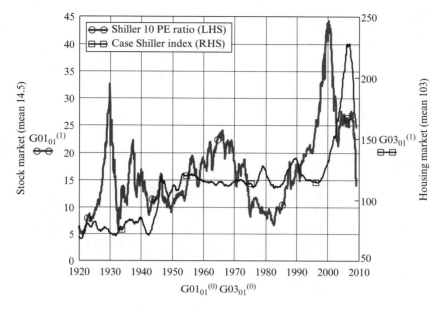

Figure 8.1   US asset market bubbles, 1920–2010

en.wikipedia.org/wiki/Greenspan_put), the Federal Reserve rescued the market from this and many subsequent financial follies. This intervention included verbal assurances of support, injections of liquidity to keep market participants solvent, and reductions in the cash rate to effectively increase the profitability of any speculative positions that had been compromised by the crash. The last policy is obvious and well known; the former were just as important, as a Federal Reserve Discussion Paper records:

> In testimony given in 1994 to the Senate Banking Committee, Chairman Greenspan indicated that '[t]elephone calls placed by officials of the Federal Reserve Bank of New York to senior management of the major New York City banks helped to assure a continuing supply of credit to the clearinghouse members, which enabled those members to make the necessary margin payments'. Contemporary newspaper articles reported similar information: 'John S. Reed, the chairman of Citicorp, has been quoted as saying that his bank's lending to securities firms soared to $1.4 billion on Oct. 20, from a more normal level of $200 million to $400 million, after he received a telephone call from E. Gerald Corrigan, president of the New York Federal Reserve Bank.' Alerted by calls about the developing credit crisis from Mr. Phelan [Chairman of the NYSE] and others, the Fed leaned heavily on the big New York banks to meet Wall Street's soaring demand for credit. (Carlson, 2007: 18–19)

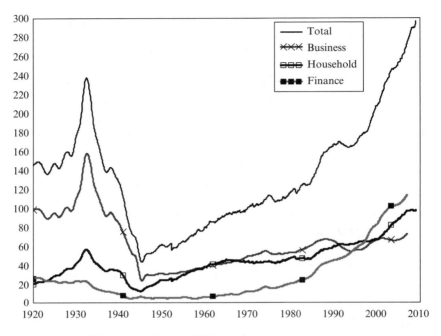

Figure 8.2   US private debt-to-GDP ratios

The 1987 intervention first led to a transference of the speculative focus from Wall Street to Main Street, with the commercial and residential property bubble that finally collapsed into the Savings and Loans crisis. An economic revival began when the rescue from that crisis encouraged private lending to accelerate once more: the USA's debt-to-GDP ratio, which had fallen from 170 per cent in mid-1991 to 163 per cent in mid-1993, began an unbroken ascent to its current peak of 290 per cent – almost 120 per cent higher than it had been when the Great Depression began, and 50 per cent higher than the peak it was driven to during the Great Depression by the effects of collapsing real output and plummeting prices.

The apparent success of the 1987 intervention encouraged its recurrent application in a series of crises, with the consequence that the recession after the dot-com bust in 2000 was unusually brief. Neoclassical econo- mists, and especially the Federal Reserve, misread this as a sign that they had finally tamed the trade cycle. Far from taming the cycle, the practice of rescuing Wall Street from its every folly, while simultaneously ignoring rising asset prices and the debt that was financing them, is the reason why this bubble has gone on so much longer, and led to so much worse an eco- nomic crisis, than ever before.

Therefore, although I differ with the Austrian school of economics in both my underlying analysis of capitalism and my preferred solutions to this crisis, I concur with them that government intervention has made this crisis far worse than it would have otherwise been. Where I differ from them is that, while they would see such a system as a nirvana, I would still expect a Minskian financial cycle that culminated every 20–30 years in a financial crisis like those that peppered the nineteenth century. They just wouldn't be as big and as systemically threatening as the one that misguided, neoclassically inspired government regulation has given us this time.

3. A JUBILEE – MAKING SURE THAT 'IT' WILL NOT HAPPEN AGAIN

Many economists, particularly neoclassical ones, are becoming 'born-again Keynesians' and recommending public debt-financed government spending, and/or inflating the money supply as solutions to this crisis. Neither will work. The former will fail because there's no point in replacing private debt with public – which is what Japan has done since its bubble economy burst at the end of 1989. The Japanese government debt to GDP ratio has exploded from 50 per cent to 180 per cent, and its economy is still mired in a depression two decades later.

The reason I expect conventional 'Keynesian' policies to fail is that deleveraging will swamp any attempt governments might make to reflate their economies. To take the example of Australia, its government has implemented a stimulus package worth A$42 billion – or more than 3 per cent of its GDP. But with private debt exceeding A$2 trillion, even a 5 per cent reduction in private debt will remove A$100 billion from circulation – equivalent to 9 per cent of its GDP. The same principle applies wherever private debt dwarfs the scale of GDP – and that is the case across the entire OECD.

Similarly, 'the logic of the printing press', to quote Bernanke (Bernanke, 2002), will fail to cause the intended inflation because the conventional 'money multiplier' model of credit creation on which it is based is wrong. While 'printing money' does cause hyperinflation in a Zimbabwe, a prerequisite is the elimination of debt so that fiat money is all there is. Achieving that end in the USA would require at least a 30-fold increase in base money, since even after Bernanke's quantitative easing in 2008, base money is still equivalent to less than one 25th of the outstanding level of private debt. I simply cannot imagine anyone in authority in the USA countenancing such an increase in fiat money.

Instead, debt has to be reduced by writedowns – a policy that is already contained in aspects of the current Obama rescue plans, but has to go much further. The question is, how much further? Before I discuss this, I'd like to propose an analogy to illustrate the dilemma this solution poses.

Imagine that you are a doctor who has as a patient a mountaineer who climbed too high with too little insulation, and now has severe frostbite in both feet. You know you must amputate them to prevent him contracting gangrene.[2] Should you operate before you receive his consent?

If you did, you could save his life – and the remainder of his legs – but he may well sue you for making him into a cripple. Your operation would be blamed for his plight, rather than his own preceding foolishness. So you have to wait until you get consent, by which time – for a particularly stubborn patient – gangrene may already have claimed a calf as well. After an operation with consent, your patient may be worse off than if you had operated immediately, but at least then he will thank you for saving his life.

I feel the same about my preferred remedy to overcome this crisis. It has been caused by the disease of excessive debt, and it will persist as long as that debt remains in excess of the capacity of the real economy to service it. So abolishing anywhere from most to all of the debt by legislative fiat would be the fastest way to end the disease. But many legacies of the disease would still remain, and the cure itself would have drastic consequences.

The legacies would include both deficient demand and deficient supply. From my monetary perspective, aggregate demand is the sum of GDP plus the change in debt.[3] By the end of this debt bubble, the increase in debt was financing up to 23 per cent of aggregate demand in the USA. Given that the change in debt is far more volatile than growth in GDP, the change in debt comes to dominate economic performance as debt levels rise relative to GDP. This is evident in the correlation revealed in Figure 8.3 between the contribution that change in debt makes to demand and the unemployment rate: there was little or no correlation in the data pre-1970, but as debt levels rose the correlation becomes unmistakable: in our debt-dependent economies, unemployment fell when the rate of change of debt increased.

The same mechanism is now working in reverse. As change in debt tends to zero and below, unemployment will inevitably skyrocket. To accelerate this process by abolishing debt immediately would make it seem that the policy caused the problem, and not the initial excessive reliance upon debt. By terminating any possibility of debt-financed consumption, it would immediately expose the 20 per cent or more hole in aggregate demand that is effectively already there.

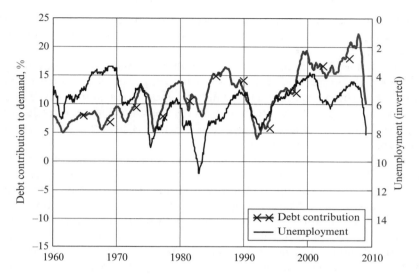

Figure 8.3   Debt contribution and unemployment, USA

The abolition of debt would also instantly bankrupt the financial system. This would not matter if it were realized that the financial system was already effectively bankrupt,[4] but the abolition of debt would be blamed for the bankruptcy of the financial system, were it done before it was apparent that the alternative was even worse.

Finally, this financial bubble has been accompanied by the movement offshore of much of the industrial capacity of the West – and the English-speaking nations in particular – with the resulting deficiency in the capacity of workers to engage in mass consumption ameliorated by rising household indebtedness. The latter will collapse – whether quickly by debt abolition, or by a continuation of the current gradual and painful adjustment.

Ultimately, nations such as the USA are going to have to confront the problem that they do not have the factories needed to employ the people who can no longer be ungainfully employed in finance, insurance, real estate and the retailing of imported durable consumer goods. If this experience of inadequate capacity to employ the unemployed is experienced after a 'pre-emptive strike' of debt abolition, the abolition rather than the debt will be blamed.

Therefore, as with the medical analogy, a policy as drastic as the abolition of debt won't be contemplated until the alternative of trying to keep the financial system afloat while pump-priming the economy has proven to be a failure. So I can't see my medium-term remedies being taken seriously for several years. With those caveats, I'll discuss my preferred solutions.

The first is debt abolition, as in a biblical 'Jubilee'. I had originally favoured the more moderate course of reducing the debt to a level that would have been responsible in the first instance – for example, in the case of housing loans, resetting them to a level whose servicing requires 30 per cent or less of household income – a policy that is already part of one of the Obama Administration's plans.

But this is to see the remedy in the light merely of overcoming our current crisis. This, I now believe, understates its importance in history. The irresponsible lending that has caused this crisis is unprecedented in the history of capitalism – and quite possibly in the history of humanity – and the responsibility for it rests firmly with the lenders rather than the borrowers.[5] We need to send a message through history that this scale of irresponsibility will never be tolerated again. A complete debt jubilee, with all debts abolished, and complete ownership of all encumbered assets transferred to the borrowers, would send that message.

That would of course cause chaos with the distribution of wealth and income, but the existing distribution itself is hopelessly mired in the insanity of the debt bubble anyway. It would eliminate the income of many retirees, who would have to go onto public pensions instead – but by then they might already be in a similar plight due to collapsing asset values. It would cause political chaos – but that will come our way anyway, and could well be far worse if decisive action were left to demagogues who had overthrown existing governments, as occurred after the Great Depression.

The financial system would also have to be nationalized for a decade or so, drastically reduced in size, and compelled while nationalized to carry out the one necessary function of a financial system – the provision of working capital for non-financial firms. Banks could then be returned to private ownership after the economy had largely recovered from the depression.

Reindustrialization will also be essential. The debt bubble went hand in hand with the deindustrialization of the West, as production was shifted from high-wage OECD nations to low-wage developing ones. This dramatically expanded the profitability of companies that could avail themselves of low wage costs, but reduced the capacity of workers to sustain a mass consumption lifestyle. The reduction was papered over by the debt bubble, but that debt-financed source of demand is now gone, and it would certainly not recur in a post-jubilee world. As a result, we face a demand deficiency of at least 20 per cent compared to current levels, while at the same time as much as 20 per cent of the workforce of nations such as the USA and the UK will be structurally unemployed. We will have to generate both the demand and the productive capacity needed to employ people who were previously unproductively employed in the FIRE economy ('finance, insurance and real estate'), and the overblown offshoots of the retail and service industries that it supported.

This reindustrialization will surely be seen as protectionism by the current political elite – but most of these won't hold on to power for long anyway, if the 1930s are any guide. Countries that can no longer employ 20 per cent of the workforce won't be able to resist pressure to reindustrialize for the benefit of their own populaces, however neoclassical economists might describe the resulting policies.[6]

Although a demand deficiency would immediately be exposed by a debt jubilee, one immediate positive aspect of debt abolition would also be a substantial boost to demand, as the proportion of income that was committed to debt servicing was eliminated.[7] That in itself could be a sufficient stimulus to increase economic activity across the globe – and indirectly benefit trading partners who might directly suffer via the rebirth of more nationalistic industrial policies. The longer-term benefit is that we set the scene for a re-engineering of our financial system in a way that would, with luck, reduce the prospects of another debt crisis in the distant future.

Once we escape from this crisis, we cannot rely on regulation to prevent a recurrence. Regulation not only failed us in the current bubble, but made it at least twice as bad as any previous one, as so-called regulators became instead cheerleaders for speculation. Minsky's comment that 'Stability – or tranquility – in a world with a cyclical past and capitalist financial institutions is destabilizing' (Minsky, 1982: 101) applies to the regulators as much as it does to the speculators.

Instead, long-term reform has to remove the incentives the current system provides that encourage the non-bank public to take on debt, since there is no prospect of designing a financial system that does not have a fundamental incentive to extend debt during periods of stable growth.[8] To tackle the problem of excessive debt, we therefore have to focus not on the supply side, which will always be willing to provide excess credit during a boom, but on the demand side.

The key incentive that entices the non-bank public to take on excessive debt is the prospect of leveraged profits from asset price speculation in both the stock and housing markets. These incentives can be reduced by relatively simple redefinitions of financial assets, which have the virtue that they would be much harder to abolish than regulations such as the Glass–Steagall Act.

The first is to redefine shares so that they last 25 years. A share would be issued for $1, it would grant voting rights and confer dividends for its life, it could be bought and sold on a secondary market, but it would be redeemed for $1 by the issuing company 25 years after it was issued. The objective of this reform is to limit the volatility in share prices, and hence to limit the prospects for gain from leveraged speculation during a bubble.

The second is to revise how houses are valued, so that valuations are based on the imputed rental income of the property and the maximum loan that can be secured against a house is some multiple (say, ten times) of the annual imputed rent. This would not eliminate speculation on house prices, but would penalize lenders who lent more than this limit by removing their security. It would also not stop buyers competing over properties, but a higher price would mean a lower level of leverage rather than a higher one as it does now. This would replace the current positive feedback loop between leverage and house prices with a negative one, so that house price bubbles would no longer occur.

These reforms are not glamorous – they may even appear pedestrian, compared to those of grandiose institutions. But grand institutions in economics have failed the test of time, over and over again. With these reforms, the only national institutions needed to enforce them would be ones with a history of independence: the law courts.

The intent of these reforms is to tame the secondary market in assets, which I see as the source of capitalism's most damaging instability. Instability is an inherent feature of a capitalist system, and in its industrial manifestations that is a good thing; but financial instability, as Minsky long ago argued and this current crisis has made critically obvious, is a very bad thing. I believe these changes would limit financial instability, without damaging the legitimate role of finance in providing working capital and investment funds for new ventures.

However, I am pessimistic about the odds of such simple yet profound reforms being enacted. The political process, even in a crisis, is dominated by expediency, and piecemeal reforms and institutional solutions to a systemic problem are far more likely to result. If so, we are likely to experience another such crisis – if we survive this one – in 50 to 70 years. I hope that by then, with the historic record of this crisis and the Great Depression before it, we will finally corral what Marx aptly named 'the roving cavaliers of credit' and limit the damage they can do to a sophisticated market economy.

NOTES

1. One example of this ignorance during the crisis was Brad DeLong's (2009) attack on a Marxist, where he opined in response to Harvey that 'it is at this point that we draw on neoclassical economics to save us – specifically, John Hicks (1937), "Mr. Keynes and the 'Classics'", the *fons et origo* of the neoclassical synthesis'. Although he chided Harvey for not having read Hicks, DeLong was clearly unaware that Hicks himself had disowned IS–LM analysis.
2. Could any medical doctors please forgive me if my analogy doesn't strictly comply with medical knowledge? I also realize that operating without consent is unthinkable.
3. This perspective necessarily combines commodity and asset markets, since aggregate spending buys both commodities and assets.
4. This realization has probably dawned in the USA, but the ideology of the free market is preventing Americans from admitting this fact and nationalizing the system.
5. At the same time, however, irresponsibility is endemic to a financial system, a topic I return to in my long-term proposals.
6. The arguments in favour of free trade are also as neoclassical, and as suspect, as the arguments in favour of deregulated finance. See Rodriguez et al. (2001).
7. The argument that such a policy wouldn't boost demand because it would simply transfer spending power from creditors to (ex-) debtors is wrong. Under the current burden of debt, borrowers are drastically reducing consumption to avoid insolvency – hence the precipitous collapse in the level of car sales and other long-lived and credit-financed consumer goods. Creditors certainly haven't taken up this consumption slack – they too are responding to the prospect of bankruptcy by reducing both consumption and investment. Debt abolition would almost certainly stimulate spending much more than it stifled it.
8. Proposals for new monetary systems based on commodity backing, or 100 per cent money schemes, ignore the evidence that a financial system is credit driven, and the simple existence of loans means that commodity-based 100 per cent money schemes will break down over time. Attempts to enforce them would also stifle the system's capacity to provide the new credit that is needed for legitimate investment by new entrepreneurs, as Schumpeter argues (Schumpeter, 1934: 95–108).

REFERENCES

Bernanke, B.S. (2002), 'Deflation: making sure "it" doesn't happen here', Remarks by Governor Ben S. Bernanke before the National Economists' Club, Washington, DC, 21 November 2002, http://www.federalreserve.gov/boarddocs/speeches/2002/20021121/default.htm.

Bernanke, B.S. (2004a), 'The Great Moderation', Remarks by Governor Ben S. Bernanke at the meetings of the Eastern Economic Association, Washington, DC, 20 February 2004, http://www.federalreserve.gov/boarddocs/speeches/2004/20040220/default.htm.

Bernanke, B.S. (2004b), Remarks by Governor Ben S. Bernanke to the Conference on Reflections on Monetary Policy 25 Years after October 1979, Federal Reserve Bank of St Louis, St Louis, Missouri, 8 October 2004, http://www.federalreserve.gov/boarddocs/speeches/2004/20041008/default.htm.

Carlson, M. (2007), 'A brief history of the 1987 stock market crash with a discussion of the Federal Reserve response', Board of Governors of the Federal Reserve, Finance and Economics Discussion Series (FEDS) 2007–13.

DeLong, B. (2009), 'Department of "Huh?": in praise of neoclassical economics', http://delong.typepad.com/sdj/2009/02/department-of-huh-in-praise-of-neo classical-economics-department.html.

Hicks, J.R. (1935), 'Wages and interest: the dynamic problem', *The Economic Journal*, **45**: 456–68.

Hicks, J.R. (1937), 'Mr. Keynes and the "Classics"; a suggested interpretation', *Econometrica*, **5**: 147–59.

Hicks, J.R. ([1980] 1982), 'IS–LM – an explanation', *Journal of Post Keynesian Economics*, **3**: 139–54, reprinted in J.R. Hicks, *Money, Interest and Wages*, Oxford: Blackwell, 1982.

Keen, S. (1995), 'Finance and economic breakdown: modelling Minsky's Financial Instability Hypothesis', *Journal of Post Keynesian Economics*, **17**: 607–35.

Keen, S. (2000), 'The nonlinear economics of debt deflation', in W.A. Barrett (ed.), *Commerce, Complexity, and Evolution: Topics in Economics, Finance, Marketing, and Management: Proceedings of the Twelfth International Symposium in Economic Theory and Econometrics*, Cambridge, New York and Melbourne: Cambridge University Press.

Keen, S. (2001), *Debunking Economics: The Naked Emperor of the Social Sciences*, Annandale: Pluto Press Australia and London: Zed Books; distributed by Palgrave, New York.

Keen, S. (2009), 'Bailing out the Titanic with a thimble', *Economic Analysis and Policy*, **39** (1): 1–23.

Minsky, H. ([1963] 1982), 'Can "It" happen again?', in D. Carson (ed.), *Banking and Monetary Studies*, Homewood, IL: Richard D. Irwin, pp. 101–11; reprinted in H. Minsky, *Inflation, Recession and Economic Policy*, Brighton: Wheatsheaf Books, 1982, pp. 3–13.

Rodriguez, F., D. Rodrik, B.S. Bernanke and K. Rogoff (2001), 'Trade policy and economic growth: a skeptic's guide to the cross-national evidence', in B.S. Bernanke and K. Rogoff (eds), *NBER Macroeconomics Annual 2000*, Vol. 15, Cambridge, MA and London: MIT Press, pp. 261–325.

Schumpeter, J.A. (1934), *The Theory of Economic Development*, Cambridge, MA: Harvard University Press.

Shafer, W. and H. Sonnenschein (1982), 'Market demand and excess demand functions', in K.J. Arrow and M.D. Intriligator (eds), *Handbook of Mathematical Economics*, Vol. II, Amsterdam: North-Holland, pp. 671–93.

9. Reflections on the global financial crisis

J.E. King[1]

1. MY MANY OBJECTIONS TO NEOCLASSICAL MACROECONOMICS

With my co-author, Mike Howard, I predicted the global financial crisis (GFC) almost a year before it occurred (Howard and King, 2008: 233–7; the manuscript of this book was sent to the publisher on 15 July 2007). I make no claim to any great powers of foresight. Anyone familiar with the work of Hyman Minsky would have made the same prediction, and the crisis has sometimes been described as a 'Minsky moment', though 'Minsky half-century' would be more accurate (Papadimitriou and Wray, 2008: 2).

Minsky was the inspiration for one of the three principal sub-schools of post-Keynesian economics, the other two being the Kaleckians and the fundamentalist Keynesians or Davidsonians (King, 2008). The three factions are in dispute on a number of important issues, but they are in broad agreement on the fundamental principles of macroeconomic theory, and the corresponding policy agenda, for an advanced capitalist economy. I myself have considerable sympathy for the Kaleckian position, due in part to my residual Marxism (on which more below), but this is tempered by an acceptance of Minsky's work on financial instability; finance was a topic on which Kalecki had very little to say.

First, though, the general principles of post-Keynesian macroeconomics must be summarized. The best brief statement remains that of A.P. Thirlwall, almost 20 years ago. The 'six central messages of Keynes's vision', he suggested, were the propositions that output and employment are determined in the product market, not the labour market; involuntary unemployment exists; an increase in savings does not generate an equivalent increase in investment; a monetary economy is fundamentally different from a barter economy; the quantity theory holds only under full employment, with a constant velocity of circulation, while cost-push forces cause inflation well before this point is reached; and capitalist economies are driven by the animal spirits of entrepreneurs, which determine the decision to invest (Thirlwall, 1993: 335–7). Thirlwall describes these propositions as 'Keynesian', without any qualifying adjective, but most or all of them would be denied by many twenty-first-century 'new Keynesians'.

What does Minsky add to this? First and foremost, there is his 'Wall Street vision' of capitalism, which places financial relations at the heart of any macroeconomic analysis; *finance*, be it noted, not (broad or narrow) money. Second, there is his almost Schumpeterian emphasis on the relentless nature of financial innovation: nothing ever remains the same for very long. Third, Minsky insisted on the inherent cyclical instability of modern capitalism: stability, he argued, is itself always an eventual source of instability. These three claims form the basis of Minsky's 'financial instability hypothesis', which I shall draw on in section 2 to explain the GFC of 2008.

How, then, does Karl Marx come into the picture? On the question of policy prescriptions to save capitalism from itself, not at all: Marx wanted to destroy the capitalist mode of production, not to rescue it. In matters of detailed macroeconomic theorizing, he can contribute very little: Marx neglected finance as a major source of crises. In any case, capitalism has moved on since his death, and as a firm advocate of historical specificity in the development of political economy he himself would have denied the relevance of *Capital* in explaining the details of a GFC that occurred almost a century and a half after he wrote it. In more general terms, however, the underlying principles of historical materialism remain substantially correct, especially when applied to advanced capitalism (see Howard and King, 2008: chs 1–2, for a justification of this position). Marx believed that capitalist economies were inherently unstable, and dismissed Say's Law as entirely wrong; on this important issue he would have found himself in agreement with post-Keynesians of all tendencies.

For my own part I am on the left or social democratic fringe of the post-Keynesian school. My socialism is of the Swedish rather than the North Korean variety (Sweden in the 1980s, before neoliberalism arrived in Scandinavia). I believe that hotels and restaurants should be kept in the private sector, while public transport networks are best left out of it. At the very least, natural monopolies should be publicly owned (and basic utilities ought therefore never to have been privatized). The market, while potentially a good servant, is a very poor master, and it requires constant vigilance and effective regulation – financial markets more than most. My proposals for dealing with the GFC, outlined in section 3, are thus broadly consistent with the 'economics of feasible socialism' that was advocated by the late Alec Nove (1991).

All this is, of course, very different from 'the standard neoclassical model'. I prefer the term 'new neoclassical synthesis' (or NNS), which is now almost universally used in the post-Keynesian literature.[2] As I understand it, the NNS operates on three levels. First, in terms of undergraduate teaching, a simple three-equation model has replaced the old IS–LM apparatus of the original neoclassical synthesis. The first is an aggregate demand curve, making real output a negative function of the rate of interest; this is the old IS curve slightly reconfigured. The second is a downward-sloping short-run Phillips curve, making the inflation rate a negative function of the output gap (itself closely and positively related to the unemployment rate). The novelty lies with the third equation, which replaces the LM curve and makes the real short-run interest rate a positive function of the central bank's expected inflation rate; this is the 'Taylor Rule' for monetary policy. Post-Keynesians can take some pleasure from the third equation, which incorporates their claims that money is endogenous and that the monetary authorities are able to control interest rates, not the stock of money. It also unwittingly acknowledges the important methodological principle that macroeconomic theory must be historically and socially specific[3] – the Taylor Rule would have been unthinkable before central bankers abandoned their monetarist illusions, and reasserted their 'independence', in the late 1980s. This does not prevent the post-Keynesians from pointing out that neither the aggregate demand function nor the Phillips curve is likely to be stable over space or time, with uncertainty (in the first case) and social conflict (in the second) being neglected in the mainstream account. In essence, then, the teaching version of the 'new consensus' model is quite similar to the 'neoclassical synthesis' that dominated mainstream macroeconomics in the 1950s and 1960s.

The second level of the NNS is the advanced theoretical analysis, with microfoundations, in which the three undergraduate relations are rigorously derived from a rational choice model of a forward-looking, utility-maximizing, classless individual agent.[4] The canonical text is Woodford (2003), a work that combines considerable scholarship and great ingenuity with considerable detachment from capitalist reality. Among the many objections to it, I shall mention three. First, and most important, it is not the economic theory of a *capitalist* economy, in which there must be *two* classes of 'representative agents' (workers and capitalists), not one, and capitalist profit expectations are what drive the entire system (Heilbroner and Milberg, 1995). Money is thus essential, since profit is defined as the difference between two sums of money: revenues and costs. In the NNS, however, as in all general equilibrium models in the Walrasian tradition, there is no clear role for money. Woodford is forced to treat it – bizarrely – as a friction or imperfection (Rogers, 2006). Second, the savings–investment relation, which must be central to any genuinely Keynesian analysis, is dealt with in a pre-Keynesian manner, equilibrium between saving and investment being established when the market interest rate equals the 'natural rate of interest'. For Keynes, as for the post-Keynesians, there is a different equilibrium (or 'natural') rate of interest for each level of effective demand, and so for every level of employment. In denying this, Say's Law has been smuggled back into the NNS. Third, the insistence on providing rigorous neoclassical microfoundations for macroeconomic theory, which is the 'defining characteristic' of the NNS, amounts to a denial of the fallacy of composition, which Keynes regarded as the methodological precondition for a separate macroeconomics in the first place. As he wrote, criticizing Edgeworth, in *Essays in Biography*:

> The atomic hypothesis which has worked so splendidly in physics breaks down in psychics. We are faced at every turn with the problems of organic unity, of discreteness, of discontinuity – *the whole is not equal to the sum of the parts*, comparisons of quantity fail us, small changes produce large effects, the assumptions of a uniform and homogeneous continuum are not satisfied. (Keynes, 1933: 262, emphasis added; see also King, 2009b)

Finally, the NNS has an operational level. For econometric estimation, forecasting and policy evaluation, practitioners of the NNS use dynamic stochastic general equilibrium (DSGE) models. They are dynamic, since they model the multi-period behaviour of rational forward-looking agents; stochastic, since they are subjected to important unexpected events, or 'shocks'; and general equilibrium, since the influence of Walrasian theory has proved more lasting among mainstream macroeconomists than it has among their microeconomist colleagues. DSGE models appear to have 'Keynesian' features, including imperfect competition, incomplete information and price and wage rigidities. However, post-Keynesian critics have concluded that these models are not in any true sense Keynesian, since they do not acknowledge the existence of involuntary unemployment and have no obvious role for money. In DSGE models the labour market is always in equilibrium; the level of employment varies only because households make intertemporal consumption–leisure substitution decisions in response to unexpected (and temporary) changes in the real wage. The output gap in such models is thus an optimal reaction to these changes. Moreover, the transversality condition[5] entails that no one ever defaults on their financial obligations. But, if you can always rely on a promise to pay, there is no point in asking for (or holding) cash. Hence there are no banks (and no entry for that word in the 21-page index to Woodford's book), no bank failures, no finance, no financial crises and no effective demand failures. Monetary policy operates only through changes in the rate of interest, and only on consumption expenditure. Post-

Keynesians conclude that DSGE models are real business cycle models in everything but name. Dullien (2008) invokes the spectre of the Trojan Horse (apparently Keynesian, but with new classical economists lurking inside). Thomas Palley (2008) uses an even more telling metaphor, describing the NNS as 'cuckoo economics': the (European) cuckoo lays its eggs in the nest of another species, leaving the unwitting host to hatch them and rear the chicks as if they were her own.

2. THE CAUSES OF THE GFC AND THE IMPENDING GLOBAL RECESSION

Some prominent mainstream economists attribute the GFC to the deep cuts in US interest rates imposed by the Federal Reserve in the early years of the new century. This is a profound mistake. A comprehensive explanation of the GFC would have to go far beyond the impact of lower interest rates on US house prices to consider the increasing financialization of the US (and the global) economy; the dismantling of much of the New Deal system of financial regulation, and the systematic evasion of those regulations that remained; the rise of a free market fundamentalism that cast doubt on the need for anything more than self-regulation of supposedly 'efficient' financial markets governed by 'rational expectations'; the lag of real wages behind the growth in labour productivity, so that workers' consumption was increasingly funded by debt; the continuing attrition of trade union power and effective government regulation of the labour market, which allowed this to happen – the whole fabric of neoliberalism, in effect. This would be a very big exercise (although identifying the transmission mechanisms that led from financial crisis to downturn in the real economy and the danger of a collapse in output and employment is, mercifully, a much less complicated task). My own very brief and selective account begins with Hyman Minsky's financial instability hypothesis.

Minsky's analysis of US capitalism placed financial relations at the centre of the analysis: labour, industry and production did not interest him very much. In his 'Wall Street vision', the crucial economic relationship is that between investment banker and client, not factory-owner and worker. His 'representative agent' is neither a classless consumer (as in mainstream economic theory) nor an industrial capitalist (as in Marxian political economy), but a financial capitalist. Borrowing and lending are the crucial transactions, not buying consumer goods or labour power. Minsky's agents are 'representative', or herd-like, only at certain stages of the business cycle: they emulate each other in the upswing, when they are all equally exuberant, and also in the downswing, when they are cautious or distinctly pessimistic. But the behaviour of atypical or non-representative agents is important at the critical turning points. At the start of a boom, someone has to have the confidence to borrow, and to lend, on a greatly increased scale. At the beginning of a financial crisis, someone has to lose faith in their clients' creditworthiness and call in their loans.

There is no suggestion that fluctuations in output and employment are caused by the decisions of the monetary authorities. For Minsky the business cycle is the result of endogenous monetary instability, which results from the behaviour of financial agents in the private sector. Government policy is not part of the problem but instead the most important part of the solution. Unlike many Marxists (and not a few Keynesians), Minsky is emphatically not a stagnationist. He sees capitalism as essentially dynamic, not least in its capacity for financial innovation, but also (and in consequence) as inherently unstable. But capitalism cannot be understood, or successfully modelled, in 'real' terms, neglecting the central role of money and finance as the supposedly 'Keynesian' growth and trade cycle models of the 1940s and 1950s had attempted to do. Minsky was thus a consistent critic of the old 'neoclassical–Keynesian synthesis', which he believed to have seriously neglected the role of money and finance. He died in 1996, before the NNS had firmly established itself as the core of mainstream macroeconomics, but he would certainly have been a severe critic of its treatment of money and its neglect of finance.

For Minsky, then, financial markets are not only crucial to the operation of capitalism but also inherently unstable. In a world characterized by fundamental uncertainty concerning future prospects, rather than quantifiable risk, the expectations of lenders and borrowers fluctuate (often dramatically) in a regularly repeated cyclical process. Depression gives way to confidence, which grows into exuberance and excitement before collapsing into despair. These mood swings are reflected in financial transactions, as caution is replaced first by optimism and then by euphoria. In the early stages of an upswing, 'hedge finance' is the general rule: borrowers are able to make both scheduled interest payments and the necessary repayments of principal from the cash flows generated by their activities. Eventually 'speculative finance' becomes more typical, and profit flows are sufficient only to meet interest bills and at best a proportion of principal commitments. (Note that Minsky's terminology was developed well before the emergence of modern 'hedge funds', whose activities are, in anyone's language, highly speculative.) As the boom nears its end, 'Ponzi finance' appears, with borrowers unable even to pay interest without incurring further debts in order to do so. 'Financial fragility' now increases rapidly, and soon the cycle turns down in a spiral of bankruptcies, 'fire sales' of assets at greatly reduced prices, falling profit expectations and declining profit flows, before confidence recovers and the entire process begins all over again.

How, precisely, does a financial crisis affect the 'real economy', according to Minsky? In mainstream macroeconomics there are two ways in which 'money' may influence the 'real world'. For monetarists, an exogenous increase in the stock of money gives rise to excess money balances, which economic agents eliminate by increasing their spending on consumer goods. In the NNS, the stock of money is endogenously determined and the monetarist story is therefore implausible. Instead, interest rates play the central role, strongly influencing consumption (and perhaps also investment) expenditure.

For Minsky, these channels are not significant. Finance is what matters, not money; neither consumption nor investment is particularly interest-elastic, and the effects of interest changes are in any case often swamped by other factors. He distinguishes three ways in which financial events have important effects on the real economy. First and foremost, changes in asset prices lead to changes in both consumption and investment spending. Two different mechanisms operate here. Consumption depends on wealth as well as income, so that increases in the price of land and financial securities induce agents to increase their consumption expenditure, and vice versa. Investment depends (*inter alia*) on the relative price of existing assets and newly produced capital goods. When asset prices collapse, due to the 'fire sales' required to meet financial commitments, the incentive to buy new capital goods falls; the reverse is true (more weakly, perhaps) when asset prices are rising.

The second way in which financial conditions affect aggregate expenditure, and therefore output and employment, is through changes in expectations. Minsky was evidently not a believer in rational expectations. Indeed, the financial instability hypothesis can be summarized as a theory of cyclically *irrational* expectations, as speculative finance gives way to Ponzi finance and then, after the credit crunch, to hedge finance once more. Minsky would, however, have insisted on the importance of the fallacy of composition in this context: what is rational for any individual financial agent (that is, lender or borrower) is often irrational from the point of view of the financial system as a whole. And there is an important sense in which Minsky's financiers are 100 per cent forward-looking: in the euphoric phase of the upswing they develop total amnesia, losing all memories of past mistakes. This turns out not to be a good thing, either for them as individuals or for the economy as a whole. Note that it is expectations concerning asset prices that really matter; 'inflationary expectations' as conventionally defined, which are about the future rate of increase of output prices, are not important.

The third channel through which finance affects output and employment is critical in the crisis and depression phases of the cycle. This is credit rationing. Whereas in the upswing and (especially) the euphoric phase almost everyone capable of asking for a loan is granted one, when the bubble bursts even solid, creditworthy borrowers will be denied finance, and will be forced to reduce their expenditure accordingly. Minsky himself emphasized the power of credit rationing in reducing business investment in the depression phase of the cycle, but he would not have been greatly surprised to discover that it also had an adverse effect on consumer expenditure, including but not confined to housing. This has little or nothing to do with interest rates. In a credit crunch, almost by definition, it is impossible to obtain finance at any price.

Thus, in Minsky's vision of financial capitalism, a crisis that begins in the financial sector (but is always conditioned by prior developments in the real economy) has pervasive effects on output and employment in all other sectors. Unemployment rises, not because workers choose leisure instead of consumer goods, but because capitalists no longer find it profitable to employ so many of them. As a short-run palliative Minsky favoured the 'job guarantee' or 'government as employer of last resort' measures introduced by Roosevelt's Works Relief Administration during the New Deal. For the longer term, he advocated policies to reduce the degree of financial fragility, including detailed supervision and regulation of financial institutions to restrain market exuberance and prevent the worst excesses of speculative (and, still worse, Ponzi) finance. This required the Federal Reserve to intervene as lender of last resort in moments of actual or potential financial crisis, in order to prevent the failure of financial institutions and the consequent collapse of asset values and investment expenditures. Minsky was well aware of the 'moral hazard' dangers of lender of last resort interventions, but he was convinced by the lessons of 1929 that non-intervention posed a much greater threat. The Fed had learned the lessons of 1929, Minsky believed, and this had contributed greatly to the increased stability of the US economy after 1945. Although financial instability could never be prevented, it could be managed, as indeed it had been in a number of postwar crises, like those of 1966 and 1987 (on which see Minsky, 1988).

In the neoliberal era, however, these important historical lessons began to be forgotten, and the amnesia that characterized financial markets now affected both the regulators and the mainstream macroeconomists who advised them (and from whom they were increasingly recruited). Hence Alan Greenspan's 'shocked disbelief' at the developing crisis in the autumn of 2008, and Ben Bernanke's continued celebration of the 'Great Moderation' of economic and financial instability as late as 2004 (Wray, 2008: 20).

The crisis of 2008 was not, of course, a simple rerun of the financial crises of the past. And Minsky would not have expected it to be so. The central dynamic of the financial instability hypothesis is provided by financial innovation: new lenders, new borrowers, new products, new ways of avoiding regulation. Minsky himself saw the importance of securitization (Minsky, 1987 [2008]), and began to think about a new stage in the development of the financial sector, which he termed 'money manager capitalism', in which 'new instruments continually eroded the bank share of assets and liabilities' (Wray, 2008: 10) and forced the banks into more and more risky forms of behaviour. He might well have been surprised by the magnitude of the US housing bubble, and perhaps also by the role of household debt, relative to corporate debt, in the unfolding of the crisis. In broad terms, though, his 'Wall Street vision' has been dramatically vindicated, and his financial instability hypothesis offers the best way of understanding it.

3. WHAT IS TO BE DONE?

Fatalistic Marxism holds no appeal for me. I agree instead with the revisionist strand of European Marxism, in which the reform of capitalism is not only possible but on occasion actually occurs. The last such occasion was during and immediately after the Second World War (Hobsbawm, 1994: ch. 9). I want to distinguish immediate and long-term policies to return the world economy to prosperity and to prevent anything like the 2008 GFC from happening again. As far as the immediate future is concerned, I agree with the broad thrust of the Bush/Obama–Brown–Sarkozy–Rudd package of bailouts, cheap money and fiscal stimulus. 'We are all Keynesians now', even if the NNS has no legitimate claim to the title and adherents to the NNS find it impossible to reconcile their support for the package with their position on matters of macroeconomic theory.

First, the bailouts (and bank deposit guarantees): almost anything would have been better than a repetition of the chain of bank failures in the early 1930s that undoubtedly deepened and lengthened the Great Depression. Whatever the nature of the monetary transmission mechanism (see section 2 above), there would have been serious consequences if any financial institution had been allowed to go under after the collapse of Lehman Brothers. It is possible to argue over the details (see, e.g., Crotty and Epstein, 2008). The bailouts certainly could and should have been designed in such a way as to punish severely the shareholders and senior managers of the institutions that were rescued, while protecting depositors, employees and (so far as possible) the taxpayer. This would have been desirable both on equity grounds and to reduce the moral hazard implications (it is strange how 'soft budget constraints' are deemed to be a serious problem only in the public sector, and in socialist countries!). In this regard the virtual nationalization of several banks by the UK government is preferable to the open-ended commitments made to private financial institutions by the US and Australian administrations. And it would have been even better if *de facto* nationalization had been converted into *de jure* nationalization, with the state in full control of the failed banks and the taxpayer receiving the full benefits of their resuscitation (on which, see below).

Second, cheap money: although in a deep recession the use of monetary policy may indeed be like 'pushing on a string' (as Keynes is supposed to have said), the alternative was certainly worse. I interpret the drastic reductions in interest rates in all the advanced capitalist economies as a *de facto* abandonment of inflation targeting in favour of employment targeting, and very welcome it is too (Arestis and Sawyer, 2008). Central bankers will probably cling to their remaining fig leaf of financial probity, claiming that their forward-looking policy has been based on the expectation of a sharp decline in inflation in 2009–10.[6] But that is not really very important. What is important is that cheap money may stimulate consumption and investment spending, and will definitely put a floor under asset (especially property) prices, and is very welcome for that reason alone. Perhaps thought will now be given to alternative anti-inflation strategies, like the incomes policy and commodity price stabilization schemes proposed by post-Keynesians such as Nicholas Kaldor (King, 2009a). To prevent new asset price bubbles from inflating themselves in the future, major changes will be needed in the financial system and the way in which it is regulated; these will be outlined below.

The third part of the package has been a substantial fiscal stimulus, entirely consistent with the post-Keynesian model of an economy threatened by collapsing aggregate demand but again very difficult to square with the implications of the NNS, which instead point towards Ricardian equivalence and the standard new classical ineffectiveness proposition. From a post-Keynesian perspective, however, the only important question about fiscal policy is whether it produces crowding out or crowding in. In all versions of classical economics (old and new) there can only be crowding out, since Say's Law applies and output is never demand-constrained.[7] In Keynesian theory output may or may not be constrained by effective demand, and so there may be crowding out or crowding in; it all depends. When effective demand is deficient, increased government expenditure (or reduced taxation) will lead to crowding in, the extent of which is summarized in the Keynesian multiplier. Thus Barack Obama,

Nicholas Sarkozy, Gordon Brown and Kevin Rudd have shown themselves to be Keynesians in the present conjuncture, as has been widely noted in the media. Again, one can object to some of the details. A fiscal stimulus can be designed to be more or less egalitarian. There is a very strong case, I think, for making direct cash payments to the poor, instead of providing tax relief for the rich. In Australia the Rudd government's December 2008 and February 2009 'bonus' payments to low- and middle-income employees, farmers, aged pensioners, disabled people and carers was a step in the right direction, but these payments were notoriously withheld from the unemployed in what seemed to be an unacknowledged act of discrimination between the 'deserving' and the 'undeserving' poor. It will be interesting to see whether the increasingly punitive attitude towards unemployed people that has become apparent in the age of neo-liberalism will survive the GFC and the probable return of double-digit 'headline' rates of unemployment.[8]

In the longer term, very substantial changes need to be made to the financial system and its regulation, and also to the operation of the real economy (Ash et al., 2009). There is substantial agreement among post-Keynesians (and many others) about the reforms that are required in the financial sector.[9] The overriding principle is the one established by Minsky: since financial innovation is ceaseless, financial regulators must be eternally vigilant, and regulations must be constantly reviewed and improved. Given this precondition, some specific suggestions follow. First, increased transparency: there must be no more off-balance-sheet transactions, and the 'sealed envelopes' full of securitized debts must be opened. Second, in order to ensure that this principle is applied in practice, there will need to be greatly enhanced regulation. A strong case can be made for the enforcement in the financial sector of the prudential principle that is operated by regulators in the pharmaceutical industry: no product should be authorized for sale unless it is both demonstrably safe and a clear need for it has been established. Third, there need to be strong restrictions on speculation in commodities, especially by pension funds and other quasi-public financial institutions. Fourth, the behaviour of credit-rating agencies must be controlled, to remove the blatant conflict of interest that arises when these agencies are paid by the same corporations whose worthless securities they give 'AAA' ratings to. Fifth, certain financial 'products' should be eliminated altogether: credit derivative swaps, to cite the most obvious example, should be outlawed, again because of the huge moral hazard issues that they raise. Sixth, central banks need additional instruments so that they can attack asset price bubbles without inflicting damage on output and employment by raising interest rates: asset-based reserve requirements, for example, or direct, quantitative controls over particular categories of lending, which were in widespread and generally successful use between 1939 and the early 1970s.

Finally, serious consideration should be given to a return to the post-1945 system of fixed exchange rates, as proposed tirelessly for a quarter of a century by Paul Davidson. Historically, the rise of global finance was made possible only by the collapse of Bretton Woods and the immense opportunities for currency speculation that were created by the post-1973 regime of floating exchange rates (Howard and King, 2008, ch. 7; LiPuma and Lee, 2004, ch. 3). I support Davidson's plan to concentrate all international payments in the hands of governments and international financial institutions, but for a different reason. Fluctuations in exchange rates may adversely affect the real economy through increased uncertainty that discourages investment, as Davidson argues, but this seems to have been exaggerated (the Australian dollar fell in value against the US dollar by almost one-third in a couple of weeks late in 2008, with no discernible effect on the local economy). Eliminating the private market in foreign exchange would, however, greatly reduce the size of the financial sector, and is thus a key component of the definancialization that is necessary if a new crisis is to be avoided.

Thomas Palley (2007) identifies distinct quantitative and qualitative dimensions of the reverse process of financialization, which began with the collapse of the fixed exchange rate system in the early 1970s. In a quantitative sense, the FIRE sector (finance, insurance and real estate) has steadily increased its share of GDP, of total employment, and of company profits. Qualitatively, short-term financial returns have come to be accepted as the sole criterion of economic success, and the interests of finance have become an increasingly dominant influence on decision-making in both the private and the public sectors. Both aspects of financialization have contributed to increasing economic instability (Hein, 2009).

Thus definancialization will entail a permanent reduction in the size of the financial sector, reflected in a smaller share of GDP, aggregate profits and total employment, and also a qualitative contraction, replacing short-term profitability with a more balanced set of indicators of economic merit. In the wake of the crisis even shareholders may be prepared to accept this, up to a point, at least, since their interests lie in the long-term viability of the enterprise. As Palley argues, the interests of other stakeholders need also to be taken into account – customers, employees, local communities and the citizenry as a whole. There is a strong case for restoring the mutual society/credit cooperative as the principal source of housing finance, and for encouraging local rather than national or global banks to service small and medium enterprises. Much of this can be achieved through favourable taxation and regulatory arrangements, and when the temporarily nationalized UK banks are returned to private ownership, it should be as credit cooperatives. Some of the principles of Islamic finance might usefully be applied to the operation of the remaining, for-profit institutions, with borrowers and lenders treated more as partners than as adversaries.

Employee interests can be advanced through profit-sharing schemes, perhaps on the ambitious scale of the (never-implemented) Swedish wage-earner funds that were proposed in the 1980s (Arestis, 1986), and through the extension of the co-determination system that was once an important constraint on the power of capital in large German companies. All these reforms will need to be bolstered by reregulation of the labour market, to re-establish collective bargaining as the principal means of protecting wages and conditions of employment. Internationally, a 'new Bretton Woods' system would have to involve much more than stable exchange rates. The international financial institutions must be released from the stranglehold of US and Western European financial interests, and the neoliberal ideology that they have imposed on poor countries must be replaced by a coherent policy programme designed to promote full employment and economic justice on a world scale. Commodity price stabilization schemes should be an integral part of this package, as Nicholas Kaldor argued in the 1970s and 1980s (King, 2009a).

There is a third dimension to the process of financialization, not discussed by Palley but arguably even more important than the other two. This is the cultural and symbolic power of finance. It is related to the Marxian themes of alienation (in which people are controlled by their own products, whether they realize it or not) and fetishism (in which they falsely attribute human powers to these products). Under capitalism, for example, workers are dominated by the machines that they themselves have made, and sometimes see these machines as being the source of their employers' profits, rather than their own surplus labour (Ollman, 1971). When finance becomes the end of all economic activity, and the production of useful goods and services becomes the means, we are in the grip of a sort of second-order alienation and fetishism, which is difficult to recognize and even more difficult to overcome. Even the most perceptive heterodox economists have neglected this question, which is, however, brilliantly dissected by the anthropologists Edward LiPuma and Benjamin Lee. Any programme of definancialization will need to overcome the culture of finance, 'a power that seems answerable to no other power' (LiPuma and Lee, 2004: 189).

I have already suggested that the crisis should induce far-reaching changes in the real economy. These changes will be beneficial in their own right, and will also reduce the degree of financial fragility in the longer term. When prosperity returns, it must be a shared prosperity. This means a return to full employment as the overriding goal of macroeconomic policy, together (as already noted) with reform of the labour market in the interests of employees, especially the low-paid. It is important to ensure that in future real wages rise at least as fast as labour productivity, or perhaps a little faster at first to restore at least some of the share of wages and salaries in GDP that was lost in the age of neoliberalism. Many of these gains should be taken in the form of increased leisure instead of higher consumption, which will be beneficial on both social and environmental grounds. This will require a firm commitment by governments in the rich countries to a reduction in hours of work, and may require legislation. It will feed back into the stability of the financial system: 'debt-financed consumption' makes some sense for the individual household, 'debt-financed leisure' much less so. Keynes argued, back in 1930, that continuing productivity growth offered the prospect that 'a hundred years hence we are all of us, on the average, eight times better off in the economic sense than we are today' (Keynes, 1930: 326). The problem of scarcity having been overcome, humanity could then enjoy an 'age of leisure and of abundance' (ibid.: 328) and be able to recognize 'the love of money' as 'a somewhat disgusting morbidity, one of those semi-criminal, semi-pathological propensities which one hands over with a shudder to the specialists in mental disease' (ibid.: 329).

In sum: the global financial crisis offers us a once-in-a-lifetime opportunity to put an end to the age of neoliberalism and to restore a more equitable, tranquil and sustainable social democratic economic order. Whether this opportunity will be taken depends above all on politics, conditioned as ever by economics. If the global recession proves to be deep and protracted, the hegemony of neoliberal finance capital may well be damaged beyond repair. If not, it will probably be 'business as usual' before very long. There is an irony here that Minsky would have appreciated. If 'crass Keynesianism'[10] does succeed in saving capitalism from itself, it will be only at the expense of renewed (and potentially even greater) crises in the future.

NOTES

1.   I am grateful to Mike Howard for assistance with an earlier draft. He is not implicated in this one.
2.   See Arestis (2008), Dullien (2008), Palley (2008) and Tamborini et al. (2008) for exposition and criticism of the NNS from a post-Keynesian perspective.
3.   Economic theory is not timeless or totally independent of the nature of social relations and social institutions. As society and economy change, their theoretical representations must also change. This is a fundamental principle of Marxian political economy, and one that most post-Keynesians would also accept.
4.   Or household, if you are happy to accept the Becker version of the neoclassical theory

of household behaviour, with all relevant decisions taken by a benevolent (male) family dictator.

5. 'The intertemporal utility optimization is based on the assumption that all debts are ultimately paid in full, thereby removing all credit risk and default. This follows from the assumption of what is known technically as the transversality condition, which means in effect that all economic agents with their rational expectations are perfectly credit worthy' (Arestis, 2008: 4).

6. In the case of the UK, the Bank of England was presumably involved in bringing it about, via the 2.5 percentage point reduction in value added tax. So much for the 'independence' of the UK central bank, and the supposed difficulty of coordinating monetary and fiscal policy!

7. Precisely how private expenditure is crowded out is an issue of secondary importance (higher interest rates? inflation? orders from the Dear Leader?).

8. When various forms of underemployment are taken into account, unemployment was always above 10 per cent, even at the height of the 1992–2008 boom (for Australian evidence see Campbell, 2008).

9. See Crotty and Epstein (2008); Palley (2008); Soros (2008). In early January 2009 even Nicholas Sarkozy and Angela Merkel were reported to agree in denouncing the 'perversion' of the financial order by 'an "amoral" form of unbridled finance capitalism' (Davies, 2009).

10. A term attributed to the German finance minister early in 2009.

REFERENCES

Arestis, Philip (1986), 'Post-Keynesian economic policies: the case of Sweden', *Journal of Economic Issues*, **20** (3): 709–23.

Arestis, Philip (2008), 'New consensus macroeconomics: a critical appraisal', University of Cambridge, mimeo, October.

Arestis, Philip and Malcolm Sawyer (2008), 'A critical consideration of the foundations of monetary policy in the new consensus macroeconomic framework', *Cambridge Journal of Economics*, **32** (5): 761–79.

Ash, Michael et al. (2009), 'A progressive program for economic recovery and financial reconstruction', New York: Schwartz Center for Economic Policy Analysis and Amherst, MA: Political Economy Research Institute, mimeo, January.

Campbell, Iain (2008), 'Pressing towards full employment? The persistence of underemployment in Australia', *Journal of Australian Political Economy*, **61**: 156–80.

Crotty, James and Gerald Epstein (2008), 'Proposals for effectively regulating the U.S. financial system to avoid yet another meltdown', Amherst, MA: Political Economy Research Institute, Working Paper No. 181, October.

Davies, Lizzy (2009), 'Leaders call for "moral" finance', *Age* (Melbourne), 10 January.

Dullien, Sebastian (2008), 'The new consensus from a post-Keynesian perspective: progress by the mainstream or a Trojan Horse for new classical economics?', Berlin: FHTW/University of Applied Sciences, mimeo, October.

Heilbroner, Robert L. and William Milberg (1995), *The Crisis of Vision in Modern Economic Thought*, Cambridge: Cambridge University Press.

Hein, E. (2009), 'A (post-)Keynesian perspective on "financialisation"', Dusseldorf: Hans Boeckler Foundation, Macroeconomic Policy Institute, IMK Studies, 1/2009.

Hobsbawm, Eric J. (1994), *Age of Extremes: The Short Twentieth Century 1914–1991*, London: Michael Joseph.

Howard, Michael C. and John E. King (2008), *The Rise of Neoliberalism in Advanced Capitalism: A Materialist Analysis*, Basingstoke: Palgrave Macmillan.

Keynes, John Maynard (1930), 'Economic possibilities for our grandchildren', in *The Collected Writings of John Maynard Keynes. Volume XI: Essays in Persuasion*, London: Macmillan for the Royal Economic Society, pp. 321–32.

Keynes, John Maynard (1933), *Essays in Biography*, London: Macmillan.

King, John E. (2008), 'Post-Keynesian Economics', in S. Durlauf and L. Blume (eds), *The New Palgrave Dictionary of Economics,* 2nd edn, Basingstoke: Palgrave Macmillan, available at http://www.dictionaryofeconomics.com/article?id=pde2008_P000135.

King, John E. (2009a), *Nicholas Kaldor*, Basingstoke: Palgrave Macmillan.

King, John E. (2009b), 'Microfoundations?', in E. Hein, T. Niechoj and E. Stockhammer (eds), *Macroeconomic Policies on Shaky Foundations: Whither Mainstream Economics?*, Marburg: Metropolis, pp. 33–53.

LiPuma, Edward and Benjamin Lee (2004), *Financial Derivatives and the Globalisation of Risk*, Durham, NC: Duke University Press.

Minsky, Hyman P. (1987 [2008]), 'Securitization', Annandale-on-Hudson, NY: Levy Economics Institute of Bard College, Policy Note 2008/2.

Minsky, Hyman P. (1988), 'Back from the brink', *Challenge*, **31** (1): 22–8.

Nove, Alec (1991), *The Economics of Feasible Socialism Revisited*, 2nd edn, London: HarperCollins.

Ollman, Bertell (1971), *Alienation: Marx's Conception of Man in Capitalist Society*, Cambridge: Cambridge University Press.

Palley, Thomas I. (2007), 'Financialization: what it is and why it matters', Amherst, MA: Political Economy Research Institute, Working Paper No. 153, November.

Palley, Thomas I. (2008), 'After the bust: the outlook for macroeconomics and macroeconomic policy', Washington DC: Economics for Democratic and Open Societies, mimeo, December.

Papadimitriou, Dimitri B. and L. Randall Wray (2008), 'Time to bail out: alternatives to the Bush–Paulson Plan', Annandale-on-Hudson, NY: Levy Economics Institute of Bard College, Policy Note 2008/6.

Rogers, Colin (2006), 'Doing without money: a critical assessment of Woodford's analysis', *Cambridge Journal of Economics*, **30** (2): 293–306.

Soros, George (2008), 'The crisis and what to do about it', *Real-world Economics Review*, **48**: 312–18 (http://www.paecon.net/PAEReview/issue48/Soros48.pdf, 6 December).

Tamborini, Roberto, Hans-Michael Trautwein and Ronny Mazzocchi (2008), 'The two triangles: what did Wicksell and Keynes know about macroeconomics that modern economists do not (consider)?', Oldenberg: University of Oldenberg, mimeo, December.

Thirlwall, A.P. (1993), 'The renaissance of Keynesian economics', *Banca Nationale del Lavoro Quarterly Review*, **186**, September: 327–37.

Woodford, Michael (2003), *Interest and Prices: Foundations of a Theory of Monetary Policy*, Princeton, NJ: Princeton University Press.

Wray, L. Randall (2008), 'Financial markets meltdown: what can we learn from Minsky?', Annandale-on-Hudson, NY: Levy Economics Institute of Bard College, Policy Brief 94, April.

10. An Islamic economic perspective on the global financial crisis

Mervyn Lewis

WHAT IS ISLAMIC ECONOMICS?

Islamic economics is a branch of knowledge that aims at analysing, interpreting and resolving economic problems with reference to the methodology of Islam. The word Islam means the 'tranquillity' and inner 'peace' (*salam*) that can be attained by submitting, surrendering or giving oneself up to the Will of God as manifest in the revealed law. The revelation (the Holy Qur'an) conceives human beings as the trustees of God on earth and bound by a covenant that is endorsed by voluntarily observing a compact (*shari'ah*) regulating life. Such compact makes no distinction between the sacred and the profane, and is inherent in the concept of trusteeship. To a Muslim, all resources are God-given, and ownership of wealth belongs to God. Individuals are only trustees and are accountable to God for their actions. Embedded in the notion of trusteeship is a call for conduct based on a code of personal ethics and a blueprint for justice.[1]

HOW DOES ISLAMIC DIFFER FROM CONVENTIONAL ECONOMICS?

In general terms, Islamic economics broadens the scope of conventional economic analysis by exploring the religious and moral aspects of economic life. In the words of Chapra (2000: 57):

> The Islamic paradigm . . . gives primary importance to moral values, human brotherhood, and socio-economic justice . . .
>   It places great emphasis on social change through a reform of the individual and his society, without which the market and the state could both perpetuate inequities.

This emphasis is understandable. Islam is an avowedly norm-based way of life seeking spiritual fulfilment in public as well as in private life, whereas conventional economics has developed into a predominantly secular discipline insisting on maintaining a difference between the positive and the normative. It can be argued that these differences hide a degree of unity at the roots: issues of public policy in the West are implicitly informed by social values that have religious (in particular, Christian) origins while the decision-making framework of the Islamic *shari'ah* explicitly recognizes the role of reason in the contextual application of religious precepts.

Nevertheless, a Muslim accepts revelation as a source of knowledge on metaphysical issues as well as on ethics and justice. By contrast, the whole evolution of standard economic methodology has been in the direction of getting rid of values and ethical theory. In particular, economics construes a person (*Homo economicus*) as a collection of preferences (attitudes, tastes, actions and laws) that adjust to the changes in the costs and benefits of resources. By comparison, Islam considers a human being as a servant and vice-regent of God on earth. In that capacity adherents ought to struggle continually to adjust their behaviour so as to bring it closer to the model laid out in *shari'ah*, whatever the cost. It is from this perspective that Islam lays great stress on keeping one eye on the material and another on the spiritual.

In pursuing this vision, Islamic economics widens the concept of utility in three ways. First, utility or satisfaction is broadened to encompass the spiritual as well as the material. Second, utility is extended temporally from this life to the hereafter. *Homo Islamicus* truly becomes the infinitely lived agent of economic theory. Third, there is recognition of communal obligations and that well-being cannot be acquired in any true sense without a concern for the welfare of others. The corollary is that the rational being is replaced by the 'faithful' being who pursues personal interests within social bounds and communal interest.

Self-interest, as such, is not denied. Indeed, the Holy Qur'an accepts that people are greedy and possessive. For instance,

> Truly Man is, To his Lord, Ungrateful;
> And to that (fact) He bears witness (By his deeds);
> And violent is he In his love of wealth.[2] (*Al-Adiyat* 100: 6–8)

Instead, self-interest is to be disciplined by moral reinforcements to produce a holistic or enlightened form of self-interest, or what Khan and Bhatti (2008: 13) refer to as a 'divinely inspired state of self-interest'. The Holy Qur'an holds that every person is a member of God's family and has a right to share in God's gift of wealth and resources.

> So fear Allah as much as ye can; Listen and obey;
> And spend in charity For the benefit of Your own souls.

And those saved from The covetousness of their own
Souls, They are the ones that achieve prosperity.[3] (*At-Tagabun* 64: 16)

Consequently the faithful person relies on moral forces such as altruism, cooperation, brotherhood, fraternity, affection and mutual respect to rein in his selfish nature and lust for riches (Ahmed, 1991).

In Islamic economics, participation in economic activity becomes a religious responsibility in which the individual is allowed to pursue his or her own personal goals while complying fully with the community's norms, values and expectations. In this respect, individual freedom of decision-making is not absolute and has to be moderated and constrained by rules designed to ensure that others enjoy similar freedoms. That, in essence, is what *shari'ah* achieves. Economic resources and human endeavours are to be employed to seek utility or satisfaction at two levels, the material and the spiritual, so that economic activity is both financially and socially beneficial. This requirement is in recognition that without spiritual enrichment achievement of material fulfilment is ephemeral and ultimately untenable, since a balance of the two is needed for the full development of the individual and society.

IMPLEMENTING THE VISION

Islam generally encourages trade and free markets, and an analysis of the behaviour of market participants in respect of pecuniary incentives is also fully admitted. Where Islam differs is on the issue of legitimizing such behaviour over all aspects of human activity. Islam takes the institution of the market neither as a benchmark nor as a reference point for a reflection on organizing other realms of human interaction. Nowhere does Islam make it explicit that the market is the natural order that ought to serve as the benchmark for reflecting on or organizing other spheres of human interaction. Instead, market behaviour stands shoulder to shoulder with all other human interactions (that constitute socioeconomic and political organization) ready to be examined and corrected with reference to the simple and complex goals of human life embodied in the precepts of justice. It is this theory of justice that holds sway over all spheres of human interaction. In fact, so much is this so that the famous Muslim scholar Ibn Sina (Avicenna) once said that justice (*adl*) maintained by law is indispensable for sustaining the life of the human species on earth (Smirnov, 1996).

These issues date back to the beginnings of the religion. Islamic economics assumed the shape of an independent discipline only in the second half of the twentieth century as intellectuals in many lands with majority Muslim populations began to reflect on alternative modes of postcolonial social organization. Until then it was an integral part of the unified and moral philosophy of Islam itself. Islam, unlike Christianity, was not born within an empire. On the contrary, it was born outside the two empires of its time and created an empire of its own that found legitimization in faith. Seen from a Muslim viewpoint, then, Islam acts as the blueprint as well the social cement of a civilization. To Muslims, all the good of that civilization can be attributed to motivation by faith and the bad to a deviation from the model set forth by the Prophet and his immediate successors during what is seen as the 'Golden Age' of Islam (Lindholm, 1996).

This different evolutionary path was significant. The Christianity that was absorbed into the remnants of the Roman Empire faced the trappings of a feudal system. In the feudal society, most exchange was in kind and, in line with Aristotelian ideas, Christianity retained for a considerable time an aversion to trading and market exchange. In contrast, Islam had to deal with the problems associated with monetized free market exchange from its inception in the Arabian towns, linked by caravan routes to each other and Asia Minor. Trading, as such, was extolled. What was needed was to elucidate what particular forms of trade and exchange were unjust. On that account there is a detailed framework that prohibits usury, gambling and *gharar*, and even condemns unequal barter exchange, encouraging instead monetized trade to avoid the potential for uncertainty in trade. This detailed framework constitutes the basis of 'justice in exchange' (Iqbal and Lewis, 2009).

Other major paradigms are silent on the issue of just exchange. The Marxist (Soviet-style) and libertarian views, for example, define two opposing poles. The former, a planned economy, has nothing akin to a market as we know it. The libertarian view not only embraces the market in full but takes the principles of 'negative freedoms' (absence of coercion and prohibitions) and 'Pareto optimality' that underlie market exchange as benchmarks. Welfare liberalism, which attempts to strike a middle ground between these positions by enforcing fair competition rules and consumer protection regimes, does not go far enough from an Islamic perspective. Its focus remains on 'external', i.e. state-sponsored, correction of market outcomes through taxation, redistribution and competition policy.

The Islamic position on these matters is that 'external' correction is needed to maintain those who fall by the wayside, but on its own its reach could be too limited. It does not strike at the root of those mechanisms or exchanges 'internal' to the market that enable accumulation through means that are unfair and keep alive the possibility of *zulm* (oppression) of people by their own kind. Consequently, while the market itself is retained, the aim is to reform it 'internally' and organize it on a more dignified and ethical footing. Prime importance is laid on the responsibility of individuals to fulfil their obligations to support themselves, parents, family, neighbours, near relatives and others. The idea is to keep those institutions and bonds intact that constitute the building blocks of a society, yet make the state responsible to step in for assistance in circumstances out of an individual's control. Again the emphasis is different. The state enters as a carrier and implementer of justice through law. Consequently, an analysis of the state's fiscal role begins with an examination of the theories of justice rather than from a study of what markets can or cannot do, and feedback from the latter illuminates how one part of the Islamic theory of justice knits with its other parts.

In order to establish justice in exchange, there are positive and negative injunctions involving ethical principles (Khan and Bhatti, 2008). The positive injunctions outlined below are designed to ensure sustainable patterns of wealth-holding and market behaviour.

Property Rights

Islam respects private property and the right of ownership is protected. Ownership rights are an effective way of fostering market efficiency and mutual cooperation, but in Islam the right of private ownership is not absolute. God is the absolute and eternal owner of everything on earth and in the heavens. However, God has appointed man His vice-regent on earth and entrusted him with the stewardship of God's possessions. Ownership of property is therefore a trust (*amanah*) to be enjoyed conditionally so long as man follows *shari'ah* and remains worthy of the trust.

Free Consent

The Holy Qur'an ordains free consent and mutual cooperation as indispensable for healthy business relations. For example,

> O ye who believe! Eat not up your property
> Among yourselves in vanities: But let there be amongst you
> Traffic and trade by mutual good-will.[4] (*An-Nisaa*, 4: 29)

Islamic law provides freedom of contract, so long as the terms do not conflict with *shari'ah* guidelines. In particular, it permits any arrangement based on the consent of the parties involved, so long as the shares of each are contingent upon uncertain gain and are a function of productive transformation of resources. Those involved should be provided with all relevant information and consent should be obtained freely without undue influence, fraud or misrepresentation in any form (Islahi, 2005).

Contractual Integrity

Commercial contracts are regarded as both legal promises and moral commitments. The general principle of the Islamic law of contract is contained in the Qur'anic verse: 'O you who believe, fulfil all obligations' (S5.1). Honesty and fair dealing are virtues in business as in all walks of life. A Muslim business person should therefore be a person of high moral values who would not set out to deceive or exploit others. Monopolies and price fixing are prohibited. Generally the market should be free and not subject to manipulation. Those engaging in trade and commerce should behave equitably. According to the Holy Qur'an, followers are required to keep records of their indebtedness:

> Believers, when you contract a debt for a fixed period, put it in writing. Let a scribe write it down fairly . . . and let the debtor dictate, not diminishing the sum he owes . . . (*Al-Baqarah* 2: 282)

Underpinning Islamic belief is the requirement that doubt and uncertainty be removed from interpersonal transactions. In business affairs, trading and the like, all parties' rights and obligations are to be fully documented for verification and exploration.

Benevolence

There are many verses in the Holy Qur'an that emphasize benevolence as one of the greatest of human virtues. Non-profit activities such as *qard hasan* (beneficence loans on a zero return basis), which make a positive contribution to society, are actively encouraged by the Holy Qur'an. The Prophet Muhammad advocated allowing a destitute debtor extra time to repay his debt, or reducing the capital sum owing, when no other protection is available. Charity enriches all: the giver, receiver and society as a whole. Almsgiving in the form of *zakat* is a compulsory levy, and constitutes one of the five basic tenets of Islam, to which all believers must adhere. It is neither a welfare programme nor a tax. Rather, *zakat* is an obligation of a Muslim not only to society, but also to Allah. In other words, *zakat* is not merely a 'contribution'; it is also a 'due' or a 'claim'. A person paying *zakat* is not primarily doing a favour to the recipient or beneficiary of *zakat*, but is rather meeting a claim on himself by purifying wealth.

There are also negative injunctions or prohibitions relating to economic behaviour.

Extravagance and Hoarding

Islam preaches moderation and a balanced pattern of consumption (both positives). Luxury and overconsumption are condemned, as is poverty (negatives). Positive values are those such as *iqtisad* (moderation), *adl* (justice), *ihsan* (kindness par excellence), *amanah* (honesty), *infaq* (spending to meet social obligations), *sabr* (patience) and *istislah* (public interest). At the same time, there are several values that are negative, and thus to be avoided: *zulm* (tyranny), *bukhl* (miserliness), *hirs* (greed), *iktinaz* (hoarding of wealth) and *israf* (extravagance). Economic activity within the positive parameters is *halal* (allowed and praiseworthy) and within the negative parameters *haram* (prohibited and blameworthy).

Fraud and Corruption

All acts such as fraud undertaken by a person to take unfair advantage of another is strictly prohibited. In this context, fraud is an act that contains elements of injustice and gains for one party at the expense of another. Corruption, in both the Holy Qur'an and the *sunnah* (the source of information concerning the practices of the Prophet Muhammad and his Companions), is condemned as a serious threat to the social, economic and ecological balance (see verses 11: 85; 28: 4,77, 83; 29: 28–30; 30: 41; 89: 12). Instead, economic activities must be based on moral and legitimate foundations. Individuals are expected to feel socially responsible for others in the community. One cannot enjoy life while others cannot. In general, the aim of the Islamic economic system is to allow people to earn their living in a fair and profitable way without exploitation of others, so that the whole society may benefit. The welfare of the community over individual rights is also emphasized, allowing the protection of the essential dignity that God conferred on all humanity.

Riba

Interest (*riba*) is strictly prohibited. Thus the payment of interest and the taking of interest as occurs in the conventional economic system is explicitly prohibited by the Holy Qur'an in four clear and forthright injunctions.[5] The first emphasizes that interest deprives wealth of God's blessings. The second condemns it, placing interest in juxtaposition with wrongful appropriation of property belonging to others. The third enjoins

Muslims to stay clear of interest for the sake of their own welfare. The fourth establishes a clear distinction between interest and trade, urging Muslims, first, to take only the principal sum and second, as noted earlier, to forgo even this sum if the borrower is unable to repay. Both the Holy Qur'an and the *sunnah* treat interest on a loan as an act of exploitation and injustice, and, as such, inconsistent with Islamic notions of fairness and property rights. The interest rate is a fixed payment specified in advance for a loan of money and whether or not the borrower gains or loses from the venture the lender uses collateral and other means to enforce payment. It is much fairer to have a sharing of the profits and losses, as occurs in profit-and-loss-sharing arrangements, which are the preferred financing method in Islam.

Gharar/Maysir

Prohibition of games of chance is explicit in the Holy Qur'an (S5: 90–91). It uses the word *maysir* for games of hazard, implying that the gambler strives to amass wealth without effort. Gambling in all its forms is forbidden in Islamic jurisprudence. Along with explicit forms of gambling, Islamic law also forbids any business activities that contain any element of gambling (Siddiqi, 1985). Another feature condemned by Islam is economic transactions involving elements of speculation, *gharar* (literally 'hazard'). In business terms, *gharar* means to undertake a venture blindly without sufficient knowledge or to undertake an excessively risky transaction. By failing or neglecting to define any of the essential pillars of contract relating to the consideration or measure of the object, the parties undertake a risk that is not indispensable to them. This kind of risk is deemed unacceptable and tantamount to speculation due to its inherent uncertainty. Speculative transactions with these characteristics are therefore prohibited.

ISLAM AND THE CRISIS

In the words of Niall Ferguson (2009), first there was the 'subprime surprise', then there was the 'credit crunch', which became the 'global financial crisis'. Now, according to the managing director of the IMF, we are in 'the Great Recession'. While the full story of the precise steps in this transition is yet to be told, salient features of the origins are well known and need not be repeated here in detail. Suffice it to say that there were many banks willing to oblige homeowners' desire to borrow for consumption purposes against the rising value of their houses ('mortgage equity withdrawal'), and they assisted others to become first-time homebuyers, by making loans that in some cases were up to and exceeding 100 per cent of valuation[6] (125 per cent in the case of Northern Rock in the UK) and lent to those with little chance of repayment once the initial 'teaser' rates adjusted to the much higher contracted levels. So was born the NINJA borrower (no income, no job and assets). By 2006, nearly 50 per cent of new US home loans were ones that did not qualify for insurance by the mortgage insurers, Fannie Mae or Freddie Mac ('subprime' loans) or loans that were higher quality than subprime but did not qualify for insurance because of little ('low doc') or no ('no doc') documentation (the 'Alt-A' mortgages).

CDOs (collateralized debt obligations) then packaged these individual loans into securities so complex that they misled credit-rating agencies, investors and the banks themselves. Issuing banks sometimes offered guarantees ('liquidity puts') to those buying CDOs that they thought would never be exercised, but came back to haunt them. All of this 'originate and distribute' lending activity was fuelled under the final years of the Greenspan Fed by the fastest growth of dollar liquidity and the lowest real federal funds rate in 30 years. Many mistakes were made, among the greatest being the poor governance by US authorities of Fannie and Freddie and the failures of regulators, bank boards and risk management committees to control the activities of banks' highly geared structured investment vehicles (SIVs).[7] The judgement of Alex Weber, president of Deutsche Bundesbank, that lax lending standards, weaknesses in the credit transfer process, and overly optimistic assessments of structured securities such as CDOs triggered the shock waves that engulfed the global financial system seems difficult to resist (Weber, 2008).

From an Islamic perspective, however, the causes are more fundamental. The Islamic critique would focus on the role of greed, *gharar,* speculation, governance, fixed interest debt (usury) and the growth of financialization.

Greed

Greed undoubtedly drove Wall Street bankers to buy mortgage loans aggressively, often with little scrutiny, in search of fees from underwriting, bundling and distributing mortgage-backed securities. Often the CDOs did not contain actual mortgage securities but derivatives such as credit default swaps (CDSs) linked to mortgages. Investment banks liked synthetic CDOs comprising CDS because they avoided having to purchase the underlying securities, while enabling the banks to create a large number of CDOs related to the same mortgage-backed bonds. Greed led to a market for the CDOs among hedge funds and other professional investors, while on the other side of the ledger banks originated loans to less creditworthy customers. Greed extended down the chain to mortgage brokers who signed up perhaps 80 per cent of the mortgages and often received higher commissions for originating mortgages that promised the higher returns (i.e. subprime and Alt-A mortgages).

Finally, greed went all the way back to the homebuyers. They were attracted by the low 'teaser rates' on offer and, in some cases, by the 'put option' that no-recourse loans provided. In this case, borrowers could bet on the continued increase in home prices, safe in the knowledge that they could return the keys to the bank if housing prices fell. It would seem that some subprime lending was to relatively affluent borrowers, who in theory could have qualified for higher-quality loans, but used the low initial rates to acquire homes as speculative investments.

The Western response to such revelations is to strengthen the 'external' constraints on participants. Under the new financial stability plan for the USA announced on 10 February 2009 there is to be enhanced transparency, accountability and monitoring of those institutions receiving exceptional federal assistance. All major banks will be subject to stress tests. Much the same is true of those banks effectively nationalized in the UK. Financial regulations generally seem sure to be tightened, and Federal Reserve Chairman Ben Bernanke has called for greater powers to do so (*Wall Street Journal*, 12 March 2009, p. 21).

In effect, much like the phenomenon of corruption, human greed, reckless behaviour and moral hazard are accepted as facts of life, endemic and incurable. They are to be countered by greater external monitoring and accountability where discipline through the market is blunted by 'too big to fail'. In Islamic eyes, the problem is a moral one and should be solved by a moral regeneration within the individuals concerned. A failure fully to explore this route is seen to be limiting in two respects. First, there will always be areas that regulations and other external constraints cannot reach, leaving self-restraint and ethical *mores* as more effective disciplines. It is simply not possible to provide enough regulatory officers, accountants and bank inspectors to verify more than a small portion of all financial transactions that take place in an economy, so that most transactions rely on voluntary compliance. In such a context, ethical norms are paramount, and society's attitudes and values can give further force to them or cause them to be weakened. Second, a reliance on external restraints may weaken inner resolve. Consider, as one leading example, the views of the famous Islamic scholar Ibn Khaldun (1332–1406 CE) (1967: 96), and the significance that he attached to 'internal' forces as opposed to 'external' law enforcement.

When laws are (enforced) by means of punishment, they completely destroy fortitude, because the use of punishment against someone who cannot defend himself generates in that person a feeling of humiliation.

In Muslim thought, there is no argument that the men around the Prophet Muhammad observed the religious laws, and yet did not experience any diminution of their fortitude, but possessed the greatest possible fortitude. When the Muslims got their religion from Muhammad, the restraining influence came from themselves, as a result of the encouragement and discouragement he gave them in the Holy Qur'an. Umar (the second Caliph) said, 'Those who are not (disciplined) by religious law are not educated by God.' Umar's desire was that everyone should have his restraining influence in himself. His certainty was that Muhammad knew best what is good for mankind (ibid.).

Gharar

Gharar signifies ambiguity, uncertainty or lack of specificity in the conditions of a financial contract. It is strictly forbidden in Islam, which insists that information be easily and equally accessible to all transactors. These requirements were almost certainly not met in the case of many option ARMs (adjustable rate mortgages), which became a staple of the subprime lending saga. The option ARM was described in *Business Week* as perhaps 'the riskiest and most complicated home loan product ever created' (Der Hovanesian, 2006: 71). Created in 1981, option ARMs were initially marketed to well-off homebuyers who wanted the flexibility they offered to make low payments most months and then pay off large amounts all at once. Instead, the product was transformed from a financial planning tool for the wealthy into an affordability tool for aspiring homeowners. 'With its temptingly low minimum payments, the option ARM brought a whole new group of buyers into the housing market, extending the boom longer than it could have otherwise lasted' (ibid.).

An option ARM generally comes with a number of payment choices. There is usually a minimum payment which does not cover the interest charges. In the meantime, the interest rate adjusts every month (say from an initial rate of 7.38 per cent p.a. rising to 7.95 per cent p.a. during the first year). When borrowers make the minimum payment, the shortfall is added on to the balance, a situation known as negative amortization. Once the balance increases by 10 or 15 per cent, the loan resets and the new balance is then amortized over the remaining life of the (generally 30-year) loan. At that point, making a minimum payment is no longer an option.

Option ARMs were not the only instrument in the market, although they grew rapidly and by 2006 they represented at least one-eighth of all mortgages written in the USA. The problem was that 80 per cent of option ARM borrowers made only the minimum payment, and once housing prices started to fall, borrowers could no longer rely on rising home equity to act as a buffer. Some borrowers were aware of the risks involved, but anecdotal evidence suggests that many did not understand how option ARMs worked, namely that the low payments were only temporary and that the less a borrower pays initially, the more is added to the balance of the mortgage (Der Hovanesian, 2006).

In these circumstances, most option ARM borrowers were not in fact paying down their loans; they were underpaying them. Interestingly, however, under GAAP (generally accepted accounting principles), the lending banks that kept option ARMs on their books (rather than securitize them) could by virtue of accrual accounting count as revenue the highest amount of an option ARM payment, that is the fully amortized amount, even when borrowers made the minimum payment. Through such deferred interest, banks can bring forward future revenue and create what has become known as 'phantom profits', since the interest may never be paid.

In a written statement provided to *Business Week*, the body responsible for overseeing GAAP, the Financial Accounting Standards Board (FASB), defended the accrual accounting standard in the context of option ARMs but did venture the opinion that the FASB is 'concerned that the disclosures associated with these types of loans [are] not providing enough transparency relative to their associated risks'. More telling still, from an Islamic perspective, is the observation in *Grant's Interest Rate Observer* that negative-amortization accounting is 'frankly a fraudulent gambit. But what it lacks in morality, it compensates for in ingenuity' (Der Hovanesian, 2006: 74).

Speculation

Speculative transactions and all forms of gambling are prohibited in Islam because they destroy the moral, economic and social fabric of socioeconomic life. Gains are made by one person at the cost of others. There is thus an aversion to conventional life insurance, seen as tantamount to taking a bet on one's own life, along with swaps, forwards, options and futures. All such activities are considered to encourage the concentration of wealth in the hands of a few and lead to socioeconomic inequalities.

The contrast with Western finance could not be sharper, as many large conventional banks evolved to be significant risk-takers. The 'old' model was that commercial banks took little or no risk other than credit risk, and it has to be said that even credit risk got them into more than enough trouble, as the third world debt crisis of the 1980s and the commercial property crash of the early 1990s revealed (Lewis and Davis, 1987; Lewis, 1994). Gradually, however, the banks moved into market risk and investment risk, expanding their trading activities into derivatives and other financial products (Das, 2008). In the USA, such multifaceted financial institutions developed when the Glass–Steagall Act of 1933 (which separated commercial and investment banking) began to be eased in 1987 and eventually repealed in 1999.

Investment banking also changed. The traditional model was one in which risks were limited to short-term underwriting risks at the time of the securities float, and the main income came from fees for organizing the flotation, handling the share trades and engaging in the corporate work that followed in terms of mergers and acquisitions (M&A). Not so long ago, the Wall Street investment banks obtained most of their revenue from fee-based activities such as M&A advisory, equity and bond underwriting, and asset management. In the new model, they too became risk-takers on a scale that dwarfed that of universal banking firms such as JP Morgan Chase and Bank of America. Consider, for example, the old Big Five (Bear Stearns, Goldman Sachs, Lehman Brothers, Merrill Lynch and Morgan Stanley). From 2000 to 2006, trading income rose from 41 per cent to 54 per cent of revenues for the Big Five, with proprietary trading accounting for most of the increase in revenue (Tully, 2008). A lot of that trading was in stocks and bonds, but they also took positions in currencies, oil futures, junk bonds and other speculative vehicles.

Underpinning the reliance on risky trading was a compensation system that meant that a sizeable proportion of the profits that resulted from the trading activity was then handed out to employees in the form of wages and bonuses. Employees of the Big Five, for example, took home 60 per cent of their firms' revenue in 2007 ($66 billion in compensation out of $110 billion) in comparison with 32 per cent at JP Morgan Chase and 28 per cent at Bank of America (Tully, 2008). However, later losses outweighed these profits. In the fourth quarter of 2008 alone, Merrill Lynch lost $15.3 billion relative to $12.6 billion of post-tax profits in 2005 and 2006 combined. *The Economist* (31 January 2009, p. 73) calls this 'the banking bonus racket'. Executives and traders took most of the profits when the market was booming, and shareholders bore the bulk of the losses during the bust.

Governance

Governance issues arise at every turn in the global financial crisis, but particularly with respect to the way in which 'the banking system was metamorphosing into an off-balance sheet and derivatives world – the shadow banking system' (Gorton, 2009: 41). In this system:

> 'Regulatory arbitrage' evolved into a business model. Required risk capital was reduced by creating the 'shadow' banking system – a complex network of off balance sheet vehicle and hedge funds. Risk was transferred into the 'unregulated' shadow banking system. The strategies exploited bank capital rules. Some or all of the real risk remained indirectly with the originating bank. (Das, 2008)

Certainly this was the experience of banks such as Citigroup, UBS and Goldman Sachs, which ran into difficulties with the specific-purpose highly geared investment vehicles (conduits, structured investment vehicles – SIVs) established off balance sheet. These subsidiaries or funds invested in assets with a high return and long duration (eg structured finance products) and financed themselves by issuing asset-backed commercial paper. An SIV is usually highly leveraged, 15–20 times the equity capital (Nyberg et al., 2008). While investors were presumably aware that these vehicles were autonomous legal entities with little or no formal recourse to the parent, when it came to the crunch the banks were unwilling to abandon the investment companies because of reputation risk. In any case, overlapping shareholders and officeholders, and the stream of management fees paid to the parents, complicated the legal standing of the bank-owned subsidiaries. In the event, as the 'runs' on them began, the SIVs were absorbed back onto the balance sheets of the sponsors. It then became apparent that

> Few outside the banks themselves knew about the growth and extent of the grey, or shadow, banking system in the guise of conduits, SIVs etc., and since a main rationale for this shadowy sub-system was regulatory arbitrage, the banks were not loudly advertising such activities. (Goodhart, 2008: 3)

Somehow all this off-balance-sheet activity seemingly escaped the regulators' attention. Bank boards also went missing and failed in their governance duty to look after shareholders' interests. Good governance in this context would mean:

> No more 'structured investment vehicles' that hold zero capital and fund their long-term lending by borrowing short-term funds. No more banks pretending they are not backstopping these entities and thus do not have to maintain a capital cushion against that lending – and then taking the failed loans on to their books anyway. (Wessel, 2008)

Governance in the Islamic system is very different because of the discipline provided by Islamic religious auditing, which is a device to solicit juristic advice and monitor compliance with Islamic precepts. This extra layer of auditing and accountability for resource use ensures that the enterprise operates as an Islamic concern in its business dealings. The processes involved in religious supervision are illustrated most clearly in the case of Islamic financial institutions (Algaoud and Lewis, 1999), but the governance principles operate across the full range of business activities. The functions of the religious auditors, as spelt out in the organization's articles of association, are threefold. First, the religious supervisors give advice to the board and the management about the religious acceptability of the firm's contractual arrangements and new product development. Second, an independent report is provided to inform shareholders as to the compliance of management with Islamic principles and to the extent that the business is run Islamically. Third, there is an audit involved with the special almsgiving levy, *zakah*, to establish that the *zakah* fund is being correctly assessed and properly administered and distributed. In these various ways, the religious supervisory process testifies that the articles of association, stipulating that the organization run its business in accordance with Islamic law, are in fact met.

Further, there is a higher authority. Accountability to God and the community for all activities is paramount to adherents to Islam. To Muslims, *shari'ah* is the essential guiding force as it encompasses all aspects of human life, and accountability is ultimately to Allah, as all deeds will be accounted, as stated in the Holy Qur'an:

> To Allah belongeth all that is in the heavens and on earth. Whether ye show what is in your minds or conceal it. Allah calleth you to account for it. (Al-Baqarah 2: 284)

The Holy Qur'an (the revelation) and *sunnah* (the Prophet's example as recorded in *hadith* or the traditions) define clearly what is true, fair and just, what are society's preferences and priorities, what are individuals' and business enterprises' roles and responsibilities, and also, in some respects, spell out specific accounting standards and accounting practices. Accountability in this context means accountability to the community of believers (*umma*) or society at large. Muslims cannot, in good faith, compartmentalize their behaviour into religious and secular dimensions, and their actions are always bound by *shari'ah* obligations and responsibilities.

Debt and Leverage

Islam prohibits *riba* (usury, interest) and all forms of interest-related transactions such as interest loans and interest debt, whether fixed rate, floating rate or zeros. Instead, in the pure theory of Islamic banking, suppliers of capital become investors or productive partners with entrepreneurs on a profit-and-loss-sharing (PLS) basis, rather than acting as creditors holding debt claims.

There is a lengthy, and not altogether conclusive, literature on the optimality of different forms of financial contracting under various assumed circumstances. Costly verification and/or monitoring points to the optimality of the standard debt contract: the borrower pays the lender a fixed payment for good outcomes, when no verification or monitoring takes place, but must hand over the whole proceeds in the event of a bad outcome, when the fixed repayment cannot be met and bankruptcy occurs (Gale and Hellwig, 1985). Hidden actions or moral hazard also point to the optimality of the same type of contract: a requirement to make debt payments independently of the state of the world may be a check against moral hazard (Harris and Raviv, 1979). Thus there would appear to be certain conditions when a debt contract is optimal, but the argument can be overstated. Some research on security design makes assumptions that virtually guarantee the optimality of a specific contract (Allen and Winton, 1995). Others focus on conflicts of the type that can more conveniently be resolved by changing managerial compensation schemes rather than adopting a certain mix of financial instruments in corporate capital structure.

These issues have been addressed within the framework of Islamic economics by W.M. Khan (1985, 1987). He sets out to compare the 'fixed return scheme' (FRS) of debt contracts with the 'variable return scheme' (VRS) of Islamic PLS partnerships. The overall comparison between the two contract types involves a tradeoff between lower monitoring costs under FRS conditions and better risk-sharing under VRS arrangements. The frequency of use of debt contracts in practice is explained by supposing that the former often outweigh the latter (Ahmed, 1989). But, equally, there undoubtedly exist situations where this position is reversed, establishing a theoretical case for Islamic banking practices for certain types of projects where monitoring and evaluation can be undertaken with relative ease. For this theoretical case to be realized in practice, however, clear contracting arrangements and monitoring procedures need to be put in place, which has proven difficult to do (Lewis and Algaoud, 2001; Hassan and Lewis, 2007a).

Where the conventional and Islamic economics literatures coalesce, however, is on the macroeconomic implications of debt. Any optimality of the debt contract in the microeconomic context comes at a cost to the macroeconomic system, where debt and leverage can magnify small economic shocks into larger investment and output fluctuations. Leading contributors to this literature are Sir Ralph Hawtrey (1932, 1950), Irving Fisher (1933) and, more recently, Bernanke and Gertler (1986).

Hawtrey outlined a stock-driven credit-fuelled trade cycle, in which a vicious cycle is set up, a cumulative expansion of production, which is fed and sustained by a continuous expansion of credit. The upswing comes to an end when the credit expansion is discontinued. When credit dries up, a vicious downward spiral ensues, the negative counterpart of the upward spiral. There are big swings of the pendulum in one or the other direction.

Fisher was motivated by events surrounding the Great Depression to argue that the severity of the economic downturn resulted from poorly performing financial markets. What made the economy initially so vulnerable, in Fisher's view, was the high leverage of borrowers in the wake of the prosperity preceding 1929. In his words, 'they [debts] were great enough to not only "rock the boat" but to start it capsizing'. The ensuing business downturn precipitated a wave of bankruptcies, and deflation redistributed wealth from debtors to creditors. Thus he maintained that the downward economic shock was magnified by a debt-deflation transmission mechanism involving, *inter alia*, debt reduction, falling asset prices and reduced net worth, higher interest rate premiums, falling confidence, lower profitability and output, contracting money and credit, and reduced velocity (in effect increased money demand). Fisher calculated that by March 1933, real debt burdens increased by roughly 40 per cent due to the sharp decline in prices and incomes. The fact that this massive deterioration in borrower balance sheets occurred simultaneously with that of output and prices lent credibility in his eyes to the 'debt-deflation' view.

In many ways, Bernanke and Gertler's model provides some formal support for Fisher's debt-deflation story. In the theoretical framework, redistributions between borrowers and lenders trigger impacts upon aggregate real activity. A transfer from debtors to creditors – due, for example, to an unanticipated decline in the price level – weakens debtors' balance sheets and reduces their ability to externally finance investments. Because the ranks of the debtors include those entrepreneurs most efficient at managing investment projects, the redistribution lowers investment and real activity.

All of this is grist for the Islamic mill. But it also resonates in terms of the current crisis. There is no doubt that high leverage among borrowers and banks alike was a striking feature of the housing market and investment banks in the USA. Among US households, the conjunction of low household saving and high investment in housing meant that the 'net acquisition of liabilities' by the household sector ballooned in the 2000s, with US consumer borrowing at 13.4 per cent of disposable income in

2005, more than double the post-Second World War average of 6.25 per cent of disposable income. Not unsurprisingly, the expansion of household borrowing produced a sharp rise in household income gearing (the stock of household debt to personal disposable income) and household interest gearing (the ratio of household interest payments to disposable income). The Federal Reserve's estimates of the household debt service ratio (the ratio of mortgage and consumer debt payments to disposable income) rose sharply after 2002 and reached a record level of 14.5 per cent by the end of 2006, despite mortgage rates remaining at historically low levels for much of this period (Iley and Lewis, 2007).

As for the Wall Street investment banks, the Big Five's leverage, measured by assets as a multiple of equity, jumped from 30:1 in 2002 to 41:1 in 2007, with the banks relying on a constant stream of short-term debt funding to finance their portfolios (Tully, 2008). Much of this increase apparently came after 2004 when the Securities and Exchange Commission eased the rules about the amount of borrowing or gearing up that the Big Five could do (Main, 2009). In addition, Adrian and Shin (2008) find that the Big Five's leverage behaved in a procyclical manner, so that the expansion and contraction of balance sheets amplified, rather than counteracted, the credit cycle. Obviously, leverage can cut both ways. It can greatly magnify earnings during a boom. But if a bank's portfolio is leveraged at 33:1, it takes only a drop of 3 per cent in the value of the portfolio to wipe out the bank's entire capital (Tully, 2008).

Financialization

The Islamic rejection of debt and adherents' preference for participatory PLS modes of financing is seriously undermined by the way Islamic banking has developed. Debt has proved indispensable in Islamic banking and constitutes by far the greater part of the system (Chapra, 2007). It would seem that PLS financing arrangements cannot cater exclusively for the peculiarities of a modern economy which is inherently cast in an interest-based mould. A major challenge facing Islamic finance was to design a more diversified set of interest-free instruments. This challenge was met by adapting permissible trading contracts, originally designed for buying and selling of real goods, for financing purposes. Broadly speaking, the prevailing instruments of interest-free finance along these lines relevant for financing can be divided into three categories: the different buying-and-selling arrangements adapted for credit financing through the process of *ijtihad* in the last three decades such as *murabaha, bai'muajjal, istisnaa*; leasing (rental) operations (*ijara*); and, most recently, Islamic bonds (*sukuk*).

On a strict interpretation there is no scope for interest- or discount-based financing instruments in Islam. Interest, that is any stipulated excess (increase) on the principal amount in money lending, is prohibited. The ideal replacement for interest-based loans is interest-free loans (*qard hasan*) for a charitable cause, and profit-and-loss-sharing arrangements for commercial purposes. Given the teething difficulties of operating PLS contracts in developing economies, however, jurists adapted some contracts for finance that in the classical interpretation were meant for engagement in the real business of buying and selling. Buying and selling and commodity trading are considered different in essence from money-lending (2: 275; 4: 29). For example, *shari'ah* does not object to a *murabaha* arrangement wherein a seller discloses his cost of goods to a buyer and a mark-up is mutually agreed in lieu of profit for the seller. These concepts, combined and adapted for Islamic banking, allow a prospective trader or a potential real-asset purchaser to approach a bank specifying his need for a real good. The bank purchases the asset and on-sells it to him, adding its mark-up covering deferred payment and the risk that it takes in owning the goods between the original purchase and its on-selling to the customer. What makes the transaction Islamically legitimate in *fiqh* is that the bank first acquires the asset for resale at profit, so that a commodity is sold for money and the operation is not a mere exchange of money for money (Wilson, 1983: 84–5). In short, the mark-up is not seen as an additional amount paid on the principal amount of a loan but is in the nature of a profit charged in a trade transaction, with attendant risks attached.

This may sound like interest lending in another guise, but there is an important difference from conventional finance. The growth of financial systems in the West has been described by a number of writers (e.g. Martin, 2002; Stockhammer, 2004; Froud et al., 2006) as driven by what is termed 'financialization'. Financialization can be seen as a process of economic change in which the structure of advanced economies has shifted increasingly towards the provision of financial services and where the value of financial assets greatly exceeds that of tangible assets. One has only to look at the situation in some European countries, where financial claims are multiples of GDP (in the UK four times and Iceland eight times) to appreciate the point. As part of this change, managerial culture and behaviour, corporate governance, executive remuneration and the distribution of income and wealth are all substantially modified by the demands of financial capital. Foster (2007) describes the process of financialization as one in which there is a decoupling of financial activity from productive tangible asset investment:

> Although orthodox economists have long assumed that productive invest-
> ment and financial investment are tied together – working on the simplistic

assumption that the saver purchases a financial claim to real assets from the entrepreneur who then uses the money thus acquired to expand production – this has long been known to be false. There is no necessary direct connection between productive investment and the amassing of financial assets. It is thus possible for the two to be decoupled to a considerable degree.

It is against this backdrop that we note the views of Chapra (2007), who considers that differences do remain between conventional lending and Islamic sales-based financing (via, say, *murabaha* or *ijara*), and that these are important in two respects. First, because the seller of goods (the financier) must legally own and possess the goods being sold, he argues that speculative short-selling is ruled out, helping to curb the type of excessive speculation that takes place and has been so evident recently in conventional financial markets. Second, the sales-based financing methods do not involve direct lending and borrowing, but comprise purchase or lease transactions based on real goods and services. Financing in the Islamic system thus tends to expand *pari passu* with the growth of the real economy, constraining excessive debt and credit creation and limiting one of the causes of instability in the international markets. Stated alternatively, unlike many financial systems in the West, Islamic financial markets are not, as yet, marked by a decoupling of financial activity from tangible asset investment.

RESOLVING THE CRISIS

Islamic precepts on financing are in the way of preventive medicine. The body politic has been made to suffer because of greed (on the part of homeowners, mortgage brokers, originating banks, investment banks doing the securitization, hedge funds and other investors), unwarranted hazard in financial contracts such as option ARMs, excessive speculative trading, poor governance of banks and other institutions, too much leverage and debt, and an explosion of financial activity relative to real tangible investment. On the other hand, if greed can be tempered internally by self-restraint, if mortgage borrowers had fully been aware of their contractual obligations, if speculation and risky trading are forbidden, if religious principles are written into bank supervision and governance, and accountability is to God and the community, if usury is banned and financing based on concrete assets, and if the financial sector does not grow much faster than real activity, then the conditions that arose under conventional financing might have been avoided and, from an Islamic economic perspective, the crisis might not have happened.

Being preventive, rather than prescriptive, medicine carries the corollary that Islamic economics offers few prescriptive insights as to how to get out of the mess. However, to the extent that the stimulus packages involve either printing money or issuing bonds to run budget deficits, Islam does have a view on them.

A strict Islamic interpretation on money would be not to allow its debasement, i.e. target a zero monetary inflation regime permitting a rate of change in money supply only to match with the demand for money. This derivation comes implicitly via analogy (*qiyas*) from the general prohibition in the Holy Qur'an (7: 85; 11: 85; 83: 1–4) of corrupting the standards of weights and measures. A more permissive stance, drawing on Islamic views on taxation, would allow monetary base finance as long as the needy are compensated. However, given the arbitrariness of an inflation tax as well as the absence of transparency in this mode of operation (i.e. what Greenspan, 1966 refers to as hidden confiscation of wealth), the former interpretation is more consistent with Islamic notions. This position does not necessarily rule out the use of monetary finance under circumstances of depression when the immediate inflationary cost is low and there are specific desirable public infrastructure needs. Tahir et al. (1999) would permit monetary finance on the following conditions: (a) exhaustion of all other means of revenue on legitimate expenditure; (b) unsatisfied and pressing needs of a public-good nature (i.e. to assist the poor, defence, debt servicing), (c) stability of money and keeping inflation within acceptable limits.

As to budget deficits in general, in Islam, the Holy Qur'an and *sunnah* constitute the two primary sources from which to seek normative guidance on all matters. Some basic principles and precedents in Islam have a bearing on the issue of budget deficits. The Prophet Muhammad borrowed in both cash and kind in his capacity as the leader of the Muslim community for emergency needs and public purposes. At times, such borrowing was undertaken to repay maturing loans. The main purpose of borrowing was to fulfil the basic needs (livelihood) of those who sought help from Muhammad as well as to strengthen defence against aggression. There was no coercion involved in such borrowings. The borrowing was undertaken on an interest-free basis and there was no instance of repudiation of borrowing; debts incurred were always repaid. Also, the Prophet Muhammad left no outstanding borrowings at the time of his death.

In view of the substantial improvement in public finances subsequent to Muhammad, there is no evidence of borrowing during the reign of the four rightly guided caliphs (Siddiqi, 1996: 77–96). Perhaps for this reason the early Islamic writers on public finance such as Abu Yusuf and Abu Ubayd al-Qasim bin Sallam (774–838 CE) are silent on this issue (Islahi, 2005). The earliest writers to talk about borrowing by the state were Abu

Yala al-Farra (990–1066 CE) and al-Mawardi (974–1058 CE), who saw it as a last resort in very rare circumstances. Their reasons seem to revolve around apprehension that the authorities may either fail to repay the loans or resort to extra taxation to do so (the burden of debt on future generations argument). Nevertheless, public borrowing was seen as permissible should regular income or payments to the *bayt al-mal* (public treasury) be temporarily delayed (Islahi, 2005). In this way the Prophet's 'urgent needs' motive was upheld. Because the *bayt al-mal* did not operate as a central bank, there was no concept of deficit financing by money creation, as can occur in the present era.

Despite these seemingly clear rules, contemporary *shari'ah* scholars have proven adept at using *ijtihad* to come up with certain asset-based debt to finance public expenditure (such as *sukuk*) based on trading, leasing and partnership instruments. While it is not easy to provide outright support or condemnation of many of these instruments by direct reference to the Holy Qur'an or *sunnah*, there can be no doubt that their innovation and use have revolutionized Islamic finance generally and the financing of public expenditures, in particular, posing challenges to public governance that have yet to be resolved (Hassan and Lewis, 2007b, 2007c, Iqbal and Lewis, 2009).

In the meantime, the precedents remain and the ban on fixed interest lies at the core of the Islamic stance. The prohibition of *riba* offers protection against many ills in the modern polity – extravagance, large governments, fiscal illusion, disregard of public opinion, and seizure of political and fiscal flexibility. Fiscal austerity ought to be accepted as a driving force in state financial management, and there should be an emphasis on instituting a sound tax system based on principles of equity. Neither inflation nor borrowing can substitute for it. The solution to the finance of deficits instead is found, on the one hand, in encouraging zero-rate loans that test the inner moral strength and whether an individual really is prepared to help fellow beings in need. On the other hand, there is the permission of PLS arrangements, which pave the way to harness self-interest in the task of general economic development through various public–private partnerships. To sum up, there is inherent in the classical Islamic preference for zero-rate loans and PLS contracts an element of economic sustainability – potential to withstand cyclical ebbs and flows of economy – that neither the interest-based loans nor the buy-and-sell-based *ijtihadi* alternatives offer.

NOTES

1. This chapter has drawn considerably upon the book written with Zafar Iqbal (Iqbal and Lewis, 2009).

2. The Holy Qur'an (1413 AH/1992). In its commentary on this passage, the Presidency of Islamic Researches notes that 'Man' refers to 'unregenerate man, in contrast to those who receive guidance and wage unceasing war with Evil, is ungrateful to his Lord and Cherisher, Him Who created him and sustains him, forgetting or denying Allah and His goodness, by misusing His gifts, or by injustice to His creatures' (p. 1995).
3. In the commentary on this *ayah*, it is noted that 'fear Allah' combined with 'as much as ye can' obviously means: 'lead lives of self-restraint and righteousness'.
4. The commentary amplifies 'all your property you hold in trust, whether it is in your name, or belongs to the community, or to people over whom you have control. To waste is wrong. In ii. 188 the same phrase occurred, to caution us against greed. Here it occurs, to encourage us to increase property by economic use (traffic and trade)' (p. 217).
5. *Surah al-Rum* (ch. 30), verse 39; *Surah al-Nisa* (ch. 39), verse 161; *Surah al-Imran* (ch. 3), verses 130–32; *Surah al-Baqarah* (ch. 2), verses 275–81.
6. According to the National Association of Realtors, banks in 2005 provided 43 per cent of US first-homebuyers with 100 per cent mortgages (Der Hovanesian, 2006).
7. For a recent account see Lewis (2009).

REFERENCES

Adrian, Tobias and H.S. Shin (2008), 'Liquidity, monetary policy, and financial cycles', *Current Issues in Economics and Finance*, **14** (1): 1–7.
Ahmed, Shaghil (1989), 'Islamic banking and finance. A review essay', *Journal of Monetary Economics*, **24**: 157–67.
Ahmed, Z. (1991), *Islam, Poverty and Income Distribution*, Leicester: The Islamic Foundation.
Algaoud, L.M. and M.K. Lewis (1999), 'Corporate governance in Islamic banking: the case of Bahrain', *International Journal of Business Studies*, **7** (1): 56–86.
Allen, Franklin and Andrew Winton (1995), 'Corporate financial structure, incentives and optimal contracting', in R.A. Jarrow, V. Maksimovic and W.T. Ziemba (eds), *Handbooks in Operations Research and Management Sciences*, vol. 9, Amsterdam: Elsevier, pp. 693–721.
Bernanke, Ben S. and Mark Gertler (1986), 'Agency costs, collateral and business fluctuations', National Bureau of Economic Research, Working Paper No. 2015, September.
Chapra, M. Umer (2000), *The Future of Economics: An Islamic Perspective*, Leicester, UK: The Islamic Foundation.
Chapra, M. Umer (2007), 'The case against interest: is it compelling?', *Thunderbird International Business Review*, **49** (2): 161–86.
Das, Satyajit (2008), 'Voodoo banking – finance on steroids', http://news.kontentkonsult. com/2008/12/voodoo-banking-finance-on-steriods.html, accessed 19 February 2009.
Der Hovanesian, Mara (2006), 'Nightmare mortgages', *Business Week*, 11 September pp. 70–81.
Ferguson, Niall (2009), *The Ascent of Money: A Financial History of the World*, London: Penguin Books.
Fisher, Irving (1933), 'The debt-deflation theory of great depressions', *Econometrica*, **1**: 337–57.
Foster, J.B. (2007), 'The financialization of capitalism', *Monthly Review*, **58**: 11, http://www.monthlyreview.org/0407jbf.htm.

Froud, J., S. Johal, A. Leaver and K. Williams (2006). *Financialization and Strategy: Narrative and Numbers*, London: Routledge/Taylor & Francis.

Gale, D. and M. Hellwig (1985), 'Incentive-compatible debt contracts: the one-period problem', *Review of Economic Studies*, **52**: 647–63.

Goodhart, Charles (2008), 'Lessons from the crisis for financial regulation: what we need and what we do not need', *Review*, **78**: 3–4.

Gorton, Gary (2009), 'The subprime panic,' *European Financial Management*, **15** (1): 10–46.

Greenspan, Alan (1966), 'Gold and economic freedom', *The Objectivist*, (July): 96–101.

Harris M. and A. Raviv (1979), 'Optimal incentive contracts with imperfect information', *Journal of Economic Theory*, **21**: 231–59.

Hassan, M. Kabir and M.K. Lewis (eds) (2007a), *The Handbook of Islamic Banking*, Cheltenham, UK and Northampton, MA: Edward Elgar.

Hassan, M. Kabir and M.K. Lewis (2007b), 'Islamic finance: a system at the crossroads?', *Thunderbird International Business Review*, **49** (2): 151–60.

Hassan, M. Kabir and M.K. Lewis (2007c), 'Product development and *shari'a* issues in Islamic finance', *Thunderbird International Business Review*, **49** (3): 281–4.

Hawtrey, Sir Ralph (1932), *The Art of Central Banking*, London: Longmans, Green & Co.

Hawtrey, Sir Ralph (1950), *Currency and Credit*, 4th edn, London: Longmans, Green & Co.

Ibn Khaldun (1332–1406 CE), Abd-ar-Rahman Abu Zayd ibn Muhammad (1967), *An Introduction to History: The Muqaddimah*, trans. from the Arabic by Franz Rosenthal, abridged and edited by N.J. Dawood, London: Routledge & Kegan Paul.

Iley, Richard A. and M.K. Lewis (2007), *Untangling the US Deficit. Evaluating Causes, Cures and Global Imbalances*, Cheltenham, UK and Northampton, MA: Edward Elgar.

Iqbal, Zafar and M.K. Lewis (2009), *An Islamic Perspective on Governance*, Cheltenham, UK and Northampton, MA: Edward Elgar (in press).

Islahi, A.A. (2005), *Contributions of Muslim Scholars to Economic Thought and Analysis* (11–905 AH/632–1500 AD), Jeddah: Scientific Publishing Centre, King Abdulaziz University.

Khan, M. Mansoor and M. Ishaq Bhatti (2008), *Developments in Islamic Banking. The Case of Pakistan*, Basingstoke, UK: Palgrave Macmillan.

Khan, W.M. (1985), *Towards an Interest-Free Islamic Economic System*, Leicester, UK: The Islamic Foundation.

Khan, W.M. (1987), 'Towards an interest-free economic system', in M.S. Khan and A. Mirakhor (eds), *Theoretical Studies in Islamic Banking and Finance*, Houston, TX: Institute for Research and Islamic Studies.

Lewis, M.K. (1994), 'Banking on real estate', in D.E. Fair and R. Raymond (eds), on behalf of the Société Universitaire Européenne de Recherches Financières, *The Competitiveness of Financial Institutions and Centres in Europe*, Dordrecht: Kluwer Academic Press, pp. 47–71.

Lewis, M.K. (2009), 'The origins of the subprime crisis: inappropriate policies, regulations, or both?', *Accounting Forum*, **33** (2): 114–26.

Lewis, M.K. and L.M. Algaoud (2001), *Islamic Banking*, Cheltenham, UK and Northampton, MA: Edward Elgar.

Lewis, M.K. and K.T. Davis (1987), *Domestic and International Banking*, Oxford: Philip Allan and Cambridge, MA: MIT Press.

Lindholm, C. (1996), *The Islamic Middle East: An Historical Anthropology*, Oxford: Blackwell.

Main, Andrew (2009), 'Bankers evolved from agents to risk-takers', *The Australian*, 26 January, p. 20.

Martin, R. (2002), *Financialization of Daily Life*, Philadelphia, PA: Temple University Press.

Nyberg, Lars, M. Persson and M.W. Johansson (2008), 'The financial market turmoil – causes and consequences', *Sveriges Riksbank Economic Review*, 1: 38–48.

Siddiqi, M.N. (1985), *Insurance in an Islamic Economy*, Leicester: The Islamic Foundation.

Siddiqi, M.N. (1996), *Role of the State in the Economy*, Leicester, UK: The Islamic Foundation.

Smirnov, A. (1996), 'Understanding justice in an Islamic context: some points of contrast with Western theories', *Philosophy East and West*, **46** (3): 337–51.

Stockhammer, E. (2004), 'Financialization and the slowdown of accumulation', *Cambridge Journal of Economics*, **28**: 719–41.

Tahir, Sayyid et al. (1999), *IIE's Blueprint of Islamic Financial System including Strategy for Elimination of Riba*, Islamabad, Pakistan: International Institute of Islamic Economics.

Tully, Shawn (2008), 'What's wrong with Wall Street – and how to fix it', *Fortune*, **157** (7): 42–6.

Weber, A.A. (2008), 'Financial market stability', *Review*, **78**: 1–2.

Wessel, David (2008), 'Big banks model is broken and must be fixed in a hurry', *The Australian*, 11 January, p. 22.

Wilson, R. (1983), *Banking and Finance in the Arab Middle East*, London: Macmillan.

11. Bankers gone wild: the Crash of 2008

Robert E. Prasch

'IT' DID HAPPEN AGAIN

By now everyone understands the broad outline of what has occurred. 'It', that is to say a financial crisis on the order of the Great Crash of 1929, has taken place. Banks across the USA, the UK and to a lesser extent in Europe, drawing upon their vast political leverage and touting their superior innovation, economic modeling, and risk-managing skills, pressed for, installed and then took advantage of deregulated and liberalized domestic and international financial markets to drive themselves off a cliff. In general, this would be unobjectionable. The problem is that they did it with other people's money and devastated much of the world's economy in the process. The damage has been so severe that more than a few people, even some of the USA political and media elite, have come to wonder if the performance of Wall Street's top five investment banks really merited the $39 billion in bonuses they awarded themselves for their 'efforts' in 2007. But what of the firms? By the end of 2008 Lehman Brothers was bankrupt, Bear Stearns and Merrill Lynch were forced into sudden and humiliating mergers to avoid bankruptcy, and Morgan Stanley and Goldman Sachs had transformed themselves into bank holding companies so that they could access the ready (and secretive) discount lending facilities of the Federal Reserve System. In short, none of these firms would survive the next year as independent investment banks.

The numbers are most likely familiar to the reader, but let us review them anyway. In the USA alone, and looking only at partial, preliminary and relatively cautious estimates, the losses are breathtaking. They include over $10 trillion in stock market valuations and $7 trillion in home equity. It is (conservatively) projected that over 6 million homes will be foreclosed on by the end of 2010. Credit card writeoffs amounted to $45 billion in 2008 and are projected to rise to well over $100 billion by the end of 2010. The official US unemployment rate, one that is widely understood to be understated, is now (June 2009) at 9.4 percent, and shows every sign of continuing to rise. Finally, the World Bank has provided the most tragic estimate of all: their figures indicate that across 59 developing countries between 200 000 and 400 000 infants (mostly girls) will perish during each of the next several years as an indirect consequence of the financial crisis within the G8 nations (Sabarwal et al., 2009). Was any of this necessary?

For over 30 years the USA, the UK, the International Monetary Fund, the World Trade Organization and the World Bank have severally and collectively led, cajoled and at times forcefully imposed the worldwide acceptance of an economic policy package that they call globalization – but that the rest of the world knows as the Washington Consensus or neoliberalism. Then, as today, there was scant scholarly proof that a policy mix of free trade, liberalized inter- and intra-national capital flows, US-style restrictions on patent and copyright, deregulated product and labor markets, and the widespread privatization of public utilities and other essential government functions enhances either economic growth or stability (Chang, 2003, 2008; Epstein, 2005; Stiglitz, 2002). But the lack of a compelling argument was never an impediment to the adoption of this agenda, so there is no reason to be surprised that it failed to slow its advance. Indeed, the political strategies periodically deployed by its architects indirectly affirm that they knew that this economic program would not be accepted on its presumptive 'merits' (MacArthur, 2000; Klein, 2007).

A most substantial, if somewhat downplayed, aspect of this new policy regime was its unwavering commitment to the deregulation of national and international financial markets. With 30 years of experience to reflect upon, almost everyone who is neither directly nor indirectly (say, through a lavishly funded think tank) on the payroll of the financial services industry has relearned what was once a commonplace understanding of the scholars and policy intellectuals who constructed the Bretton Woods system. This is that unfettered financial markets are inherently unstable, and that financial crises can spread quickly, thereby destroying the 'real economies' of economically interdependent nations (Skidelsky, 2000, chs 7 and 8–10; Helleiner, 1994).

It was both predictable and predicted that our deregulated financial markets would result in one economic crisis after another, accompanied by an endless series of bankruptcies, lender-of-last-resort actions by central banks, and massive direct bailouts of financial institutions by governments. The Savings and Loan fiasco, Mexico's foreign exchange crisis, Russia's boom and collapse, Long-Term Capital Management, the East Asia crisis, the Clinton dot-com bubble, Iceland's fantastic bank crisis, and the still ongoing Crash of 2008 are only a few of the highlights (Baker, 2009; Black, 2005; Lowenstein, 2000; Shiller, 2005; Wade, 2009). What is remarkable about this monumental period of instability is not that it has occurred, but that it has failed to generate sufficient political discontent, much less the political will, to bring about substantive reform. This fact, more than anything else, speaks to the hegemony of the financial services industry over the political imagination of the collective citizenry of the G8 nations, and in particular over the construction of the limited range of ideas that political, financial and media elites are willing to certify as 'responsible' or 'respectable'.

This economic instability, with its periodic bouts of economic destruction and insecurity for the masses of the world's people, who are now, and will remain, employed in the real sector – to say nothing of those who simply hope to hold onto their home or see a pension someday – might have been worth it in the event that faster economic growth, greater equality of income or enhanced opportunity had followed from these policies (Epstein, 2005; Lazonick and O'Sullivan, 2000; Orhangazi, 2008; Stockhammer, 2004; Weisbrot et al., 2006). But, as was predicted, it did not. Since 1980, US and world economic growth have been approximately one percentage point lower than that which reigned during the Bretton Woods era, which spanned from 1945 to 1973. Since 1973, despite ongoing gains in labor productivity, the inflation-adjusted average hourly earnings of Americans has, with a few interruptions, generally trended downwards (Economic Report of the President, 2009, Table B-47). Another alarming and disconcerting trend comes from a well-regarded empirical study of intergenerational economic mobility within the USA. It concludes that it had 'increased from 1950 to 1980, but has declined sharply since 1980' (Aaronson and Mazumder, 2005).

Stated simply, the verdict on neoliberalism in general, and financial deregulation in particular, remains what it ever was: an economic policy of the wealthy, by the wealthy and for the wealthy. That it is supported by politicians whose campaigns and post-political careers are so lavishly supported by the financial sector is a fact that cannot be numbered among the greater mysteries of US or UK politics (Phillips, 2009; 169–74). More distressing is that, at the time of this writing, those who advanced the 'financialization' agenda, and who were its direct and often substantial beneficiaries, have emerged from virtually every crisis with greater political influence. True, they have experienced a few setbacks – such as the bankruptcy of Lehman Brothers or the modest reform known as the Sarbanes–Oxley Act – but at the time of this writing all indications are that the Obama Administration shares the unshakable commitment of its several predecessors that in the event of a crisis the financial sector should be recapitalized and revitalized, rather than reconstituted or reconstructed. There appears to be little understanding (perhaps a wilful misunderstanding?) that the national and international financial system has profound structural flaws. There seems to be little understanding that these flaws necessarily promote widespread instability, a perverse misallocation of productive resources, and lend support to outright corporate misconduct, irresponsibility and fraud. William Black, a former senior bank regulator who is now a professor of law and economics, nicely summarizes the almost-laughable futility of the situation in which we find ourselves: 'We have failed bankers giving advice to failed regulators on how to deal with failed assets. How can it result in anything but failure?' (Black, 2009).

THE BROADER THEORETICAL ISSUES: ASSETS CONSIDERED AS A MARKET

Much of mainstream economics is based on what I have elsewhere called 'the simple exchange story' (Prasch, 2009). This label denotes the presentation of the 'typical' transaction featured in the earliest chapters of introductory economics textbooks. These exchanges are characterized by perfectly informed individuals bartering in a spot market, on their own account, for a commodity with well-understood properties, that they do not need.

This simplistic understanding of the logic of exchange reveals its flaws when it is applied to the market for financial assets, including stocks, bonds, foreign exchange and options, etc. Sensing that it represents an unsatisfactory analogy, the simple exchange story has been modified periodically to introduce assumptions designed to provide something of a fix, although their real purpose is to suppress or elide a coherent sense of time (Currie and Steedman, 1990). For example, it is notorious that everything happens at once in the canonical model of general equilibrium. It is perhaps trivial to observe that this is not an especially useful way to conceptualize the structure of time when one wishes to study a contract exchanging money today for a promise, under specified conditions, of money tomorrow.

The first, and most important, of these 'fixes' for avoiding the problem of time is to assume that all parties to the contract have perfect information. Such an assumption effectively eliminates the importance of time because all contingencies are now known and fully accounted for in every trade. A second fix, only slightly removed from the first, is to assume that the structure of risk, including its mean and variance, are fully known to every market participant. While surprises can occur, such an assumption implies that all contingencies are fully anticipated and priced appropriately. A third fix assumes that every current and future exchange can be costlessly recontracted. Zero costs include no bankruptcy costs. There are variants on each of these approaches, but the themes are as evident as the underlying agenda – through one or another device, the messy idea of time as it is experienced by human beings must be eradicated from consideration. This is essential if mainstream theories and policy nostrums, such as a *laissez-faire* attitude toward financial market regulation, are to be upheld.

Nevertheless, most thinking adults understand that time matters in the 'real world'. If only by intuition, most people understand that assets are quintessentially 'experience goods'. That is to say that, by contrast to 'inspection goods', it is only with the passage of time that we come to understand whether or not it made sense to buy the asset (or item) in question. In many of today's transactions, which are increasingly 'fee' oriented, as in the case of credit default swaps or mortgage- and asset-backed securities, the revenue is booked at the time that the contract is made, but any potential downside is revealed only with the passage of time. Optimistic expectations or, to put it bluntly, a bank running what is in effect – if not in actual intent – a Ponzi scheme (consider the increasingly aggressive lending activities of Washington Mutual or Northern Rock even after it was evident that the real-estate markets had peaked in 2006), will encourage and directly reward their staff for taking on ever-greater quantities of risk while assuming, hoping, or perhaps just not caring, that things will work out in the end. Such a business model can at best be termed 'faith-based banking'.

Even when investors, traders or bankers make a deliberate and sincere effort to anticipate the future, the best that they – or any of us – can do is to put together an 'expectation'. This, as psychologists and behavioral economists have shown, is a very human activity and for that reason often fraught with error (Shiller, 2005). The trivial reason for this is that, despite the assertions of mainstream economic models, we simply do not know the future, we do not know the structure of risk, and we cannot costlessly recontract. Most real human beings are highly conscious of these parameters as they undertake risky activities.

An important implication of the existence of irreducible uncertainty is that even after expectations are formed, they may be held with varying degrees of confidence. John Maynard Keynes called this the 'weight' of our expectation (Keynes, 1936: ch. 12). Stated simply, how readily and upon how much additional evidence will we change any given one of our expectations? Will a modicum of evidence or a mere market rumor induce a reassessment? Or does it require something more substantial? Under some conditions, the collective expectations of investors can be subject to radical recalculation over surprisingly short periods of time, and upon the basis of seemingly inconsequential or trivial information. At other times investors seem to hold an unwavering faith despite the revelation of a series of alarming facts concerning a given class of investments. (Examples would include Russia in the early 1990s or dot-com stocks a few years later.)

That the future is unknown and that expectations have the potential for sudden reversals are conditions that embody important consequences for asset markets, especially those with a high degree of liquidity – as is the case for many financial markets. High liquidity means that changes in expectations will be rapidly reflected in the price of the underlying assets. If a firm has borrowed against the (presumed) value of these assets, it will be forced to turn elsewhere for the financing it requires to support these loans, at least until it can 'unwind' these positions. This latter move often means selling the underlying assets into distressed markets, which could threaten the viability of the bank or enterprise. In the event of a financial crisis, not knowing which of its counterparties are, or are not, struggling to stay afloat in the turbulence of a declining market has, as we have seen over the last year or two, profound and dire implications for the quantity and price of lending between banks, and between banks and business firms or individuals. This type of concern has clearly contributed to the severity of the current credit crisis (Rosengren, 2009, especially figures 4 and 5).

HYMAN MINSKY'S CONTRIBUTION TO ECONOMIC THEORY AND POLICY

Throughout his career, but especially during the 1980s, Hyman Minsky wrote several important books that cut against the grain of what was then the conventional wisdom of the economics profession (Minsky, 1982, 1986). To understand the extremes of Minsky's heresy, we must recall that by the early 1980s the mainstream of economists could not imagine, much less consider, the idea that financial markets were anything but a paragon of 'rational expectations'. According to this theory, the only appropriate way to model the knowledge of economic agents was to suppose that (1) they had access to all available information of interest or concern to anyone operating in any given market, and (2) that all agents could identify and understand the 'true' economic model underlying economic relationships. Accepting these assumptions, mainstream economists deduced that markets 'must have' strong tendencies to achieve a stable equilibrium at prices accurately reflecting underlying economic relationships, including supplies, demands and the state of technology. That such propositions failed numerous empirical tests, to say nothing of common sense or the 'grin test', was never considered to be a point against them.

Minsky, by contrast, was then advancing the argument that financial markets were inherently unstable. Moreover, markets could only hope to achieve some semblance of stability only in the event that they were supervised by an alert and engaged government with extensive regulatory capacity, and the ability to provide adequate aggregate demand in a timely and targeted fashion in the event of financial turmoil (Minsky, 2008 [1986], chs 12–13). In light of trends then dominating the economics profession and politics more generally, it is an understatement to say that Minsky's work was found to be unacceptable. Nevertheless, he did gain a following among those economists who placed considerations of accuracy and knowledge ahead of career.[1]

Minsky's work was broad ranging, falling largely into three categories. The first was an in-depth critique of mainstream economic theory. In several places, but most completely in his *Stabilizing an Unstable Economy*, he criticized the then-dominant 'neoclassical synthesis', including that theory's application to the understanding and regulation of financial markets, and its role in the consequent failure to maintain economic stability or full employment. Second was his reformulation of economic theory along lines initially pioneered by John Maynard Keynes and Michal Kalecki. Of particular interest was that his reconstituted economic theory was explicitly designed to include the changes that occur to the balance sheets of business firms making forward-oriented decisions to invest in fixed assets such as plant, equipment, inventories or distribution networks. He placed particular emphasis on the fact that the purchase and installment of fixed productive assets implied that profit-seeking firms were, of necessity and simultaneously, undertaking risky liability structures. His third contribution was to sketch the contours of how economic policy should be reconstituted in light of his reformulation of economic theory. In particular, he stressed the importance of the absolute level of prices in a world of interlinked liabilities and debt contracts. He emphasized that he was not opposed to markets, and that he appreciated their important role in the distribution of products and the preservation of a free society, but he dismissed the notion that markets in general and financial markets in particular could be counted upon to be self-regulating. Neither did he believe that they should be exclusively permitted to establish or manage our most important social objectives and commitments:

> The general view sustained by the following analysis is that while the market mechanism is a good enough device for making social decisions about unimportant matters such as the mix of colors in the production of frocks, the length of

skirts, or the flavors of ice cream, it cannot and should not be relied upon for important, big matters such as the distribution of income, the maintenance of economic stability, the capital development of the economy, and the education and training of the young. (Minsky, 2008 [1986]: 112)

But Minsky's most important and – to economists working in the classical and neoclassical traditions – most heretical idea was that an extended period of economic stability was itself an independent cause of economic instability (Minsky, 1986: chs 7–9; Wray, 2008). Think about it. Minsky was not simply denying the proposition that markets were able to bring about stability from a position of instability. He was affirming the direct opposite. He proposed that even in the event that we could begin with a free market system in a state of stability, this condition would itself be sufficient, on its own, to bring about instability. Rather than self-stabilizing, financial markets were self-destabilizing.

The core of Minsky's argument was that a period of prolonged stability would modify the expectations of underwriters and creditors (commercial and investment banks, finance companies, insurance companies etc.). Revised expectations, working in conjunction with competitive pressures, would induce profit-seeking firms to engage in ever-more risky financial transactions. The reason is that during tranquil and relatively prosperous periods firms are pleased to discover that the default rate on risky assets is lower than predicted by their (historically based) models. With their recent financial decisions validated by apparent success, financial firms and individuals come to reassess their understanding and estimation of the risks they face. Specifically, they come to believe that transactions or positions that they once perceived to be overly risky should be reclassified as acceptable risks, and what they once classified as a marginally acceptable risk should be reclassified as overly cautious, etc. Competition and rivalry among firms for access to financing, revenues with which to compensate senior staff, profits for investors, and the ever-present rivalry over market share each and severally accelerates this tendency to reassess and reclassify risk during extended periods of market tranquillity. Those banks or financial institutions that are quickest to reassess risk, and act on their revised understanding, will be the first to reap rewards (Minsky, 1986: chs 9 and 10).[2]

Over the short period, these higher returns will raise the firm's stated performance. This, in turn, leads to higher reported profits and readier (and cheaper) access to financing in commercial paper, bond and equity markets. An immediate consequence is that the bank will see its earnings and price per share rise. This, in turn, readily translates into larger bonuses for middle- and upper-level employees, and simply wonderful bonuses for senior executives. Financial journalists and mainstream economists will fall over each other to tout these rewards as well-deserved compensation for innovation and risk-taking that 'must be' making the economy more efficient and productive (Frank, 2000; Cassidy, 2002).

Throughout the ages economists have argued that remunerative activities will be repeated and imitated by others. It follows that, after a lapse of time, the higher profits that initially accrue from any financial innovation will be reduced with the inevitable expansion of the volume of business and the entry of competitors and imitators. Banks and other financial institutions, especially those trading with other people's money, will wish to protect their superior return on equity performance by seeking out the 'next new thing', which, in all likelihood, will be an even riskier innovation, often one that is poorly understood by investors and perhaps even by the management of the firm. Sadly, many of these highly touted 'innovations' are really, in an important sense, not at all innovative. When one gets past the specifics and takes a broader look, it is too often the case that many of them were simply variations on the age-old financial practice of taking on ever-greater leverage, that is to say taking on a very high debt-to-equity ratio so that the firm could purchase a greater number of earning assets. The downside, of course, is that a firm holding 33 or more dollars of assets for each dollar of equity will be effectively bankrupt in the event that the assets they have purchased fall by only 3 percent in value. Nevertheless, when such highly leveraged positions are validated by apparent success, the competitive process will again whittle away profit margins as more and more firms come to imitate the strategy. This means that, once again, even more risky positions must be undertaken if the firm's return-on-equity targets are to be met, and on it goes. Absent the intervention of a regulator, there can be little doubt as to how such a process will end. But that it will end is a certainty, the only question is the exact date of the disaster.

Simply observing that in a world of perfect information and perfect competition financial institutions should understand the risks they are undertaking neglects the critical role of time and competitive pressures in decision-making. In an increasingly fee-driven market for banking and financial services, reward makes itself evident well before downside of any given level of risk.[3] As a matter of pure theory, or what I sometimes call 'blackboard economics', after a bank or finance company subtracts its costs from its revenues it is left with a sum that is partially profit and partially a risk premium. The problem is that in the 'real world' it is far from evident which proportion should be attributed to each category, and human nature is such that there is a clear bias toward minimizing the portion perceived to be a risk premium that needs to be set aside in a loan-loss reserve. Throughout the recent bubble it is evident that firms were booking what were essentially risk premiums as profit and then distributing it as dividends, bonuses and other payments. As intimated, the exact proportion of a firm's after-cost revenue that should be ascribed to profit or the risk premium can be readily ascertained on a blackboard, but less easily calculated in the proverbial 'real world', especially one in which short-term success tends to draw in investors to the firm, and facilitates outsized rewards for senior management.

At least initially, many financial innovations appear to be ingenious ideas delivering supernormal profits without enhancing the firm's risk profile. The firm's leadership, its public relations department, inside and outside financial economists, and a generally 'bullish' financial press can be counted upon, in the main, to trumpet 'the good news' of the firm's genius for financial innovation. As the super-profits roll in, average opinion finds that its initial assessment has been affirmed and reaffirmed, and for that reason validated. Against this juggernaut of apparent success – success amply marinated in self-interest – inside and outside analysts, regulators, and media pundits must be exceptionally brave to sound an alarm, much less push for decisive action. Regulators are especially exposed as they will get little support from the elected politicians who are keen to receive 'generous' contributions from these firms to fund their re-elections or hire them into lucrative post-political careers in the financial services industry (Black, 2005; Prasch, 2007; Swan, 2009).[4]

Of course, to the mainstream of economic thought, the neutralization or suborning of the political and regulatory system is not a concern – on the contrary, it is generally welcomed. The reason is that mainstream economists have long supposed that the most effective and efficient controls of financial excesses are external to the firm but internal to the market system. In the absence of regulatory checks on the part of a firm's management, it is argued that the self-interested integrity of credit-rating agencies and market analysts, or the equally self-interested trading decisions of counterparties and risk-arbitrageurs, should each and severally be more than sufficient to check any tendency on the part of a firm or any set of firms to undertake more risk than they can manage. The market, working as suggested by the textbooks, is the true source of the 'checks and balances' required to manage the financial system.

By contrast to the above narrative, Minsky's sense of history and politics is too astute to overlook the fact that regulators – be they internal, external or working for government agencies – will be subject to a wide range of pressures to approve financial innovations or understate their risk to the firm and the system as a whole. Sadly, mainstream economists commonly misunderstand the relationship of prominent firms, including financial firms, to the laws or regulations of a democratic polity. John Q.

Citizen faces the choice of obeying or disobeying the law. By contrast, a prominent firm faces a threefold choice: obey the law; disobey the law (often at the cost of lengthy litigation followed by a fairly modest civil penalty in which 'no guilt is acknowledged'); or act to get the law modified or repealed (Prasch, 2004). A highlight of the second approach would be the bi-partisan Congressional vote to release the major US telecom firms from all civil liability for participating in the surveillance program that President George W. Bush initiated seven months before 9/11. A highlight of the third would be the repeal of Glass–Steagall after an extended period of partial repeals through rule-changes quietly undertaken by the Federal Reserve. Other examples include the Financial Services Modernization Act (1999), the Commodity Futures Modernization Act (2000), the appointment of political hacks and industry lobbyists to key regulatory agencies, the defunding and demoralizing of those same agencies, or the 'capture' of regulators who are almost always subject to tempting job offers in the industries they regulate. Such maneuvers may appear less crass if their opponents allow themselves to become 'caught up' in the excessively bullish conventional wisdom of the time. This latter process is greatly facilitated by the intellectuals of 'think tanks' or academe who, in exchange for direct compensation, consulting fees or 'research' grants, can be counted upon to tirelessly and relentlessly advance the Panglossian message that 'whatever the market does, is always and everywhere for the best'.

SOME UNIQUE QUALITIES OF THE SUBPRIME CRISIS

While the Crash of 2008 shares many qualities of earlier financial crises, it also has several unique characteristics. One is the organization of the US mortgage market. Under the (relatively) recent innovation now known as the 'originate and distribute' model of mortgage lending, finance companies and banks have earned the bulk of their profits from the fees they charge to originate and service loans. This is distinct from the older model, as exemplified by the classic Jimmy Stewart movie *It's a Wonderful Life*, where a building and loan bank drew upon its close relationships with the savers and homeowners of a community to assess the underlying risk of the loans that it originated and kept on its books to maturity. These loans were supported by the passbook savings of other community members. In this earlier, and increasingly antiquated, model of mortgage lending profits were dependent upon the 'spread' between the interest paid on passbook savings and the rate charged for the mortgage. Risk was minimized in two ways: first, by issuing loans to worthy borrowers with good underlying collateral; and second, by means of the bank owner's and manager's reputation in the community as a person of unimpeachable character and conservative values who would be an unquestionable guardian of the savings entrusted to him (and it was almost always a 'him'). After the New Deal reforms, the reputation of bank owners and managers was directly enhanced by government-directed programs that insured the deposits of most small and medium depositors.

In today's 'originate and distribute' model of lending, the earnings based on the interest rate 'spread' are increasingly irrelevant as mortgage lenders look increasingly to profit from the fees generated by the processes of originating and servicing housing debt, including debts from the original mortgage and second mortgages, such as the increasingly popular home equity loans. Under such a reward structure, it is not hard to see that maximizing fee income implies that traders, bankers and bank executives will come to develop a business model biased toward maximizing the quantity of underlying fee-driven activity. An unsurprising consequence is that increasingly less attention will be paid to the underlying quality of the mortgage loans generated in such a process.[5] Early in the boom this neglect occurred because of an expectation that this debt would be passed on to others. Later in the boom, banks were increasingly likely to hold on to the 'super senior' tranches of the CDOs they created (Tett, 2009: ch. 13). In addition, to enhance liquidity in the commercial paper markets, many banks issued lines of credit to the SIVs that they had created off of their balance sheets to buy, hold and manage bundled asset-based securities and other risky assets.[6] When these commercial paper markets dried up in the summer and fall of 2007, commercial banks found that they were, suddenly and unexpectedly, obliged to make good on these lines of credit. Not having anticipated this eventuality, and for that reason not having set aside adequate reserves, they suddenly found themselves overstretched. Worse yet, as there was a minimal market for these asset-backed securities, any 'forced sale' would take place at prices that would make the banks insolvent. This, in short, was how a liquidity problem came to be a solvency problem. Moreover, it is not a solvency problem that might soon resolve itself after a recovery in the value of the underlying housing assets, as the collapse of the housing bubble and the consequent decline in US incomes has raised the default rate on subprime and even prime mortgage loans (Kregel, 2007, 2008a, 2008b; Wray, 2008).

One mystery is why some financial institutions, such as Citigroup or AIG, would retain or even purchase so much of the 'super senior' tranches of the CDOs created out of these subprime mortgages. In some instances it appears to be because the (*ex ante*) perceived risk on these assets was so low that it did not make sense to sell them. This view may have been bolstered as banks increasingly came to believe in their own genius for creating financial innovations that dissipated risk. Another explanation was that some banks thought that they would sell these assets eventually; they failed to understand that the reason that the market for such assets was slow was that buyers were beginning to sense a problem. Acting as if they wished to compound the problem, some institutions, such as Citibank, issued 'liquidity puts' for buyers. These obliged banks to receive troubled assets back onto their books in the event that the market was tanking. As with the lines of credit, no reserves had been set aside for such an eventuality, so there was no 'cushion of safety' to absorb the losses from such a contingency (Tett, 2009).

As we have seen, under the modern 'originate and distribute' model of mortgage lending, banks faced a peculiar, one might even say perverse, set of incentives. Payment for short-period performance enhanced the problem as it rewarded and encouraged the myopia that has long been an inherent quality of financial markets (Crotty, 2008; Epstein, 2005; Orhangazi, 2008). The consequence was something akin to organized irresponsibility. That misconduct and even fraud were to emerge should not be too surprising.

THE NEUTRALIZATION OF THE MARKET'S 'GATEKEEPERS'

The 'Efficient Markets' Theory

According to a longstanding tradition in economic thought – one that has persisted through the classical, neoclassical and neoclassical synthesis schools – market economies are self-correcting. While different economists and different schools have periodically debated the speed at which market economies could adjust to a stable, full-employment equilibrium, and whether or not it made sense to wait that long, that such a position exists and that the price system would bring about such an adjustment was not subject to question. Relative prices guide this adjustment in the goods market, interest rates guide the financial markets, and relative wages guide the labor markets. The balance of trade is assured by changes in the exchange rate. The fact that the economic system is not in balance at any given moment is explained by the existence of 'exogenous shocks' and 'adjustment lags', with the latter being, notoriously, 'long and variable'.

By the mid-1970s many economists had come to believe that, by contrast to the markets for goods, services and labour, financial markets could be supposed to be highly 'efficient'. That is to say that the prices prevailing in financial markets at any given juncture were the best possible reflection of the 'true' value of the underlying assets. This idea depends on the existence and free play of 'smart money' and the market's rapid adjustment to equilibrium. Formalized, this idea came to be known as the 'theory of rational expectations'.

Speculation is not Arbitrage

This brings us to an important error made by too many economists. This is a tendency to look upon speculation as a form of arbitrage and, on the basis of this analogy, announce that it is inherently benign, even a force for good. But the underlying analogy is flawed. Arbitrage, to review, is a trade across space or different markets. So if grain is selling for a higher price in market A than in market B, then an arbitrageur can earn a virtually risk-free profit by simultaneously buying in market B and selling in market A. The only substantial risk such a trader undertakes is that a counterparty may fail to meet their obligations.

By contrast, speculation is an exchange that takes place over time. That is to say that a firm buys or sells an asset at time A with the intention of selling or buying it for a profit at time B. Because the future is uncertain, it should be evident that the risk undertaken by a speculator is qualitatively different. For this reason arbitrage is not speculation and vice versa. Treating, and regulating, speculation as if it were merely a form of arbitrage substantially misses the point and ignores the systemic risk, and consequent misallocation of productive resources, that can occur in the event that financial markets come to be dominated by speculation. This misallocation occurs in the upswing, but is most painfully evident in the economic turmoil that occurs in the wake of a crash.

Does the 'Smart Money' Correct Prices?

A cherished belief of mainstream economics that is implicit in the error described above is that any 'market anomaly' in the form of 'incorrect' prices or quantities can and will be readily traded away through the self-interested actions of 'better-informed' market actors in search of easy profits. This is the time-honored role of what is conventionally called the 'smart money'. Indeed, the existence and self-interested action of this smart money is, as may be evident, critical to the claim that a free market economy – and especially its financial sector – is self-correcting and self-stabilizing. The corollary is, of course, that such a system neither needs nor desires intervention by government regulators (Galbraith, 2008; Prasch,

2008, conclusion). But our repeated experience with financial markets over the past 30 years forces us to ask whether the smart money is really engaged in stabilizing the market system.

Why the 'Smart Money' may also be Destabilizing

In a most insightful chapter on the subject of expectations formation and the organization of asset markets, John Maynard Keynes argued that unless traders are operating independently with their own funds, they will soon discover that it is difficult to take a contrarian position in the financial markets. He gave several reasons to support his conclusion.

One was the outlook and disposition of the vast majority of traders:

> It needs *more* intelligence to defeat the forces of time and our ignorance of the future than to beat the gun. Moreover, life is not long enough; – human nature desires quick results, there is a peculiar zest in making money quickly, and remoter gains are discounted by the average man at a very high rate. (Keynes, 1936; 157; italics original)

While such *bon mots* on the human condition are interesting, and have been verified by behavioral economists, his case does not rest solely upon them. On the contrary, Keynes made a *structural* argument for the institutionalization and dominance of myopic investing. Alarmingly, the structures supporting myopia that he identified over 70 years ago are even more dominant today.

A crucial consideration is whether the trader works for himself or for others. Specifically, is he trading with other people's money? The reason for this question is that employees or agents investing other people's money will soon discover that their performance will be compared with that of others. Contrarian investing, if it is an idea with any meaning at all, implies accepting the substantial chance that for several short periods our (presumably 'smart' or better-informed) trader will underperform his or her peers. It is reasonable to expect that this observable underperformance will induce a degree of unease or nervousness among members of the board to whom the trader reports (or outside investors if the trader is the manager of a fund). Since our hypothetical example supposes that these board members or outside investors are less informed or 'smart' than the person they have hired to manage their portfolio, they might be forgiven for wondering if the maverick they have hired really will win out in the end. Human nature, self-interest and a fairly normal degree of risk aversion will likely induce them to become impatient before too long, and our insightful but contrarian trader will find him- or herself without a portfolio to manage, perhaps even out of a job. Keynes makes the case rather succinctly: 'an investor who proposes to ignore near-term market fluctuations needs greater resources for safety and must not operate on so large a scale, if at all, with borrowed money . . ..' His conclusion captures another insightful aspect of how groups come to judge contrarians:

> For it is the essence of his behaviour that he should be eccentric, unconventional and rash in the eyes of average opinion. If he is successful, that will only confirm the general belief in his rashness; and if in the short run he is unsuccessful, which is very likely, he will not receive much mercy. Worldly wisdom teaches that it is better for reputation to fail conventionally than to succeed unconventionally. (Keynes, 1936: 157–8)

In light of the above, it should not surprise us that the most important 'contrarian' investors of our era tend to be individuals who have sufficient wealth to trade largely on their own account. George Soros and Warren Buffett come readily to mind. Usually, those making purchase and sale decisions feel that they cannot act with such a level of independence. Even someone as prominent and powerful as the CEO of Citigroup, Charles Prince, indicated that he felt highly constrained by market conditions and the conventional wisdom: 'As long as the music is still playing, we are still dancing – and the music is still playing' (Tett, 2009: 148).

What of Gatekeepers such as the Credit-Rating Agencies?

The above argument that financial markets can be expected to be 'efficient' depends upon a second longstanding tenet of mainstream economic thinking – although this idea has a greater merit. It is the proposition that persistent market failures (such as the misrepresentation of the quality of a product or service) create an incentive to develop a solution in the form of new norms of behavior, or even the establishment of a formal institution that itself earns an income by improving the efficiency of the market. If self-interested firms caught up in the competitive pressures of the marketplace have a tendency to engage in myopic behavior by selling bonds that are riskier than represented, then an opportunity is created. Seeing an opportunity, credit-rating firms will emerge who will make it their business to present a disinterested perspective on the value of these bonds. Such agencies will, one might suppose, succeed or fail on the basis of their reputation for providing accurate assessments of risk.

But we now know that disinterested ratings have been increasingly less likely to emerge from the ratings process. The reason is that over the past several decades the business of rating bonds has undergone dramatic changes. Regrettably, these changes have compromised the capacity of these agencies to act as independent evaluators, thereby diminishing their value as market gatekeepers. As with the housing bubble, this unfortunate outcome was both predictable and predicted (Partnoy, 1999, 2006; Muolo and Padilla, 2008, ch. 12). What happened?

Thirty years ago, those firms that the Securities and Exchange Commission identified as Nationally Recognized Statistical Rating Organizations (NRSROs) earned their relatively modest, but comfortable, incomes by formulating and selling ratings to prospective bond buyers. Depending on buyers for their incomes, firms such as Moody's, Standard & Poor's and Fitch had a clear incentive to assess the quality of these assets accurately. This is not to say or imply that they always got it right, but rather that one could reasonably suppose that what economists call 'incentive alignment' existed between these firms and their clients – the aforementioned buyers of bonds.

That was then, but this is now. For a variety of reasons that need not detain us, by the mid-1990s these agencies had come to be increasingly in the business of rating the quality of debt at the behest of underwriters – the banks. Competing with one another for the lucrative repeat patronage of the major banks issuing the bulk of the new mortgage- and asset-backed securities and other increasingly exotic financial instruments induced the NRSROs to give ever-higher ratings to these assets. They were materially assisted in this effort by the increasing complexity of these assets and the fact that, as innovations, there was little solid historical data available with which to rate prospective performance. Indeed, because of the uncertainty surrounding the underlying value of these assets and the absence of organized markets, buyers and even regulators came to be increasingly reliant on the evaluations of the NRSROs to assess risk or – in the case of regulators – make determinations of capital adequacy (Partnoy, 2006).

As ratings came to be more important to the banks, and repeat patronage in an increasingly competitive environment came to be more important to the NRSROs (who by this time had all abandoned their partnership structure to become publicly traded corporations), the latter firms became much more profitable and much more subject to systemic bias. Indeed, there is evidence that major banks were openly 'ratings shopping' among the agencies. But it would be a stretch to suggest that the agencies were aggressively resisting these pressures. Indeed, in a move seemingly designed to compound these already-powerful conflicts of interest, ratings agencies set up consulting branches to work with bond issuers to devise the optimal structure of debt, and thereby enhance the assigned rating. While the ratings agencies would like us to believe that this new business model embodied creative 'synergies' that added value, it would now seem that what was being exploited was a substantial and irresolvable conflict of interest (Partnoy, 2006; Muolo and Padilla, 2008: ch. 12).

Indeed, after incorporation, it would not be inaccurate to suggest that NRSROs had a fiduciary responsibility to their shareholders to maximize profits by every legal means. This tendency has been compounded by the position taken by the NRSROs, one thus far upheld by the courts, that their ratings are a form of 'journalism' and for that reason represent 'protected speech'. Such an argument, so long as it is accepted, protects the NRSROs from lawsuits claiming damages from the biased ratings that follow from a flawed business model. Frank Partnoy has argued that this ruling must be changed if these agencies are to fulfill their role as disinterested intermediaries (Partnoy, 2006).

The theory that financial markets are self-stabilizing depends upon the self-interest of individuals and firms, the existence of 'smart money' to correct deviations from correct underlying values, and the emergence of intermediary institutions to correct market failures that may emerge as a consequence of inadequate information or other systemic faults. As this section has illustrated, there are substantial reasons to believe that these either do not or cannot exist. We have also seen that intermediary institutions such as credit-rating agencies can be compromised by major clients. At one time, in the early 1930s, this was well understood. The problem has not been a lack of experience or understanding; it is rather that the banks never accommodated themselves to the regulatory structure of the New Deal and have worked for years to undermine it (Helleiner, 1994). By the 1980s they had succeeded, and we are now paying the price for that success.

CONCLUSION

As the reader most likely knows, the ratings agencies were far from the only instance of institutional failure. Failures occurred in the political and regulatory process. Both major parties came to be 'captured' by Wall Street interests and as a consequence we saw a bi-partisan effort to deregulate the financial sector in exchange for campaign contributions and lucrative speakers' fees and 'consulting' jobs for politicians who have rotated out of office. The Federal Reserve under its much-vaunted 'maestro' Chairman Alan Greenspan failed in its most basic function – to protect Americans from a systemic financial collapse. The Securities and Exchange Commission, also 'captured' by Wall Street, failed to perform its most elementary task as a watchdog. Indeed, it allowed rule-changes that enabled investment banks to work with breathtaking degrees of leverage. It also looked the other way while multiple Ponzi schemes emerged and fleeced Americans of their wealth. With a few noteworthy exceptions, the business press has failed to keep voters and investors properly informed of important trends and risks in the financial system. The only agency that we might completely exonerate from blame is the Office of the Comptroller of the Currency. Ostensibly, it is in charge of overseeing federally chartered commercial banks. But since there is little record of it ever having provided such oversight, we cannot be disappointed by its neglect of its official duties.

Detailing the specific failures of each of these institutions would require a treatise, and I do not doubt that several are now being written. But lest we lose hope in our fellow man, let us recall that there were also many instances of individuals, or even small groups of individuals, with a sense of integrity and intellectual honesty who, often at great risk to their own careers and incomes, 'did the right thing' and directed our attention, or the attention of their firms' management, to the alarming trends and mounting risks. It is now evident that they were unable to make much of an impact on the collective psyche or the political institutions of the nation. Some of them were dismissed from their jobs, and few of them are recognized today. Even fewer of them have been asked to participate in the reconstructing of our financial system.

NOTES

1. It has been a longstanding presumption of liberal political theory that ignorance on the part of some portion of the citizenry or elite opinion can be addressed through 'education' or 'conversation'. This is a flawed view. As in all human societies and organizations, knowledge is filtered through power, access and interest. Unfortunately, the conventional perspective ignores what philosopher Slavoj Žižek calls a 'will to ignorance'. The point, as most good propagandists and advertisers know, is that there is an essential difference between an 'excuse to believe' and a 'compelling argument'. When important economic, political, ethnic, or religious interests are at stake, 'an excuse to believe' backed by sums of money large enough to provide constant repetition is usually enough to validate an action taken for less than publicly minded reasons.
2. Minsky's understanding of this profit-driven push toward instability is nicely affirmed in a recent book by *Financial Times* journalist Gillian Tett (Tett, 2009), although it was no part of her agenda. Her history recounts how the swaps department at J.P. Morgan developed many of the derivatives that were so critical to the subprime boom, but also how the relatively risk-averse corporate culture of J.P. Morgan meant that the firm was not inclined to use these new tools to ramp up risk (and thereby its annual return on equity). The consequence was that throughout the latter 1990s, J.P. Morgan appeared to underperform most of the banks that it considered to be its peers. The, almost inevitable, end was that the firm allowed itself to be essentially taken over by Chase Manhattan Bank. To Wall Street of the late 1990s, Chase Manhattan looked like a bank that 'clearly understood' the 'new economy' and for that reason was a 'top performer'. Soon after the merger, many of Chase's most important clients, including Enron, Global Crossing and Worldcom, were revealed to have been major accounting frauds and spectacular business failures. Of course, by that time it was too late to point out that the former J.P. Morgan had taken a prudent strategy during the previous frenzy, and that while it was highly

profitable during those years, it only appeared to have been underperforming against its peers as it had steered clear of some (but not all) of the greatest excesses of that time (Tett, 2009: chs 3–5).

3. Post-Keynesian economists stress the importance of Frank Knight's concept of 'uncertainty', which refers to a subset of risks that are known to exist, but whose mean and variance are unknown and most likely unknowable. So, for example, the (very small) chance of my earning the Nobel memorial prize in economics is not readily subject to calculation in the same way that I might calculate the possibility of my drawing the Queen of Hearts from a fair deck of cards. The importance of this distinction for understanding financial markets is, of course, both legitimate and important. However, in the text I am making a somewhat different and perhaps somewhat obvious – but necessary – point. Christian Schmidt's edited volume provides an interesting and insightful overview of how the issues of risk and uncertainty have been handled throughout the history of economic thought (Schmidt, 1996).

4. In light of what is now so painfully evident about the risk/reward profile of so many of these loans and other derivatives, it would appear that the *ex ante* risk premiums that should have been assessed would have left the expected profitability of many of these financial assets significantly less than zero. In short, there was no economic rationale for many of these transactions, as there was so little chance that the underlying positions would actually pay off. When one observes the persistence of profoundly ill-advised behavior in a financial market, behavior that repeatedly works to the systemic advantage of decision-makers, one has at least to entertain the possibility that these decision-makers, no matter how influential or admired by the community, may actually be engaged in fraud. Knowing whether or not serious fraud was a factor during the recent boom in mortgage-backed securities would require a proper and detailed investigation. It is evident, however, that the Obama Administration is simply unwilling to entertain such an idea. Or is it, as several wags have suggested, that the system as a whole has become 'too Ponzi-like to prosecute'?

5. Early in the crisis we were repeatedly told that 'No one saw this coming'. While demonstratively false, such claims are useful as they establish the guilt of all, and thereby support the idea that no one in particular is responsible or culpable. It follows that having the public believe that 'no one saw it coming' is very important to the well-being and income of a number of very prominent and influential people. Of course a substantial number of people did, in fact, see this debacle coming and some of them were brave, naïve, or foolish enough to say so out loud. Those within banks were either silenced or, if they persisted, dismissed. Those outside of banks were patronized or ignored. This, of course, is to be expected as the marginalization and silencing of dissenting voices is a normal and routine aspect of financial bubbles. The reason is that bubbles must be accompanied by a narrative that rationalizes or justifies what is clearly implausible if they are to persist. When someone within or without a bank makes a claim that flies in the face of the pecuniary interest of a number of well-placed persons – and the perceived or anticipated pecuniary interest of many more – there is a strong tendency, really a need, to see to it that their ideas do not attract attention. Too much is at stake and self-interest, in this case collective self-interest, is more than adequate to ensure a more or less coordinated response.

6. See Richard J. Rosen (2007) for a useful and brief overview of the terminology of modern mortgage markets.

REFERENCES

Aaronson, Daniel and Bhashkar Mazumder (2005), 'Intergenerational economic mobility in the U.S., 1940 to 2000', Working Paper 2005-12. Chicago, IL: Federal Reserve Bank of Chicago.

Baker, Dean (2009), *Plunder and Blunder: The Rise and Fall of the Bubble Economy*, Sausalito, CA: PoliPointPress.
Black, William K. (2005), *The Best Way to Rob a Bank is to Own One: How Corporate Executives and Politicians Looted the S&L Industry*, Austin, TX: University of Texas Press.
Black, William K. (2009), 'The lessons of the savings-and-loan crisis', Barron's interview, 13 April, available at http://online.barrons.com/article/ SB123940701204709985.html?page=sp.
Cassidy, John (2002), *dot.con: The Greatest Story Ever Sold*, New York: HarperCollins.
Chang, Ha-Joon (2003), *Kicking Away the Ladder: Development Strategy in Historical Perspective*, London: Anthem Press.
Chang, Ha-Joon (2008), *Bad Samaritans: The Myth of Free Trade and the Secret History of Capitalism*, New York: Bloomsbury Press.
Crotty, James (2008), 'Structural causes of the global financial crisis: a critical assessment of the "new financial architecture"', Working Paper No. 180, Political Economy Research Institute, Amherst, MA: University of Massachusetts.
Currie, Martin and Ian Steedman (1990), *Wrestling with Time: Problems in Economic Theory*, Ann Arbor, MI: University of Michigan Press.
Economic Report of the President (2009), available at http://www.gpoaccess.gov/ eop.
Epstein, Gerald (ed.) (2005), *Financialization and the World Economy*, Cheltenham, UK and Northampton, MA: Edward Elgar.
Frank, Thomas (2000), *One Market Under God: Extreme Capitalism, Market Populism, and the End of Economic Democracy*, New York: Doubleday.
Galbraith, James K. (2008), *The Predator State: How Conservatives Abandoned the Free Market and Why Liberals Should Too*, New York: Free Press.
Helleiner, Eric (1994), *States and the Reemergence of Global Finance: From Bretton Woods to the 1990s*, Ithaca, NY: Cornell University Press.
Keynes, John Maynard (1964 [1936]), *The General Theory of Employment, Interest and Money*, New York: Harcourt, Brace.
Klein, Naomi (2007), *The Shock Doctrine: The Rise of Disaster Capitalism*, New York: Henry Holt.
Kregel, Jan (2007), 'The natural instability of financial markets', Working Paper, No. 523, The Levy Economics Institute of Bard College, Annandale-on-Hudson, New York.
Kregel, Jan (2008a), 'Minsky's cushions of safety: systemic risk and the crisis in the U.S. subprime mortgage market', Public Policy Brief No. 93, The Levy Economics Institute of Bard College, Annandale-on-Hudson, New York.
Kregel, Jan (2008b), 'Changes in the U.S. financial system and the subprime crisis', Working Paper No. 530, The Levy Economics Institute of Bard College, Annandale-on-Hudson, New York.
Lazonick, William and Mary O'Sullivan (2000), 'Maximizing shareholder value: a new ideology for corporate governance', *Economy and Society*, **29** (1): 13–35.
Lowenstein, Roger (2000), *When Genius Failed: The Rise and Fall of Long-Term Capital Management*, New York: Random House.
MacArthur, John R. (2000), *The Selling of 'Free Trade': NAFTA, Washington, and the Subversion of American Democracy*, New York: Hill & Wang.
Minsky, Hyman P. (1982), *Can 'It' Happen Again?*, Armonk, NY: M.E. Sharpe.

Minsky, Hyman P. (2008 [1986]), *Stabilizing an Unstable Economy*, New Haven, CT: Yale University Press.

Muolo, Paul and Mathew Padilla (2008), *Chain of Blame: How Wall Street Caused the Mortgage and Credit Crisis*, Hoboken, NJ: John Wiley & Sons.

Orhangazi, Ozgur (2008), *Financialization and the U.S. Economy*, Cheltenham, UK and Northampton, MA: Edward Elgar.

Partnoy, Frank (1999), 'The Siskel and Ebert of financial markets: two thumbs down for the credit rating agencies', *Washington University Law Quarterly*, **77** (3): 619–712.

Partnoy, Frank (2006), 'How and why credit rating agencies are not like other gate-keepers', in Yasuyuki Fuchita and Robert E. Litan (eds), *Financial Gatekeepers; Can They Protect Investors?*, Washington, DC: Brookings Institution Press.

Phillips, Kevin (2009), *Bad Money: Reckless Finance, Failed Politics, and the Global Crisis of American Capitalism*, updated edn, New York: Penguin.

Prasch, Robert E. (2004), 'Shifting risk: the divorce of risk from reward in American capitalism,' *Journal of Economic Issues*, **38** (2): 405–12.

Prasch, Robert E. (2007), 'The economics of fraud', manuscript, Middlebury College Department of Economics.

Prasch, Robert E. (2008), *How Markets Work: Supply, Demand and the 'Real World'*, Cheltenham, UK and Northampton, MA: Edward Elgar.

Prasch, Robert E. (2009), 'Markets, states, and exchange: an introduction to economics,' in Hassan Bougrine and Mario Seccareccia (eds), *Introducing Macroeconomic Analysis: Issues, Questions, and Competing Views*, Toronto, ON: Emond Montgomery.

Rosen, Richard J. (2007), 'The role of securitization in mortgage lending', *Chicago Fed Letter*, no. 244 (November): 1–4.

Rosengren, Eric S. (2009), 'The impact of liquidity, securitization, and banks on the real economy', Remarks by the President of the Federal Reserve Bank of Boston at the Conference on Financial Markets and Monetary Policy (9 June 2009), Washington, DC: Federal Reserve Board.

Sabarwal, Shwetlena, Nistha Sinha and Mayra Buvinic (2009), 'The global financial crisis: assessing vulnerability for women and children', World Bank: PREM Working Paper 09-1 (March), pp. 1–4.

Schmidt, Christian (ed.) (1996), *Uncertainty in Economic Thought*, Cheltenham, UK and Brookfield, USA: Edward Elgar.

Shiller, Robert (2005), *Irrational Exuberance*, Princeton, NJ: Princeton University Press.

Skidelsky, Robert (2000), *John Maynard Keynes: Fighting for Britain, 1937–1946*, New York: Penguin.

Stiglitz, Joseph E. (2002), *Development and Its Discontents*, New York: Norton.

Stockhammer, Engelbert (2004), 'Financialization and the slowdown of accumulation', *Cambridge Journal of Economics*, **28** (5): 719–41.

Swan, Peter L. (2009), 'The political economy of the subprime crisis: why subprime was so attractive to its creators', *European Journal of Political Economy*, **25**: 124–32.

Tett, Gillian (2009), *Fool's Gold: How the Bold Dream of a Small Tribe at J. P. Morgan Was Corrupted by Wall Street Greed and Unleashed a Catastrophe*, New York: Free Press.

Wade, Robert (2009), 'Why Iceland flew too close to the sun', *Challenge* (May–June): 5–33.

Weisbrot, Mark, Dean Baker and David Rosnick (2006), 'The Scorecard on development: 25 years of diminished progress,' DESA Working Paper No. 31, New York: United Nations Department of Economic and Social Affairs.

Wray, L. Randall (2008), 'Financial markets meltdown: what can we learn from Minsky?', Public Policy Brief No. 94, The Levy Economics Institute of Bard College, Annandale-on-Hudson, New York.

12. The governance of financial transactions

Martin Ricketts

In this chapter the new institutional economics is used to explore the origins of the financial crisis. Economists such as Oliver Williamson, Harold Demsetz and Armen Alchian in the later part of the twentieth century developed the insights that Ronald Coase first introduced in the 1930s. Essentially these ideas derived from the observation that all contractual relations give rise to transactions costs. Organizations are then structured, under conditions of competitive adaptation, to gain the greatest benefits from exchange net of these costs. The governance of transactional relations is greatly affected by public regulatory intervention. The substitution of publicly imposed for privately evolved governance can be seen as a significant factor underlying the malfunctioning of financial markets.

INTRODUCTION

At times of economic crisis it is to be expected that established institutions will be subject to scrutiny as explanations for relative hardship and disruption are sought. In times of stability and generally rising standards of living, cumulative day-to-day events seem to validate the established order and give rise to an unnoticed complacency. As events shatter expectations and undermine confidence in the future, long-held assumptions are revisited and the institutional framework is viewed from a new and less flattering perspective. This institutional reappraisal can be wide-ranging. It embraces criticism of institutions in the sense of particular organizations set up to achieve given ends – for example the commercial banks or other financial institutions and the regulatory bodies charged with their oversight. It also can extend to criticism of institutions in the more abstract sense of 'ways of doing business', legal conventions or even the evolved customary attitudes, manners and behaviour of the population – for example a preference for contractual relations involving high-powered incentives, low levels of trust or excessive insouciance with respect to indebtedness.

The depression years of the 1930s witnessed growing interest in the institutionalism of economists such as Veblen (1899, 1904) or Berle and Means (1932). Veblen regarded the modern industrial economy that had developed in the USA as the product of 'imbecile institutions' – institutions that pandered to the pursuit of status or 'ceremonial' distinctions or to the more predatory instincts of people. The structure of industry with its 'absentee owners' and the consumption behaviour of the population reflected an obsession with 'business' (or money-making) over 'industry' or the making of goods.[1] Berle and Means particularly emphasized the increasing 'division of ownership from control' and the power thereby exercised in large corporations by a growing managerial elite. In each case an important purpose was to throw into relief a perceived disjunction between the foundations of received economic doctrine and the apparent realities of life. People's choices were governed not merely by their autonomous preferences combined with reason, but by drives closer in nature to the Greek idea of *thymos* – the desire for distinction or recognition by others – a desire that has important ramifications in political as well as economic theory.[2] Further, their business dealings were far removed from the world of small-scale competitive enterprise and were conducted within the context of corporate entities that changed the social as well as the economic relations of the participants.

This 'institutionalist' tradition in economics did not come to dominate during the twentieth century and the generally accepted explanations for the malfunctioning of markets in the 1930s drew very little on institutionalist thinking. Once the basically Keynesian idea became established that involuntary unemployment (the most socially damaging symptom of malfunctioning markets) was the result of deficiency of aggregate demand and that this could be rectified by suitable government action (whether monetary or fiscal), 'institutionalist' criticism seemed no longer relevant. Those institutions and corporate structures that so offended the institutionalists could continue in existence, and criticism could be interpreted as normative sociological or political comment rather than as a serious scientific assault on the sustainability of the established economic system.

Nevertheless, mainstream thinkers have gradually taken up some elements of the institutionalist critique. In particular, the 'new institutional economics' is a broad label given to research that attempts to explain the institutional and organizational structures that are observed within a 'free market' economy. This literature did not evolve out of the old institutionalism as a radical critique of established theory, but originated independently as a means of using established theory to address what was perceived to be a new set of issues. Gradually, however, the dominance of the neoclassical paradigm has been undermined until a recent article in the *Economist* could assert that 'today's economists show no great attachment to the rational model of behaviour' and even that 'economic theory has become so eclectic that ingenious researchers can usually cook up a plausible model to explain whatever empirical results they find interesting'.[3] Whether or not this judgement is sound need not detain us here. It is certainly a questionable conclusion if we define economics not as recommended by *The Economist* – 'economics is what economists do' – but somewhat more objectively as 'what the big-selling textbooks contain' or 'what economists teach'.

If economists have become more eclectic in the sense of drawing on various schools of thought and spending less time in fruitless methodological and doctrinal disputes, it is still helpful to be able to distinguish between these schools so as to appreciate their relative strengths and to see where they are complementary and where irreconcilable. In this spirit, therefore, this chapter discusses the main features of the neoclassical school and contrasts it with the 'new institutionalism'. It then investigates whether the new institutional approach to economics has anything to contribute to the understanding of the present financial crisis and what, if any, conclusions can be drawn about the appropriate response of public policy.

A NEOCLASSICAL STRAW MAN

At the heart of conventional economic theory, its principal building block and the main target for most criticism, is the rational calculating individual. People know what they want to achieve but the scarcity of resources means that they have to choose between alternatives. It is assumed that they can always place a list of alternative outcomes (usually thought of as alternative baskets of desired ends or 'goods') in order of preference, and that they know what outcomes are potentially achievable with the resources at their disposal. Of all the privately achievable outcomes, each person picks the one he or she perceives to be 'best' – and this is logically equivalent to ensuring that, for each resource under a person's control, the extra benefit received from using the last unit or increment is the same irrespective of the desired end to which it is directed. If a person is constrained by time, he or she should find that the last minute devoted to each activity yields the same extra benefit. If this were not true, it would obviously suggest that the person should reassign some of his or her time away from activities yielding relatively small marginal benefits and towards activities yielding relatively large marginal benefits. This is the celebrated 'equi-marginal condition' for utility maximization – the condition that must hold if a person is to be maximizing his or her satisfaction and to have achieved 'equilibrium'.

From the above brief description it is evident that the pure logic of rational choice is fundamental to neoclassical microeconomics. It is not the entire story, however. Everyone is familiar with the idea that neoclassical theory is also heavily concerned with the use of market prices to guide resource allocation. People do not sit outside their caves maximizing their own satisfaction in a state of mutual isolation. The power of trade, and thus of cooperation with others, to increase the satisfaction of all participants has been at the centre of 'political economy' from the time of David Hume and Adam Smith. In the neoclassical treatment of trade, the market prices of all goods and resources determine the 'outcomes that are potentially achievable' – the constraints that face the participants in the market. People can specialize in the production and sale of particular goods and meet their varied demands for other goods through purchases on the market. Market prices therefore will determine the pattern of specialization and exchange.

All these individual decisions to supply or demand goods and factors have to be mutually compatible. Decisions by some agents to supply cabbages and demand potatoes require to be reconciled with decisions by other agents to demand cabbages and supply potatoes. Prices in the neoclassical model accomplish this end by adjusting up or down until quantities supplied and demanded are the same and 'market equilibrium' is established. Whether prices can be relied upon to settle at equilibrium levels and precisely what mechanism is supposed to bring about this result have been major concerns of economic theory for at least one hundred years. At times of crisis and instability the descriptive plausibility of the model seems unpersuasive, but there is no doubt that it exercises a powerful and indeed almost aesthetic appeal. The 'correct' set of prices will induce economic agents to make self-interested decisions that will be perfectly compatible with everyone else's self-interested decisions and that, in ideal conditions, will result in the achievement of all available gains from specialization and exchange. As a theoretical attempt to formalize the case for decentralized markets and to encapsulate the power of Adam Smith's 'invisible hand', it is vulnerable to many and powerful objections, some of which will be discussed below, but it is difficult not to come partially under its seductive sway.

Neoclassical thinking may still represent the dominant paradigm, but it has always faced criticism from theorists chafing at some of its most fundamental features. Were people really quite so calculating and rational as the theory assumed? Could they be completely described by the twin attributes of appetite and reason, with no mention of the more animating but suspect characteristics of desire for worldly success and distinction? Did they have stable preference orderings? Did the immense complexity of the real world allow for calculation as required by the theory? Did people have the information about opportunities, technology, resources and prices that would permit them to make optimal decisions? These and similar questions have been levelled at the neoclassical framework by psychologists, behaviouralists, thoroughgoing subjectivists and others.

A significant neoclassical answer to these questions in the 1950s and 1960s was a purely methodological one. The model was not supposed to be a realistic description of the world but an abstraction that enabled scientific analysis to take place. The only really mortal wound that could be inflicted would be a refutation of its predictions. Why worry if people were psychologically more complicated than the model assumed or frequently faced more complex environments than they could be expected to handle by pure calculation? If the aim was to construct a theory that predicted qualitative responses to particular exogenous disturbances such as the introduction of taxes, subsidies, price controls, technological innovations and so forth, the model was capable of yielding results that were, in principle, testable. The challenge to the critics was to come up with something better.

THE NEW INSTITUTIONALIST CRITIQUE

It is possible that this methodological impasse played some part in encouraging the development of the new institutional economics. This particular branch of economic theory was not initially aimed at upsetting neoclassical orthodoxy. Much was derived from a paper by Coase (1937) that was concerned simply with explaining aspects of the world that appeared out of reach of the established doctrine. In particular, the central challenge faced by Coase was to offer an explanation for the differing structure of firms and industries that could be observed – why, for example, were some industries made up of highly specialized firms trading intermediate goods as value was added through the production chain, whereas other industries comprised vertically integrated enterprises? This did not seem to be an unreasonable question for an economist to ask and yet it was not at all easy to answer within the established theoretical framework. Indeed, as noted above, the individualist foundations of the subject provided no particular account of the existence of 'firms' at all. Firms were simply individual profit-maximizing entities constrained by the technological limitations of a 'production function'. There was no 'internal structure' discernible.

The usual attitude of neoclassical theorists up to the mid-1960s is perhaps
well represented by Machlup's (1967: 13) remark that 'Frankly, I cannot
quite see what great difference organizational matters are supposed to
make to the firm's price reactions to changes in conditions.' Why clutter
up the analysis with 'realistic' firms if all we want to do is predict output
and price changes to 'changes in conditions'?

The response to Machlup's statement by those economists who developed the new institutionalist critique was to show that organizational
matters were not irrelevant to the prediction of a firm's behaviour.
Further, they showed that by asking questions about organizational
matters, the inadequacy of the purely competitive model of 'markets' was
revealed in a particularly instructive way. For Coase's seminal observation
was simply that organization within the firm and organization through
the use of market contracts were substitutes. 'The market' did not dominate exclusively because 'there would seem to be a cost of using the price
mechanism' and firms could sometimes handle transactions internally
at lower cost. Transactions were assigned where they could be handled
most cheaply, and the boundary of the firm was to be found where the
cost of the marginal transaction was the same both in the 'firm' and in the
'market' – a satisfyingly 'neoclassical' conclusion.

Neoclassical it might have been in its references to familiar concepts
– the availability of substitutable methods, the existence of opportunity
costs and the explanatory power of rational cost-minimizing 'marginal
conditions', but it was also deceptively subversive. The whole thrust of
analysis was subtly diverted away from individual constrained choice (a
somewhat formal and mathematically well-structured problem) towards
the study of contractual relations (a more obviously 'social' and less
mathematically tractable subject).[4] If 'the firm' had advantages over
'the market' for coordinating the efforts of transactors or vice versa, the
reasons were presumably related to the differing contractual settings.
There is a 'cost of transacting in markets' and there is a 'cost of transacting in firms', and the obvious questions concern why and how they differ.
Looking at economics as the study of competitive markets, it was possible
to ignore the internal structure of firms. Looking at economics as the study
of exchange and hence 'contract', ignorance of what went on within firms
was no longer so easily defended from a methodological point of view.
Pace Machlup, the structure of firms did matter because organizations
were structured to cope with the most fundamental economic problem of
all – achieving the gains to trade.

When people trade, they face inevitable problems. Can they trust one
another? Will they deliver on their promises or will they renege? Is their
behaviour observable at low cost? Is it possible to specify precisely what

the respective promises are – or are they too complex fully to identify in a written document? Will they try to change the terms of the contract as time advances? Is one contractor more vulnerable than the other to 'contractual opportunism'? Is it possible for a third party to adjudicate in the event of contractual breakdown or are certain terms inherently 'unverifiable'? These and other contractual problems would not exist, of course, if everyone were always and everywhere costlessly and fully informed. Thus, implicitly, it is the social and organizational response to the 'information problem' that underlies transaction cost economics. Where information is incomplete and unequally distributed between the contractors, contracting will present formidable obstacles and contractual relations will require 'governance' – the governance supplied by third parties and courts of law, and the governance supplied within firms.

THE GOVERNANCE OF FINANCIAL TRANSACTIONS

In financial markets the importance of institutional economics is particularly obvious and the danger inherent in overlooking problems of governance and in confining economic analysis to the elaboration of increasingly complex exercises in constrained maximization is particularly acute. Of all the exchange problems that can be envisaged, that of transferring purchasing power from a set of lenders to a set of borrowers so that productive investments can be financed and returns paid out of profits in the future must rank as among the most hazardous. Particularly hazardous, we might think, would be agreements to pay a protracted sequence of premiums over a whole working life in exchange for promises of payments (a pension) in old age. All financial transactions, however, give rise to similar problems. Agreements to pay sums of money in the event of fire or ill health, or of changes in the price of oil or other commodities, in exchange for specified payments – state-contingent contracts – cannot avoid the transaction cost problem and hence the issue of contractual governance.

What makes financial intermediation – commercial and investment banking, life assurance, fire and health insurance, the raising of finance by means of bond issues and equity stock – contractually hazardous is that these activities are all subject to extreme forms of information asymmetry and pervasive uncertainty. If one contractor promises to pay another a sum of money if the latter suffers a loss through theft or fire, how is the former to know whether the fire or 'theft' really was an 'act of God' rather than a deliberate act of the insured? This 'moral hazard' (deriving from the inability to observe the actions of contractors) is even more obviously associated with banking. A depositor in a bank will naturally fear that the banker might abscond with the money, or, more subtly, might be tempted to take extravagant risks with the funds and find it impossible to repay. The same would be true of people committing funds to a pension fund. Thus, sometimes it is necessary to think of ways of enabling an insurance provider to trust the people it is insuring, and sometimes it is necessary to think of ways of enabling the depositors or savers to trust the bank or pensions provider. There is a need for trust on both sides of all transactions – and particularly of financial transactions.

From the point of view of the new institutional economics, financial institutions would be expected to evolve so as to engender trust and to reduce the cost of transacting. A major strand in this theory is that an important method of reassuring vulnerable contractors is to offer them control rights.[5] People with control rights are effectively the 'owners' of a firm. Their relationship is not contractual. The owners of a firm hold residual rights – all those rights in the firm's assets that have not explicitly been contracted away remain with the owners and it is the owners who decide how these residual rights are used. Usually they would be expected to appoint agents (managers) to run the firm, but the owners can determine the policy of the firm and remove managers who do not comply with their wishes. Ownership imposes the cost of making decisions about the policy of the firm and of appointing and policing managers to run it. It also implies the bearing of the costs of uncertainty. Owners receive what remains after all contractual obligations are settled – a residual return to their residual control rights.

Proponents of Coase's 'transactions cost' view of the firm argue that governance matters. A competitive system would be expected to select those forms of enterprise that produced the greatest net gains after allowing for transactions costs and ownership costs. The costs of 'doing business' must be taken into account and the assignment of ownership rights and the contractual methods used to bind the participants will determine the chances of survival. It would be expected, therefore, that groups of people who faced high costs of transacting with the firm relative to the costs of ownership would tend to hold the control rights and become 'owners'. Hansmann (1996) shows, for example, how firms can be controlled by their consumers (as in retail cooperatives), the purchasers of resource inputs (as in agricultural supply cooperatives), their suppliers (as in marketing cooperatives), their workers (as in labour-managed firms) or a subset of workers (as in professional partnerships), their investors (as in the public limited company) or their members (as in clubs and mutuals). In each case it is possible to argue that governance is a cost-reducing response to transactional hazards.

Retail cooperatives emerged as a response to local monopoly power as well as the delivery of poor quality and the exploitation of consumer ignorance in the new luxury markets of the nineteenth century. Similar forces led to agricultural supply cooperatives and cooperatively owned electricity companies in the USA. Worker control is observed as a response to vulnerability and dependence on the firm (situations where a person has skills that are specific to a particular organization and cannot be traded outside), and where the costs of ownership are low (for example if mutual monitoring and peer pressure are effective and homogeneous interests ensure that collective decision-making is not too costly). The dominance of the investor-owned public limited company is explained mainly by the relatively low collective decision-making costs associated with outside suppliers of finance. Investors will be concerned mainly with the return on their equity stakes, whereas consumers and workers might have many and diverse interests that increase the costs of making collective decisions. Mutual governance emerges in situations of great uncertainty and where the dangers of moral hazard and adverse selection are extreme. If a 'price' cannot be negotiated in the face of contractual hazards – for example the price to insure a factory against fire – the businesspeople of an area might form a 'club' and agree to cover their members. The advantages of the 'club' are that the members would be expected to know one another and be knowledgeable about the methods that might be employed to reduce the risk of fire. Living locally, they might also be able to monitor compliance and discourage insurance fraud.

It is hardly surprising in the light of this brief discussion of the logic of enterprise governance that mutual ownership has been historically extremely important in the development of the financial services industry. The Amicable Society for a Perpetual Assurance Office that later became the Norwich Union and is now 'Aviva' was established in 1706 as a mutual society. The same could be said for many other institutions, including Scottish Widows and the unfortunate Equitable Life Assurance Society that retained its mutual status but discovered to its cost in the House of Lords[6] (2000) that it might as well not have done so since 'contractual' promises made to a subgroup of its policy-holders would always in law take precedence over the broader rights and obligations of 'club membership'. The provision of housing finance was historically addressed by the development of mutual 'building societies' or, in the USA, 'savings and loan associations'. In savings banks, mutual and non-profit arrangements survived for many years as reassurance to depositors and, when joint stock commercial banks were established with limited liability (after 1857), large reserves of capital were kept. Only one-quarter of the share capital of the Birmingham Joint Stock Bank was called – the remainder being security for depositors. As Sayers (1957: 219–20) noted, 'The stress laid on these measures is an indication of the importance previously attached, as a protection to depositors, to the unlimited liability of shareholders.'

INSTITUTIONS AND THE FINANCIAL CRISIS

The business cycle is hardly new and in each era there are plenty of apparently plausible reasons for explaining away 'irrational exuberance' as a perfectly rational response to unprecedented technological or other opportunities. Given a pervasive and instinctive desire for relative status and success, as distinct from the simple desire to optimize scarce resources, it is not altogether surprising that market economies with fractional reserve banks are prone to get out of hand at intervals and that this can in turn result in painful readjustments.[7] The ultimate causes have been debated for centuries – waves of technical change, sun-spots, monetary disturbances, wars, changes in government spending and so forth. However, there is always an institutional dimension to these crises and the present one has already given rise to suggestions that institutional failure has occurred.

Clearly the financial sector has been at the centre of the turmoil. Mortgage lenders have contributed to a speculative boom in house and other asset prices and seem (with the advantage of hindsight) to have greatly underestimated the risks associated with their activities. Financial innovation has occurred on a massive scale and the extent to which the directors of the financial institutions understood the trade in which their subordinates were engaged is widely questioned. Financial instruments were created and traded simply as impersonal 'state contingent claims' with wide implicit acceptance that the value of such claims could reasonably be calculated on scientific 'market' principles irrespective of their complexity. Bonus payments were offered to traders and executives on the basis of annual turnover, growth or profit figures rather than sustained longer-term investment performance – a practice that did not necessarily align the interests of owners with those of managers.

Future scholarship will no doubt try to determine what importance is to be ascribed to these issues – the adequacy of 'risk assessment models', the methods of 'pricing risk', the incentive packages of the various economic actors, the within-firm auditing and control mechanisms and so forth. But the overarching question is why the dangers, long inherent in financial markets, were not recognized by the participants and why the established protections embodied in the prevailing governance arrangements proved inadequate. Was the apparent failure of governance in the area of financial transacting itself part of the momentum towards a 'bubble economy' and thus a symptom of the failure of free agents to contrive suitable frameworks for governing their dealings – a type of 'market failure'? Or was the apparent failure of governance the result of flawed public policy – a type of 'government failure'? Much of the immediate response to the crisis has adopted the former position. The financial collapse is, according to this view, the result of 'unregulated financial capitalism'. The new institutional economics, by contrast, suggests a very different perspective.

THE EFFECT OF STATE REGULATION ON ENTERPRISE GOVERNANCE

A notable characteristic of 'governance' arrangements in the financial sector at the end of the twentieth century and the beginning of the twenty-first in the UK was the relative decline of 'mutual' status and the dominance of the public limited company. Building societies, banks, insurance companies, savings institutions and stock exchanges abandoned mutual status in large numbers.[8] Instead of a financial sector containing a range of competing organizational forms, the dominance of the public limited company seemed to be almost complete. Trends both towards and away from mutual ownership have occurred in the past, and the aftermath of a major financial crisis often coincides with a reappraisal of the case for mutual governance.[9] However, the main issue here concerns the impact of the growth of government regulation on the incentive to adopt particular corporate forms. Whether the regulatory system adopted by governments is 'light touch' or 'heavy handed', the perception that the state is policing the financial markets changes more than is normally realized, for government regulation is a substitute for private governance.

State regulation undermines the competitive position of mutual institutions, friendly societies or cooperative banks and in general makes it very difficult to build a competitive advantage based on the idea of greater safety and the avoidance of financial hazards. Whereas in the nineteenth century and earlier in the twentieth century people would have been aware of, and interested in, the governance of the banks or life assurance companies to which their savings were committed, it is much less clear that any real judgement has characterized the choices of more contemporary depositors and investors.[10] The search for higher returns was all that mattered because the authorities could be relied upon to make sure all financial institutions were equally safe. This confidence in the ability of regulatory agencies to ensure compliance with rules that protect depositors and investors actually increases the danger of adverse selection. All players in the market 'look' similar because they can all claim to be subject to government-approved regulatory mechanisms. Unless these mechanisms are very reliable and enforceable at relatively low cost, participants in the market will be tempted to lower quality (in this case safety) in pursuit of higher profits. Mechanisms once seen as important signals of safety and important guarantors of conservative policy – such as directors appointed by depositors (in mutual institutions) or very high levels of 'uncalled' capital (in joint stock institutions) or unlimited liability (in the case of professional partnerships) – have been swept aside in the rush for higher returns.

Looking at the present financial crisis from the perspective of the new institutional economics therefore suggests a somewhat different interpretation both of the crisis itself and of the policy response. It is certainly not argued here that institutional failure was the sole cause of the crisis or that without government regulation of financial markets financial excesses would not occur. Clearly financial capitalism has been subject to speculative frenzies since it became recognizable as a feature of the 'modern' world in Renaissance Italy. However, it is not exactly obvious that the substitution of ever-more centralized regulation as a replacement for what little remains of the 'anxious vigilance' of millions of savers, depositors and investors is the best response, even if in the immediate future it is the most likely. National and international regulators will find it necessary to impose restrictions that are simultaneously simple and draconian in order to make them enforceable. The costs in terms of a less innovative and responsive system will be difficult if not impossible to gauge. In the very long run they might not even be proof against future excesses.

Institutional economics would suggest, in contrast, a more decentralised system in which governance arrangements evolve and respond to transactional hazards in the market. Such competitive adaptation is only possible, however, if risk–return tradeoffs are much more obvious to market participants than they have been in the recent past, if the failure of more risky institutions is common enough to engender caution without threatening the stability of the wider system, and if people accept that 'safety' cannot be a free lunch provided by state agencies. It is a matter of political rather than economic judgement whether these requirements are likely to make a return to an institutionally more diverse financial sector a realistic possibility.

NOTES

1. For a review of this 'Veblenian dichotomy' see Waller (1994).
2. For example, Francis Fukuyama's (1992) book *The End of History and the Last Man* is

an extended discussion concerning the question of whether the universal and reciprocal recognition associated (in principle) with Western liberal democracy can satisfy the demands of thymotic drives and deliver perpetual peace.

3. 'International bright young things', *The Economist*, 30 December 2008.
4. The view that economics was most productively seen as the study of voluntary exchange is reflected strongly in the work of Williamson (1975, 1985), as well as 'property rights' theorists such as Alchian (1965) and Demsetz (1967), and 'public choice' economists such as Buchanan and Tullock (1962). See Williamson (2008) for a discussion of the progress of transaction cost economics from the 1920s to the 1970s. So-called 'Austrian' economists such as Kirzner (1973) also reject the calculating and maximizing basis for neoclassical 'equilibrium', but their emphasis thereafter is more on the role of the entrepreneur as an intermediary in a dynamic 'market process' rather than on the role of institutions in the governance of this process. Kirzner pays very little attention to the governance of firms.
5. Alchian and Woodward (1987) argue that vulnerable firm-specific assets will seek control of the firm while Hart and Moore (1990) see the allocation of control rights as a means of encouraging 'non-verifiable' *ex ante* investment in a contractual relationship.
6. *The Equitable Life Assurance Society* v. *Alan David Hyman* (2000).
7. This observation has been central to so-called 'Austrian' approaches to the economic cycle for many years – see De Soto (2006).
8. The causes of 'demutualization' and the trend towards publicly quoted investor-owned companies were discussed by the present author in Ricketts (1999, 2000, 2003).
9. For example, the Armstrong Commission in the United States (1905) encouraged a move towards mutual status after financial abuses were uncovered at the beginning of the twentieth century.
10. In recent years, for example, large numbers of UK individuals and local authorities invested in Icelandic banks, seemingly with little idea that any greater risk was involved than in any other depository institution. The point is not that these banks were in any way fraudulent. The point is that any institution failing to promise similarly high returns was doomed, and mechanisms that stood in the way of generating these returns were perceived as threats rather than protections.

REFERENCES

Alchian, A.A. (1965), 'Some economics of property rights', *Il Politico*, **30** (4): 816–29.
Alchian, A.A. and S. Woodward (1987), 'Reflections on the theory of the firm', *Journal of Institutional and Theoretical Economics*, **143** (1): 110–36.
Berle, A.A. and G.C. Means (1932), *The Modern Corporation and Private Property*, New York: Harcourt, Brace & World.
Buchanan, J.M. and G. Tullock (1962), *The Calculus of Consent*, Ann Arbor, MI: University of Michigan Press.
Coase, R.H. (1937), 'The Nature of the Firm', *Economica*, **4** (16): 386–405.
De Soto, J.H. (2006), *Money, Bank Credit, and Economic Cycles*, trans. M.A. Stroup, Auburn, AL: Ludwig von Mises Institute.
Demsetz, H. (1967), 'Towards a theory of property rights', *American Economic Review*, **57** (2): 347–59.
Fukuyama, F. (1992), *The End of History and the Last Man*, New York: Free Press.
Hansmann, H.B. (1996), *The Ownership of Enterprise*, Cambridge, MA: Harvard University Press.

Hart, O. and J. Moore (1990), 'Property rights and the nature of the firm', *Journal of Political Economy*, **98** (6): 1119–58.
Kirzner, I. (1973), *Competition and Entrepreneurship*, Chicago, IL: University of Chicago Press.
Machlup, F. (1967), 'Theories of the firm: marginalist, behavioral, managerial', *American Economic Review*, **62** (1): 1–33.
Ricketts, M. (1999), *The Many Ways of Governance: Perspectives on the Control of the Firm*, Research Report 31, Social Affairs Unit, London.
Ricketts, M. (2000), 'Competitive processes and the evolution of governance structures', *Journal des Economistes et des Etudes Humaines*, **10** (2/3): 235–52.
Ricketts, M. (2003), 'Alternative explanations for changes in ownership structures', *Journal of Institutional and Theoretical Economics*, **159** (4): 688–97.
Sayers, R.S. (1957), *Lloyds Bank in the History of English Banking*, Oxford, Clarendon Press.
Veblen, T. (1899), *The Theory of the Leisure Class*, republished (1934), New York: Modern Library.
Veblen, T. (1904), *The Theory of Business Enterprise*, New York, Charles Scribner's.
Waller, W. (1994), 'Veblenian dichotomy and its critics', in G.M. Hodgson et al. (eds), *The Elgar Companion to Institutional and Evolutionary Economics*, Aldershot, UK and Brookfield, USA: Edward Elgar, pp. 368–72.
Williamson, O.E. (1975), *Markets and Hierarchies: Analysis and Antitrust Implications. A Study in the Economics of Internal Organization*, New York: Free Press, Collier Macmillan.
Williamson, O.E. (1985), *The Economic Institutions of Capitalism: Firms, Markets, Relational Contracting*, London: Collier Macmillan.
Williamson, O.E. (2008), 'Transactions cost economics: the precursors', *Economic Affairs*, **28** (3): 7–14.

13. Excess debt and asset deflation

Jan Toporowski

INTRODUCTION: THE FAILURE OF ECONOMIC THEORY

The financial crisis that is spreading out from countries with the most 'advanced' financial systems to the rest of the world has not been well served by economic theory. That is to say, economic theories did not, as they should, prepare policy-makers and practitioners for the crisis, and few theorists have been able to illuminate the course of the crisis and its implications with anything other than the insights that had conspicuously failed to prepare us for such a crisis.

In the mainstream, new classical economics has modelled a very attenuated financial system, driven by 'rational' individuals exchanging real resources to obtain such allocations in general equilibrium that maximize utility functions now and over time. Disturbances arise because of unanticipated 'shocks', following which general equilibrium is resumed. This unworldly philosophy ignores the very apparent macroeconomic imbalances that built up over many years (and therefore can hardly be described as 'unanticipated shocks') and that are now working themselves out in the deflation of economies. However, that philosophy still plays a very real part in the thinking of policy-makers. Their general equilibrium models still reassure us that what is clearly emerging as a lengthy deflationary process is a temporary response to the shock of bank defaults, and that stable growth will be shortly resumed (Bank of England, 2008).

The new Keynesians have also been intellectually hamstrung by a methodological addiction to general equilibrium. This was used to model underemployment equilibria due to market 'rigidities'. The more dynamic 'financial accelerator' model has a credit cycle driven by fluctuations in net wealth. However, this is still within a general equilibrium framework and with little explanation of the financial mechanics that have now broken down. Such mechanics are replaced by arbitrary constraints and lags imposed on the general equilibrium model, in order to generate a cycle (Bernanke and Gertler, 1989). Among behavioural economists Robert Shiller stands out for his embrace of what he regards as more realistic financial economics that rejects 'realism', i.e. the notion that monetary and financial relations are a mere veil over real economic relations.

Outside the mainstream, post-Keynesians have traditionally emphasized low growth and high unemployment as consequences of the departure from 'Keynesian policies', which range from cheap money to fiscal activism (Coddington, 1983; Tily, 2007; Chick, 1973: ch. 8). For post-Keynesians, almost without exception, instability arises out of some combination of speculation and financial deregulation (e.g. Kregel, 2008; Wray, 2008). Over the years since post-Keynesianism emerged in the 1970s, its partisans have had one major methodological advantage over new classical and new Keynesian economists, namely the post-Keynesians' rejection of general equilibrium. This advantage is now apparent, but that was of precious little benefit to post-Keynesians in the meantime and led to their being cast out of the mainstream. The rejection of general equilibrium inspired post-Keynesians to embrace an approach to financial market dynamics that I describe below as 'market process'. Within this, post-Keynesians have emphasized the generation of economic disequilibrium because of uncertainty, perverse or fluctuating expectations, highlighting in particular the role of speculation in financial markets as a factor in capitalist instability.

Outside the mainstream have also been old Keynesian critics of financial markets, such as Charles P. Kindleberger and John Kenneth Galbraith. Their economic-historical approach to their subject, rejection of the scientific pretensions of modern quantitative finance theory, and doom-laden forecasts as the markets rose, caused their ideas to be marginalized in their senior stratum of their profession.

The present crisis has not dealt kindly with any of these schools of thought. The principal flaws have not been either a devotion to the efficiency of financial markets, or a belief in the inefficiency of those markets, since the former was, superficially at least, right through the long financial boom, and the latter is quite clearly right in the current crisis.

Perhaps the greatest casualties have been suffered by new classical ideas. The attenuated view of financial markets put forward by their most mathematically sophisticated exponents such as Michael Woodford has left them with little in the way of diagnostic equipment to bring to the analysis of the crisis. The equilibrium business cycle idea that real economies are briefly disturbed by 'shocks' is clearly inconsistent with not only the long-term structural disequilibria, most notably the macroeconomic imbalances of the USA, that preceded the crisis, but also the deflation now unfolding in the world economy.

The new Keynesian approach, focusing on information asymmetries, is also unsuitable for dealing with long-term imbalances. At best it produced a financial cycle based on *ad hoc* lags and restrictions. For all of their claimed insight into credit market operations, new Keynesians offer little in the way of a theory of credit or liquidity, other than a balance sheet of net wealth, that is supposed to respond to changing financial conditions by inflating or deflating the economy. Their cousins, the behavioural finance school, have the disadvantage of being led by someone whose touching faith in the ability of futures markets to secure us against all economic disasters is dramatically out of tune with what we now know about the risk-reducing efficiency of financial derivatives (Shiller, 1993).

The 'old Keynesians' of Kindleberger and Galbraith seem to be amply vindicated by the events of the crisis. Their accounts of greed, enrichment through financial manipulations, the hubris of finance leading to the nemesis of depression, cannot be read without evoking vivid parallels with our times. Nevertheless, their insights, however profound, do not add up to a systematic analysis, in the sense of laying out the market mechanisms by which financial markets are inflated and then deflated. In the final analysis, attributing financial boom and collapse to some nebulous 'confidence', or 'euphoria' followed by a 'loss of confidence', or 'panic' reduces experience to perceptions of that experience, rather than explaining events (cf. 'Bagehot's *Lombard Street* is the psychology of finance, not the theory of it': Keynes, 1915).

Related considerations apply to post-Keynesian accounts of the crisis, attributing it to either speculation or deregulation. The post-Keynesian view, as indicated above, is firmly rooted in the market process in the financial markets. However, it provides for weak accounts of business cycles. In the version put forward by Keynes and Kaldor, speculation and volatile expectations are permanent conditions of financial markets (Keynes, 1936: ch. 12, Kaldor, 1939). They may provide an explanation of economic or financial instability, in the sense of something approaching stochastic changes in output and financial variables, but more is needed to account for *extended* financial booms and collapses. As for deregulation as a factor in the financial crisis, it may be a necessary condition of the crisis, but it is not a sufficient one. The major dismantling of financial regulations in the USA and the UK took place in the 1970s and the 1980s. By the 1990s it was virtually complete. Yet it took another decade and a half for the deregulated edifice to collapse. If anything, this would suggest that deregulation provided the economy with a stable boom, rather than financial disorder. An additional complication in the post-Keynesian case, perhaps, is that Keynes himself opposed 'Schachtian' policies of financial regulation except in the international monetary sphere.

The crisis has also provided some vindication of the views of Marxists and institutionalist followers of Veblen, whose analyses of capitalism rested to some extent at least on the immanence of its failure. We now know much more about the financial theories of Marx and Veblen, and can marvel at the sophistication of their analysis and even their antici- pations of certain aspects of twenty-first-century financial capitalism. However, by clinging to the original observations of those masters, their followers today have been unable to develop any theory of money and finance for modern financial capitalism that can provide insights to match or even go beyond those of Keynes, Kalecki, Steindl and Minsky.

The laurels for anticipating the crisis must assuredly go to Hyman P. Minsky, the leading late twentieth-century exponent of the inherent instability of modern financial capitalism. In his work, more than in that of any other economist, may be found the essential ideas and concepts that are necessary to understand the generation of the crisis and its con- sequences. The flaws in his work arise not because his insights were incor- rect but because, put together into a systematic analysis, they contain inconsistencies in monetary analysis (see Toporowski, 2008). Central to Minsky's explanation of crisis is the emergence of over-indebtedness in the economy, i.e. excessive debt in relation to the income that is supposed to service it. This he drew from the debt-deflation theory of Irving Fisher (Fisher, 1933). However, over-indebtedness is difficult to reconcile with the boom in equity financing since the 1980s, and in the years preceding the 1929 Crash. By all accounts equity financing is a stabilizing feature of financial systems rather than a destabilizing one ('the greater the weight of equity financing in the liability structure, the greater the likelihood that the unit is a hedge financing unit': Minsky, 1992: 7).

In general, the financial crisis, like the 1929 Crash and the Great Depression that succeeded it, has confounded general equilibrium theo- rists and justified those critics of capitalism who view the system as prone to crisis. But if the crisis reveals the credulity of general equilibrium theo- rists, the catastrophists have an equivalent defect in their argument. This is in their failure to explain the relative stability of financial capitalism in the decades before the crisis, with only peripheral, if no less catastrophic for the markets concerned, crises up to 2007. Monetarists have sought to explain this stability and subsequent collapse by attributing it to loose monetary policy before a tightening in 2007–08. This view has two flaws. In the first place, monetary policy was hardly loose in the countries now most affected by the crisis, such as the UK. More importantly, monetar- ists never put forward financial crisis as a possible consequence of loose monetary policy. In their view, loose monetary policy was supposed to generate inflation in wages and product markets, rather than in the finan- cial markets. The absence of such wage and product market inflation prior to the crisis is an inconsistency in the monetarist explanation.

In sum, economists have failed to predict the crisis and those who now claim to have predicted it failed to predict the extent of the boom that preceded it. This chapter presents an explanation of the crisis rooted in a theory of financial inflation that has injected excess debt into the economy. The next section looks at some of the methodological issues in credit cycle analysis. A further section presents an explanation of the crisis using elements of Minsky and my own theory of capital market inflation. The final section considers some distributional aspects of financial inflation and crisis.

THREE METHODOLOGICAL APPROACHES

It is perhaps natural that, in a situation of largely unanticipated financial crisis (unanticipated in a new classical sense that, had market participants anticipated the crisis, then they would have hedged or insured against it and the crisis would not have occurred), questions have been raised about the role of risk models and recently even of the macroeconomic models that the Bank of England uses as a guide to policy. In those models it has increasingly been accepted, in line with the new classical approach to macroeconomic dynamics, that changes in variables over time are responses to shocks or stochastic disturbances, i.e. random events with a known probability distribution, affecting a system that starts in general equilibrium, and then reverts to a different general equilibrium. This may be contrasted with an older tradition in economic analysis attributing catastrophic economic events to particular market processes, perhaps most famously described in Kindleberger's *Manias, Panics and Crashes* (Kindleberger, 1989). Early on in his work Minsky made clear that he regarded theories that give no account of market process as defective (Toporowski, 2008).

The two analytical approaches are not necessarily incompatible, since the outcomes of market processes, such as prices, may be modelled as variables exhibiting particular kinds of distribution. However, the two approaches are certainly not equivalent, at least not for policy-makers. While stochastic disturbance modelling provides satisfying simulations of crises, and even pre-crisis anticipations of crisis, the hallmark of any actual financial crisis is an inability to clear complex transactions between assets and liabilities that were previously settled in a routine way. In such a situation, an awareness that particular incidents have a stochastic distribution is not very helpful to those responsible for clearing up the mess. Unravelling those complex transactions, in order to clear payments and settle liabilities, and setting up new transactions routines requires a careful analysis of actual market processes. This abstraction of stochastic modelling from really existing situations is what Marx had in mind when, discussing 'abstract forms of crisis', he observed:

> how insipid the economists are who, when they are no longer able to explain away the phenomenon of over-production and crises, are content to say that these forms contain the possibility of *crises*, and that it is therefore *accidental* whether or not crises occur and consequently their occurrence is itself merely a *matter of chance*. (Marx, 1975: 512)

There is, moreover, another serious deficiency of the stochastic disturbance or 'shock' approach. This is that such shocks and the apparently dynamic (because they occur over time) adjustments to which they give rise are inevitably transitory before market-clearing general equilibrium is restored. In practice, as we are now much more aware, the structural shift that has occurred with the financial crisis is an outcome of much more deep-rooted and sustained macroeconomic imbalances. These have been most apparent in the USA, where the trade and fiscal deficits have been widening for nearly ten years. In China, the investment boom that is now coming to an end has been sustained for nearly 30 years. These are therefore very persistent 'shocks' and those who think in new classical business cycle terms need more than just vague allusions to generic market rigidities to explain their persistence. Moreover, in the present economic situation any new classical economists who may believe that a new market-clearing general equilibrium is emerging are, I think, very much mistaken or are using the notion of market-clearing (which includes full employment) rather loosely.

The approach to financial crisis that regards it as a structural shift following an extended period of expanding disequilibria, followed by a new period of extended imbalances, most notably in the labour market, suggests a different way of analysing financial crisis. This would be by examining the mechanisms by which macroeconomic imbalances were accommodated over the initial period. (Such mechanisms, for example, were provided in the period before the crisis by a process of what I have called capital market inflation: Toporowski, 2000: Part 1.) The analysis of crisis can then move on to examining the reasons why those accommodating mechanisms broke down and thereby precipitated the crisis. The subsequent economic decline can then be examined by regarding that decline as an outcome of a new set of macroeconomic imbalances reinforced by mechanisms generated in the crisis (see, e.g., Perelstein, 2009).

In the next section, I present my own view of how long-term structural imbalances were accommodated by the financial markets through stabilizing mechanisms that broke down in the months preceding the outbreak of the crisis in 2007.

INFLATING THE CREDIT MARKETS

The account of corporate borrowing that is put forward by virtually all schools of thought in economics presents it as a 'voluntary' phenomenon, undertaken to generate the income that will service and repay that borrowing, with Keynesians, new Keynesians and post-Keynesians dissenting only to highlight the uncertainty that surrounds future income. It is precisely that uncertainty that makes lending against future income the most hazardous kind of lending, so that for 200 years and more banks have preferred to lend against collateral. However, collateralized lending is vulnerable to asset inflation, leading to lending against prospective capital gains. In a book criticizing the quantity theory of money, a book that was roundly condemned by Keynes, who refused thereafter to publish his work in the *Economic Journal*, John Atkinson Hobson recognized collateralized lending against financial assets as a key source of credit expansion and pointed to the inflationary potential of the equity market in this regard (Hobson, 1913: 89–92). Hobson did not foresee that when those gains fail to materialize, debt becomes excessive in the sense that it can only be serviced through the sale of assets, or reduced expenditure. This is how asset inflation creates excess debt, which in turn creates deflation in the form of falling prices and demand.

As indicated in the first part of this chapter, the systems of general equilibrium that are commonly used to analyse asset markets routinely ignore the market process that actually occurs in such markets. Those markets do not fix prices that make supply equal to demand, except in a notional sense. Financial markets typically operate for extended periods of disequilibrium, itself the counterpart of the structural disequilibrium of the real economy that they are accommodating. When the demand for financial securities exceeds the amount of money that holders and issuers of those securities are prepared to take out of the market, prices rise. As prices rise, demand for those assets, far from falling off, is enhanced by a speculative demand for assets to benefit from capital gains. However, not all securities are equal, and prices of securities do not rise equally. Short-term securities and bonds usually have the price at which they are repaid written into the terms of the bond. As the date of their repayment approaches, their market price converges on their repayment price. The market price of such bonds will only exceed that repayment price by a small margin, reflecting any differences between the interest payable on such a bond and the interest payable on equivalent new issues. Excess demand for new securities will therefore inflate most of all equities (common stocks) that do not have any fixed repayment value.

The majority of securities are issued by financial intermediaries and bought by other financial intermediaries. This issue therefore does not constitute any net expansion of credit, or of the balance sheets of non-financial businesses, such as would take out of the markets any excess net inflow of money into those markets. The non-financial sectors that do take money out of the markets are governments and corporations. The finance that governments take out of the markets is limited by their fiscal position (the balance between government income and expenditure). An excess demand for securities, such as was set off by the inauguration of funded pension schemes in the UK and the USA therefore impacts most directly on the balance-sheet operations of corporations. During the 1980s, corporations that issued securities in the capital markets found that they could issue shares cheaply. In large part this is because the return on shares is not just in the form of dividends paid out of company profits, but also in the form of capital gains, which are not paid by the company but by other buyers in the market for the shares.

As a result of the excess demand for shares, corporations have issued capital in excess of what they need to finance their commercial and industrial operations. In the past, the overcapitalization of companies might have been avoided because it would have involved the 'watering down' of profits (sharing a given amount of profits among more shareholders), or loss of control by the directors of a company who could no longer control the majority of shares at a company general meeting. However, today's shareholders are mostly institutions whose large diversified portfolios are subcontracted to professional fund managers and rated on financial returns, rather than on their interventions in the running of companies. Those financial returns include the appreciation of the value of stocks through financial inflation, a return that is paid by other participants in the market, rather than by the issuer of the securities. By and large fund managers have too many diverse holdings to take any other than a financial interest in a company. At the same time, new techniques of senior management remuneration have tended to replace profit-related pay with share-price-related pay, through stock options. Along with new techniques of debt management, stock option remuneration has removed inhibitions about the overcapitalization of companies.

Excess capital has been used to replace bank borrowing with cheaper long-term capital. Replacing borrowing with shares also has the advantage that pre-tax profits can be made to rise by the reduction in interest cost. Where excess capital has not been used to reduce debt, it has been used to buy short-term financial assets. Alternatively, excess capital is committed to buying and selling companies. Hence the extended festival of merger and takeover activity and balance-sheet restructuring that has characterized corporate finance since the 1980s.

The overall effect on banks of company overcapitalization has been to make them more fragile. Before the 1970s, the largest, most reliable borrowers from banks were large corporations. From the end of the 1970s, such corporations found that they could borrow much more cheaply by issuing their own bills (company paper) or directly from the interbank market. If banks want to hold company loans, they have to buy them in the market at yields that give banks no profit over their cost of funds in the capital or money markets. The loss of their best customers has turned banks towards fee-related business in derivatives and debt obligations markets, and towards lending into the property market and to other risky customers that banks had hitherto treated with much more caution. The overall effect, from the savings and loans scandals of the early 1980s, to the subprime market crisis since 2007, has clearly been to make banking markets much more prone to crisis.

This capital market inflation is behind the long equity financing boom since the 1970s. In the housing market, the deregulation of housing credit since the 1980s has increased the amount of credit entering the housing market, driving up house prices. In a sense, this is the paradigmatic example of asset inflation with collateralized lending. The more house prices rise, the more credit comes into the market because housing is a necessity, and the prospects of capital gains may be set against the costs of greater indebtedness. Indeed, as house prices rise, the housing market becomes more liquid and more capital gains can be realized to reduce the debt induced by the inflation of housing assets (Toporowski, 2009; see also below).

Furthermore, asset inflation improves the quality of loan collateral, not only by making that collateral more liquid, but also by increasing its value, so that the margin between the loan and the asset value increases. With competitive lending and turnover in the housing market, the prospective capital gain on housing collateral comes to be incorporated into the loan. Whereas at the start of the housing boom, during the 1980s, house purchasers were offered typically 80 per cent of the value of the property as a mortgage loan, in the 1990s they could obtain 100 per cent mortgages. Three years ago, borrowers in the UK were being offered 120 per cent mortgages.

Unlike the Bernanke–Gertler financial accelerator model, this asset inflation was clearly a disequilibrium process. (The determining variable of the financial accelerator is a fluctuating net worth of economic agents, whereas in this analysis it is an unconstrained rise in asset values.) But asset inflation had two stabilizing features which put off the Minskyan crisis until 2008. The first was the overcapitalization of large non-financial companies: excess capital held in the form of liquid assets makes those companies more financially stable and capable of surviving a longer period of negative cash flow. The other stabilizer was the support for consumption expenditure from a debt-inflated housing market, whose capital gains could be extracted by the greater liquidity of that market. The use of capital gains for consumption reduced household saving and made firms' investment a more effective generator of cash flow for the business sector (Toporowski, 2009). Rising asset values thus hedged speculative and Ponzi financing structures with capital gains.

The financial crisis results from the breakdown of these two stabilizers. In the capital market the emergence of debt-financed private equity funds, which bought out companies and transferred those funds' debt onto the companies' balance sheets in order to resell the companies (and debts), transformed the process of capital market inflation. The trend towards equity financing was now converted into a process of converting the debts used to inflate the equity market into company debt. (In his exhaustive analysis of the 1929 Crash, Schumpeter (1939: 877) had noted 'the ominous increase in the flotations of securities of investment trusts and financial and trading companies since 1926 . . . '.) In the housing market, there was clearly a limit to which young people, at the start of their careers, could indebt themselves, even with the prospect of capital gains in their later middle age. It is significant that the housing boom broke not where houses were most expensive, where capital gains may be said to have been the greatest, and hence where a speculative 'bubble' may have been most distended. The boom broke where incomes were lowest, in the subprime sector of the market, where the market in the asset was least liquid, and therefore excessive debt could be serviced only out of a low and unreliable income, rather than out of capital gain.

With a reduction in the credit entering the capital and housing markets, relative to the credit being taken out of those markets, asset inflation reverts to asset deflation. Collateralized lending now chokes off the supply of credit even further. The proportion of housing value that mortgage lenders in the UK will advance has, in recent months, reduced to between 60 per cent and 75 per cent. This obliges purchasers to put more of their own money into house purchase. The higher deposit requirement has reduced the number of borrowers capable of meeting the standard for prudent collateralized lending. Moreover, with falling asset values, homeowners find that the excess of collateral value over outstanding loan value disappears, and may even become negative. Debt that previously could be written off against capital gain must now be paid out of income.

In the company sector, the equivalent process involves reducing firms' investment, which then reduces the cash inflow of the firm sector as a whole. In both sectors a reluctance to borrow is accompanied by an increased desire to repay debt. Contrary to official opinion, the reduced lending of banks is not because banks are unwilling to lend, but because their customers are unwilling to borrow. In terms of Minsky's financing structures, financing obligations previously hedged by capital gains are made speculative by the fall in asset values, and speculative structures are turned into Ponzi financing structures when income and asset values cannot generate sufficient cash flow to settle financing obligations.

Throughout the process of asset inflation and the subsequent deflation, companies, households and banks are behaving rationally and prudently in terms of what their recent experience tells them about their prospects. The problem lies in the mutually reinforcing combination of asset inflation and collateralized lending, inducing over-indebtedness in the economy. Modern finance theory presents borrowing as a financing activity to generate future income which is then supposed to service that borrowing. From this is derived the economic function of the rate of interest in neoclassical, Keynesian, new Keynesian, new classical and even many post-Keynesian theories, as a regulator of business investment. However, in speculative markets it ceases to have that function. More importantly, as long as asset inflation continues, asset markets remain liquid, allowing the build-up of collateralized debt. Contrary to Minsky, Fisher, Kindleberger and their followers, it is not business investment that causes company over-indebtedness. As recently as 2006, around 90 per cent of non-financial business investment in the USA was financed from retained profits. Companies succumb to excess debt through asset inflation and the intervention of investment funds and private equity funds in the capital market inflation process. Such financial intermediaries raise funds that are transferred as debts onto the balance sheets of non-financial companies.

ECONOMIC INEQUALITY AND ASSET INFLATION

In the discussion on the financial crisis, one important factor has been overlooked, namely the distribution of income and wealth. It is obvious that the social consequences of the financial crisis have been made much more painful by the growing inequalities of income and wealth in the USA and the UK. But there are also connections between such inequalities and financial instability. These have been highlighted by many critics of financialized capitalism. For example, Hobson argued that inequalities of wealth and income gave rise to oversaving, and hence economic stagnation. More recently, the late John Kenneth Galbraith noted the connection between tax cuts for the rich and asset inflation (Galbraith, 1988: Foreword).

Asset inflation and income and economic inequalities are intimately linked. When the asset is housing, its inflation is especially pernicious. The housing market then redistributes income and wealth, from young people earning less at the start of their careers and indebting themselves hugely in order to get somewhere decent to live to people enjoying highest earnings at the end of their careers. But housing inflation is also like a pyramid banking scheme because it requires more and more credit to be put into the housing market in order to allow those profiting from house inflation to realize their profits.

Nevertheless, even those entering the system with large debts hope to be able to profit from it. Such has been the dependence of recent governments and society in general on asset inflation that the political consensus is 'intensely relaxed' about such regressive redistribution of income. That consensus has encouraged the belief that the best that young people can do to enhance their prospects is to indebt themselves in order to 'get on the property ladder', i.e. enrich themselves (or at least improve their housing) through housing inflation.

Those at the bottom of the income distribution inevitably suffer most from rising house prices because, living in the worst housing, they have the least possibility to accommodate their house purchase to their income by buying cheaper, smaller housing. Because households in this social group have little other option but to over-indebt themselves in order to secure their housing, default rates among them are also most likely to rise with house price inflation. This inequality lies behind the problems in the subprime market in the USA and the equivalents of that market in the UK and elsewhere. Paradoxically, a more equal distribution of income and wealth is more likely to keep the housing market in equilibrium, because any increase in house prices above the rate of increase in income and wealth is more likely to result in a fall in demand for housing. Where income and wealth are already unequally distributed, and house prices rise faster than incomes, a fall in demand from those who can no longer afford a given class of housing is offset by the increased demand for that class of housing among households that previously could afford better housing. In this way, the redistribution of income and wealth from those with more modest incomes to those with higher incomes also facilitates asset inflation in the housing market.

Thus asset inflation has increased inequalities of wealth and income, and those inequalities have further fed that inflation. Such inflation is therefore a self-reinforcing pathology of financial markets and society, rather than, as the economics establishment tells us, a temporary disequilibrium (a 'bubble') in the markets. Financial stability rests not only on sound banking and financial institutions; it also requires a much more equal distribution of income and wealth.

CONCLUSION

The present financial crisis is not the result of euphoria, followed by panic and a rush to sell, but the outcome of asset inflation in the dual price system that Minsky took over from Irving Fisher, in a setting of collateralized lending. Measures to stabilize asset values are an essential element in financial reconstruction. Furthermore, financial reconstruction must deal with more than just the stability of the banking system, or the broader financial system. Here it needs to be recognized that one of the functions of financial intermediation is to absorb risks that arise in the course of business. Stabilizing a banking system without stabilizing the economy makes any regulated financial system vulnerable to arguments from bankers and economists that if only the regulations were made lighter, or preferably removed altogether, the credit system would automatically alleviate those imbalances, and bring the economy back to equilibrium. And who then would argue against them, since we all teach our students that the credit system functions to accommodate economic imbalances and has done so quite effectively for decades, with only recent disastrous results. The radical conclusion of Minsky's work remains that without stabilizing the economy at large, banking stabilization is unlikely to hold. To this must be added recognition that the inequalities of income and wealth that have scarred the most financialized economies are not incidental to asset inflation, but are a part of its pathology.

ACKNOWLEDGEMENT

I am grateful to Ms Fatima Tariq for her assistance.

REFERENCES

Bank of England (2008), *Financial Stability Report*, No. 24, October.

Bernanke, B.S. and M. Gertler (1989), 'Agency costs, net worth, and business fluctuations', *The American Economic Review*, **79** (1): 14–31.

Chick, V. (1973), *The Theory of Monetary Policy*, London: Gray–Mills Publishing.

Coddington, A.C. (1983), *Keynesian Economics: The Search for First Principles*, London: Allen & Unwin.

Fisher, I. (1933), 'The debt deflation theory of Great Depression', *Econometrica*, **1** (1): 337–57.

Galbraith, J.K. (1988), *The Great Crash*, London: André Deutsch.

Hobson, J.A. (1913), *Gold, Prices and Wages with an Examination of the Quantity Theory*, London: Methuen.

Kaldor, N. (1960 [1939]), 'Speculation and economic stability', in N. Kaldor,

Essays on Economic Stability and Growth, London: Gerald Duckworth & Co., pp. 17–58.

Keynes, J.M. (1915), Review of Mrs. Russell Barrington (ed.), *The Works and Life of Walter Bagehot. Economic Journal*, in Donald Moggridge (ed.), *The Collected Writings of John Maynard Keynes Volume XI: Economic Articles and Correspondence Academic*, London: Macmillan and Cambridge University Press for the Royal Economic Society, 1973.

Keynes, J.M. (1936), *The General Theory of Employment, Interest and Money*, London: Macmillan & Co.

Kindleberger, C.P. (1989), *Manias, Panics and Crashes: A History of Financial Crises*, London: Macmillan.

Kregel, J.A. (2008), 'Minsky's cushions of safety: systemic risk and the crisis in the U.S. subprime mortgage market', *Public Policy Brief*, No. 93, New York: The Levy Economics Institute of Bard College.

Marx, K. (1975), *Theories of Surplus Value Part II*, Moscow: Progress Publishers.

Minsky, H.P. (1992), 'The financial instability hypothesis', Working Paper No. 74, New York: The Levy Economics Institute of Bard College.

Perelstein, J.S. (2009), 'Macroeconomic imbalances in the United States and their impact on the international financial system', Working Paper No. 554, New York: The Levy Economics Institute of Bard College.

Schumpeter, J.A. (1939), *Business Cycles A Theoretical, Historical, and Statistical Analysis of the Capitalist Process*, New York: McGraw-Hill Book Company.

Shiller R.J. (1993), *Macro Markets Creating Institutions for Managing Society's Largest Economic Risks*, Oxford: The Clarendon Press.

Tily, G. (2007), *Keynes's General Theory, the Rate of Interest, and Keynesian Economics: Keynes Betrayed*, Basingstoke, UK: Palgrave Macmillan.

Toporowski, J. (2000), *The End of Finance: The Theory of Capital Market Inflation, Financial Derivatives and Pension Fund Capitalism*, London: Routledge.

Toporowski, J. (2008), 'Minsky's *Induced Investment and Business Cycles*', *Cambridge Journal of Economics*, **32** (5): 725–37.

Toporowski, J. (2009), 'The economics and culture of financial inflation', *Competition and Change*, **13** (2): 147–58.

Wray, L.R. (2008), 'Financial markets meltdown: what can we learn from Minsky?', *Public Policy Brief*, No. 94, New York: The Levy Economics Institute of Bard College, April.

14. An institutionalist perspective on the global financial crisis

Charles J. Whalen

INTRODUCTION

This chapter presents an institutionalist perspective on the financial crisis that has been at the center of world attention since mid-2008. It is divided into three sections. The first provides a brief history of the institutionalist understanding of how an economy operates, with special attention to how this understanding differs from that offered by neoclassical economics. The second outlines an institutionalist explanation of the global financial crisis. The third identifies some of the public-policy steps that are required to achieve a more stable and broadly shared prosperity in the USA and abroad.

The particular variant of institutional economics that informs this chapter is what can be called post-Keynesian institutionalism (PKI). This strand of institutionalist thought, which emerged in the USA in the early 1980s, is rooted in the contributions of Thorstein B. Veblen (1857–1929), Wesley C. Mitchell (1874–1948) and John R. Commons (1862–1945), but also benefits from the insights of John Maynard Keynes (1883–1946) and even Joseph A. Schumpeter (1883–1950). The publications of Hyman P. Minsky (1919–96) were a model of PKI in the 1980s and 1990s, and his ideas remain relevant today. In addition to the author of this chapter, recent contributors to PKI include Martin H. Wolfson, David A. Zalewski, Kenneth P. Jameson, Slim Thabet, Chris Niggle, Fadhel Kaboub, Eric Tymoigne, L. Randall Wray and Zdravka Todorova.[1]

HOW AN ECONOMY OPERATES

In a 1996 essay, institutionalist William M. Dugger observed that institutional economists have traditionally been 'notoriously independent cusses, so getting them all within the perimeters of a manageable definition is not easy – it is a bit like herding stray cats' (Dugger, 1996: 31). In this chapter, that challenge is underscored by recognition that PKI draws on several strands of economic thought. Thus, instead of a roundup, this section offers an aerial survey: a historical overview of relevant institutionalist perspectives on how an economy operates, with attention to their divergence from mainstream economics.

Scope, Focus and Point of View

Institutional and neoclassical economics have always differed in scope. Neoclassical economics involves the study of market economies; its theories are not equipped to study a command economy or pre-capitalist economy. In contrast, institutional economics involves the much broader study of 'social provisioning' – it is interested in the what, how and why of all aspects of production and distribution by human beings, regardless of whether those processes involve markets or not (Dugger 1996).

This difference in scope leads to an essential difference in focus. Neoclassical economics focuses on the price mechanism, and considers the adjustment of prices to be the key regulating force in an economy. In contrast, institutionalism focuses on social institutions, and views them as the key to economic regulation. Indeed, according to institutionalist Yngve Ramstad, a 'central insight' of the institutional school is that institutional adjustment is 'the balancing wheel of the economy' (Ramstad, 1985: 509).

To be sure, institutionalists study market economies, but their different focus yields an alternative conception of how such economies operate. Since the days of Veblen, institutionalists have stressed that the difference between their approach to studying capitalist economies and the approach of the mainstream boils down to a different 'point of view:' neoclassical economics assumes the price system is self-regulating, while institutional economics does not (Veblen, 1898). Institutionalists recognize system tendencies, but are unwilling to assume self-reinforcing or self-regulating forces dominate *a priori*. It all depends on the social institutions.

Veblen, Mitchell and Commons

The neoclassical and institutionalist conceptions of market economies produce divergent research streams. Mainstream economics devotes much attention to identifying the normal conditions and long-run tendencies that are consistent with its fundamental preconception regarding price adjustments. Institutional economics seeks instead to understand the actual evolution of social institutions. In fact, this was the orientation Veblen advocated in 1898, when he wrote, 'There is the economic life process still in great measure awaiting theoretical formulation' (Veblen 1898: 387).

Financial crises were among the aspects of the economic life process incorporated into the theories of Veblen and his student, Mitchell (see, e.g., Veblen, 1904 and Mitchell, 1927). That is not surprising; such crises appeared to be an integral part of the business cycles that occurred regularly in their lifetime. However, such crises and cycles received little attention from conventional economists. As Mitchell noted in 1927, 'It was not the orthodox economists who gave the problem of crises and depressions its place in economics'; to scholars in the economic mainstream, such issues did not rank 'among the central problems of economic theory' and were 'of secondary interest' at best (Mitchell, 1927, 3–4).

While Mitchell was much more interested in using theory to resolve immediate economic problems than Veblen, perhaps the most outspoken 'problem-solver' of the early institutionalists was Commons. Motivated by an interest in the issues of concern to working people, Commons was drawn to a study of the credit system and business cycles. According to Commons, 'Unemployment is *the* outstanding defect of capitalism'; the business cycle was the most important cause of unemployment; and the credit cycle was at the root of the business cycle (Lewisohn et al., 1925: 52; Commons, 1922). Thus, attacking these issues was at the heart of his career-long attempt to 'save capitalism by making it good' (Commons, 1934, 143).

Keynes and the Keynesian Revolution

Keynes, of course, was in many respects on the same mission as Commons (Atkinson and Oleson, 1998). Moreover, Keynes and Commons corresponded and occasionally exchanged papers. In one letter to Commons, Keynes famously wrote, '[T]here seems to be no other economist with whose general way of thinking I feel myself in such genuine accord' (Keynes, 1927).

In a series of lectures and articles written in the 1920s and 1930s, Keynes distinguished his view of how the capitalist system operates from that of mainstream economists. He differed from the mainstream, Keynes argued, due to rejection of the conventional belief that 'the existing economic system is in the long run self-adjusting' (Keynes, 1935: 35). As he wrote in 1925,

> On the one side the Treasury and the Bank of England are pursuing an orthodox nineteenth-century policy based on the assumption that economic adjustments can and ought to be brought about by the free play of the forces of supply and demand. . . .On the other side, not only the facts, but public opinion also, have moved a long distance away in the direction of Professor Commons's epoch of stabilization. (Keynes, 1972: 305)

The 'epoch of stabilization' to which Keynes refers is a stage of world economic history outlined in 'Reasonable Value', a 100-page manuscript that Commons eventually developed into *Institutional Economics* (Commons, 2008). From Keynes's discussion of Commons's eras of scarcity, abundance and stabilization (which appears in two 1925 essays), it is clear both economists appreciated that institutional change affects an economy's performance and policy needs (Keynes, 1972, 1981). The institutionalist literature has even demonstrated that the determinants of national output and employment presented in Keynes's *The General Theory of Employment, Interest and Money* are historically contingent and institutionally determined (Chase, 1975; Foster, 1981; Crotty, 1990).[2]

Despite Keynes's affinity with the non-neoclassical ideas of Commons, the Keynesian revolution in economics was quickly defused and *The General Theory* was soon co-opted by the economic mainstream. Through the work of John R. Hicks, Paul A. Samuelson, James Tobin and others, Keynes's insights became merely a special case in a macroeconomic theory compatible with the pre-Keynesian mainstream and neoclassical microeconomics. In the 1950s and 1960s, that macro theory reached the peak of its popularity and was widely regarded as an adequate guide to US fiscal policy and aggregate-demand management, which boiled down to 'fine-tuning' in response to exogenous disturbances. Instead of adopting a dynamic, business-cycle perspective, macroeconomic analysis was heavily oriented toward comparative statics.

In the 1970s and early 1980s, however, the Keynesian–neoclassical synthesis was under attack for inadequately addressing stagflation and the resurgence of financial instability. In the realm of theory, the macroeconomic mainstream distanced itself further from Keynes by embracing the notion of a natural rate of unemployment and even new classical macroeconomics, which defines away the problem of unemployment by dismissing the possibility that joblessness can be involuntary. With respect to policy, meanwhile, the mainstream moved toward monetarism and later to inflation targeting. The case for activist demand management became more dependent than ever on the existence of 'market imperfections', such as rigid wages, which could rarely be used to justify more than short-term government action.

Post-Keynesian Institutionalism

A number of institutionalists responded to the assault on mainstream Keynesianism in a very different manner: by emphasizing the common ground between their approach and that of Keynes. This opened the door to the emergence of post-Keynesian institutionalism (PKI). Wallace C. Peterson, for example, used his 1976 presidential address before the institutionalists' Association for Evolutionary Economics (AFEE) to underscore the overlapping 'bedrock, seminal ideas in institutionalism and Keynes'. He began, not surprisingly, by drawing attention to the fact that *The General Theory* describes an economic system 'inherently flawed' due to 'intractable cyclical instability' and by observing that 'the neoclassical synthesis cut Keynes loose from real, historical time'. According to Peterson, 'Leaving history and its uncertain movement out of the analysis imparts a false sense of determinacy and predictability to the economic process' (Peterson, 1977: 202, 213–14).

Dudley Dillard, W. Robert Brazelton and Robert R. Keller also helped pave the way for PKI. Dillard stressed that financial institutions play a critical role in the economics of Veblen, Mitchell and Keynes, and that each had 'what may be called a monetary theory of production' (Dillard, 1980: 255). Brazelton drew attention to microeconomic and macroeconomic compatibilities in institutional economics, *The General Theory*, and the emerging post-Keynesian economics associated with the work of Sidney Weintraub, Daniel R. Fusfeld and a small number of other Americans (Brazelton, 1981). Keller, meanwhile, highlighted institutionalist and post-Keynesian complementarities; for example, the former gave more attention to the case for constructive state involvement in the economy, while the latter produced more detailed analyses of problems such as stagflation (Keller, 1983).

Stagflation is one of the central problems addressed in the first book to analyze the economy from a PKI perspective, *An Inquiry into the Poverty of Economics* by Charles K. Wilber and Kenneth P. Jameson (1983). Drawing on Keynes's belief that the economy is inherently unstable, and on the institutionalist tradition pioneered by Veblen, Mitchell and Commons, Wilber and Jameson gave special attention to John Kenneth Galbraith's notion of a bifurcated economic system – a 'planning sector' with about a thousand oligopolistic corporations and a 'market sector' with millions of small firms wielding little or no market power. Key chapters of their book focused on how the interplay of these two sectors and government affected output, employment and prices.

In a rapidly changing economy, however, the Wilber and Jameson volume fell out of date quickly. Even more than a book centered on the condition of stagflation, PKI needed attention to the dynamics of business cycles and postwar capitalist development. In the wake of *An Inquiry into the Poverty of Economics*, Hyman P. Minsky came closest to providing what was required. He also integrated key insights from Schumpeter into the PKI conception of how the contemporary economy operates.

Minsky's PKI

Although Minsky may have been most often labeled a 'post-Keynesian' economist, he maintained a close relationship with institutionalists throughout his career and eventually considered himself both an institutionalist and a post-Keynesian. In the early 1980s, Minsky and his colleague Steven Fazzari were selected to contribute an article on monetary policy to a special economic-policy issue of AFEE's *Journal of Economic Issues* (Fazzari and Minsky, 1984). In the late 1980s, another special issue of that journal was organized to highlight institutionalist research, and Minsky's ideas on financial instability were featured prominently in the chapters on money and macroeconomics (Dillard, 1987; Peterson, 1987).

Minsky's main contribution on financial instability is called the 'financial instability hypothesis'. Stated simply, it maintains that the capitalist financial system tends to cycle endogenously from a conservative state of affairs called hedge financing, to a more risky form called speculative financing, to an unsustainable form called Ponzi financing and then back to hedge financing for another round. This hypothesis contrasts sharply with mainstream's 'efficient market hypothesis', which assumes investors, lenders and other financial market participants are not collectively predisposed to overconfidence and other biases. Without timely and appropriate public intervention, the financial instability cycle can have far-reaching macroeconomic consequences: a period of moderate prosperity can be quickly transformed into a boom, which can even more rapidly unravel and produce a deep recession (Minsky, 1992a, 1986a: 206–13).

According to Minsky, the financial instability hypothesis is rooted in a view of the world shared by Keynes and Mitchell. Both of those earlier economists looked at the economy of their time and saw a world in which Wall Street and other major financial centers played a critical role (Minsky, 1990: 72, 1993, 1975: 57–8). In contrast to conventional macroeconomics, which Minsky viewed as having simply added money and financial assets to an analysis based on a barter economy, Minsky argued that the insights of Keynes and Mitchell could be fashioned into what might be called the 'modern Keynesian' view:

> The modern Keynesian view begins with the creation and control of resources under actual (real world) capitalist conditions. Keynesian analysis is institutionally specific; it analyzes a capitalist economy with a sophisticated banking and financial system whose principal activity is financing business. This means that in each period capital-asset-owning and -using businesses have to pay funds to banks because prior financing contracts fall due. The Wall Street vision of businesspeople and bankers negotiating liability structures to finance asset holdings and activity, and these liability structures being validated or

repudiated by events that happen in calendar time, is the essential theoretical and institutional structure upon which Keynesian theory is based. (Fazzari and Minsky, 1984: 106)

In Minsky's modern Keynesian view, financial instability and business cycles are inherent in a capitalist economy with a 'Wall Street' institutional structure and expensive, long-lived capital assets (i.e. specialized types of plant and equipment). However, Minsky also recognized that business cycles are not simply fluctuations within a fixed economic structure. Instead, cycles represent both a cause and consequence of changes to that structure (Minsky, 1986a). As Mitchell wrote decades earlier, a major challenge for the business cycle theorist is that 'each new cycle presents idiosyncrasies' (Mitchell, 1941: ix).[3]

Minsky outlined his modern Keynesian perspective in a book and articles published in the mid-1970s (including Minsky, 1975, 1982: 59–70), but by the mid-1980s he was concerned that decades of cumulative changes in US financial relations and institutions had produced a new form of capitalism (Minsky, 1986b). As a result, he turned to the writings of Schumpeter, his professor and graduate advisor at Harvard, for insight into long-term capitalist development. In an essay written for the hundredth anniversary of the birth of Keynes and Schumpeter, Minsky wrote:

> Further progress in understanding capitalism may very well depend upon integrating Schumpeter's insights with regard to the dynamics of a capitalist process and the role of innovative entrepreneurs into an analytical framework that in its essential properties is Keynesian. Capitalism has exhibited both fragility and resiliency over the century since the death of Marx and the birth of Keynes and Schumpeter. Keynes's analytical structure enables us to understand and even cope with the fragility of capitalism. Schumpeter's vision of entrepreneurship helps us understand the resilience of capitalism and in particular how policy reactions to slumps that reflect Keynesian insights lead to resilience and add new dimensions to the fragility of financial structures. (Minsky, 1986c: 113)

Summarizing his position, Minsky added:

> The task confronting economics today may be characterized as a need to integrate Schumpeter's vision of a resilient intertemporal capitalist process with Keynes's hard insights into the fragility introduced into the capitalist accumulation process by some inescapable properties of capitalist financial structures. (Minsky, 1986c: 121)

The result is Minsky's theory of US capitalist development. According to this theory, the evolution of capitalism is shaped by the institutional structure, which is always changing as a consequence of profit-seeking activity. The financial system takes on special importance in this theory because while production precedes exchange, finance precedes production. In addition, as Minsky learned directly from Schumpeter, 'Nowhere are evolution, change and Schumpeterian entrepreneurship more evident than in banking and finance and nowhere is the drive for profits more clearly the factor making for change' (Minsky, 1993: 106). Moreover, since there is a symbiotic relationship between finance and industrial development, financial evolution profoundly affects the course of capitalist development.

Public policy is also an essential element in Minsky's theory. Government action is an inescapable determinant of capitalist evolution: policy affects 'both the details and the overall character of the economy', wrote Minsky in 1986. Thus 'economic policy must be concerned with the design of institutions as well as operations within a set of institutions' (Minsky, 1986a: 7). In addition, the shaping of an economy requires a definition of goals. There is no price mechanism or other invisible hand that can be relied upon to ensure optimal economic well-being; there is only a social system shaped by individual and collective choices (ibid.: 7–9). Further, since the economy evolves endogenously, no policy regime can provide a once-and-for-all solution to economic problems: 'We cannot, in a dynamic world, expect to resolve the problems of institutional organization for all time' (ibid.: 7, 333).

Minsky's theory of US capitalist development traces the American economy through a series of stages. The most recent transition involves the shift from managerial capitalism, ushered in by the New Deal, to money-manager capitalism, which, according to Minsky, emerged in the early 1980s. According to this theory, US capitalism evolved in the decades after the Second World War from a form driven by corporate executives to one controlled by managers of pensions, mutual funds and other investment institutions, who endeavor to maximize the value of the assets they manage (Minsky, 1990, 1993, 1996). The theory can be seen as an extension of analyses of US economic and industrial development found in both Veblen and Commons (Whalen, 2001).

Contemporary PKI

Although Minsky did not live to see the Asian financial crisis of the late 1990s, the dot-com era bubble and bust, or the current global financial crisis and economic downturn, other scholars continue to apply and build on the foundation he left behind. For example, a 1998 essay by Jan Kregel used Minsky's ideas to diagnose and prescribe policies for the Asian crisis at a time when mainstream economists were admitting they had little to offer (Kregel, 1998).[4] In the wake of the 'irrational exuberance' and subsequent economic difficulties that greeted the start of the new millennium, Zalewski (2002) applied the notion of money-manager capitalism to explain rising US retirement insecurity and Wolfson (2002) extended Minsky's theory of financial crises to the international economy. Niggle (2006), Wray (2008) and Whalen (2008a; 2008b) are among those offering more recent applications and extensions.

The economic contributions of Minsky and other institutionalists are products of careers devoted to understanding economic performance through time. In contrast, conventional economists have sought to focus on how markets operate at any moment in time, without giving attention to how those markets develop over time. However, as Douglass C. North – who served as Minsky's colleague at Washington University – asked in his Nobel Prize lecture in 1993, 'How can one prescribe policies when one doesn't understand how economies develop?' As North's lecture suggests, because neoclassical theory assumes institutions and time do not matter, that theory is 'simply an inappropriate tool' for analyzing and prescribing real-world policies (North, 1994: 359).

EXPLAINING THE GLOBAL FINANCIAL CRISIS

PKI incorporates Minsky's (1975: 9) assumption that the 'basic path' of real-world capitalism is cyclical and Mitchell's recognition that each cycle has its own idiosyncrasies. PKI also recognizes that such idiosyncrasies are largely a product of ongoing institutional evolution. Therefore it seems appropriate to sketch this institutionalist analysis of the current crisis by drawing attention to the underlying tendency toward financial instability and then adding institutional elements unique to the latest cycle.

Financial Instability

From the perspective of PKI, the financial structure of our economy becomes more and more fragile over a period of prosperity. In the early stages of prosperity, enterprises in highly profitable segments of the economy are rewarded for taking on increasing amounts of debt. And their success encourages other firms to engage in similar behavior.

This pattern was certainly evident in the high-tech sector during the late 1990s and in the housing sector during the early and mid-2000s. In fact, construction companies and contractors were not the only ones taking on more debt in the 2000s. Homebuyers were also taking on more debt as the housing market began heating up, in part because interest rates were low and the stock market had become less attractive in the wake of the dot-com boom and bust. While it had long been customary for US homebuyers to make a 20 percent down payment on a home, 42 percent of first-time home purchasers and 13 percent of buyers who were not first-time purchasers put no money down to acquire homes in the mid-2000s (Baker, 2009a; Irwin, 2005).[5]

In retrospect, it seems that enterprises and homebuyers should have resisted the impulse toward increasing indebtedness, but the incentives at the time were just too great. As Gary Dymski and Robert Pollin explain in a 1992 essay, nobody in a robust sector of the economy wants to be left behind due to underinvestment:

> Even if market participants did have full knowledge of the Minsky model, and were aware that financial crises will occur at some point, that would still not enable them to predict when the financial crisis will occur. In the meantime, aggressive firm managers and bank loan officers will be rewarded for pursuing profitable opportunities and gaining competitive advantages. Cautious managers, operating from the understanding that boom conditions will end at some uncertain point, will be penalized when their more aggressive competitors surpass their short-run performance. (Dymski and Pollin, 1992: 45)[6]

As the preceding quote indicates, lenders as well as borrowers fuel the tendency toward greater indebtedness in an expansion. The same climate of expectations that encourages borrowers to acquire more risky financial liability structures also eases lenders' worries that new loans might go unpaid (Minsky, 1975). Moreover, it is not just that borrowing and lending expand in the boom. There is also financial innovation. In fact, in a 1992 essay, Minsky wrote that bankers and other financial intermediaries are 'merchants of debt, who strive to innovate with regard to both the assets they acquire and the liabilities they market' (Minsky, 1992a: 6).

The boom cannot continue forever, however; we eventually arrive at what some observers have called the 'Minsky moment' (Lahart, 2007: 1). That is when it becomes clear that some borrowers have become over-extended and need to sell assets to make their payments. In the current crisis, early high-profile cases involved the mortgage broker Countrywide and two hedge funds run by Bear Stearns.[7]

Then the problem spreads. Since bankers and investors hold subjective views about acceptable debt levels, once a shortfall of cash and a forced selling of assets materialize somewhere in the economy, there can be a widespread reassessment of how much debt or lending is appropriate. Moreover, the build-up can go on for years, but when anything goes wrong the revaluation can be sudden (Minsky, 1982, 67).

When banks decide to rein in their lending, we find ourselves in a credit crunch. It is easy to think of the present economic crisis as something that began with the worldwide stock market downturn in the autumn of 2008.

In fact, though, the difficulties of 2008 were preceded by a credit crunch that began in the summer of 2007, and signs of trouble – traceable in large part to the 'subprime' mortgage market – were evident as early as March 2007 (Magnus, 2007; Foley, 2007; *BBC News*, 2009).

Once a credit crunch emerges, financial difficulties are no longer confined to one sector. In fact, a crunch threatens not only business investment, but also household consumption. This means that when a sectoral bubble bursts – in the high-tech sector nearly a decade ago or in the housing sector more recently – the collapse threatens to trigger an economy-wide recession.

And that sort of recession is what the USA and much of the world now experiences. Moreover, it is pretty clear that the situation has gone beyond a Minsky 'moment' and is more akin to an economic 'meltdown', at least with respect to US housing, banking and stocks. The Dow Jones industrial average, for example, fell 37 percent between 1 April 2007 and 1 April 2009 (Yahoo Finance, 2009). Meanwhile, the US unemployment rate rose from 4.4 percent in March 2007 to 8.5 percent in March 2009 (the latest monthly data available as of this writing), and is widely expected to continue rising through 2009 (US Department of Labor, 2009).

Institutional Features

While the analysis above provides some insight into the current crisis, the picture becomes clearer when distinctive institutional features of the crisis are brought into focus. The origin of today's economic difficulties can be traced in large part to four financial sector innovations: unconventional mortgages, securitization, the rise of hedge funds and the globalization of finance. The importance of these items underscores the value of two major contributions Minsky made to PKI: introduction of Schumpeter's emphasis on financial system evolution and invention of the notion of money-manager capitalism.

At the heart of the current financial crisis are home mortgages that deviate from the traditional US home-loan arrangement, which involved a long-term loan on fixed-rate terms. Many of these unconventional – some have even called them 'exotic' – mortgages have adjustable interest rates and/or payments that balloon over time. Federal law has allowed banks to issue adjustable-rate mortgages since 1982, but their use and complexity have exploded in the past decade. For example, industry experts estimate that a variant called the 'option adjustable rate mortgage' (option ARM), which offers a low 'teaser' rate and later resets so that minimum payments skyrocket, accounted for about 0.5 percent of all US mortgages written in 2003, but close to 15 percent (and up to 33 percent in many US communities) in 2006. More precise figures are unavailable because banks have not been required to report how many option ARMs they originate (Der Hovanesian, 2006).

Many of these mortgages were created to target less creditworthy customers, including those in what the banking industry calls the subprime market (Baker, 2009a). Others were marketed to people who wanted to speculate in the booming housing market, people who intended to buy and then quickly resell property. However, many unconventional loans were marketed to ordinary working families who could have handled conventional mortgages (Marks, 2008).

Unfortunately, it was clear from the outset that many of these exotic mortgages could never be paid back. (For an eye-opening look at the aggressive marketing of unconventional mortgages, see Morgenson, 2007.) But why did this happen? Why did the mortgage market evolve in this dangerous direction?

This is where securitization comes into the picture. Securitization is simply the bundling of loans – which can include auto loans, student loans, accounts receivable, and, of course, mortgages – and the subsequent selling of bundle shares to investors. In the mid-1980s, Minsky returned home from a conference sponsored by the Federal Reserve Bank of Chicago and wrote that securitization was emerging as a key, new financial innovation. 'That which can be securitized, will be securitized', he wrote (Minsky, 1990: 64). He was right, but way ahead of his time. Securitization of mortgages exploded onto the scene in the past decade.

After the dot-com bubble burst in 2001, housing in the USA looked like a safer and more appealing investment than ever to many Americans, especially with low interest rates in place due to Federal Reserve policy. Still, returns on conventional mortgages were too mundane to satisfy the aims of most money managers. As a result, what Minsky and Schumpeter might have called the 'financial-innovation machine' turned its attention to housing and shifted into high gear.

Securitization of mortgages meant that home-loan originators could be less concerned about the creditworthiness of borrowers than in the past. Thus they had an incentive to steer customers toward the most profitable types of mortgages, even if they were the riskiest (which, of course, they were) (Der Hovanesian, 2006). The result was the explosive growth in option ARMs and in 'no money down' and 'no documentation (of income)' loans. Minsky warned of all this in 1992, when he observed that securitization means that mortgage originators are rewarded as long as they avoid 'obvious fraud' (Minsky, 1992b: 22–3).[8]

Securitization worked like magic upon risky mortgages. Instead of 'garbage in, garbage out', risky loans went into the securitization process, but out came bundles that received high credit ratings from agencies like

Standard and Poor's. According to Christopher Huhne, a member of the UK Parliament and former rating-agency economist, part of the challenge of rating the bundles was that 'financial markets fall in love with new things, with innovations, and the [important] thing about new things is that it is very difficult to assess the real riskiness of them because you don't have a history by definition' (Huhne, 2007).

Another problem is that the rating agencies do not verify the information provided by mortgage issuers. Instead, they base their decisions on information received from intermediaries that, as Minsky put it, 'do not hazard any of their wealth on the long term viability of the underlying [loans]' (Minsky, 1992b: 23).

Moreover, there are so many middlemen in the mortgage securitization game, including a number permitted to operate in a largely unregulated manner, that no one person or organization can be easily assigned blame in the event of default. The chain between the borrower and the investor includes realtors, home appraisers, mortgage brokers, mortgage originators, investment banks that bundled the mortgages, agencies that rated the bundles, and even companies (like American International Group) that insured many of the bundles.[9]

Trillions of dollars worth of mortgage-backed securities were bundled and sold as shares to investors. In late 2008, Fannie Mae and Freddie Mac alone held $4.1 trillion (Lanman and Kopecki, 2008).

Many of the underlying mortgages are now in foreclosure or are headed there. In 2008, 2.3 million US homes went into foreclosure, up 81 percent from 2007 and 225 percent from 2006 (RealtyTrac, 2009). There were another 290 000 filings in February 2009 (the most recent period for which data are available as this chapter is being written), up 6 percent from the previous month (El Nasser, 2009).

Mortgage delinquencies are also up sharply. In February 2009, 7 percent of US homeowners with mortgages were at least 30 days late on their loans, an increase of more than 50 percent from a year earlier. Among subprime borrowers, that month's delinquency rate was 39.8 percent (Chernikoff, 2009). (Again, these are the latest available figures as of April 2009.)

There has been much public discussion over the past year or so in the USA about reckless homebuyers, but mortgage seekers could not and did not bring the economy to its knees on their own. Behind both the exotic home loans and mortgage securitization is money-manager capitalism. As Minsky stressed at a pair of professional conferences in the late 1980s and early 1990s, there is a symbiotic relationship 'between the growth of securitization and managed money'; fund managers 'have outgrown the orthodox high quality stocks and bond portfolios of fiduciaries' (Minsky, 1990: 71; 1992c: 32).

From the perspective of PKI, the economic participants most responsible for bringing down the economy are hedge funds and other investment funds, investment banks and other financial institutions. Looking at hedge funds offers a glimpse at what happened. Although the following discussion focuses on hedge funds because they are a relative newcomer to the scene and have become infamous for operating beyond the reach of much government regulation, the investment banks and other institutions played a similar role.

Some of the biggest purchasers of securitized mortgages have been hedge funds. The first of these funds were established in the first few decades after the Second World War for the purpose of seeking absolute returns (rather than beating a benchmark stock market index). They were indeed 'hedged' funds, which sought to protect principal from financial loss by hedging investments through short selling or other means. The number of hedge funds and the assets under their management expanded in the 1990s and grew even more rapidly in the 2000s. At the same time, these assets became increasingly concentrated in the top ten firms and funds became more diverse in terms of the strategies their managers employed. In mid-2008, the Alternative Investment Management Association estimated that the world's hedge funds (based primarily in the USA) were managing $2.5 trillion, although it acknowledged that other estimates were as high as $4 trillion (Ineichen and Silberstein, 2008: 16).

The total value of assets under hedge fund management is uncertain because such funds are typically restricted to wealthy individuals and institutional investors, which exempts them from most financial sector reporting requirements and regulation. Taking advantage of their largely unregulated status, managers of hedge funds used their mortgage-backed securities as collateral to take out highly leveraged loans. They then purchased an assortment of financial instruments, including still more mortgage bundles. As a result, the world's hedge funds used securitized mortgages to lay an inherently flimsy foundation for a financial 'house of cards' (Freeman, 2009; Holt, 2009).

The current crisis is unmistakably global. It is having economic and political ramifications on all continents (*BBC News*, 2009). The trouble is even affecting unexpected places like rural China: factories in cities along that nation's coast are laying off workers and sending them back to their villages (Lee, 2009).

The global nature of the current situation would not have surprised Minsky, who stressed early on that money-manager capitalism 'is international in both the funds and the assets in funds' (Minsky, 1990: 71). Looking ahead to the current crisis, Minsky wrote: 'The problem of finance that will emerge is whether the . . . institutions of national governments can contain both the consequences of global financial fragility and an international debt deflation' (Minsky, 1995: 93). He worried that the USA would be unable to serve as 'the guardian angel for stability in the world economy' and stressed the need for 'an international division of responsibility for maintaining global aggregate gross profits' (Minsky, 1986d: 15; 1990: 71).

In short, from the perspective of PKI, the global economy is now reeling from the consequences of a classic Minsky crisis. Its origins are in a housing boom fueled by rising expectations, expanding debt and financial innovation. Then the bubble burst, creating a credit crunch, followed by a broader banking and stock-market crisis, and now a recession.

The consequences have been staggering. In the housing sector, an unprecedented one in nine US homes (14 million) sits vacant, while another 9.4 million are for sale (El Nasser, 2009). The US stock market lost an unprecedented $1.2 trillion of value in just a single day in late September 2008 (measured by the Wilshire 5000), and for 2008 overall the Dow Jones Industrial Average (the Dow) had its worst year since 1931 (Blaine 2008). The unemployment rate may soon hit double digits in the USA; joblessness has already reached double digits in some parts of Europe.

Since 2007, the global banking industry has seen an unprecedented shakeout (*BBC News*, 2009), but there is still uncertainty about how much more difficulty lies ahead. As the Bank for International Settlements indicated in a report released in June 2007:

> Assuming that the big banks have managed to distribute more widely the risks inherent in the loans they have made, who now holds these risks, and can they manage them adequately? The honest answer is that we do not know. Much of the risk is embodied in various forms of asset-backed securities of growing complexity and opacity. They have been purchased by a wide range of smaller banks, pension funds, insurance companies, hedge funds, other funds and even individuals, who have been encouraged to invest by the generally high ratings given to these instruments. (Bank for International Settlements, 2007: 145)

Warren Buffett made the point more vividly: 'You only learn who has been swimming naked when the tide goes out' (Buffett, 2008: 3). Although the risks are now being laid bare, it will still be some time before the world learns the full extent of the financial exposure.

TOWARD RENEWED PROSPERITY

The current global economic situation requires a two-pronged economic-policy strategy: recovery and reform. Beyond stabilizing the troubled financial sector and preventing the current downturn from becoming more severe, the overarching policy objective should be greater macroeconomic stability and broadly shared prosperity in the USA and abroad. The discussion below is intended merely to highlight some of the important issues and necessary steps; a comprehensive revitalization plan would require considerably more space than is available and deserves to be fashioned by a team, rather than by an individual. The focus of this discussion is the USA, not merely because the economic trouble originated there, but also because my training and experience have been heavily oriented toward studying and addressing the functioning of that economy.

Recovery

A government strategy for recovery must have at least three components: monetary policy, fiscal policy and financial-market policy. Each is considered in turn.

US monetary policy is on the right track. The Federal Reserve has been trying to stabilize the financial sector and the overall economy for well over a year. It has aggressively cut interest rates, allowed banks to borrow from it at nominal rates, and given banks cash in exchange for risky assets (promising to take on the risk if those assets prove worthless). The Fed has also engineered bank mergers and worked with other central banks to increase the supply of dollars worldwide. In a very short time, Fed Chairman Ben Bernanke has moved a long way from the days when he was known as a proponent of inflation targeting.

US fiscal policy has also been moving in the right direction, but has been too timid. The first stimulus attempt, passed in early 2008, included $100 billion in tax rebates and helped prop up consumer spending (Broda and Parker, 2008), but the bill also included tens of billions in less stimulative business tax cuts. More recently, President Barack Obama signed into law a stimulus package totaling $787 billion over two years. However, Paul Krugman was probably correct when he suggested that the package should have been twice as big and even more tilted toward spending (as opposed to tax cuts), especially since recent data revisions show that fourth-quarter US GDP fell by 6.3 percent, not 4.0 percent as reported originally (Earnshaw, 2009; Krugman, 2009a).[10]

Financial-market policy at the US Treasury Department, however, has been woefully inadequate. The Troubled Asset Relief Program, more commonly known as the $700 billion Wall St Bailout, seemed designed to clean up bank balance sheets by purchasing their bad assets. Instead, the Treasury was soon writing banks checks and buying large quantities of bank stocks. The underlying problem of the 'toxic' assets remained unresolved, banks remained reluctant to lend, and much of the added liquidity was transformed into bank stock dividends.

The Treasury's latest plan, a 'public–private partnership' that creates a market for troubled assets with government loans and guarantees, is not much better. The plan offers what Joseph E. Stiglitz calls a 'win–win–lose proposal: the banks win, investors win – and taxpayers lose'. He argues that the plan encourages investors to bid high in that market and socializes the losses that are likely to follow. In attempting to account for this proposal, Stiglitz writes: 'Perhaps it's the kind of Rube Goldberg device that Wall Street loves – clever, complex and nontransparent, allowing huge transfers of wealth to the financial markets' (Stiglitz, 2009).

Minsky, who admired how the administration of President Franklin D. Roosevelt closed insolvent banks and assisted solvent ones during the Great Depression, would have almost certainly called for a more hands-on sorting-out of the financial mess by means of bank restructuring. Today, Krugman (2009b; 2009c), Dean Baker (2009b), and James K. Galbraith (2009) call for similar action. As Galbraith writes,

> If the subprime securities are truly trash, most of the big banks are troubled and some are insolvent. The FDIC should put them through receivership, get clean audits, install new management, and begin the necessary shrinkage of the banking system with the big guys, not the small ones. (Galbraith 2009)

The Obama Administration recently ordered federal regulators to conduct 'stress tests' to gauge the condition of the nation's banks. As a next step, the receivership approach makes more sense than creation of a government-subsidized market for toxic assets.

Another aspect of financial-market policy that needs attention is home mortgages. Throughout 2008, the USA largely avoided addressing the unaffordable mortgages that are at the heart of the current problem (Marks, 2008). The Obama Administration has been encouraging the financial industry to voluntarily restructure those loans, but industry pressure has made many in the nation's capital reluctant to require it. For example, federal legislators have so far refused to let bankruptcy judges insist on home-loan restructuring, despite the fact that judges can demand a restructuring of all loans except the mortgage on a homeowner's residence (legislation is stalled in the US Senate as of this writing).

Reform

Looking beyond the current downturn, a reform agenda must include stricter regulation and supervision of the financial system, a national commitment to the challenges facing the USA's working families, and US participation in efforts that promote international economic stability and job creation.

Minsky believed that those responsible for government regulation and supervision of the financial system are in a 'never-ending struggle' with financial markets (Minsky, quoted in Phillips, 1997: 512). As he wrote in 1986, 'After an initial interval, the basic disequilibrating tendencies of capitalist finance will once again push the financial structure to the brink of fragility' (Minsky, 1986a: 333). Still, he always believed it was necessary for regulators to continue the struggle. Today's institutionalists hold the same view.

Greater industry transparency, more rigorous bank examinations and broader regulatory oversight would be a good place to start. If policy-makers had better information about the extent to which financial insti-tutions were making use of option ARMs and other exotic instruments, perhaps at least a few would have more aggressively sought to address the mounting problem. It also seems appropriate to revive Minsky's notion of a cash-flow approach to bank examinations, which is 'designed to use the examination process to generate information on not only the liquid-ity and solvency of particular institutions, but also on threats, if any, to the stability of financial markets' (Minsky, quoted in Phillips, 1997: 513). Similarly, mortgage brokers, hedge funds and other institutions that have gained increasing importance in the past decade deserve greater scrutiny from financial-system regulators.[11] In light of the current economic crisis, stricter oversight of securitization and other recent financial innovations are clearly overdue, but the additional need is for regulators to be on the lookout for future innovations in an effort to head off future crises before they occur.[12]

At the very least, the US government should not block state efforts designed to protect citizens from gaps in federal law. Today, most Americans know about the 2008 Valentine's Day in Washington that cost former New York Governor Eliot Spitzer his job, but of greater national importance was his guest column that appeared in *The Washington Post* that day. It described how the federal government stopped states from cracking down on predatory lending practices. As Spitzer's essay documents,

> Not only did the Bush Administration do nothing to protect consumers, it embarked on an aggressive and unprecedented campaign to prevent states from protecting their residents from the very problems to which the federal govern-ment was turning a blind eye . . . The tale is still unfolding, but when the dust settles, [the Bush Administration] will be judged as a willing accomplice to the lenders who went to any lengths in their quest for profits. (Spitzer, 2008)

In the age of managerial capitalism, it may have been sufficient to focus on full employment, low inflation and steady economic growth. In the age of money-manager capitalism, these goals are still important, but the challenges facing the USA's working families require more direct attention as well. Americans, like citizens elsewhere around the world, want the opportunity to develop and utilize their talents and to increase their standard of living in the process. They also want the prospect of an even better life for their children.

Unfortunately, rising worker insecurity is the flipside of money-manager capitalism. Under pressure from money managers, corporate executives have largely put aside the employer–employee social contract of the New Deal and the early decades following the Second World War. They have moved increasingly toward treating labor as just another 'spot market' commodity (Minsky, 1996; Minsky and Whalen, 1996–97).

Thus the economic challenges facing the USA extend far beyond stabilizing the financial system and preventing a long and deep recession. The nation needs to spur the growth of domestic jobs that pay family-supporting wages and to ensure that Americans have access to the education and training such jobs require. It needs to find a way to promote partnerships between workers and managers, so that companies can compete on the basis of innovation, quality and customer service, rather than by outsourcing jobs or slashing wages and benefits. It needs to provide adjustment assistance to workers displaced by international trade (including service workers excluded from some existing benefits programs) and public service employment to those unable to find private sector work. And it needs health-care reform, retirement-system reform and labor-law reform to address not only medical and retirement insecurity, but also the insecurity of workers who seek to exercise their legal right to engage in union organizing and collective bargaining.[13]

Finally, pursuit of greater economic stability and broadly shared prosperity cannot end at the borders of the USA. Americans must be active in helping to fashion international institutions that not only contain global financial instability, but also enhance labor rights and promote job growth. According to Stiglitz,

> During my three years as chief economist of the World Bank, labor market issues were looked at through the lens of neoclassical economics. 'Wage rigidities' – often the fruits of hard-fought bargaining – were thought part of the problem facing many countries. A standard message was to increase labor market flexibility. The not-so-subtle subtext was to lower wages and lay off unneeded workers. (Stiglitz, quoted in Komisar, 2000)

He concludes, 'They had a strategy for job destruction. They had no strategy for job creation' (ibid.). Institutionalists in the USA need to work with like-minded economists in other nations to develop that missing strategy.

CONCLUSION: STANDING ON THE SHOULDERS OF GIANTS

Minsky used to say we should stand on the shoulders of giants to better understand the economy; PKI seeks to do just that. Veblen, Mitchell, Commons, Keynes and Schumpeter provided a foundation. Minsky and other post-Second World War post-Keynesian institutionalists built upon the foundation. The present generation of institutionalists is now applying and adapting the inherited framework as a way of interpreting and addressing the current situation. If PKI is successful, it will leave the next generation both a more prosperous global economy and a more evolutionary and institutionally grounded economic science.

NOTES

1. Since economic conditions are changing rapidly as the current crisis evolves, it should be noted that this chapter was written in April 2009. A version of this chapter with a more extensive bibliography can be found online at http://digitalcommons.ilr.cornell.edu/intlvf/27/.
2. For a discussion of what is 'general' in *The General Theory*, see Crotty (1990).
3. According to Mitchell, 'Business history repeats itself, but always with a difference' (Mitchell, 1941: ix). For this reason, he stressed that 'history and theory supplement each other' (Mitchell, 1927: 57).
4. In an October 1998 essay published in *The New Republic*, Paul Krugman wrote the following regarding the Asian financial crisis: 'Suppose that you were to buy a copy of the best-selling textbook on international economics. What would it tell you about how to cope with such a sudden loss of confidence by international investors? Well, not much. (Trust me – I'm the coauthor of that textbook.)' (Krugman, 1998: 23).
5. Homeowners were also able to fuel a consumption boom by taking on even more debt. That is partly because rising home prices encouraged banks to increase customers' credit-card limits and to heavily promote home-equity loans.
6. Dymski and Pollin add: 'When boom conditions do end, aggressive managers will already have been promoted, while cautious managers will have been demoted, if not dismissed. Moreover, during the slump, all aggressive managers will fail together, so no single individual will be singled out for blame. This is in contrast to the boom, where the miscalculating cautious will have been isolated' (Dymski and Pollin, 1992: 45).
7. Of course, Bear Stearns itself was to be a casualty of the crisis in early 2008.
8. Here are some figures that indicate the magnitude of US mortgage securitization: in early 2007, about 65 percent of mortgages were being turned into bonds via securitization, up from 40 percent in 1990; and, in the years 2004–06, nearly $100 billion per year in option ARMs were sold to investors (Pittman, 2007; Der Hovanesian, 2006).
9. Mortgage brokers, who operate without much government regulation, accounted for 80 percent of all US mortgage originations in 2006, double their share a decade earlier (Der Hovanesian, 2006).

10. Another reason for suggesting that the 2009 stimulus was too timid is that the first-year tax-cut multipliers estimated by Christine Romer and Jared Bernstein were considerably below 1.0 (Romer and Bernstein, 2009: 12). Thus, modifying the package in the direction of tax cuts (to ensure passage) seemed ill advised from a macroeconomic perspective.
11. The use of leverage by hedge funds (and other financial institutions) and the writing of no-documentation home-loans are among the practices in greatest need of regulatory attention.
12. As this chapter was being prepared for publication, the US Treasury Department released (in mid-June 2009) a promising financial regulatory reform proposal.
13. To address the challenges facing the USA's working families, the Obama Administration has created a Middle Class Task Force, headed by Vice President Joe Biden. Its goals suggest an awareness of the issues discussed above ('About the Task Force', 2009).

REFERENCES

'About the Task Force', *The White House Blog* (30 January 2009), http://www. whitehouse.gov/blog_post/about_the_task_force_1/ (accessed 13 April 2009).

Atkinson, Glen and Theodore Oleson Jr (1998), 'Commons and Keynes: their assault on laissez faire', *Journal of Economic Issues*, **32** (4): 1019–30.

Bank for International Settlements (2007), *77th Annual Report*, Basel, Switzerland: Bank for International Settlements Press and Communications.

Baker, Dean (2009a), 'The economic crisis: how we got here', PowerPoint Presentation, Labor and Employment Relations Association Annual Meeting, 3 January, San Francisco, CA.

Baker, Dean (2009b), 'Geithner's plan will tax Main Street to make Wall Street Richer', *The Huffington Post* (30 March), http://www.huffingtonpost.com/dean-baker/geithners-plan-will-tax-m_b_181021.html (accessed 13 April 2009).

BBC News (2009), 'Timeline: credit crunch to downturn', *BBC News* (3 April 2009), http://news.bbc.co.uk/2/hi/business/7521250.stm (accessed 13 April 2009).

Blaine, Charley (2008), 'Wall Street says "good riddance!" to 2008', *MSN Money* (31 December), http://articles.moneycentral.msn.com/Investing/Dispatch/worst-year-since-1931-123108.aspx (accessed 13 April 2009).

Brazelton, W. Robert (1981), 'Post Keynesian economics: an institutional compatibility', *Journal of Economic Issues*, **15** (2): 531–42.

Broda, Christian and Jonathan Parker (2008), 'The impact of the 2008 tax rebates on consumer spending: preliminary evidence', Working paper (July), http://faculty.chicagobooth.edu/christian.broda/website/research/unrestricted/ Research.htm (accessed 13 April 2009).

Buffett, Warren E. (2008), Letter to shareholders, Berkshire Hathaway Inc., 2007 Annual Report.

Chase, Richard X. (1975), 'Keynes and U.S. Keynesianism: a lack of historical perspective and the decline of the new economics', *Journal of Economic Issues*, **9** (3): 441–61.

Chernikoff, Helen (2009), 'U.S. mortgage delinquencies up 50 percent', Reuters UK, http://uk.reuters.com/article/economyNews/idUKTRE5374LT20090408 (accessed 13 April 2009).

Commons, John R. (1922), 'Unemployment prevention', *American Labor Legislation Review*, **12** (1): 15–24.

Commons, John R. (1934), *Myself*, New York: Macmillan.
Commons, John R. (2008), 'Reasonable Value', in Warren J. Samuels (ed.), *Research in the History of Economic Thought and Methodology, Volume 26-B*, Bingley, UK: Emerald, pp. 239–307.
Crotty, James R. (1990), 'Keynes on the stages of development of the capitalist economy: the institutional foundation of Keynes's methodology', *Journal of Economic Issues*, **24** (3): 761–80.
Der Hovanesian, Mara (2006), 'Nightmare mortgages', *Business Week* (11 September), http://www.businessweek.com/magazine/content/06_37/b4000001.htm (accessed 13 April 2009).
Dillard, Dudley (1980), 'A monetary theory of production: Keynes and the institutionalists', *Journal of Economic Issues*, **14** (2): 255–73.
Dillard, Dudley (1987), 'Money as an institution of capitalism', *Journal of Economic Issues*, **21** (4): 1623–47.
Dugger, William M. (1996), 'Redefining economics: from market allocation to social provisioning', in Charles J. Whalen (ed.), *Political Economy for the 21st Century: Contemporary Views on the Trend of Economics*, Armonk, NY: M.E. Sharpe, pp. 31–43.
Dymski, Gary and Robert Pollin (1992), 'Minsky as hedgehog: the power of the Wall Street paradigm', in Steven Fazzari and Dimitri B. Papadimitriou (eds), *Financial Conditions and Macroeconomic Performance: Essays in Honor of Hyman P. Minsky*, Armonk, NY: M.E. Sharpe, pp. 27–61.
Earnshaw, Aliza (2009), 'Krugman: stimulus needs to be twice as big', *Portland Business Journal* (2 February), http://www.bizjournals.com/portland/stories/2009/01/26/daily68.html (accessed 13 April 2009).
El Nasser, Haya (2009), 'Open house anyone? 1 in 9 homes sit empty', *USA Today*, http://www.usatoday.com/money/economy/housing/2009-04-09-vacant homes_N.htm (accessed 13 April 2009).
Fazzari, Steven and Hyman P. Minsky (1984), 'Domestic monetary policy: if not monetarism, what?', *Journal of Economic Issues*, **18** (1): 101–16.
Foley, Stephen (2007), 'Anatomy of a credit crunch', *The (London) Independent* (27 July), http://www.independent.co.uk/news/business/analysis-and-features/anatomy-of-a-credit-crunch-459209.html (accessed 13 April 2009).
Foster, John Fagg (1981), 'Economics', *Journal of Economic Issues*, **15** (4): 857–67.
Freeman, James (2009), 'How the money vanished', *The Wall Street Journal* (6 March), http://online.wsj.com/article/SB123630340388147387.html (accessed 13 April 2009).
Galbraith, James K. (2009), 'The Geithner plan won't work', *The Daily Beast* (24 March), http://www.thedailybeast.com/blogs-and-stories/2009-03-24/the-geithner-plan-wont-work/full/ (accessed 13 April 2009).
Holt, Christopher (2009), 'A graphical look at hedge fund leverage', *Seeking Alpha* (8 March), http://seekingalpha.com/article/124783-a-graphical-look-at-hedge-fund-leverage.
Huhne, Christopher (2007), Comments on credit rating agencies and the US credit crunch, *World Business Review*, BBC World Service (1 September).
Ineichen, Alexander and Kurt Silberstein (2008), *AIMA's roadmap to hedge funds*, London: The Alternative Investment Management Association.
Irwin, Gloria (2005), 'No money down gains more buyers', *Akron Beacon Journal* (31 July), http://www.policymattersohio.org/media/

ABJ_No_money_down_gains_more_buyers_2005_0731.htm (accessed April 13, 2009).

Keller, Robert R. (1983), 'Keynesian and institutional economics: compatibility and complementarity', *Journal of Economic Issues*, **17** (4): 1087–95.

Keynes, John Maynard (1927), Letter to John R. Commons, 26 April. Reproduced in John R. Commons Papers, microfilm edition, reel 4. Madison, WI: State Historical Society of Wisconsin.

Keynes, John Maynard (1935), 'A self-adjusting economic system?', *The New Republic*, **82** (1055): 35–7.

Keynes, John Maynard (1972), 'Am I a liberal?' in Donald Moggridge (ed.), *The Collected Writings of John Maynard Keynes, Volume 9, Essays in Persuasion*, London: Macmillan, pp. 295–311. Based on an address delivered in the UK, summer 1925.

Keynes, John Maynard (1981), 'The economic transition in England', in Donald Moggridge (ed.), *The Collected Writings of John Maynard Keynes, Volume 19, The Return to Gold and Industrial Policy*, New York: Macmillan, pp. 438–42. Address delivered in Moscow, September 1925.

Komisar, Lucy (2000), 'Interview with Joseph Stiglitz', *The Progressive* (June), http://www.progressive.org/0901/intv0600.html (accessed 13 April 2009).

Kregel, Jan (1998), 'Yes "it" did happen again: a Minsky crisis in Asia', Working Paper No. 234, The Levy Economics Institute of Bard College.

Krugman, Paul (1998), 'The confidence game', *The New Republic*, **219** (14): 23–25.

Krugman, Paul (2009a), 'Stimulus arithmetic (wonkish but important)', *The New York Times* (6 January), http://krugman.blogs.nytimes.com/2009/01/06/stimulus-arithmetic-wonkish-but-important/ (accessed 13 April 2009).

Krugman, Paul (2009b), 'Despair over financial policy', *The New York Times* (21 March), http://krugman.blogs.nytimes.com/2009/03/21/despair-over-financial-policy/ (accessed 13 April 2009).

Krugman, Paul (2009c), 'Geithner plan arithmetic', *The New York Times* (23 March), http://krugman.blogs.nytimes.com/2009/03/23/geithner-plan-arithmetic/ (accessed 13 April 2009).

Lahart, Justin (2007), 'In time of tumult, obscure economist gains currency', *The Wall Street Journal* (8 August), 1.

Lanman, Scott and Dawn Kopecki (2008), 'Fed commits $800 billion more to unfreeze lending', Bloomberg.com (25 November), http://www.bloomberg.com/apps/news?pid=20601103&refer=us&sid=a.IQxmdJnJMc (accessed 13 April 2009).

Lee, Don (2009), 'Migrant factory workers at a loss as China's economy slumps', *Los Angeles Times* (23 January), http://articles.latimes.com/2009/jan/23/business/fi-chinamigrant23 (accessed 13 April 2009).

Lewisohn, Sam A., Ernest Gallaudet Draper, John R. Commons and Don D. Lescohier (1925), *Can Business Prevent Unemployment?*, New York: Alfred A. Knopf.

Magnus, George (2007), 'The credit cycle and liquidity: have we arrived at a Minsky moment?', *Economic Insights – By George*, UBS Investment Research, London (March).

Marks, Bruce (2008), 'Bailout must address the foreclosure crisis', *The Boston Globe* (24 September), http://www.boston.com/bostonglobe/editorial_opinion/oped/articles/2008/09/24/bailout_must_address_the_foreclosure_crisis/ (accessed 13 April 2009).

Minsky, Hyman P. (1975), *John Maynard Keynes*, New York: Columbia University Press.

Minsky, Hyman P. (1982), *Can 'it' happen again? Essays on instability and finance*, Armonk, NY: M.E. Sharpe.

Minsky, Hyman P. (1986a), *Stabilizing an Unstable Economy*, New Haven, CT: Yale University Press.

Minsky, Hyman P. (1986b), 'The evolution of financial institutions and the performance of the economy', *Journal of Economic Issues*, **20** (2): 345–53.

Minsky, Hyman P. (1986c), 'Money and crisis in Schumpeter and Keynes', in Hans-Jurgen Wagener and Jan W. Drukker (eds), *The Economic Law of Motion of Modern Society: A Marx–Keynes–Schumpeter Centennial*, Cambridge, UK: Cambridge University Press, pp. 112–22.

Minsky, Hyman P. (1986d), 'Global consequences of financial deregulation', *The Marcus Wallenberg Papers on International Finance*, **2** (1): 1–19.

Minsky, Hyman P. (1990), 'Schumpeter: finance and evolution', in Arnold Heertje and Mark Perlman (eds), *Evolving Market Technology and Market Structure: Studies in Schumpeterian Economics*, Ann Arbor, MI: The University of Michigan Press, pp. 51–74.

Minsky, Hyman P. (1992a), 'The financial instability hypothesis', Working Paper No. 74, The Levy Economics Institute of Bard College.

Minsky, Hyman P. (1992b), 'The capital development of the economy and the structure of financial institutions', Working Paper No. 72, The Levy Economics Institute of Bard College.

Minsky, Hyman P. (1992c), 'Reconstituting the United States' financial structure: some fundamental issues', Working Paper No. 69, The Levy Economics Institute of Bard College.

Minsky, Hyman P. (1993), 'Schumpeter and finance', in Salvatore Biasco, Alessandro Roncaglia and Michele Salvati (eds), *Market and Institutions in Economic Development: Essays in Honour of Paulo Sylos Labini*, New York: St Martin's Press, pp. 103–15.

Minsky, Hyman P. (1995), 'Longer waves in financial relations: financial factors in the more severe depressions II', *Journal of Economic Issues*, **29** (1): 83–95.

Minsky, Hyman P. (1996), 'Uncertainty and the institutional structure of capitalist economies', *Journal of Economic Issues*, **30** (2): 357–68.

Minsky, Hyman P. and Charles J. Whalen (1996–97), 'Economic insecurity and the institutional prerequisites for successful capitalism', *Journal of Post Keynesian Economics*, **19** (2): 155–70.

Mitchell, Wesley C. (1927), *Business Cycles: The Problem and Its Setting*, New York: National Bureau of Economic Research.

Mitchell, Wesley C. (1941), *Business Cycles and their Causes*, Berkeley, CA: University of California Press.

Morgenson, Gretchen (2007), 'Inside the Countrywide lending spree', *The New York Times* (26 August), http://www.nytimes.com/2007/08/26/business/yourmoney/26country.html?hp (accessed 13 April 2009).

North, Douglass (1994), 'Economic performance through time', *The American Economic Review*, **84** (3): 359–68.

Niggle, Chris (2006), 'Evolutionary Keynesianism: a synthesis of institutionalist and post Keynesian macroeconomics', *Journal of Economic Issues*, **40** (2): 405–12.

Peterson, Wallace C. (1977), 'Institutionalism, Keynes and the real world', *Journal of Economic Issues*, **11** (2): 201–21.

Peterson, Wallace C. (1987), 'Macroeconomic theory and policy in an institutionalist perspective', *Journal of Economic Issues*, **21** (4): 1587–621.

Phillips, Ronnie J. (1997), 'Rethinking bank examinations: a Minsky approach', *Journal of Economic Issues*, **31** (2): 509–16.

Pittman, Mark (2007), 'Subprime bondholders may lose $75 billion from slump', Bloomberg.com (24 April), http://www.bloomberg.com/apps/news?pid=2060108 7&sid=aq3flDbwBCbk&refer=home (accessed 13 April 2009).

Ramstad, Yngve (1985), 'Comments on Adams and Brock paper', *Journal of Economic Issues*, **19** (2): 507–11.

RealtyTrac (2009), 'Foreclosure activity increases 81 percent in 2008', RealtyTrac.com, http://www.realtytrac.com/ContentManagement/pressrelease. aspx?ChannelID=9&ItemID=5681 (accessed 13 April 2009).

Romer, Christina and Jared Bernstein (2009), *The Job Impact of the American Recovery and Reinvestment Plan*, Washington, DC: Presidential Transition Team, 9 January.

Spitzer, Eliot (2008), 'Predatory lenders' partner in crime', *The Washington Post*, http://www.washingtonpost.com/wp-dyn/content/article/2008/02/13/AR2008021 302783.html (accessed 13 April 2009).

Stiglitz, Joseph E. (2009), 'Obama's ersatz capitalism', *The New York Times* (31 March), http://www.nytimes.com/2009/04/01/opinion/01stiglitz.html (accessed 13 April 2009).

US Department of Labor (2009), 'Employment situation summary', Economic News Release, Bureau of Labor Statistics, http://www.bls.gov/news.release/ empsit.nr0.htm (accessed 13 April 2009).

Veblen, Thorstein B. (1898), 'Why is economics not an evolutionary science?', *The Quarterly Journal of Economics*, **12** (4): 373–97.

Veblen, Thorstein B. (1904), *The Theory of Business Enterprise*, New York: Charles Scribner's Sons.

Whalen, Charles J. (2001), 'Integrating Schumpeter and Keynes: Hyman Minsky's theory of capitalist development', *Journal of Economic Issues*, **35** (4): 805–23.

Whalen, Charles J. (2008a), 'The credit crunch: a Minsky moment', *Studi e Note Di Economia*, **13** (1): 3–21.

Whalen, Charles J. (2008b), 'Toward "wisely managed" capitalism: post-Keynesian institutionalism and the creative state', *Forum for Social Economics*, **37** (1): 43–60.

Wilber, Charles K. and Kenneth P. Jameson (1983), *An Inquiry into the Poverty of Economics*, Notre Dame, IN: University of Notre Dame Press.

Wolfson, Martin H. (2002), 'Minsky's theory of financial crises in a global context', *Journal of Economic Issues*, **36** (2): 393–400.

Wray, L. Randall (2008), 'The commodities market bubble: money manager capitalism and the financialization of commodities', Public Policy Brief No. 96, The Levy Economics Institute of Bard College.

Yahoo Finance (2009), Dow Jones Industrial Average: Historical Prices, http:// finance.yahoo.com (accessed 13 April 2009).

Zalewski, David A. (2002), 'Retirement insecurity in the age of money-manager capitalism', *Journal of Economic Issues*, **36** (2): 349–56.

15. Minsky, the global money-manager crisis, and the return of big government

L. Randall Wray[1]

MONEY-MANAGER CAPITALISM AND THE CRISIS

As of spring 2009, the world faces the worst economic crisis since the 1930s. Even some mainstream economists have labeled it a depression. References to Keynesian theory and policy are now commonplace, with only a few fringe economists and policy-makers arguing against massive government spending to cushion the collapse, and reregulation to prevent future crises. A variety of explanations has been proffered for the causes of the crisis: lax regulation and oversight, rising inequality that encouraged households to borrow to support spending, greed and irrational exuberance, and excessive global liquidity – spurred by easy money policy in the USA and by US current account deficits that flooded the world with too many dollars. Unfortunately, these do not recognize the systemic nature of the global crisis, even if some of them contain an element of truth.

Hyman Minsky's work has enjoyed unprecedented interest, with many calling this the 'Minsky moment' or 'Minsky crisis' (Cassidy, 2008; Chancellor, 2007; McCulley, 2007; Whalen, 2007). However, I have argued that this is not a 'moment' that can be traced to recent developments (Wray, 2008a). Rather, as Minsky argued for nearly 50 years, what we have seen is a slow transformation of the global financial system toward what Minsky called 'money-manager capitalism'. Hence I argue that this is a crisis of money-manager capitalism. While I shall focus on the USA (where the current crisis was triggered), money-manager capitalism is global.

Of course, we have had a long series of crises, and the trend has been toward more severe and more frequent crises: real-estate investment trusts in the early 1970s; developing-country debt in the early 1980s; commercial real-estate, junk bonds and the thrift crisis in the USA (with banking crises in many other nations) in the 1980s; stock market crashes in 1987 and again in 2000 with the dot-com bust; the Japanese meltdown from the late 1980s; Long Term Capital Management (LTCM), the Russian default and Asian debt crises in the late 1990s; and so on. Until the current crisis, each of these was resolved (some more painfully than others – impacts were particularly severe and long-lasting in the developing world) with some combination of central bank or international institution (IMF, World Bank) intervention plus a fiscal rescue (often taking the form of US Treasury spending of last resort to prop up the US economy to maintain imports that helped to generate rest of world growth).

Minsky always insisted that there are two essential propositions of his 'financial instability hypothesis'.[2] The first is that there are two financing 'regimes' – one that is consistent with stability and the other that subjects the economy to instability. The second proposition is that 'stability is destabilizing', so that endogenous processes will tend to move a stable system toward fragility. While Minsky is best known for his analysis of crises, he argued that the strongest force in a modern capitalist economy operates in the other direction – toward an unconstrained speculative boom. The current crisis is a natural outcome of these processes – an unsustainable explosion of real-estate prices, mortgage debt and leveraged positions in collateralized securities and derivatives in conjunction with a similarly unsustainable explosion of commodities prices. Add to the mix an overly tight fiscal policy (so that growth required private sector deficits) and it was not hard to see the crisis coming (Wray, 2003).

Hence the problem is money-manager capitalism – the economic system characterized by highly leveraged funds seeking maximum returns in an environment that systematically underprices risk. With little regulation or supervision of financial institutions, money-managers concocted increasingly esoteric and opaque financial instruments that quickly spread around the world. Contrary to economic theory, markets generate perverse incentives for excess risk, punishing the timid. Those playing along are rewarded with high returns because highly leveraged funding drives up prices for the underlying assets – whether they are dot-com stocks, Las Vegas homes or corn futures. We are now living with the aftermath as positions are deleveraged, driving down prices of the underlying collateral (homes, commodities, factories). Previous financial crises were sufficiently limited that only a portion of the managed money was wiped out so that a new boom inevitably rose from the ashes. However, this current crisis has already destroyed a considerable part of the managed money and led to national and international calls for thoroughgoing financial reform. And, in spite of the unprecedented efforts of Fed Chairman Bernanke and Treasury Secretary Geithner to save the money-managers, I believe they will fail to restore 'business as usual'.

THE GOLDEN AGE OF CAPITALISM

The first generation of the postwar period generally enjoyed the best performance ever seen – not just in the USA or even in developed nations, but also in developing nations. That was the so-called Keynesian era. I do not want to dredge up a debate about the accuracy of the nomenclature. Hyman Minsky (1986) emphasized the following characteristics that he believed contributed to the robust performance:

- High wage/high consumption bias: strong unions pushed up wages, allowing growing domestic consumption based on income (not debt); this also promoted labor-saving innovation and technological advance.
- High government debt ratios/low private debt: we emerged from the Second World War with private balance sheets stuffed full of very safe government debt; in Minsky's terminology we had a 'robust' financial sector with highly liquid assets.
- External markets for US output: thanks to the Marshall Plan, which provided the financial wherewithal to purchase US exports (as well as some destruction of productive capacity in war-torn Europe and Japan), the USA could sell abroad.
- Government spending 'ratchet' (the term comes from Vatter and Walker, not Minsky – see Wray, 2008c): government spending grew faster than GDP, supplementing private sector demand and thereby keeping labor, plant and equipment operating near to full capacity.

No doubt there are other factors, but these will allow me to make several relevant and related points. While much of the postwar 'Keynesian' policy tried to push private investment (tax credits for saving and investing), some economists (Domar, Minsky, and Vatter and Walker – again, see Wray, 2008c) long recognized that this is problematic for several reasons that I can only briefly summarize here. First, it tends to introduce inflationary pressures, since at the aggregate level prices of consumer goods must be marked up over the wage bill required to produce those goods so that the workers that produced them cannot consume all of them – this leaves consumption goods for workers (and others) in other sectors to consume. Second, it tends to promote inequality since wages and profits in the investment sector are higher due to greater economic power (of unions and firms). Third, it creates excessive productive capacity unless demand rises sufficiently (with capital-saving innovations, it is likely that the supply-side effects of investment outstrip the demand-side effects – leaving capital idle and depressing demand). Finally, as emphasized by Minsky, modern investment goods are expensive and long-lived, requiring complex financial instruments and relations. This is related to the point I shall discuss below: investment-fueled economic growth will at the same time tend to produce growing private debt ratios that increase financial fragility. For this reason, Minsky always argued that government-spending-led growth is more sustainable because it allows private sector spending to grow based on income rather than private debt.

We now see why the four factors I listed above are interrelated. It was the hot war of the Second World War plus the following cold war that ended the Depression and set the stage for the 'Golden Age'. The government deficit reached 25 percent of GDP during the war, providing the massive amount of private sector saving in the form of safe financial assets that strengthened balance sheets. From 1960, the baby boom drove rapid growth of state and local government spending so that even though federal government spending remained relatively constant as a percentage of GDP, total government spending grew rapidly until the 1970s. This pulled up aggregate demand, private sector incomes, and thus consumption. Note that in spite of the conventional wisdom, the early postwar 'Keynesian golden era' of rapid government growth actually resulted in very small budget deficits because robust economic growth generated rising tax revenues. Further, growth reduced government debt ratios – in effect, Treasury bonds were 'leveraged' to generate the postwar boom.

Economists have long recognized a macroeconomic turning point in the early 1970s. Government spending began to grow more slowly than GDP; inflation-adjusted wages stagnated; poverty rates stopped falling; unemployment rates trended upward; and economic growth slowed. Intensified efforts to promote saving and investment (on the belief that this would restore growth) only made matters worse: saving depressed demand, and investment produced fragility. Another major transformation occurred in the 1990s with innovations in the financial sector that increased access to credit, as well as changed attitudes of firms and households about prudent levels of debt. Now consumption led the way, but it was financed by debt rather than by growing income. Robust growth returned, but this time fueled by deficit spending of the private sector. The rest, as they say, is history: thrift-financed commercial real-estate that faced an excess supply (Wray, 1994); Nasdaq IPO (initial public offering) pet-dot-coms; securitized NINJA (no income, no job, no assets) subprimes (Wray, 2008a); and pension-fund-fueled index speculation in commodities futures (Wray, 2008b).[3] With no more bubbles on the immediate horizon, we are left with debt deflation and deepening recession.

STABILITY IS DESTABILIZING

Hyman Minsky saw this crisis coming as early as the late 1950s (Papadimitriou and Wray, 1998). To the extent that we really did have what Chairman Bernanke called The 'Great Moderation' in the decade or so that led up to the crisis, it would have fueled the longer-run transition toward fragility that had been developing over the entire postwar period (Wray, 2008a). Indeed, 1996 saw for the first time ever persistent private sector deficit spending (taken as a whole, US firms and households were spending more than their incomes) (Wray, 2003). This continued without let-up through to 2008 (with a brief respite during the depths of the Bush recession). So there was something to the claims about a 'great moderation' – in that there was an absence of fear that helped to generate debt-fueled bubble after debt-fueled bubble – although those promulgating these claims never understood the true ramifications. All of that was building toward what Minsky called 'it' (as in 'Can "it" happen again?'): a Fisher-type debt deflation process.

Turning to the other side of the private sector deficits coin, we find the Clinton budget surpluses. Of course these were widely proclaimed as beneficial (supposedly enhancing our future ability to take care of retiring baby-boomers – particularly ironic as we now watch our pension funds disappear). Those familiar with macro accounting recognize that the non-government sector balance must be equal to the government sector balance (sign reversed). If the government runs a budget surplus, the non-government must run a deficit of the same size. The Clinton government surplus sucked income and net financial wealth out of the private sector – leading to the Bush recession at the beginning of the 2000s. That is not something to be wildly celebrated and emulated as fiscally responsible policy.

The non-government sector balance can be further broken down to a domestic (US) private sector deficit and a foreign sector surplus (in dollars, the rest of the world runs a budget surplus against the USA, as the USA runs a trade deficit). To conclude, US domestic private sector deficit spending was equal to the US government budget surplus plus the foreign sector surplus. Even when the Clinton budget surpluses morphed to Bush budget deficits, they were too small to allow the domestic private sector to run balanced budgets. As a result, the US private sector continued to run up deficits and go more deeply into debt. In spite of the Bush tax cuts, federal tax revenue was actually growing at a near-record pace until this finally took the steam out of the economy in 2007 (Papadimitriou and Wray, 2007). From 2005 leading up to the financial crash, US tax receipts grew even faster than they had during the Clinton surplus! This, again, sucked income out of the private sector. With all this fiscal drag (plus a trade deficit drag), the only way for the economy to grow was through private deficits and exploding debt (Papadimitriou and Wray, 2007). At the same time, commodities prices exploded (most relevantly, oil prices), adding to household burdens (Wray, 2008b). And, finally, the Fed began to raise interest rates in 2004, increasing debt service burdens. This triple whammy ensured that the private sector would eventually cut back its borrowing. We are now witnessing the unraveling of all of that debt, with snowballing defaults reducing its value. This is what Irving Fisher identified as a debt deflation process, which he believed had made the Great Depression so, well, 'great'.

That (probably) won't happen again. We've got the 'big government and big bank' to constrain the natural market processes (Minsky, 1986). The 'big bank' (Fed) took far too long to recognize the scope of the problem as well as the solution: lend without limit. While it took a couple of trillion dollars, Bernanke et al. have just about accomplished that task. Yes, financial institutions still faced solvency problems, but those did not have to be resolved immediately (the various Paulson plans – continued so far by Secretary Geithner – were unnecessary, and impotent in any case) (Papadimitriou and Wray, 2008). What we need now is the 'big government' Treasury to ramp up spending. The federal budget deficit has already grown well beyond $1 trillion annually – and it will continue to grow, allowing the private sector to strengthen its balance sheet by running budget surpluses.

There is a real danger in the belief that all we need is a big but short-lived fiscal stimulus. As I summarized above, what we really need is a 'ratchet' – more government spending in the 'depression' to provide needed effective demand, and then continued fiscal stimulus in the recovery to ensure we can operate the new plant and equipment that will be put in place. The problem is that the 'supply-side' effect of private (and public) investment (in terms of added capacity) is far greater than the 'demand-side' effect of that investment (the textbook 'multiplier' impact). Unfortunately, policy-makers around the globe promise an eventual return to 'fiscally responsible' budgets once the crisis is past. This could throw us back into depression – just as President Roosevelt's budget balancing caused the economy to plunge in 1937.

SHORT-RUN POLICY RESPONSE

US financial institutions have already written off far more than $1 trillion of bad assets, while the Treasury has injected about $700 billion of 'bailout' funds through asset purchases, by taking non-voting equity shares, and by subsidizing mergers. A US fiscal stimulus of $800 billion has been allocated – although little had actually been spent by the beginning of summer 2009. Thus, while the US budget deficit grew to more than $1.2 trillion, most of this was simply due to the automatic stabilizers (tax revenue plummeted). The Fed's balance sheet had expanded to nearly $2 trillion as it lent reserves to US banks and to foreign central banks, and Chairman Bernanke has hinted that it is willing to increase its lending and purchases by another $2 trillion. The current US government commitment already totals about $9 trillion – counting fiscal stimulus, financial bailouts and guarantees of toxic assets. Many other nations have also committed funds, with China standing out because its fiscal stimulus package is even larger than that of the USA (relative to the size of its economy). And the IMF is preparing to lend up to $1 trillion globally. Even conventional projections expect another $2 trillion of bank writedowns in the USA, and perhaps more than that in Europe. Note that the total securitized universe was only $10 trillion, of which subprimes were $2.5 trillion. It is clear that the losses incurred and expected to be incurred are not simply a matter of some bad mortgage loans made to low-income borrowers to buy suburban mansions they could not afford. Rather, this is a crisis of the whole money-manager system. And because so much of it is unregulated (more properly, 'self-regulated'), unreported, and off balance sheet, there is no way to even guess the ultimate scale of losses.

Two kinds of responses are required: first we must deal with the immediate crisis; and second we need to formulate policy that will put economies on a sustainable path. Ideally, these should be integrated and coherent. Most policy-makers have assumed that the best way to deal with the crisis is to restore liquidity through loans and bailouts targeted at financial institutions, and to promote private sector spending with a quick but moderate fiscal boost. In the USA, there is great concern that the bailouts have not restored credit flows – with banks chastised because they will not lend. I think this is mostly wrong-headed: the US private sector is already overburdened with debt (as is the case in many other nations), and financial institutions have already made trillions in bad loans. The last thing we need is another credit boom. While it is true that we had to resolve the liquidity crisis through prompt central bank intervention as a lender of last resort, the Fed accomplished that task many months ago. The problem now is that many financial institutions are massively insolvent.

The approach taken by both former Treasury Secretary Paulson and current Secretary Geithner is to preserve the status quo – to save institutions by injecting capital and taking toxic assets off their balance sheets. It is believed that somehow we can restore the outsized role that money-managers have played over the past two decades. The problem is that managed money was far too large and far too leveraged as taste for risk grew even as ability to perceive risk became ever scarcer. (Minsky, 1986 attributed this to fading memories of the Great Depression; many of today's money-managers cannot even remember the 1980s – much less the 1930s.) As a result, we had – we might say – command over too much money chasing too few good asset classes with what are perceived to be acceptable returns. The answer is to massively downsize the financial sector. This means that we must stop trying to bail out Wall Street in the hopes that somehow economic growth will trickle down. The $9 trillion committed so far will not be nearly enough, and even if this worked, it would just mean that money-managers would have to target yet another asset class for a bubble. In any case, the voting public seems to have already had enough and will not tolerate many more give-aways to Wall Street.

Policy should avoid promotion of financial institution consolidation – a natural result of financial crises that can be boosted by policy-arranged bailouts. Minsky (1986) always preferred policy that would promote small-to-medium-sized financial institutions. Unfortunately, policy-makers who are biased toward 'free markets' instinctively prefer to use public money to subsidize private institution takeovers of failing financial firms. Indeed, consolidation was a stated goal of Secretary Paulson's plan, and Geithner has not publicly rejected it (Papadimitriou and Wray, 2008). The Roosevelt alternative should be adopted: a 'banking holiday' that gives time to identify failing institutions, which are placed into receivership. Insured depositors are paid off, and the institutions are resolved (in some cases, institutions will be closed and assets sold; in other cases, the institutions will be dismantled with pieces sold). This is what Minsky advocated during the thrift crisis of the 1980s. Instead, what we have now is 'too big to fail' doctrine – even Geithner's 'stress test' promised that no institution examined would be allowed to fail, no matter how the results turned out. Policy should instead foster competition by adopting a 'too big to save' doctrine, with a bias against consolidation in favor of dissolution, and with greater regulation of the banking, protected, sector.

In other words, financial losses must be accepted and collateral damage must be managed by directly targeting the 'real' part of the economy (households and productive firms, as well as state and local governments) rather than the financial sector. Pension funds and banking deposits will be threatened; thus depositors and pensioners will need to be rescued – the former through deposit insurance, the latter through a combination of restoration of a portion of private pensions plus permanent increases to publicly provided pensions. Time and economic growth can go a long way in restoring financial health – if incomes can grow sufficiently, it becomes easier to service debt. But the US private sector cannot be the main source of demand stimulus as it has been running up debt, spending more than its income for a decade. While the US government budget deficit is already growing as the economy slows, this results from deterioration of employment and income (which lowers taxes and increases transfers) – thus it will not proactively create growth although it will help to constrain the depths of recession. What is needed is a massive fiscal stimulus – probably two or three times the $800 billion that President Obama obtained – and then a permanently larger fiscal presence to allow growth without relying on private sector debt. Government spending will need to be several percentage points larger relative to GDP in the future, and will need to grow on trend somewhat faster than GDP as a whole.

The USA (as well as some other nations that experienced real-estate booms) also needs mortgage relief. President Roosevelt created an agency, the Home Owners' Loan Corporation (HOLC), to take on the tasks of successfully refinancing 20 percent of the nation's mortgages, issuing bonds to raise the funds. While a fifth of those loans eventually were foreclosed, the HOLC actually earned a small profit on its activities, which was paid to the Treasury when it was liquidated in 1951. Clearly, there are lessons to be learned from that experience: refinance is preferable to foreclosure as it preserves homeownership and communities. Congress must promulgate regulations on mortgage originators to establish new licensing requirements, put restrictions on saddling borrowers with riskier loans, and provide liability for financial institutions that sell mortgages. In addition, Congress should set new standards to be met by originators regarding ability of borrowers to make payments. New regulations of appraisers, risk-rating agencies and accounting firms will be required.

Minsky (1986) argued that the Great Depression represented a failure of the small-government, *laissez-faire* economic model, while the New Deal promoted a big government/big bank highly successful model for financial capitalism. The current crisis just as convincingly represents a failure of the big government/neoconservative (or, outside the USA, what is called neoliberal) model that promotes deregulation, reduced supervision and oversight, privatization, and consolidation of market power. It replaced the New Deal reforms with self-supervision of markets, with greater reliance on 'personal responsibility' as safety nets were shredded, and with monetary and fiscal policy that is biased against maintenance of full employment and adequate growth to generate rising living standards for most Americans. The model is in trouble – and not just with respect to the current global crisis, as the USA faces record inequality and destruction of the middle class, a health-care crisis, an incarceration disaster, and other problems beyond the scope of this chapter (see Wray, 2005a; 2000).

Hence we must use this opportunity to return to a more sensible model, with enhanced oversight of financial institutions and with a financial structure that promotes stability rather than speculation. We need policy that promotes rising wages for the bottom half so that borrowing is less necessary to achieve middle-class living standards. And we need policy that promotes employment, rather than transfer payments – or worse, incarceration – for those left behind. Monetary policy must be turned away from using rate hikes to pre-empt inflation and toward a proper role: stabilizing interest rates, direct credit controls to prevent runaway speculation, and supervision. Fiscal policy will need to play a bigger role in the future, providing a larger share of aggregate demand; only government can operate against the boom-and-bust-trend that is natural for the private sector.

GLOBAL RESTRUCTURING

If anything, prospects facing the rest of the world are worse. The Fed has become the global lender of last resort, providing up to $600 billion in loans to foreign central banks. Further, it is widely understood that the bailout of US financial institutions (most prominently, of American International Group – AIG) helps to protect foreign financial institutions (AIG is the biggest supplier of CDS 'insurance' for debt held by European banks). Still, the run to relative safety in US Treasuries has threatened exchange rates and increased risk spreads around the world. Social and political unrest is growing in the periphery nations. Many economies will not recover until the USA does. While I believe that the USA has at its disposal ample policy space to resolve its crisis (although its political will remains in question), many other nations do not. In particular, most of those nations that have 'dollarized' or pegged exchange rates to foreign currencies do not have sufficient domestic policy space to deal with this crisis. I include even Euroland in this category because individual nations do not have the ability to operate independent monetary and fiscal policy. Further, while the IMF has promised to play a bigger role in helping nations deal with the global crisis, this will finally result in even greater dollar-denominated debt around the globe – a major source of the financial instability we have seen in developing countries over the past three decades.

This makes it all the more imperative that nations with the ability to use fiscal stimulus (including the USA, China, the UK, Brazil and Japan) do so as quickly as possible. Euroland needs to restructure its unification, preferably putting greater fiscal authority in the hands of the

European Parliament (which should ramp up its spending from about 1 percent of Euroland GDP toward 15 percent). This will help to restore European and thus global growth. In addition, more financial aid (not in the form of dollar loans) should be provided to developing nations. Debt relief will become a more pressing issue. For the longer term, developing nations need an alternative to the Washington Consensus (which is itself based on neoliberal policies that promoted the interests of global managed money) to promote job creation and sustainable growth with equity and equality. Extended discussion of these topics is beyond the scope of this chapter, but interested readers are referred to the growing body of work on use of job guarantee programs as part of long-term development strategy (Bhaduri, 2005; Felipe et al., 2009; Hirway, 2006; Minsky, 1965; Mitchell and Wray, 2005; Tcherneva and Wray, 2005; Wray, 2007).

The global crisis offers grave risks as well as opportunities. Global employment and output are collapsing faster than at any time since the Great Depression. Hunger and violence are growing – even in developed nations. The 1930s offers examples of possible responses – on the one hand, nationalism and repression, on the other a New Deal and progressive policy. There is no question that finance has played an outsized role over the past two decades, both in the developed nations where policy promoted managed money and in the developing nations which were encouraged to open to international capital under control of global managed money. Households and firms in developed nations were buried under mountains of debt even as incomes for wage earners stagnated. Developing nations were similarly swamped with external debt service commitments, while the promised benefits of neoliberal policies usually never arrived. It is time finally to put global finance back in its proper place as a tool to achieving sustainable development. This means substantial downsizing and careful reregulation. Government must play a bigger role, which in turn requires a new economic paradigm that recognizes the possibility of simultaneously achieving social justice, full employment, and price and currency stability through appropriate policy.

Minsky insisted that 'the creation of new economic institutions which constrain the impact of uncertainty is necessary', arguing that the

> aim of policy is to assure that the economic prerequisites for sustaining the civil and civilized standards of an open liberal society exist. If amplified uncertainty and extremes in income maldistribution and social inequalities attenuate the economic underpinnings of democracy, then the market behavior that creates these conditions has to be constrained. (Minsky, 1996: 14, 15)

It is time to take finance back from the clutches of Wall Street's casino.

BUT CAN WE AFFORD BIG GOVERNMENT?

Unfortunately, by late spring 2009, President Obama was publicly fretting about the growth of the budget deficit, going so far as to claim that the USA had 'run out of money'. Why, in the face of the biggest economic catastrophe this nation has faced since the 1930s, would Obama lose his courage? The three *I*s have it: inflation, investment crowding out, insolvency. In this penultimate section, I shall address those fears.

First, inflation. Price pressures can arise from many sources – excess demand, commodity price hikes, bottlenecks, wage or profit pressures, composition of demand (trade surpluses and private investment tend to be inflationary for reasons mentioned above), and so on. Most fear that too much government spending will drive demand beyond full capacity, generating wage and price pressures. However, in current circumstances, that is highly unlikely with global demand plummeting, unemployment rising, and commodity prices busting. Still, I have called for faster growth of government even after this crisis passes. So the key is to ensure that government spending grows at a pace just consistent with the required level of fiscal stimulus. Further, it does make a difference where government demand is directed – to avoid bottlenecks, to add to productive capacity, toward underutilized resources, and toward resources whose prices are rising below the average rate of price increase. Right now, it probably doesn't matter too much what the government spends for (the often-quoted Keynes statement about digging holes comes to mind); but for the longer run the composition and nature of government spending are critical. This is for two reasons: first, to maintain public support for big government, it has got to spend in a way that has obvious benefits for Americans. Second, government has to avoid spending that fuels accelerating inflation. Even fairly mainstream economists such as Paul Krugman and Brad DeLong have seemed to accept that moderate and stable inflation is not a bad thing – a position with which I am sympathetic – but rising inflation is not acceptable.

Second, investment crowding out. There are two main kinds of crowding out – resource and financial. If the government were to hire away all of the competent engineers, investment projects that required engineers could get crowded out for the simple reason that the government has an unlimited checking account and can always win any bidding war. At full employment (as in the Second World War), additional government hiring crowds out private hiring. The solution to resource crowding out is pretty simple: to avoid it, don't hire away the resources the private sector needs. When the economy is well below full employment, this is easy enough; when it is close to full employment, care is required. Usually, however, economists worry more about financial crowding out – which can occur even with unemployed resources. There are different versions, but the most important ones boil down to the argument that government deficits push up interest rates as its borrowing competes with private borrowing. Again, since the government has a bigger checking account, it will win the competition because its spending is not interest-sensitive. Private spending that is sensitive (supposedly, investment and real-estate spending are) is reduced. For a long time, economists of the big government persuasion argued that empirical results are mixed – we find many cases of rising budget deficits and falling interest rates, and falling budget deficits and rising interest rates – so even if the theory is correct, the real-world results don't necessarily comply. But it is simpler than that: the theory is just plain wrong. All central bankers everywhere now admit that they target the short-term interest rate; and they hit their targets within a self-determined margin of error. It makes no difference whether the budget deficit reaches a Japan-like 10 percent of GDP (with zero interest rates), or a USA-like 25 percent of GDP (during the Second World War, with interest rates at 3/8 of 1 percent), or a USA-like budget *surplus* of 2 percent of GDP (under Clinton – accompanied by rising rates!). The Fed determines the short-term interest rate. Period. Yes, it might raise the rate in response to budget deficits – but that is a policy decision. If Congress doesn't like that, it should change the instructions it provides to the Fed.

There are two further points to be made here. The central bank operates with an overnight rate target, but it can choose the maturity it likes – indeed, Bernanke's Fed is now experimenting with longer maturity targets under cover of the label 'quantitative easing'. This seems important because one objection is that the Treasury issues longer-term debt and while it is true that the central bank sets overnight rates, longer rates are 'market determined' and crowding out in the longer maturity markets is still possible. However, the maturity of Treasury debt is a policy variable – and there is no reason in principle why the Treasury could not operate only at the short end (even overnight debt!) to avoid crowding out.

For those who are still skeptical, let me move to the second, more important, point. Government spends by crediting bank accounts (bank deposits go up, and their reserves are credited by the Fed). All else equal, this generates excess reserves that are offered in the overnight interbank lending market (fed funds in the USA), putting downward pressure on overnight rates. Let me repeat that: government spending pushes interest rates down. When they fall below the target, the Fed sells bonds to drain the excess reserves – pushing the overnight rate back to the target. Continuous budget deficits lead to continuous open market sales, causing the NY Fed to call on the Treasury to soak up reserves through new issues of bonds. The purpose of bond sales by the Fed or Treasury is to substitute interest-earning bonds for undesired reserves – to allow the Fed to hit its interest rate target. (In the old days, these reserves earned no interest; Bernanke has changed that, effectively eliminating the difference between very short-term Treasuries and bank reserves. It also entirely eliminates the need to issue Treasuries – but that is a topic for another day.) We conclude: government deficits do not exert upward pressure on interest rates – quite the contrary: they put downward pressure that is relieved through bond sales.

On to the final phobia: insolvency. Let me state the conclusion first: a sovereign government that issues its own floating rate currency can never become insolvent in its own currency. (While such a currency is often called 'fiat', that is somewhat misleading for reasons I won't discuss here – I prefer the term 'sovereign currency'.) The US Treasury can always make all payments as they come due – whether it is for spending on goods and services, for social spending, or to meet interest payments on its debt. While analogies to household budgets are often made, these are completely erroneous. I do not know any households that can issue Treasury coins or Federal Reserve Notes (I suppose some try occasionally, but that is a dangerously illegal business). To be sure, government does not really spend by direct issues of coined nickels. Rather, it spends by crediting bank accounts. It taxes by debiting them. When its credits to bank accounts exceed its debits to them, we call that a budget deficit. The accounting and operating procedures adopted by the Treasury, the Fed, special deposit banks and regular banks are complex, but they do not change the principle: government spending is accomplished by crediting bank accounts. Government spending can be too big (beyond full employment), it can misdirect resources, and it can be wasteful or undesirable, but it cannot lead to insolvency.

Constraining government spending by imposing budgets is certainly desirable (Galbraith et al., 2009). We want to know in advance what the government is planning to do, and we want to hold it accountable; a budget is one lever of control. At this point, it is impossible to know how much additional government spending will be required to get us out of this deep recession. Whether the Obama team finally settles on $850 billion worth of useful projects, or $1.5 trillion, voters have the right to expect that the spending is well planned and that the projects are well executed. But the budgets ought to be set with regard to results desired and competencies to execute plans – not out of some preconceived notion of what is 'affordable'. Our federal government can afford anything that is for sale in terms of its own currency. The trick is to ensure that it spends enough to produce sustainable growth and other desired outcomes while at the same time ensuring that its spending does not have undesirable outcomes such as fueling inflation or taking away resources that could be put to better use by the private sector.

LONGER-RUN POLICY

For the medium to longer term, we need to put into place policies that will encourage sustainable economic growth. Here I conclude by discussing eight important areas for reformulation of policy.

1. Green policy: economic sustainability will require more attention to the environment. This is an area that President Obama has already identified as important, and I have no special expertise here. I would simply caution that economic recovery could reverse the course of oil prices (likely back toward $80 per barrel – the break-even price for high-cost producers). Some combination of pressure on oil producers, subsidies for alternative energy and conservation, and energy costs relief for low-income households will be needed.

2. Payroll tax reform: payroll taxes are regressive, discourage work and employment, are inflationary because they add to labor costs, and reduce US competitiveness against all countries that do not tax work. Further – and this might come as a shock to readers who have bought into the claims made by intergenerational warriors financed by the Concorde coalition – the taxes are far too high, generating revenue that is about one-third higher than necessary to equal all OASDI (Social Security) spending. As part of my package of policies to deal with the current crisis, I recommended a payroll tax holiday. To placate the 'intergenerational warriors' who continually claim that Social Security is going broke, we can have the Treasury directly make all Social Security payments during the holiday (they do it anyway, even when we are not on holiday), and credit the Trust Fund with the one-third extra tax revenue that would have been received (again they do that anyway since the Trust Fund is just a Treasury promise to pay Social Security payments when they come due) (Galbraith et al., 2009). Now what should we do when the holiday comes to an end? I have the 'audacity of hope' (President Obama's campaign mantra) to believe that we can end the intergenerational fighting, that we will finally recognize that promised Social Security benefits can and will be paid as they come due, and that we can end the nonsense about accumulating Trust Funds (Treasury IOUs owed by the Treasury to itself) to take care of future retiring baby-boomers. Unless baby-boomers

can eat Trust Fund IOUs, they are no better off if the Trust Fund is filled with quadrillions of Treasuries than they would be without a Trust Fund at all. So let us stop pretending, recognize Social Security promises for what they are (commitments by sovereign government to credit bank accounts on schedule), accept the social commitment to ensure a decent retirement for all Americans (which will depend on our capacity to produce the real stuff retirees will want, plus our ability to import), and come up with a better way to redistribute resources from those of working age to those of retirement age. After all, that is really what payroll taxes are all about (taking income away from those accruing it to ensure they don't consume everything). It makes far more sense to tax all sources of income, in a progressive manner, to share the burden of taking care of a growing elderly population. Can we financially afford growing numbers of baby-boomer retirees? Of course. (See the previous section on affordability.) Can we ensure they get enough real resources to achieve the standard of living they expect at retirement? Probably, but that has nothing to do with affordability or payroll taxes. All it requires is that we (a) provide sufficiently large credits to their bank accounts, and (b) put at their command a sufficient quantity of real resources.

3. State and local government revenue: the 'devolution' that has taken place since the early 1970s puts more responsibility on state and local governments; in response they have increased (mostly) regressive taxes such as sales and excise taxes. As discussed above, they need immediate assistance because tax revenue is plummeting. Once the crisis is past, we also need to encourage them to move away from regressive taxes (in the average state, poor people pay twice as much of their income in state and local taxes as do the rich). I suggest we offer federal government funding to states that agree to eliminate regressive taxes, on a dollar-for-dollar basis.

4. Inequality: the rise of inequality is a major contributing factor to the run-up of household debt: stagnant real wages for most Americans in the face of rising expectations (largely thanks to emulation of Hollywood and Wall Street) encouraged the debt binge. Hence the current financial crisis is indeed related to the rise of inequality – both because of stagnant incomes at the bottom and because of soaring incomes at the top. Many processes contributed to rising inequality; and I have already alluded to the reversal of the early postwar trend that saw poverty rates fall by half by the mid-1970s – and then virtually no further reduction since. I won't go into all of this in detail, but the emphasis on stimulating private investment as well as the public subsidies of consolidation and the promotion of finance over

industrial enterprise all encouraged rising inequality. The weakening of unions played an important role. What Galbraith (2008) has called the 'predator state' has also played a major role as Vice President Dick Cheney and his minions richly rewarded their friends. We need to reverse those trends. Thankfully, Wall Street has already taken care of most of the excessively rich, downsizing their wealth and incomes to an extent not seen since 1929. Now we only need to drive a stake through the heart of finance to ensure it cannot recover. Next we need to get incomes rising at the bottom – more below.

5.   Health care: while much is made of the 'unfunded entitlements' of the public leg of the US health-care stool, the other two legs (the employer-funded leg as well as the patient-funded leg) are also broken and collapsing. In our 'global economy' one could not imagine a worse design for health care than the one that has evolved in the USA – highly inefficient and employment-killing as it saddles employers with costs. Sooner or later, it will be reformed. We might as well do it now: nationally funded and universal access to reasonable health care, with a much smaller privately funded system for nose jobs and other elective treatments. Note: non-price rationing will be necessary. It makes no sense to devote 80 percent of health-care spending to the last dying gasps of life. Those unwilling to accept rationing of care will need to buy extra insurance and build up savings.

6.   Infrastructure and social spending: I have argued that government spending needs to operate like a ratchet: increase in bad times to get us out of recessions, and increase in good times to generate demand for growth of capacity. What should we spend on? Infrastructure, social programs and jobs. We've got a nearly $2 trillion public infrastructure deficit – just to bring the USA up to the minimal standard expected by today's civil engineers. I hope that all readers concede that is a low standard. I can remember when all the kids expected levitating bullet trains coast to coast and perhaps even rocket ship transport to Martian seas vacations by the early twenty-first century. Here we are a half century later stuck in traffic in gas-guzzling dinosaurs that aren't that far removed from the finned Buicks our grandparents drove. If anything, our relative dearth of public services is even worse than it was when Galbraith brought it to our attention. And our needs are much greater – wealthy (and aging) societies need services, many of which are best provided outside the for-profit sector. The long-fashionable belief that the market knows best, that it is well suited to providing everything from elder care to health care and to education, now seems crazily improbable. Heck, the market couldn't even do a relatively simple thing such as determine whether someone

with no income, no job, and no assets ought to be buying a half-million-dollar house with a loan-to-value ratio of 120 percent! Jimmy Stewart's heavily regulated thrifts (in the movie *It's a Wonderful Life*) successfully financed far more housing with virtually no defaults or insolvencies, and with none of the modern rocket-scientist models that generated the subprime fiasco.

7. Financial reform: the market has decisively spoken – it is not capable of self-regulation. It cannot tell who is creditworthy. It cannot be trusted to innovate new products. It cannot be relied upon to determine compensation schemes. It makes terrible credit allocation decisions. It cries out for downsizing and heavy-handed re-regulation. In short, it is telling us that government of money-managers, by money-managers, and for money-managers is no way to run a country or an economy. President Obama needs to listen. Admittedly, this is an extremely complex and difficult topic, but fundamental reform will be required.

8. Jobs: I have saved the most controversial proposal to last. I believe that anyone who is willing and ready to work ought to be working. I even believe that able adults ought to work, rather than relying on handouts. These beliefs have been labeled radical, but I think they are consistent with capitalism and with the United Nations Declaration on Human Rights. Here are the problems: first, capitalism has no internal processes to ensure full employment of labor resources; second, policy always acts to ensure that full employment will not be reached in the belief that it will generate inflation. John Maynard Keynes explained the first point: firms hire the amount of labor they need to produce the amount of output they expect to sell. The existence of unemployed labor will not induce employers to hire more, even at lower wages, for the simple reason that additional production is not warranted by expected sales. The second point was developed as Marx's reserve army of the unemployed argument, updated as a Phillips curve tradeoff, further transformed as Milton Friedman's natural rate hypothesis, later bastardized as the Lucas surprise hypothesis, rejected by real business cycle claims, and finally revived as the new monetary consensus. Transcripts from Federal Open Market Committee meetings conclusively demonstrate that the Fed fights against falling unemployment by raising its target interest rate in an attempt to slow economic growth. Whether these policy actions have the desired effect is beside the point. What is clear is that policy-makers oppose provision of a sufficient supply of jobs to satisfy the demand for them, in the belief that if everyone is working, inflation will result. Let that sink in for a moment: if everyone is gainfully

employed producing the stuff we Americans want to consume, that will be more inflationary than an economy in which we maintain, say, 10 percent of the employable population in enforced idleness, subsisting on handouts and producing nothing of use. Only an economist could come up with such an outrageous proposition. It sounds silly because it is. (Joan Robinson used to argue that one should study economics in order to identify the lies economists tell.) I do not have the space here to explain what is wrong with the conventional views or to detail an alternative. Let me just say that Obama is on the right track when he sets a goal of creating millions of new jobs, many of which will be created through programs modeled on the New Deal. He can and should go much further: there is no reason to constrain the supply of jobs. Provide them without limit to anyone willing and ready to work. Give them useful things to do (see above for ideas). And here is the most important thing to do to ensure this will not be inflationary: set a fixed price (nominal wage) and float the quantity (hire those that show up to work). Offer a living wage and package of benefits but do not bid against the private sector if it is willing to pay more. In this way, the government's jobs program will operate like a buffer stock, expanding in recession when private jobs are scarce and their wages are falling, and shrinking in a boom when the private sector bids workers away. This also makes the government's budget move countercyclically: more spending in recession; less in expansion. Earlier I noted that a key to ensuring that government spending is not inflationary is to make sure it doesn't increase demand beyond full employment. The job program I am describing here is an automatic stabilizer: spending increases up to the point of full employment, and then no further. Full employment without generating inflationary pressures. But can we afford it? You bet we can: government can afford to buy anything for sale in its own currency – including unemployed labor – simply by crediting bank accounts.

This package of policies will help to restore sustainable economic growth, putting the USA on a new path to an even better Golden Age. It will reduce inequality, shift the emphasis away from private investment toward consumption (out of earned income, not debt or welfare) and public spending, reduce the role of high finance, and provide better services and more secure retirements for our aging baby-boomers. Still, as Minsky argued, we have to be diligent because the stability created by these policies will encourage experimentation by profit-seekers to push risky practices. This means that the policy-maker's work is never done. New challenges will arise – but that is no reason to forego Golden Ages.

NOTES

1. See Wray (2008a, 2008b, 2009) for more detailed discussions of the crisis.
2. See Minsky (1986, 1993) and Papadimitriou and Wray (1998) for a summary of Minsky's approach.
3. In addition, see Wray (2003, 2006, 2008c) and Masters and White (2008).

REFERENCES

Bhaduri, Amit (2005), *Development with Dignity: A Case for Full Employment*, India: National Book Trust.
Cassidy, John (2008), 'The Minsky moment', *The New Yorker*, 4 February, www.newyorker.com.
Chancellor, Edward (2007), 'Ponzi nation', *Institutional Investor*, 7 February.
Felipe, Jesus, William Mitchell and L. Randall Wray (2009), 'A reinterpretation of Pakistan's "economic crisis" and options for policymakers', manuscript, Asian Development Bank.
Galbraith, J.K. (2008), *The Predator State: How Conservatives Abandoned the Free Market and Why Liberals Should Too*, New York: Free Press.
Galbraith, J.K., L. Randall Wray and Warren Mosler (2009), 'The case against intergenerational accounting: the accounting campaign against Social Security and Medicare', Levy Economics Institute Policy Brief 98, http://www.levy.org/download.aspx?file=ppb_98.pdf&pubid=1119.
Hirway, Indira (2006), 'Enhancing livelihood security through the National Employment Guarantee Act: toward effective implementation of the Act', Levy Economics Institute Working Paper No. 437, January, www.levy.org.
Masters, Michael W. and Adam K. White (2008), 'The accidental Hunt Brothers', Special Report, 31 July, www.accidentalhuntbrothers.com.
McCulley, Paul (2007), 'The plankton theory meets Minsky', *Global Central Bank Focus*, PIMCO Bonds, March, www.pimco.com/leftnav/featured+market+commentary/FF, accessed 8 March 2007.
Minsky, Hyman P. (1965), 'The role of employment policy', in M.S. Gordon (ed.), *Poverty in America*, San Francisco, CA: Chandler Publishing Company, pp. 175–200.
Minsky, Hyman P. (1986), *Stabilizing an Unstable Economy*, New Haven and London: Yale University Press.
Minsky, Hyman P. (1993), 'Finance and stability: the limits of capitalism', Working Paper No. 93, Levy Economics Institute, May, http://www.levy.org/pubs/wp93.pdf.
Minsky, Hyman P. (1996), 'Uncertainty and the institutional structure of capitalist economies', Levy Economics Institute Working Paper No. 155, April.
Mitchell, W.F. and L.R. Wray (2005), 'In defense of employer of last resort: a response to Malcolm Sawyer', *Journal of Economic Issues*, **39** (1): 235–45.
Papadimitriou, Dimitri B. and L. Randall Wray (1998), 'The economic contributions of Hyman Minsky: varieties of capitalism and institutional reform', *Review of Political Economy*, **10** (2): 199–225.
Papadimitriou, Dimitri B. and L. Randall Wray (2007), 'The April AMT shock',

Policy Note 2007/1, Levy Economics Institute, available at http://www.levy.org/vtype.aspx?doctype57, last accessed 12 May 2009.

Papadimitriou, Dimitri B. and L. Randall Wray (2008), 'Time to bail-out: alternatives to the Paulson Plans', Policy Note 2008/6, Levy Economics Institute, available at http://www.levy.org/vtype.aspx?doctype57, last accessed 12 May 2009.

Tcherneva, Pavlina and L. Randall Wray (2005), 'Gender and the job guarantee: the impact of Argentina's *Jefes* program on female heads of poor households', Center for Full Employment and Price Stability, Working Paper No. 50, December, http://www.cfeps.org/pubs/.

Whalen, Charles (2007), 'The U.S. credit crunch of 2007: a Minsky moment', Levy Public Policy Brief No. 92, www.levy.org.

Wray, L. Randall (2000), 'A new economic reality: penal Keynesianism', *Challenge*, **43** (5): 31–59.

Wray, L. Randall (2003), 'The perfect fiscal storm', *Challenge*, **46** (1): 55–78

Wray, L. Randall (2005a), 'The ownership society: Social Security is only the beginning', Public Policy Brief No. 82, Levy Economics Institute, August, available at http://www.levy.org/vtype.aspx?doctype59, last accessed 12 May 2009.

Wray, L. Randall (2005b), 'Manufacturing a crisis: the neocon attack on Social Security', Policy Note 2005/2, The Levy Economics Institute, available at http://www.levy.org/vtype.aspx?doctype57, last accessed 12 May 2009.

Wray, L. Randall (2006), 'Can Basel II enhance financial stability?', Public Policy Brief No. 84, Levy Economics Institute, May, available at http://www.levy.org/vtype.aspx?doctype59, last accessed 12 May 2009.

Wray, L. Randall (2007), 'The employer of last resort programme: could it work for developing countries?', Economic and Labour Market Papers, 2007/5, International Labour Office, Geneva.

Wray, L. Randall (2008a), 'Financial markets meltdown: what can we learn from Minsky?', Public Policy Brief 94, Levy Economics Institute, April, available at http://www.levy.org/vtype.aspx?doctype59, last accessed 12 May 2009.

Wray, L. Randall (2008b), 'The commodities market bubble: money-manager capitalism and the financialization of commodities', Public Policy Brief 96, Levy Economics Institute, available at http://www.levy.org/vtype.aspx?doctype59, last accessed 12 May 2009.

Wray, L. Randall (2008c), 'Demand constraints and big government', *Journal of Economic Issues*, **XLII** (1): 153–74.

Wray, L. Randall (2009), 'Return to big government: policy advice for President Obama,' Public Policy Brief No. 99, Levy Economics Institute, available at http://www.levy.org/vtype.aspx?doctype59, last accessed 12 May 2009.

Index